The Architecture of Government

Since the days of Montesquieu and Jefferson, political decentralization has been seen as a force for better government and economic performance. It is thought to bring government "closer to the people," nurture civic virtue, protect liberty, exploit local information, stimulate policy innovation, and alleviate ethnic tensions. Inspired by such arguments, and generously funded by the major development agencies, countries across the globe have been racing to devolve power to local governments.

This book reexamines the arguments that underlie the modern faith in decentralization. Using logical analysis and formal modeling and appealing to numerous examples, it shows that most such arguments are based on vague intuitions or partial views that do not withstand scrutiny. A review of empirical studies of decentralization finds these as inconclusive and mutually contradictory as the theories they set out to test. The book's conclusion – that one cannot generalize about when decentralizing will be beneficial and when harmful – promises to prompt a rethinking of both the theory of political decentralization and current rationales for development aid.

Daniel Treisman is a professor of political science at the University of California, Los Angeles. He is the author of *After the Deluge: Regional Crises and Political Consolidation in Russia* (1999) and (with Andrei Shleifer) *Without a Map: Political Tactics and Economic Reform in Russia* (2000). A recipient of fellowships from the John Simon Guggenheim Foundation, the German Marshall Fund of the United States, the Hoover Institution, and the Smith Richardson Foundation, he has published broadly in academic journals, including the *American Political Science Review*, the *American Economic Review*, the *British Journal of Political Science*, and *World Politics*, as well as policy journals such as *Foreign Affairs* and *Foreign Policy*.

Cambridge Studies in Comparative Politics

General Editor
Margaret Levi   *University of Washington, Seattle*

Assistant General Editor
Stephen Hanson   *University of Washington, Seattle*

Associate Editors
Robert H. Bates   *Harvard University*
Peter Lange   *Duke University*
Helen Milner   *Princeton University*
Frances Rosenbluth   *Yale University*
Susan Stokes   *Yale University*
Sidney Tarrow   *Cornell University*
Kathleen Thelen   *Northwestern University*
Erik Wibbels   *University of Washington, Seattle*

Continued after the Index

The Architecture of Government

RETHINKING POLITICAL DECENTRALIZATION

DANIEL TREISMAN

University of California, Los Angeles

CAMBRIDGE
UNIVERSITY PRESS

CAMBRIDGE UNIVERSITY PRESS
Cambridge, New York, Melbourne, Madrid, Cape Town, Singapore, São Paulo, Delhi

ML

Cambridge University Press
32 Avenue of the Americas, New York, NY 10013-2473, USA

www.cambridge.org
Information on this title: www.cambridge.org/9780521872294

© Daniel Treisman 2007

First published 2007

Printed in the United States of America

A catalog record for this publication is available from the British Library.

Library of Congress Cataloging in Publication Data

Treisman, Daniel.
The architecture of government : rethinking political decentralization / Daniel Treisman.
    p.   cm. – (Cambridge studies in comparative politics)
Includes bibliographical references and index.
ISBN-13: 978-0-521-87229-4 (hardback)
ISBN-13: 978-0-521-69382-0 (pbk.)
1. Decentralization in government.   2. Central-local government relations.
3. Federal government.   4. Comparative government.   I. Title.   II. Series.
JS113.T74   2007
320.8 – dc22   2006032899

ISBN   978-0-521-87229-4 hardback
ISBN   978-0-521-69382-0 paperback

To Alex and Lara

Contents

Figures and Tables

Figures

Tables

Preface

This book has been a long time in the making. It began as an empirical project. I wanted to see what difference decentralized political institutions make for economic performance and the quality of government. The common presumption in Western democracies seemed to be that devolving power to autonomous local governments produced a number of important benefits. In the developing world, international aid agencies were backing reforms to decentralize responsibilities and resources in an ever-lengthening list of countries. Studying the politics of postcommunist Russia and reading about Latin America, I had grown skeptical that powerful local governments were quite as unmixed a blessing as was generally believed. I thought I would examine the empirical record.

Having collected data about the structure of government in countries around the world, I set aside what I thought would be a couple of months to work through the logic of the arguments about decentralization I would use the data to test. Five years went by. Along the way, I became convinced that – with one exception – there was no compelling reason to think that decentralized political institutions have any predictable effect at all. The one more persuasive argument – that some kinds of decentralization slow the pace of policy change – had no implications about whether decentralization was good or bad: It could be either, depending on what kind of change was being prevented.

During this unplanned journey into the recesses of institutional theory, I have benefited tremendously from conversations with and suggestions from a great many colleagues, all of whom are, of course, blameless for any defects in the final result. Some read bits and pieces, some listened and responded, others suggested directions worth exploring. I am grateful to Yoram Barzel, Pablo Beramendi, Tim Besley, Richard Bird, Thierry de Montbrial, J. R. DeShazo, Alberto Diaz-Cayeros, Tim Frye, Stephan Haggard, Stephen Hanson, Michael Hechter, Torben Iversen, Edgar Kiser, Herbert Kitschelt, Anirudh Krishna, Margaret Levi, Kirstie McClure, Scott Morgenstern, Aseem Prakash, Antonio Rangel, Karen Remmer, Jonathan Rodden, Ron Rogowski, Gérard Roland, Tom Romer, Ken Scheve, Matt Singer, David Soskice, Mariano Tommasi, Michel Treisman, Barry Weingast, Susan Whiting, Erik Wibbels, and two anonymous readers, as well as seminar participants at Princeton; the University of Washington; Duke University; University of California, San Diego; and the American Political Science Association meetings. I imposed more than once on the intellectual firepower of Andrei Shleifer, George Tsebelis, and Jean-Laurent Rosenthal, and I am grateful for their generosity. I owe a great debt to my collaborator, Hongbin Cai, with whom I have been working on the logic of decentralization; Hongbin's contributions are very evident in this book. Yi Zhang, Ani Sarkissian, Linda Choi, Matias Iaryczower, and Rolf Campos provided excellent research assistance. I thank Margaret Levi and Lew Bateman at Cambridge University Press for their patient interest in the manuscript and the John Simon Guggenheim Foundation, the German Marshall Fund of the United States, and the UCLA Academic Senate and Social Sciences Division for financial support.

I am grateful to my family for continuing to ask how the book is coming along. I thank my wife, Susi, for her encouragement and companionship. I dedicate this book to Alex and Lara, whose lives have overlapped with its gestation. Although they do not yet know how to spell *decentralization*, both are strong believers that many decisions in the Treisman household – especially those concerning ice cream and bedtime – would be better made if decentralized to those with the most direct interest in the outcome.

Glossary of Main Notation Used

M $(m = 1, 2, \ldots M)$	indexes citizens
J $(j = 1, 2, \ldots J)$	indexes tiers of government
N $(n = 1, 2, \ldots N)$	indexes governments within a tier
I $(i = 1, 2, \ldots I)$	indexes government official within a particular government
T $(t = 1, 2, \ldots T)$	indexes time period
W $(w = 1, 2, \ldots W)$	indexes public good or service provided by a particular government
l	labor supply of individual
$L \equiv \sum_m l_m$	total labor supply
k	capital endowment of individual
$K \equiv \sum_m k_m$	total capital endowment
I	public infrastructure investment
g	subnational provision of public goods or services
G	central provision of public goods or services
$H(\cdot), h(\cdot), q(\cdot), v(\cdot), z(\cdot)$	increasing, concave subutility functions
t	subnational lump-sum tax level
T	central lump-sum tax level
τ	subnational income tax rate
T	central income tax rate
r	according to context: cash transfer; interest rate; share of shared tax
R	government revenue
y	income, output of individual
$Y \equiv \sum_m y_m$	total income, output

c	government consumption
s	consumption by citizens of privately supplied goods
$f(\cdot)$	increasing, concave production function
$\gamma(g_{-n})$	utility of residents of jurisdiction n from externalities from spending in other jurisdictions at the same tier
μ	community size
δ	discount rate

1

─────────────────────────────────────

Introduction

The Mexican novelist Carlos Fuentes believes that federalism may be the only way to preserve local cultures in a world of increasing economic integration. *The Federalist Papers*, he has argued, "should be distributed in the millions." When British Prime Minister Tony Blair set out to modernize his country, he made devolving power outside Westminster a key element in the campaign. This was necessary, he said, to protect Britons' "fundamental rights and freedoms" and to "develop their sense of citizenship." In the 1990s, the diplomat and historian George Kennan confessed to dreaming of a United States reconstituted as a confederation of twelve regional republics, each of which would be small enough to provide "intimacy between the rulers and the ruled."[1]

For anyone who might not yet have noticed, political decentralization is in fashion. Along with democracy, competitive markets, and the rule of law, decentralized government has come to be seen as a cure for a remarkable range of political and social ills. Enthusiasm extends across geographical and ideological boundaries, uniting left and right, East and West, and North and South. It is hard to think of any other constitutional feature – except perhaps democracy itself – that could win praise from both Bill Clinton and George W. Bush, Newt Gingrich and Jerry Brown, François Mitterrand and

---

[1] Carlos Fuentes' comments are in "Where Have All The Leaders Gone? Federalism Is the Great Healer," *Los Angeles Times*, December 16, 1990, p. M1. For Tony Blair's opinions, see his "Britain Speech" in *The Guardian Unlimited*, March 28, 2000, at http://www.guardian. co.uk/britain/article/0,2763,184950,00.html, downloaded March 27, 2005, and his speech at the Council of Europe Summit, October 10, 1997, from the prime minister's web site at www.number-10.gov.uk/output/Page1062.asp, downloaded March 27, 2005. Kennan's remarks are in Kennan (1993, pp. 143–51).

1

Jacques Chirac, Ernesto Zedillo and Vicente Fox, Mikhail Gorbachev and Boris Yeltsin.[2]

Political decentralization means different things to different people, and I will discuss definitions in Chapter 2. But most would agree that a political system is more decentralized to the extent that local officials are chosen locally and have the right to make final decisions on important policy issues. Political decentralization differs from mere administrative decentralization, under which the central government delegates some policy responsibilities to its appointed local agents but retains the right to overrule its agents' decisions. Complete political and administrative centralization – found only in small, unitary states such as Monaco – exists if all policy decisions are made and implemented by a single central government and its centrally located agents.

The belief that political decentralization is a good thing has been reshaping government across the globe. In Western Europe, Italy, Spain, and France created directly elected regional legislatures in recent decades, and Belgium turned itself into a federal state. The United Kingdom introduced parliamentary assemblies in Scotland and Wales, reversing centuries of precedent, and revived one in Northern Ireland.[3] In the postcommunist East, countries from Poland to Kyrgyzstan have been strengthening local

[2] For Clinton on decentralization see "Transcript of President Clinton's Remarks to National Building and Construction Trades Department Conference," April 5, 1995, U.S. Newswire, downloaded from Factiva database, August 20, 2006. For Bush, see his memoir, *A Charge to Keep* (Bush 1999, p. 235). For Gingrich, see R. W. Apple Jr., "You Say You Want a Devolution," *The New York Times*, January 29, 1995, Section 4, p. 1. For Brown, see "Luncheon address by Jerry Brown" to the American Society of Newspaper Editors, April 14, 1999, at http://www.asne.org/kiosk/archive/convention/conv99/jerrybrown.htm, downloaded March 28, 2005. On Chirac and Mitterrand, see Robert Graham, "Chirac gives blessing to Raffarin's radical decentralization proposals," *The Financial Times*, October 17, 2002, p. 8. For Zedillo, see his speech at the International Forum of Federations, Mont-Tremblant, Canada, Wednesday, October 6, 1999, at http://zedilloworld.presidencia.gob. mx/PAGES/library/sp_07oct99.html, downloaded March 28, 2005. For Fox, see Elisabeth Malkin, ed., "Vicente Fox on the Transition, NAFTA, Corruption, Drugs, the Economy . . ." *Business Week*, July 17, 2000, downloaded March 29, 2005, from http://www. businessweek.com/2000/00_29/b3690043.htm. For Gorbachev, see "Gorbachev considers that disintegration of the USSR was avoidable," Interfax, Moscow, December 24, 2001, wherein Gorbachev discusses his attempts to decentralize the Soviet Union in 1990–1 and insists that "Reform, the broadest decentralization, was the correct strategy." On Yeltsin's commitment to decentralization, see Aron (2000, p. 394).

[3] On Western Europe, see Hooghe and Marks (2001, pp. 205–6), European Union (2001, pp. 48–9).

governments. ("Before the Decentralization Program, we were like camels," one Kyrgyz village leader enthused to a visiting aid worker, "but now we are horses.") In Latin America, Argentina, Bolivia, Brazil, Chile, Colombia, Paraguay, Peru, Venezuela, and many of their Central American neighbors introduced local or provincial elections, and most devolved responsibilities to subnational bodies. In Africa, Ethiopia adopted a federal constitution, and post-*apartheid* South Africa gave its provinces considerable autonomy. Seventeen other countries – from Benin to Zimbabwe – introduced elections for local councils. In Asia, India rewrote its constitution to empower rural *panchayat* governments, and post-Suharto Indonesia shifted functions and resources to its subnational units. The Philippines transferred responsibilities for health care, education, social services, and the environment to localities. Even China, not to be left out, began holding village elections in the late 1980s and authorized the elected committees to arbitrate civil disputes and provide local services.[4]

Although the impetus has come from many directions, international development agencies have been energetic – and generous – cheerleaders. Calculating how much such agencies have spent promoting decentralization is difficult, but in recent decades it has surely run into the billions. According to its Web site, the Inter-American Development Bank approved $671 million in loans to support "decentralization and subnational government" in Latin America between 1961 and 2005.[5] In 1997–2003, the World Bank was allocating about $300 million–500 million *a year* on loans to projects with a decentralization component.[6] Besides this, the Bank claimed to have 180 members "holding meetings, sponsoring seminars and workshops, and developing Web sites to ensure that the latest

---

[4] On Eastern Europe and the former Soviet Union, see Bird, Ebel, and Wallich (1996). The Kyrgyz village leader is quoted in Pandey and Misnikov (2001). On Latin America, see Burki, Perry, and Dillinger (1999). On Africa, see Brosio (2000), and on South Africa, Inman and Rubinfeld (2005). On Indonesia and the Philippines, see chapters in Brillantes and Cuachon, eds. (2002). On India, see Singh (1994). On Chinese village elections, see, for instance, Alpermann (2001).

[5] Information from its web site, http://www.iadb.org/projects/index.cfm?language=english#, "Approved Loans by Sector/Subsector," downloaded March 9, 2005.

[6] See http://www1.worldbank.org/publicsector/decentralization/operations.htm, downloaded March 9, 2005. It is not clear from the published statistics how large the "decentralization component" was in each of these. Some projects probably involved improving the quality of government at lower levels within already decentralized states rather than getting states to decentralize in the first place.

thinking on [decentralization] is widely available" (Ayres 2003, p. 74). According to the same report, half the education projects supported by the Bank recently included "decentralization strategies in their design" (ibid., p. 76).

Various United Nations agencies have also done their part. As of 2000, the UN Development Program was supporting decentralization programs in ninety-five countries (UNDP 2002). The UN's Capital Development Fund and Food and Agriculture Organization were both financing decentralization and local government in Africa (Morell 2004). The European Union provides grants, as do many of its member countries.[7] The Asian Development Bank allocates loans and grants for decentralization in Asia. The U.S. Agency for International Development said in 2000 it was "supporting decentralization and democratic local governance initiatives in some 50 countries" (Dininio 2000, p. 2). Its funding for "democracy and local governance" averaged $141 million a year recently, some of which went to decentralization projects.[8] In part, such flows probably aimed to make already decentralized structures more effective rather than to stimulate further decentralization. But for a developing country short of money, devolving power must look like an easy way to cash in on the rich world's desire to help.

Behind these aid dollars stands a series of arguments. Many have a familiar, common-sensical feel to them. Decentralization brings government "closer to the people." It focuses authority at a level at which governments must compete against one another – like firms in a market – to please footloose voters or investors. It makes it easier for citizens to hold their representatives accountable. Devolving power to local governments makes better use of local knowledge, protects individual liberty, encourages citizen participation, nurtures civic virtue, and alleviates ethnic grievances. Decentralized units can serve as "laboratories" of democracy, hosting parallel policy experiments. Besides being intuitive, these arguments have a distinguished provenance. Many date to the work of political thinkers such as Montesquieu, Rousseau, Tocqueville, or John Stuart Mill. Others are

---

[7] For instance, in January 2004, the EU announced aid of €20 million for decentralization in Guatemala and €21 million for education decentralization in Nicaragua (Commission of the European Communities, press release, IP: 04/63, "Commission approves co-operation actions for EUR 250 million in Latin America" January 16, 2004, downloaded from Lexis-Nexis, March 24, 2005).

[8] Table 3b, from USAID web site, downloaded March 22, 2005, http://www.usaid.gov/policy/budget/cbj2004/summary_tables_table3.pdf. The average is for fiscal years 2001–4.

associated with great twentieth-century economists such as Friedrich Hayek and James Buchanan.

Not all scholars are sure that decentralization is always beneficial. Skeptics have argued that empowering local governments can undermine macroeconomic discipline because of "common pool" problems or "soft budget constraints" that lead governments to overspend (Prud'homme 1996, Tanzi 1996). Others have been disappointed by the record of decentralization reforms in practice. Sophisticated advocates of decentralization have taken such reservations in stride. While remaining enthusiastic about the objective, they have sought simple rules to guide how countries should decentralize, as well as remedies for the inconveniences decentralization might generate.

The goal of this book is to reexamine these arguments – both those of decentralization's advocates and those of the skeptics. In the chapters that follow, I consider a dozen or so of the most common and influential arguments about how decentralization affects economic and political outcomes. I use formal modeling where useful to clarify the logic underlying each of these, to test for consistency, and to see what conditions or assumptions each presupposes. Are there reliable reasons to think that decentralizing government will in general have the effects the arguments predict? Even if the effects are not fully general, can one identify precise, observable conditions under which the arguments do hold?

The short answer to both these questions turns out to be no. When examined closely, neither the arguments about benefits of decentralization nor those about macroeconomic dangers are general at all. Some are simply invalid. Others do hold given certain conditions. But the conditions are so complicated and difficult to observe that the results provide little basis for empirical work or policy advice. One argument withstands scrutiny a little better, but even this implies nothing general about when decentralization is beneficial and when it is harmful. Although it might seem a waste of time given this conclusion even to review empirical studies of the consequences of decentralization, I do so briefly in Chapter 11. I find there that, as one would expect given the uncertain and conditional results of theory, almost no robust empirical findings have been reported about the consequences of decentralization.

To be clear, I do not find that decentralization is generally bad. In fact, the arguments against decentralization appear to be as partial and inconclusive as those for it, and the empirical evidence for them is just as weak and inconsistent. Rather, decentralization's consequences are complex and obscure. Many effects pull in different directions, leaving the net result indeterminate. To choose to decentralize, in most settings, requires a leap of faith rather than the application of science. To devote hundreds of millions of dollars to persuading others to decentralize, given the current state of knowledge, seems odd to say the least. The emperor may not be completely naked. But he is dressed in little other than his underwear.

This conclusion will seem controversial and unappealing to many readers, and I do not expect it to be readily accepted. Critics will find points to question in my treatment of the arguments. I think it is harder to question the general picture that emerges. At the least, the analysis should cast doubt on certain widely shared assumptions and challenge advocates of decentralization to develop a more systematic and compelling theoretical case.

1.1 A Quick Look Back

The question of how governments should be organized must be as old as the study of politics.[9] From Aristotle to Polybius and Cicero, classical authors debated whether public authority should be entrusted to a monarch, a senate of aristocrats, a popular assembly, or some mixture of the three. The advantages of different constitutions were scrupulously examined.

Almost all the ancient scholarship focused on the institutions of central government. It is striking how little, by comparison, classical thinkers had to say about the vertical structure of government – the division of states into several tiers and the distribution of responsibilities among them. Local government did not entirely escape notice. Cicero, who served himself as governor of Cilicia, expounded on the duties of provincial governors, and Plutarch offered memorable advice to Greek municipal councilors on how to deal with their Roman overlords.[10] But both – like other writers – seem

---

[9] The following pages focus on the history and political theory of decentralization in the West, for no other reason than my lack of familiarity with Eastern sources. It should not be taken as a comprehensive survey.

[10] On Cicero, see Lacey and Wilson (1970, pp. 275–89), as well as his famous prosecution of Gaius Verres, the corrupt former governor of Sicily (Cicero 1960 [70 B.C.], pp. 35–57). In his *Moralia*, Plutarch instructs the Greek municipal councilor that he should not stir up the common people with tales of ancient heroes and should remember "the boots of Roman soldiers just above [his] head." Maintaining some autonomy, Plutarch argued, required keeping one's distance. Those "who invite the sovereign's decision on every decree, meeting of a council, granting of a privilege, or administrative measure, force their sovereign to be their master more than he desires" and risk wholly destroying the city's "constitutional government, making it dazed, timid, and powerless in everything" (Plutarch 1936, pp. 798–825).

to have taken the existing vertical structure for granted. How functions should be divided among central and local organs does not appear to have struck them as an interesting or relevant question.[11]

This is strange because multi-tier states have been common since the beginning of recorded history. The Sumerians, who left some of the oldest writing, inhabited a network of twelve or so theocratic city-states, each of which was divided into villages or rural communities, which were in turn subdivided into hamlets (Diakonoff 1974, pp. 8–10; Crawford 1991; Finer 1997, vol. 1, pp. 104–27). Every unit had its own priest-ruler. All the great empires – from Egypt to Persia – were administered by territorial governors, viziers, satraps, or other agents. The Israelite tribes and the Greek city leagues compete for the credit of having invented the confederation (Larsen 1968, Elazar 1987). The Roman republic and its provinces were integrated by an innovative system of administrative law, in which centrally appointed provincial governors could be sued, after leaving office, by those they had governed. Even the polis, that symbol of unitary, direct democracy, was not as flat as might be thought. Athens, after Cleisthenes' reforms of 508–507 B.C., was divided into 139 *demes* – city wards or rural villages – that served as both administrative subdivisions and "self-contained and self-determining units of local government in their own right" (Whitehead 1986).[12]

Scholarly analysis of multilevel systems seems to have begun with a few paragraphs in Aristotle's *Politics* (1996).[13] Aristotle begins by deconstructing

[11] Finer (1997, vol. 1, p. 380) wonders at the apparent silence of the Greeks about composite states: "Unless there is a corpus of political literature that has not come down to us, it seems that they did not develop any explicatory theory relative to this class of states." Whitehead (1986, p. 51), in his study of local government in Attica, notes with surprise that neither Plato nor Aristotle shows "any interest whatever in the Attic demes as an object of study in themselves." Larsen (1968, p. xi) is puzzled by Aristotle's and Polybius' "failure[s] to give adequate attention to the federal state." (Polybius, in his discussion of the Roman constitution [1979, Book 6], discusses only the three key elements of central government – the consuls, the Senate, and the people – and does not address how they relate to lower-tier actors such as the provincial governors or municipal organs.) J. P. Genet (1981, p. 20) makes a similar observation about medieval political thought: "No theorist was concerned with 'local communities' as one of his central themes ... A distinct characteristic of late medieval theory is its failure, both in France and in England, to insert local communities into the framework of the *politia*."

[12] Besides Athens, Rhodes was also divided into *demes*. Sparta contained 5 villages or *obae*. And in Alexandria, the structure consisted of 5 *phylai*, 60 *demes*, and 720 *phratries* (Ehrenberg 1960, p. 30).

[13] Plato's ideal polity, Magnesia, described in *The Laws* (1970 [350s–340s B.C.] Book 5), is divided into twelve territorial segments, each inhabited by a different tribe. Teams of five "country wardens" and sixty young men, all from the same tribe, rotate through the twelve

the Greek city into a three-tier hierarchy of households, villages, and the polis, each of which aims at a different good. In fact, only the third of these is political. The household exists to "supply men's everyday wants" – material provision and procreation (ibid., pp. 12, 1252a–b). The polis is the setting in which a citizen can participate in self-government, realizing his nature as a being capable of practical wisdom. What purpose there is for something in between is not spelled out. Aristotle says only that the village aims at "something more than the supply of daily needs." He does not mention the *demes* (the word used for "village" is *kômê*).[14] In short, the passage does not so much justify multilevel government as explain why some nonpolitical communities are needed to supplement the uniquely political one.

Medieval Christian scholars, starting from this passage, stretched Aristotle's city into a five- or six-tier hierarchy – rising from the *domus* (household) to the *imperium* (Empire) – that more closely approximated their own world (Gierke 1966, p. 277). The particular function of each tier was often left vague. However, Dante, in *De Monarchia*, provided a reason why multiple levels were necessary. Only in a pyramid of different-sized, nested communities could the full multiplicity of human potential be realized all at once:

There is, then, some distinct function for which humanity as a whole is ordained, a function which neither an individual nor a household, neither a village, nor a city, nor a particular kingdom, has power to perform. . . . [This function is] to actualize continually the entire capacity of the possible intellect, primarily in speculation, then, through its extension and for its sake, secondarily in action. (Dante 1904 [c.1314–20], Book 1, chs. 3–4)

God created the multi-tiered Empire as the stage on which the different dramas of human life could be simultaneously and peacefully enacted.

Aristotle's and Dante's images of social organization may seem foreign. But the notion that different public functions should be assigned to different-sized units in a hierarchy, so that multiple goals can be achieved simultaneously, continues to inform constitutional thinking. Another source of modern ideas about decentralization was the medieval – and, before that, Roman – association of law with custom. As the Institutes of

territories, providing justice and defense. However, Plato provides no explicit reasons why this arrangement is to be preferred to any other. Thomas More offers a parody in *Utopia* (More 1965 [1516], pp. 70–1).
[14] In his *Constitution of Athens*, Aristotle describes Athenian local institutions in some detail (1996, p. xxi).

Justinian put it, "immemorial custom approved by consent of those who use it supplies the place of law" (quoted in McIlwain 1932, p. 128). In the fragmented world of medieval Christendom, reverence for custom led naturally to the empowerment of local groups and individuals. Because customs were clearly rooted in particular places, judging what was and was not customary required consulting the locals. In medieval society "the normal way to prove custom was to have it stated by a body of people who represented the community within which it applied" (Reynolds 1984, pp. 42–3). In England, as described by Blackstone, that meant asking a twelve-man jury of local citizens.[15] Local tribunals such as the hundred courts, gathering together freemen to interpret custom, established a tradition of local assemblies and popular participation in the administration of justice that extended across the feudal world (Bloch 1961, vol. 2; Reynolds 1984, p. 19). This history implanted a close association between local government, freedom, and democracy into the subconscious of Western societies.

As nation-states solidified in the early modern period, the interaction between central authorities and local communities became a more common preoccupation of political thinkers. One can trace the emergence of three counterposed, ideal-type representations of this relationship. The first casts the state as a top-down hierarchy, in which local officials are subordinate agents of an all-powerful sovereign. The purest exponent is Hobbes, for whom state officials are mere mechanical devices, resembling "the Nerves, and Tendons that move the severall limbs of a body naturall" (Hobbes 1968 [1651], p. 290). So long as these agents faithfully implement the sovereign's orders, the subjects have an obligation to obey them. Bodin (1992 [1576]) also placed complete authority with the crown but argued for some enlightened – always reversible – delegation.[16]

A second image conceives the state as the creation of freely associating, self-governing local units, which covenant among themselves to delegate

---

[15] "The trial ... (both to shew the existence of the custom, as 'that in the manor of Dale lands shall descend only to the heirs male, and never to the heirs female;' and also to shew that the lands in question are within that manor) is by a jury of twelve men, and not by the judges, except the same particular custom has been before tried, determined, and recorded in the same court" (Blackstone 1979 [1765–9], Vol. 1, p. 76).

[16] "Monarchies become corrupted when little by little the privileges of bodies and cities are taken away, and when, instead of limiting themselves to a general supervision, which is alone worthy of a sovereign, princes want to rule everything alone without intermediary." Quoted in Norton (1994, p. 6); see also Hoffmann (1959, p. 115).

authority upward while retaining their individual sovereignty. This is Montesquieu's "federal republic" – really a confederation – a "society of societies that make a new one" (Montesquieu 1989 [1748], Part II, Book 9, ch. 1). The image, taken up by American Antifederalists such as Melancton Smith, reaches its extreme expression in Proudhon's ideal state, in which higher governments are the strictly accountable and highly constrained agents of local governments, subject to recall at any time, and limited to contractually pre-specified tasks (Vernon 1979, p. xxiv).[17]

The third ideal type – that of the "compound republic," later the "federal state" – appears first in the writing of Harrington (1992 [1656]), Milton, Hugo, and Leibniz, and then in practice in the U.S. Constitution of 1789.[18] This conception seems at first to fall between the first two, but in fact it is distinct from both. In a compound republic, neither central nor local governments command the other; they act in parallel, deriving separate grants of authority from a common sovereign. The supreme power, James Wilson declared, "*resides* in the PEOPLE, as the fountain of government . . . The power both of the general government, and the State governments, under this system, are acknowledged to be so many emanations of power from the people" (Wood 1969, pp. 530–1). While sovereignty remained inalienable and undivided, it could be exercised simultaneously by several mechanisms. These separate mechanisms – state and federal governments – were equally legitimate, authorized by the sovereign's consent and by the constitutional compact that defined them and their powers.[19]

---

[17] Some might also include in this category the German legal theorist Johannes Althusius, who in 1603 described the state as an "association of associations," in which each type of association – from the family, to the collegium, city, province, and state – is constituted by a covenant between the units at the lower level and serves its own particular purpose. Sovereignty, in Althusius' scheme, was not held by a particular actor but inhered in the *ius regni*, or fundamental laws of the realm (Carney 1964, p. xxiv). However, Althusius' vision of the state is not easy to classify. Others would characterize him as an early disciple of federalism (Gierke 1966, Elazar 1987), or as a theorist of medieval constitutionalism (Riley 1976). On Melancton Smith's invocation of Montesquieu, see Storing (1981, p. 334).

[18] Some might argue that the Holy Roman Empire around this time was also a compound republic.

[19] In the American case, this formulation reflected a political compromise that both sides regretted having to make rather than a sudden stroke of genius (see, e.g., Riley 1976). The Federalists hoped for something much more centralized; the Antifederalists, for a reinvigorated confederation. Madison, as late as the spring of 1787, favored "a due supremacy of the national authority," with local authorities tolerated only "so far as they can be subordinately useful" (quoted in Wood 1969, p. 525).

This early modern competition to locate sovereignty within complex states opened the way to the subsequent explosion of thought about political institutions. With the Enlightenment, curiosity about the diversity of political arrangements combined with the revolutionary notion, asserted in Philadelphia and Paris, that constitutions could be chosen and crafted rather than just inherited. Scholars began to pose new questions about practical utility, accountability, and individual liberty. Many of the arguments made today by advocates and critics of political decentralization can be traced to insights of the great Enlightenment and nineteenth-century political theorists. With the marginal revolution in economics in the late nineteenth century, it became possible to pose and answer precise questions about the efficiency consequences of different constitutional arrangements. A final way of thinking about decentralization developed from the formal analyses of politics and public finance that became popular in the second half of the twentieth century.

The main ideas about the consequences of political decentralization that emerged from these disparate sources are the subject of this book. These arguments entered public consciousness in various ways. Some seeped out from historical debates by osmosis. Others were pulled from library books with scholarly tweezers. Some are to be found in academic journals, while others seem to hover in the air, somewhere between conventional wisdom and cliché. In the next section, I identify the main arguments, along with an instant preview of why their claims do not seem to me to be general and convincing. The rest of the book develops these critiques.

1.2 The Arguments

1.2.1 Decentralization – Good or Neutral

1. Administrative efficiency. Multi-tier government makes it possible to satisfy citizens' demands for public goods and services more precisely and cost-effectively. If it is most efficient to provide some public outputs in small units and others in large ones, or if tastes for some outputs vary geographically, provision in a multi-tier structure can be tailored to these cost and demand conditions. (See Oates 1972, Montesquieu 1989 [1748].)

Critique In fact, only administrative – not political – decentralization is required for this. An all-powerful central government, implementing a plan via subordinate field agents, could achieve the same efficiencies, so to demonstrate the superiority of political decentralization some other argument is needed. Moreover, a multi-tier structure only makes such efficiencies *possible*. It also makes possible provision plans that are even less efficient than unitary provision (suppose all services are assigned to units of the "wrong" scale). To know whether more tiers lead to greater efficiency, one must know how functions are allocated. And given that increasing the number of tiers and governments is costly, this argument establishes only that some administrative decentralization may be beneficial, not how much. It is an argument for cost-benefit analysis, not for a particular structure of government or direction of reform.

2. Local competition. Competition among local governments to attract mobile residents or investment induces them to be more honest, efficient, and responsive. Such competitive pressures are weaker among nation-states. Therefore, one should give more responsibilities to local governments. (See Hayek 1939, Tiebout 1956.)

Critique The conditions for vigorous competition among local governments are so restrictive they will rarely be met even approximately in real countries. If, however, the conditions *are* met, competition may for many reasons be perverse, leading to less efficient or less desirable outcomes. If competition among local governments would be both vigorous and beneficial, an all-powerful central government would in most cases be both motivated and able to achieve the same benefits by introducing similar competition among its appointed field agents.

3. Fiscal incentives. Increasing local governments' share in a shared tax should increase their motivation to support local economic activity, resulting in better performance nationwide.

Critique Increasing local governments' share means decreasing the shares of other levels of government. If local governments become more motivated to support economic performance, the other levels of government will become less motivated. Because, for better or worse, all levels of government can influence economic performance, the resulting net effect on performance is indeterminate.

4. Democracy. Decentralization, by reducing the scale of government, increases citizen participation and cultivates civic virtue. It also enhances electoral accountability because voters have better information about local than about central government performance, because dividing responsibilities up among multiple levels makes it easier for voters to attribute credit or blame among them, and because voters in small groups can coordinate better on a voting strategy. (See Tocqueville 1969 [1835], Mill 1991 [1861], Jefferson 1999 [1774–1826].)

Critique In all but the tiniest communities, only a small fraction of citizens can participate directly in local government. In any case, participating in government may cultivate either civic virtue or corruption, depending on whether preexisting practice in that government is virtuous or corrupt. There is no reason why citizens could or would participate more *indirectly* (signing petitions, voting, demonstrating, etc.) in a decentralized than in a centralized system. As for electoral accountability, it is not clear why voters would be better informed about local than central government performance. (One can observe whether the Central Bank is keeping inflation low as directly as one can observe whether a local school board is managing schools well.) Multiple tiers may make it harder, not easier, to attribute credit and blame – suppose, as often occurs in federal states, that responsibilities are shared across levels rather than neatly assigned to one level or another. Coordinating in small groups is significantly easier only if the groups are extremely small, and incumbents at any level of government can undermine such voter coordination by playing groups of voters off against one another, using "divide and conquer" strategies.

5. Checks, balances, and liberty. In decentralized orders, strong local governments will check central government abuses and protect individual freedoms. (See Tocqueville 1969 [1835], Weingast 1995, Madison 1999 [1772–1836], Hamilton 2001 [1769–1804].)

Critique Local governments can usually defeat a central government only if they coordinate. They will often fail to coordinate, and their attempts to do so can easily be undermined by central "divide-and-conquer" strategies. In any case, local governments that succeed in blocking central interventions are just as likely to do so to protect local abuses – slavery, school segregation – as to protect the freedom of individuals.

6. Veto players and change. By making policy changes depend on more actors, decentralization tends to increase policy stability. (See Proudhon 1979 [1863], Hume 1994 [1752], Tsebelis 2002.)

Critique This is the most convincing argument. Still, because decentralization does not always increase the number of veto players with divergent policy preferences, the prediction should hold only on average. When the claim does hold, there are no general normative implications. Policy stability is good when the policies entrenched are good, but bad when the policies entrenched are bad, however one defines "good" and "bad."

13

7. Local information and policy innovation. Local governments are better able to elicit and make use of local information, or are more motivated to do so. Decentralization should increase policy experimentation. (See Turgot 1775, Brandeis 1932, J. S. Mill 1991 [1861].)

Critique On examination, it is not clear why local governments would be better able to extract local information, or more motivated to do so. As for policy innovation, central governments in centralized systems can also introduce local policy experiments, and electoral pressures will usually make them *more* motivated to do so than local governments in decentralized systems. A central government has more to gain from local discoveries (which it can use to increase its support in other regions), and it has less to lose electorally if an experiment in one region goes wrong than the government of that region.

8. Ethnic conflicts. Political decentralization defuses ethnic conflicts by satisfying limited demands for autonomy, splitting the prizes and lowering the stakes of politics, creating checks on the central government, socializing ethnic politicians into cooperative behavior, and refocusing party development onto very small ethnic groups.

Critique First, decentralization can help only geographically concentrated minorities. By the same token, it may create new ethnic minorities within smaller units. And it may strengthen local groups' capacity to press *unlimited* demands for autonomy. Second, distributing political offices among different ethnic groups may avoid excluding any; but it may turn conflicts between ethnic groups into ethnically motivated conflicts between different levels of government. Constitutional constraints on central policies can lower the stakes of politics just as effectively as decentralization. Third, the central government is sometimes the solution, not the problem. If decentralization prevents central government interventions, it will prevent both abusive interventions and humanitarian actions to stop one local ethnic group from massacring another. Fourth, local governments may socialize ethnic politicians into cooperation – or they may turn into schools of intolerance and ethnic hatred. Fifth, refocusing the party system on smaller, local ethnic parties may reduce the scale of conflicts, but it may sometimes render them more intense. Small ethnic groups may feel more threatened than larger ones. The strategy may fail because nationwide inter-ethnic coalitions are still needed to contest central positions. If it succeeds, it may reduce inter-ethnic cooperation learned in multi-ethnic national coalitions. In sum, all the effects can go both ways.

1.2.2   Decentralization – Bad

1. Fiscal pressures. Politically strong local governments undermine fiscal and macroeconomic discipline by pressuring the central government for aid. Local governments undervalue central fiscal balance because they view the central budget as a "common pool" – if they do not drain it of fish, others will. And they exploit "soft budget constraints" to extract transfers from the center.

Critique   Because central aid to some regions must be financed by central taxation of others, strengthening all regional governments should empower opponents as well as supporters of fiscal transfers. Those pressing harder for aid should be offset by those pressing harder for less taxation. If the effects are geographically uneven, this could generate either greater fiscal imbalance or greater restraint. Local governments seeking to extract central aid may either "overspend," hoping for a bailout, or "undercollect taxes" to prompt central revenue transfers. In the second case, this should reduce – rather than increase – final spending. And the center may say no even to constitutionally powerful local governments. It may play local units off against one another, neutralizing their lobbying power, or invest in a reputation for toughness. What matters is not just the extent of local powers but how well local governments can coordinate and how long is the central government's time horizon.

2. Fiscal coordination. Decentralization leads to failures of fiscal coordination across levels of government that result in inefficiency. When local and central governments can independently tax the same base or are expected by voters to spend on the same items, they may tend to overtax or underspend.

Critique   This is the most convincing negative argument. However, the pressures to overtax and to underspend may offset each other.

1.3   A Note on Methods: Formal Modeling

Before examining these arguments in more detail, I should say a few words about my methods. Although I review empirical studies in Chapter 11, the analysis in this book is primarily theoretical. I evaluate the logic of particular arguments and try to establish how general their conclusions are. In doing so, I often find it useful to recast arguments as formal models. Because formal modeling can be used in a number of ways, my explaining here how I use it may avoid confusion.

Models come in various shapes and sizes. One type of model is a miniature replica of the world, within which "real world" phenomena can be simulated. Sometimes the easiest way to understand the causes of complex outcomes is to try to create such outcomes on a smaller scale. Paul Krugman (1995, pp. 68–73) discusses the meteorological researcher Dave Fultz, who placed a dishpan of water on a slowly rotating turntable with an electric heating element on one side. With this simple physical model of the world, Fultz was able to re-create key elements of global climate systems – from the temperature differences between the equator and the poles to the flow of the jet stream and tropical cyclones. By reproducing complex outcomes in simpler settings, one can identify factors that are sufficient to generate them.

A second type of model is an extrapolation from observations. Forecasters sometimes use such models as tools for making predictions. They assume that two variables are related by a particular form of function and use observations to estimate the function's parameters. The "model" then consists of the function with inductively derived parameter estimates filled in. Such forecasting tools help to identify patterns in the world. If the patterns do not change, such models can predict future relationships.

The models I explore in this book are neither simulations nor forecasting extrapolations. They are models of a third kind – mathematical representations of logical arguments. Such models consist of a set of symbols, assumptions about the relationships among these symbols, and implications that are deduced from the assumptions. Many informal verbal arguments can be translated into such formal models by means of a set of definitions (which equate particular symbols in the formal model to concepts used in the verbal argument).

Formal models of this type are tools that can be used for various purposes. A first use is to communicate ideas precisely and economically. Certain claims are simply easier to write and understand using mathematical symbols than using words. To write "$F = Gm_1m_2/d^2$" takes fewer keystrokes than to write "the gravitational force of attraction between two objects is equal to the product of the mass of the two objects times the gravitational constant divided by the distance between them squared." Clarity and precision of communication are important because evaluating whether a claim is true and what else it implies is easier when the claim is clearly expressed.

Besides helping scientists communicate, formalization can also help them to think systematically and creatively. To quote Bertrand Russell, commenting on a conjecture of Wittgenstein's: "a good notation has a subtlety and suggestiveness which at times make it seem almost like a live teacher. Notational irregularities are often the first sign of philosophical errors, and a perfect notation would be a substitute for thought" (Russell 1961 [1922], p. xiv). Just as translating a work of literature into a foreign language sometimes reveals unnoticed aspects of the writer's art, translating ideas into mathematical symbols can produce a deeper understanding of their meaning.

In this vein, formal models can be used to test the internal consistency of arguments. By stating the assumptions precisely and checking whether all deductions follow the rules of logic, one discovers whether an intuitively plausible argument is, in fact, valid. Some arguments are simple enough that one can confidently assess their validity without resort to mathematical symbols. But arguments that seem plausible often turn out, on closer inspection, to make faulty inferences or to imply contradictions.

At the same time, models help to determine what assumptions are necessary for a particular argument. Without knowing this, one cannot judge how generally the argument will apply. If the necessary assumptions are unlikely to be met, then the argument – even if valid – will be relevant only in exceptional cases. Yet another use is to generate additional, previously unrecognized implications. By applying the rules of formal logic to an argument's propositions, one can sometimes unlock implications and derive predictions that would not have suggested themselves were the argument expressed verbally. These predictions can be used both to assess the argument's explanatory power relative to that of other arguments and – if the predictions prove accurate – to explain other phenomena.

In this book, I use formal modeling to clarify the content of arguments, to check for internal inconsistencies, and to identify what assumptions are necessary for the result. I emphasize that I use modeling here as a *critical tool*. I am not trying to simulate reality – to reproduce the world in a series of equations – but only to analyze the validity and generality of particular arguments. The aim is to express the logic of these arguments faithfully, simply, and where possible in the terms that leading advocates or critics of decentralization themselves use.

Anyone expecting a general theory of political decentralization will not find it here. Another approach might be to try to build a super-model, incorporating all the relevant mechanisms and effects simultaneously. Using such a model, one might attempt to simulate how politically decentralized states operate and to observe decentralization's net effects. By the end of

17

the book, it should be clear why I do not think such an approach would be fruitful. There are simply too many effects, interacting in too many ways, with results dependent on conditions that are too numerous and obscure. The practical impossibility of netting out the different effects of decentralization so as to form contingent predictions that are useful for policy analysis and political judgments is, in fact, my main conclusion.

A fallback option sometimes adopted by economists is to choose two effects with opposite implications – one favoring centralization, one favoring decentralization – and model the tradeoff between them. This has the attraction of simplicity. But whatever conclusions one derives in this way might be undone by including more of the relevant effects. And the conclusions will differ depending on which two counterposed effects one chooses to model. For instance, Oates (1972) and Alesina and Spolaore (2003) focus on the classic tradeoff between economies of scale in the provision of a given public good and heterogeneity of preferences across local units. They show that if heterogeneity is great enough it will be more efficient to let each local government provide the good autonomously. But now suppose that giving local governments this power enables them to game the center in a way that undermines fiscal stability. And that making local governments more autonomous in a heterogeneous country exacerbates demands for secession, provoking ethnic conflict. And that central governments are more motivated than local ones to try out innovative new ways of providing the good. And, perhaps, that local governments in the country in question happen to be notoriously corrupt. Clearly, modeling just the particular tradeoff we started with would not be very useful – or, if taken as a guide to reality, would be extremely misleading. But putting all these effects in a single model would make it intractable.

The arguments I examine consist of two parts: first, claims about how different rules of the game (centralization or decentralization) lead to different outcomes, given certain assumptions, and second (explicit or implicit), claims about which outcomes are more desirable. They are, thus, both positive and normative. For example, in Chapter 8, I discuss an argument that decentralization protects individual liberty more effectively than centralization. The positive argument is that empowering local governments enables them to resist central government violations of individuals' rights. The normative part is the implicit claim that individual liberty is good. In this book, I evaluate only the positive parts of the arguments. I leave it to the reader to decide whether individual liberty is a good thing, or how important it is relative to other values. Because I conclude that decentralization has almost no general consequences, whether the alleged consequences are good or bad is usually beside the point.

I will criticize the way in which arguments about decentralization have been presented and used to motivate policy. Some arguments establish only that a certain outcome is *possible*, yet they are used to justify general policy recommendations or empirical predictions. Some make assumptions that beg the question at issue. Some leave important, empirically relevant actors out of the game. Some focus on a subset of effects that push in a certain direction, ignoring other effects that pull the opposite way. (Of course, any model simplifies reality; the question is whether the way one simplifies predetermines the result. If focusing on different subsets of effects leads to opposite conclusions, the predictive power and normative relevance of a given model is limited.) Most frequently, arguments turn out to require long lists of restrictive assumptions that are unlikely to be met in most real cases.

These criticisms should not be taken as an attack on previous work on this subject. On the contrary, this book owes a great debt to the contributions of a variety of political economists. There are often good reasons why scholars studying a certain question in a certain context make assumptions that seem problematic if one seeks to generalize their results more broadly. My critique aims more at the way particular analyses have been interpreted and aggregated. The careful hedging of claims tends to get pruned away as arguments migrate from the academic journals to policy briefs. Final results, rather than the many assumptions necessary to reach them, are emphasized. Or an accumulation of weak arguments is taken as adding up to a strong one, rather than as repeated evidence of weakness. As with any important subject, an occasional reconsideration may be useful.

1.4 Overview

The next chapter introduces some notation and concepts that will help in the subsequent analysis: Then Chapter 3 begins examining the arguments, starting with those that concern administrative decentralization. Given a sovereign central government, will establishing subordinate administrative tiers help implement a given public policy more efficiently? If so, how many tiers should the government create? Subsequent chapters move on to political decentralization. For a given administrative structure, are there benefits or costs to letting local communities choose their own political leaders and policies? I start by considering how political decentralization interacts with fiscal factors. Chapter 4 examines arguments that local governments will be disciplined in desirable ways by competition to attract mobile capital or residents. Chapter 5 takes up arguments that empowering local governments will cause fiscal instability and that competition among local governments will keep them from redistributing income. In Chapter 6, I explore whether increasing the number of tiers of government with the power to tax leads them to extract more from citizens in the aggregate, and whether giving local governments larger shares of tax revenue improves economic performance by motivating them to choose more business-friendly policies.

Chapters 7 and 8 examine several purported political benefits of decentralization. I consider whether political decentralization nurtures civic virtue, renders governments more accountable, and protects individual liberty. I also discuss the claim that decentralization, by increasing the number of veto players, makes central policies harder to change. Chapter 9 turns to questions of information acquisition. I study whether autonomous local governments will generally be better informed about local tastes and conditions than a central government, and whether decentralization tends to stimulate policy experimentation. Chapter 10 looks at arguments that political decentralization tends to reduce ethnic conflict and dampen the demand for secession.

Chapters 3 to 10 analyze the logic of theoretical arguments. In Chapter 11, I briefly review attempts by scholars to identify empirical relationships between decentralization and various political and economic outcomes, using cross-national data. I survey statistical studies of the quality of government, economic performance, ethnic conflict, democracy, and the durability of policies. Chapter 12 summarizes the previous findings and draws some conclusions.

2

The Political Process

In this chapter, I introduce some concepts and a formal notation that will be useful for examining arguments about the consequences of decentralization. Of course, there are many ways one might think about the political process, and the conceptualization I offer here is chosen for convenience. I begin by defining various types of decentralization.[1]

2.1 Defining Decentralization

"'Centralization' is now a word constantly repeated but is one that, generally speaking, no one tries to define accurately," Tocqueville wrote in 1835 (Tocqueville 1969 [1835], p. 87).[2] These days, the problem is more that people define centralization and decentralization in many different ways, and any two scholars or policy makers who sit down to debate the subject will usually have different things in mind. Some also try to squeeze several concepts under a single label. I find it helpful to distinguish different types or aspects of decentralization. The definitions I suggest here are useful primarily for making and analyzing theoretical arguments. To adapt these to cross-national empirical comparison would take a great deal of additional thought.

---

[1] For another way one might differentiate types of decentralization, see Bird and Vaillancourt (1998).

[2] He did not help much himself. Tocqueville's distinction between "administrative" centralization – the concentration of control over interests that are "of special concern to certain parts of the nation" – and "governmental" centralization – the concentration of control over "interests . . . common to all parts of the nation" does not give much guidance about what these common and special interests are.

Before defining decentralization, I need to define a few other terms. Each state governs a particular territory, or set of points in space. A *jurisdiction* is a subset of the territory consisting of contiguous points. While some jurisdictions contain others, I assume the borders of jurisdictions do not cross.[3] The largest jurisdiction comprises the state's entire territory, and I call this the *first tier* jurisdiction. All those jurisdictions that are proper subsets of the first tier jurisdiction – but of no others – are second tier jurisdictions. Those that are proper subsets of only first and second tier jurisdictions are third tier jurisdictions, and so on.[4] I call those jurisdictions that do not contain any smaller ones "bottom tier" jurisdictions. Each citizen lives within one jurisdiction at each tier (for example, each citizen might live within one municipality, one county, one state, and one country).

Each jurisdiction is associated with at least one *governmental body*. Governmental bodies are the organizations – executive, legislative, judicial – that together make and implement *policies*. Policies are authoritative decisions that are binding on citizens, and they typically include laws, executive directives, decrees, regulations, court orders, and so on. Governmental bodies are staffed by *officials*, who are usually a subset of citizens. I refer to the set of governmental bodies associated with a particular jurisdiction as *the government* of that jurisdiction. Any policies made by this government are binding within its jurisdiction. (Note that the definitions so far say nothing about the relationship between governments at different tiers. Lower tier governments might be completely independent of higher tier ones or they might be completely subordinate to them, consisting of centrally appointed field agents authorized only to implement policies imposed from above.) Often it will be convenient to treat a given government as though it were a single decision maker, rather than a set of governmental bodies that interact in various ways. A system of *multilevel* or *multi-tier government* is one in which jurisdictions and governmental bodies exist at more than one tier.

To orient discussion, consider now the ideal type of a completely *centralized* regime. A single government exists, based in the nation's capital, with the whole national territory as its jurisdiction. This government directly

---

[3] This is a simplification that excludes such cases as municipalities that straddle a state line or local service providers whose jurisdictions overlap. It also excludes jurisdictions that are different shapes and sizes for different branches of government – for instance, U.S. federal judicial circuits, which do not correspond to individual states. For alternative approaches, see the discussion in Hooghe and Marks (2003).

[4] For a similar discussion, see Breton and Scott (1978, ch. 3).

chooses all public policies for all parts of the territory and implements and adjudicates them itself. It can, of course, implement different policies in different parts of the territory if it so chooses. Different types of decentralization represent different departures from this extreme case.

First, suppose the government of an otherwise centralized regime employs field agents located in lower tier jurisdictions to implement at least one policy. Suppose the agents are appointed by and subordinate to the central government. I then say the government is *administratively decentralized*. By "subordinate to the central government" I mean that the agent has no right to overrule the central government's instructions or appeal them to some other body (except for the right all citizens may have to challenge in court the legality of the content of a particular order). The local official is analogous to the locally based employee of a corporation, although he may or may not be paid for his service. I call tiers that house only officials of this type *administrative tiers*. Chapter 3 examines several arguments about the optimal number of administrative tiers within a state and the allocation of functions among them.

Administratively decentralized systems differ in various ways. They may have one or more administrative tiers. In systems with two or more subnational tiers, governments at intermediate levels (e.g., states or provinces) may have the right to command those at lower levels (e.g., municipalities). So long as no tier has the right to overrule or appeal the central government's instructions and all agents are appointed by and subordinate to governments at higher tiers, the system is still just administratively (and not politically) decentralized. Such systems differ also in the proportion of policies that local agents implement and the proportion that the central government (and its centrally based agents) implements itself. At the same time, subordination, even when clear in theory, is never absolute in practice. The central government may not be able to observe its agents' actions perfectly, in which case the relationship may be subject to "principal–agent" problems. Higher tier governments may also delegate authority to their agents to make local policy decisions. For this to remain just administrative decentralization, the superior government must retain the right to reverse such delegation and to overrule decisions its agents make.

I contrast administrative decentralization with various types of *political decentralization*. These all involve either assigning some decision-making authority to lower tiers in a way that is difficult to reverse or assigning residents of lower-level jurisdictions some rights to select lower-level officials, or both. Within a multi-tier structure, authority to make policy decisions might be divided among the governments in various ways. Authority over particular groups of issues might be assigned exclusively to one or the other tier. For instance, a central government might have exclusive authority to legislate on national defense and local governments to legislate on education. Alternatively, the right to decide on a particular issue might be shared between tiers in some way. I say that some degree of *decision-making decentralization* exists if at least one subnational tier of government has exclusive authority to make decisions on at least one policy issue.[5] In addition, to distinguish decision-making decentralization from mere administrative delegation, the subnational government's right to decide on this issue must be entrenched in a way that is difficult for the central government to reverse. Or, with Breton and Fraschini (2003), we could invoke the analogy to the theory of incomplete contracts and say that the subnational government *owns* this decision-making power.

A second type of decentralization concerns the choice not of policies but of officials. Government officials at a given tier may be selected and appointed either by governments at other levels (either higher or lower) or by some subset of the residents of the relevant jurisdiction.[6] I say that some degree of *appointment decentralization* exists if government officials at at least one subnational tier are selected and appointed by residents of that government's jurisdiction, independent of higher-level governments. Such local appointment might be democratic – involving local elections – or not – involving, say, acclamation by a local elite.

My definition of *decision-making decentralization* corresponds to one classic definition of *federalism*. Riker argues that a state is federal if it meets two conditions: (a) it must have (at least) two levels of government, and (b) each level must have "at least one area of action in which it is autonomous." The second requirement must be formally guaranteed, for instance in a constitution (Riker 1964, p. 11). For Robert Dahl, also, federalism is "a system in which some matters are exclusively within the competence of certain local units – cantons, states, provinces – and are constitutionally

---

[5] I distinguish the assignment of decision-making authority across tiers from the question of how decisions are made at different tiers. For instance, suppose that in two systems, A and B, local legislatures have the right to decide on education policy, but in A unanimity of the local legislators is required to pass bills whereas in B only a strict majority is required. I would consider both to be politically decentralized.

[6] They could also serve by virtue of some inherited status, as for instance the sultans in some of the Malaysian states.

beyond the scope of the authority of the national government; and where certain other matters are constitutionally outside the scope of the authority of the smaller units" (Dahl 1986, quoted in Stepan 2001, p. 318). However, some would add that officials of the subnational units must also be locally appointed or elected. (Some might argue that this is implied by the Riker and Dahl definitions.) In this case, *federalism* would correspond to a certain combination of *decision-making* and *appointment* decentralization.[7]

As already noted, authority to make policy in a particular area might be shared between different-tier governments. In some cases, the constitution gives subnational governments an explicit role in the central government's decision making. An extreme example is a loose confederation in which each state has the right to veto all central government decisions. A weaker form occurs when subnational government representatives get to vote on central legislation, with less than unanimity required. For instance, the upper house of the German national parliament, the Bundesrat, consists of representatives appointed by the Land governments. The Bundesrat can veto certain central bills. In Russia between 1996 and 2001, the leaders of regional governments and legislatures themselves served *ex officio* in the central parliament's upper house and could require a supermajority in the lower house to pass some legislation.[8] Because such constitutional devices enable local constituencies to influence central government policy, they are sometimes regarded as a form of decentralization. I refer to a system in which subnational governments or their representatives have formal rights to participate in central policy making as *constitutionally decentralized*. I refer to *decision-making, appointment*, and *constitutional decentralization* as different types of *political decentralization*.

Finally, some arguments concern what scholars call *fiscal decentralization*. This can mean various things.[9] Sometimes what is meant is decision-making decentralization on questions of taxation or expenditure. A more fiscally decentralized state, in this sense, is one in which lower tier governments have greater autonomy to define their own tax bases, set their own tax rates, and determine their own public spending. In other settings, "fiscal

---

[7] There are, of course, many other conceptions of "federalism" – so many, in fact, that it is easy to agree with Proudhon that "calling for 'federalism' *tout court* is about as helpful as calling for happiness without further explanation" (Proudhon 1979 [1863], p. xxiii).

[8] Since 2001, the upper house has been filled with appointees of the regional executives and legislatures.

[9] See Ebel and Yilmaz (2002) for a discussion.

decentralization" is used to refer to the *ex post* division of tax revenues – or expenditures – between levels of government, regardless of whose decisions led to this division. In this sense, a state in which subnational governments receive a larger share of total tax revenues – or account for a larger share of total state expenditures – is more fiscally decentralized.[10] These different usages are relevant to different arguments. For instance, some have suggested that fiscal decentralization *in the first sense* leads to greater fiscal responsibility. Others have argued that fiscal decentralization *in the second sense* strengthens local officials' motivation to support economic activity and thus expand their tax base (see section 6.2).[11]

I have kept these definitions as simple as was consistent with the goal of the book – to analyze a particular set of arguments.[12] Most of these arguments claim that (some kind of) political decentralization tends to produce outcomes that are better in some way than those produced by administrative decentralization or complete centralization. For instance, decision-making decentralization is said to improve the quality of policy decisions because local officials tend to have more accurate information or a stronger impulse to innovate (see Chapter 9). Constitutional decentralization is thought to entrench central policies by increasing the number of veto players whose agreement is necessary to change them (see Chapter 8). Various other arguments focus on how equilibrium outcomes change when a particular policy responsibility is reassigned from central to local governments.

People often refer to countries as being more or less decentralized overall, without specifying which aspects they have in mind. This raises enormous conceptual problems. Even to assess a country's "overall" degree of just *decision-making* decentralization would require resolving many tricky questions. First, when the right to make policy on a given issue is shared between actors from different tiers, it is difficult to measure the extent of

---

[10] This is essentially the indicator of decentralization chosen by Lijphart (1984, p. 177). It has been used in numerous other studies. The *ex post* division of revenues or expenditures is often treated as a proxy for the constitutional division of policy responsibilities. However, it seems more like a social outcome than an exogenous institution.

[11] Fiscal decentralization, in either of the senses discussed, admits various additional nuances. For instance, do subnational governments have greater autonomy over defining tax bases, tax rates, or both? For all their taxes or just some? Is the division of revenue just a *de facto* outcome, or do governments have the right to a given share? Do subnational governments collect their taxes themselves? Such issues are often highly relevant to particular arguments.

[12] For other recent discussions of the meaning of decentralization, see Rodden (2004) and Schneider (2003).

their respective rights.[13] Second, if two countries differ in more than one policy assignment, it is not clear how to add these up.[14] Is a system in which local governments make education policy and central government makes health policy more or less decentralized than one in which the assignments are reversed? How does one compare two three-tier systems, A and B, when in A one-third of the issues are assigned to each of the tiers, while in B 90 percent of issues are assigned to the middle tier and 5 percent each to the top and bottom tiers?[15] These questions have no obvious answers. Fortunately, the arguments I discuss in later chapters generally do not require me to answer them.

2.2 Modeling Politics

2.2.1 Three Games

I develop here a very simple formalization of the political process, into which many of the arguments about decentralization can later be transposed. I introduce some notation that I will re-use throughout the book and discuss a few modeling elements that will reappear later.

I start by considering the political process in a single, isolated unit and then adapt this to politics in multi-tiered states. Consider a country inhabited by M citizens (indexed $m = 1, 2, \ldots, M$), where M is large. One may think of the country's citizens and officials as playing three repeated games. In the *leadership selection game*, certain citizens (or outsiders) are chosen to become officials for the next period. In the *policy game*, officials choose public policies for the country. (Citizens may also participate in this game by lobbying officials over policies.) In the *economic game*, citizens decide on economic actions: They allocate time between work and leisure, invest capital, pay or evade taxes, and consume privately and publicly supplied goods and services. The first two of these are "games" in the strict sense – that is, actors are strategic, taking into account the reactions of others when making their

---

[13] Various constitutions – those of India, Malaysia, Germany, Russia, and Brazil, for instance – assign certain policy areas "concurrently" to central and subnational authorities. In other cases, one tier may have primary responsibility, but its laws or regulations may be overturned by bodies at another tier.

[14] Cf. Riker (1964, p. 7): "There is no mechanical means of totting up the numbers and importance of areas of action in which either kind of government is independent of the other."

[15] Oates (1972, p. 196) notes this problem.

Table 2.1. *Types of decentralization*

1. Administrative decentralization	At least one policy is implemented not by the central government directly but by locally based agents appointed by and subordinate to the central government.
2. Political decentralization	
Decisionmaking decentralization	At least one subnational tier of government has exclusive authority to make decisions on at least one policy issue.
Appointment decentralization	Government officials at one or more subnational tiers are selected by local residents, independent of higher level governments.
Federal state	a. Decisionmaking decentralization. b. Decisionmaking decentralization + appointment decentralization (at the same tier).
Constitutional decentralization	Subnational governments or their representatives have a formal right to participate (in some non-trivial way) in central policymaking.
3. Fiscal decentralization	a. Decisionmaking decentralization on tax or expenditure issues. b. Subnational governments account for a large share of total government revenues or spending.

choices. I will often treat the economic game in simpler, decision-theoretic terms, assuming that because there are many citizens, each takes the wage, interest rate, and other prices as given. The policies chosen, along with the economic decisions of citizens, determine economic outcomes – the size of the public budget, employment level, economic output, and so on.

As an analytical simplification (but not a philosophical position!) I assume that the basic preferences of the actors are fixed before the three games begin. Actors rationally maximize their payoffs, given their preferences, the constraints created by the rules of the game, and the anticipated reactions of others. In fact, the process is endlessly repeated, so the preferences of actors at the start of any round might be determined (in part) by the outcomes of previous rounds (that is, individuals' preferences may be shaped by their histories, rather than genetically implanted). Nevertheless, to understand an iterated process one must begin somewhere, and the point at which

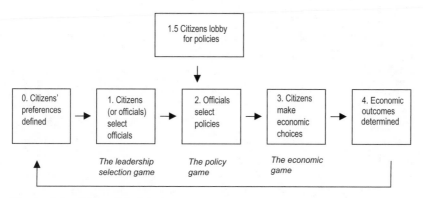

Figure 2.1. The political process

preferences are already defined is a useful starting point. The political process is summarized in Figure 2.1.

2.2.2 Preferences of Actors

I make a standard assumption that citizens care about two things: their consumption of privately supplied goods and their consumption of public goods and services. Focusing for now on a single period, denote spending on public goods and services as g and citizen m's consumption of privately supplied goods as s_m. It will often be convenient to assume a quasilinear form of each citizen's payoff function:

$$U_m = \theta_m h(g) + s_m \tag{2.1}$$

where $h' > 0, h'' < 0, h(0) = 0, \underset{g \to 0}{Lim}\, h'(g) = \infty$, and $\theta_m \geq 0$ is a constant that indexes citizen m's relative preference for public over private spending.[16] Where the heterogeneity of citizens' tastes is not important, I will often assume $\theta_m = 1$ for all m and drop it from the equation. I will do so for the rest of this chapter.

Let citizen m have pre-tax income y_m. Suppose first that the government levies a lump sum tax of t on each citizen and pays a cash transfer of $r_m \geq 0$ to citizen m. Suppose also that citizens do not save any of their income. Then, $s_m = y_m - t + r_m$. If, by contrast, the government levies a proportional tax

---

[16] I assume here that $h(\cdot)$ is the same for all citizens, although it may sometimes be useful to relax this.

on income at rate τ, then citizen m's private spending is $s_m = (1 - \tau)y_m + r_m$. When cash transfers are not important to the argument, I will abstract from them and set $r_m = 0$ for all m.

Quasilinear payoff functions like that in (2.1) have been used by political economists in many applications,[17] and – as I will show in this chapter – they can be viewed as a reduced form consistent with a variety of more complicated underlying models. Such preference functions embody three key assumptions. First, the marginal utility that citizens derive from publicly provided goods and services falls as the level of provision rises. The first million dollars of government services are more valuable to citizens than the first hundred. Second, the marginal utility from private consumption does not diminish.[18] This also means that, once a certain level of public goods and services has been provided, citizens will wish to spend any additional income on private consumption. The third assumption is a greater simplification, and more open to question: Utility is additively separable in public spending and private consumption. That is, the utility that citizens derive from public goods and services does not vary with their level of private consumption – public and private consumption are neither complements nor substitutes.

How should one characterize the preferences of government officials? Of course, officials' preferences are constrained by the political game, as discussed below. But to analyze how the political game affects outcomes, one must know something about what officials would choose if they were not constrained.

Political economists often make either of two extreme assumptions. Some assume that government officials are entirely predatory, maximizing their private gains from public office with no concern for the well-being of citizens. Such private gains may be legal – an official salary – or illegal – funds corruptly embezzled. I denote such (after-tax) consumption of the budget by officials as c. Others assume that officials are entirely benevolent, maximizing the well-being of the citizens they govern. Although I will sometimes adopt one of these extreme positions – for instance, to evaluate arguments that themselves make these assumptions – I will more generally suppose that government officials are partially benevolent and partially

---

[17] See, for instance, Persson and Tabellini (2000, p. 48).

[18] This is a useful although inaccurate simplification. But it does seem reasonable to think that individuals' marginal utility from private consumption diminishes more slowly than their marginal utility from public services. Assuming just this would usually yield similar results, although after more complicated algebra.

predatory. Even if they were unconstrained, officials would want to maximize some combination of their own private benefits and the utility of (at least some subset of) citizens.

Supposing that the government contains just one official, we can write the government's payoff in a given period as: $a \sum_{m \in F} (h(g) + s_m) + dq(c)$ where I suppose that the official cares equally about each citizen within a subset, F, and not at all about those outside this group; $q' > 0, q'' < 0$, $q(0) = 0$, and $\underset{c \to 0}{Lim}\, q'(c) = \infty$; and $a, d \geq 0$ are constants. Define M_F as the number of members of the favored group, F, and $\bar{x}_F \equiv \sum_{m \in F} x_m / M_F$ as the average value of variable x among members of F. After a few manipulations and a normalization, we can rewrite the objective as:

$$V = h(g) + \bar{s}_F + bq(c) \tag{2.2}$$

where $b \geq 0$ is a constant.[19] ($\bar{s}_F = \bar{y}_F + \bar{r}_F - t$ under lump sum taxation, and $\bar{s}_F = (1 - \tau)\bar{y}_F + \bar{r}_F$ under proportional taxation.) The government's budget constraint is $c + g + \sum_m r_m \leq tM$ for lump sum taxation and $c + g + \sum_m r_m \leq \tau \sum_m y_m$ for proportional taxation. This is a very general formulation of policy makers' basic preferences that encompasses everything from pure representation of the average citizen's preferences ($b = 0$, $M_F = M$) to pure predation ($b \to \infty$), as well as various gradations of motivation in between.

2.2.3 The Leadership Selection Game

The leadership selection game determines who has authority to make policy decisions. No single model can capture all the important variations in how leaders emerge in different regimes. It is useful, therefore, to look for some simple, general conceptualizations that can be adapted to particular problems.

The leadership selection game can perform either or both of two functions. First, it can select certain types of candidates for office – in the language of Equation (2.2), it may choose candidates with desired versions of the $q(\cdot)$ function, of the parameter b, and of the subset F. Second, the leadership selection game may shape candidates' choices once in office. Instead of

---

[19] In fact, the government would wish to maximize $a M_F V$, but so long as the size of the favored group is fixed, this is just a linear transformation that does not change anything important.

simply maximizing (2.2) subject to the budget constraint, officials may take into account how their actions at time 2 in one round affect their chance of being reappointed at time 1 in the next round.

I first consider democratic, and then authoritarian, regimes. In democracies, leaders are selected in elections. As I will show, various models of elections can be seen as constraining officials' payoffs, producing constrained payoff functions that still take the form of Equation (2.2). In some applications, modeling elections explicitly is important. But in others, it is reasonable to ignore the details of the leadership selection game and simply start from a constrained preference function like that in (2.2). Three approaches to modeling elections are currently popular. These differ on two main dimensions. First, models differ on whether candidates and parties can credibly commit to particular policies before elections. Second, assuming that commitments are *not* credible, models differ on whether elections are conceived as a selection device or as a mechanism to discipline incumbents.

2.2.3.1 Policy Precommitment Hotelling (1929) and Downs (1957) developed one of the first formal models of electoral competition. In the simplest version, two candidates or parties compete for votes by committing themselves to policies, measured on a single dimension. They care only about getting elected, and not at all about policy per se. All citizens vote. Whichever candidate wins more votes then implements the policy he promised. If each voter has single-peaked preferences (that is, she has a unique favorite policy, and her utility drops monotonically as policy rises above or falls below this point), the only Nash equilibrium is for both candidates to choose the policy preferred by the median voter.[20] The policy game is telescoped into the election itself, which selects not just an official but a particular policy. Because the median voter has preferences of the form of (2.1), the winning candidate seeks to maximize a quasilinear function of this type.

The model can be adapted straightforwardly to competitions between two parties for seats in a majority-rule legislature. Before the election, each party commits to a policy on the single dimension. The one that wins more than half the seats gets to implement its policy. The result depends on the electoral rule. If seats are allocated by proportional representation, both parties' policies converge on that favored by the median voter nationwide.

[20] See, for instance, Osborne (1995).

If candidates run in separate districts (and all care sufficiently about their party's electoral performance as well as their own), the unique equilibrium is for both parties to propose the policy favored by the median voter in the median district (when districts are ordered by the favored policy of the local median voter) (Hinich and Ordeshook 1974).

The standard Downsian model has important limitations that have been widely noted. First, if voters' preferences are not single-peaked, or if the policy space is multidimensional, there may be no pure-strategy equilibrium. That is, there may be no pair of policy vectors (x_A, x_B) such that x_A maximizes party A's expected utility given that party B chooses x_B and vice versa. Given the citizen preferences in (2.1) and assuming $r_m = 0$ for all m, preferences are single-peaked, and a median-voter equilibrium will exist in which the parties or candidates converge on the policy preferred by the citizen with the median income.[21] But, if g were multidimensional – a vector of different types of public spending, say – this would not necessarily be the case. When the issue space is multidimensional, a pure-strategy equilibrium will exist only by fluke, if there happens to be a policy vector such that every hyperplane through it divides the distribution of citizen ideal points in half (Davis, DeGroot, and Hinich 1972).[22]

One can guarantee a pure-strategy equilibrium even given multiple policy dimensions by making several additional assumptions. Suppose, first, that at least one policy dimension cannot be manipulated by the candidates or parties. Grossman and Helpman (2001, chapter 2) distinguish "fixed positions" that candidates cannot change from "pliable positions" that they manipulate to secure votes. Dixit and Londregan (1996) contrast permanent "ideological" positions and flexible "tactical promises." Fixed positions might represent historically generated reputations or strong preferences on particular issues. Suppose, in addition, that policies can differentiate among subgroups of voters, each of which contains more than one voter and has a known cumulative distribution function for preferences on the fixed policies

---

[21] Under lump sum taxation, the budget constraint is $g \leq Mt$; assuming as before that $\theta_m = 1, \forall m, dU_m/dt = h_g(g)M - 1$, from which we see that U_m increases to a maximum at $g^* = h_g^{-1}(1/M)$, and then falls. Under proportional taxation, the budget constraint is $g \leq \tau \sum_m y_m$; $dU_m/d\tau = h_g(g) \sum_m y_m - y_m$, from which U_m increases to a maximum at $g^* = h_g^{-1}(y_m/\sum_m y_m)$, and then falls. Persson and Tabellini (2000, p. 49) show that such preferences satisfy the Gans–Smart single-crossing condition, which guarantees an equilibrium.

[22] A pure-strategy equilibrium may also exist if not all citizens vote (Hinich, Ledyard, and Ordeshook 1972).

that is quasiconcave.[23] An equilibrium will, then, exist. Alternatively, if pliable policies can differentiate between individual voters, one can guarantee an equilibrium by assuming some uncertainty on the part of candidates about the voters' fixed policy preferences, and a probability distribution for these that meets some plausible technical conditions.[24]

In the equilibria of such models, the candidates choose pliable positions that maximize a weighted average of the utilities of the voters, with the weights measuring how responsive the voter (or group) is to the pliable policies at the equilibrium. More responsive voters (or groups) get greater weight. Because the candidates converge on sets of pliable policies that provide the same weighted average of utilities, the winner is determined by the fixed positions.

Because in equilibrium the parties or candidates maximize a weighted average of voters' preference functions, their maximand will look like $\sum_m \beta_m[h(g) + (1 - \tau)y_m]$, for the proportional tax case, where $\{\beta_m\}$ represents the weights, which we can normalize so that they sum to M. Dividing everything by M, the maximand becomes $V = h(g) + (1 - \tau)(\sum_m \beta_m y_m)/M$, which resembles Equation (2.2) with $b = 0$, except that average after-tax income is replaced by a weighted average of after-tax incomes. In the special case in which $\beta_m = 1$ for all m and all citizens are in the favored group, the two are identical. There is a subtlety in that the weights, $\{\beta_m\}$, are determined endogenously, because they measure the sensitivity of voter m to budget policy *at the equilibrium*. However, assuming there is such an equilibrium, the actual level of the weights will not usually concern us. We can view policy makers as simply maximizing a function of this form – that is, one that is quasilinear in a weighted sum of citizen income.

Three limitations of the Downsian model – even versions of it that could accommodate multiple policy dimensions – motivated a search for richer conceptualizations of electoral competition. First, the Downsian model assumed that officials consumed no rents (i.e., $b = 0$). This followed from the unrealistic assumption that all policies must be honestly described in

---

[23] This is the approach of Dixit and Londregan (1996). Although they provide a more complicated set of conditions (p. 1149), it would seem to be enough for their proof to assume quasiconcavity of the cumulative distribution function because an increasing function of a quasiconcave function is quasiconcave. Almost any reasonable cdf will be quasiconcave.

[24] This is the approach of Lindbeck and Weibull (1987). If campaigning is costly, uncertainty may also be necessary to ensure that both parties believe they have a chance of winning and so choose to enter the race (see Grossman and Helpman 2001, ch. 2).

full before each election – a candidate who admitted she would consume rents would always lose to an otherwise identical rival who promised not to. This meant the model could not be used to analyze situations in which officials do consume rents. Second, the assumption of only two parties or candidates begged the question of how citizens decide whether or not to run for office. This was a key focus of a subsequent wave of models.

Finally, the assumption that candidates can credibly commit themselves to particular policies before an election struck some political economists as dubious. In fact, empirical studies – not to mention casual observation – suggest that far from all campaign promises are kept. Fishel (1985) found that U.S. presidents tried to keep their promises only 63 percent of the time.[25] Voters are certainly not naïve about this. Ringquist and Dasse (2004) cite one 1989 poll which found that 71 percent of American respondents thought that "to win elections, most members of Congress make campaign promises they have no intention of fulfilling." The interest of a given candidate – or especially a party – in preserving a reputation for honesty might lead it to keep promises if the game has a long time horizon (Alesina 1988, Austen-Smith and Banks 1989). But this depends on the discount rate, and in some models on the degree of political polarization.

2.2.3.2 *Elections as Selection Device; No Policy Precommitment* Osborne and Slivinski (1996) and Besley and Coate (1997) develop models that do not assume candidates can commit to policies. They also model the choice of citizens to run for office. In the first stage of the game, citizens decide whether to pay a small cost and become candidates. Those who enter the race announce their preferred policy. (They are assumed to do so honestly.) Then voters vote for candidates, and the one with a plurality wins. Candidates cannot commit to particular policies, and so when elected they just maximize their own preferences subject to any constraints of the policy game. Including the entry stage in the game makes it easier to ensure that an equilibrium exists even when policy is multidimensional. Besley and Coate show that, if mixed strategies are permitted in the entry stage, the game always has at least one equilibrium. In fact, it has many. There will generally be equilibria with one, two, and more candidates entering the race (for details, see Besley and Coate 1997, Persson and Tabellini 2000, chapter 5). In the one- and two-candidate equilibria, voters vote sincerely

---

[25] Cited in Ringquist and Dasse (2004). Some studies find higher proportions – but none come close to 100 percent.

and pick the candidate whose preferences are closest to their own. In the multicandidate equilibria, strategic voting often occurs.

The model has various advantages over its Downsian predecessor. It accommodates elections in which there are more than two candidates or parties, and it models their entry endogenously. Moreover, it does not require one to assume that politicians are bound by their promises. However, the citizen–candidate model in its original form has two drawbacks. Like Downsian models, it assumes that candidates honestly announce their preferences, without providing any mechanism to ensure such truth telling. And the related assumption that all candidates take no rents (because they announce their preferences sincerely, and voters reject all who would take some) is implausible.

In reality, all candidates claim to be honest and frugal, and almost all profit from office in some way, legal or otherwise. Their assertions are appropriately treated as uninformative. One could adapt the citizen–candidate model to suppose that all candidates take some rents – most simply, by assuming that all have the same concavely increasing $q(\cdot)$ function. Because they cannot use elections to select candidates with a lower preference for rents, voters simply ignore this.[26] I will call the citizen–candidate model adapted in this way to incorporate a positive taste for rents the "adapted citizen–candidate model." It is consistent with this model to suppose that each winning candidate maximizes some payoff function of the form of Equation (2.2).

2.2.3.3 Elections as Source of Discipline; No Policy Precommitment A third approach treats elections as a device to control the extraction of rents. Rooted in the principal–agent model of hierarchies, such formalizations assume that citizens vote "retrospectively" to punish candidates who fail to supply desired policies at low cost or who reveal incompetence. Like the citizen–candidate models, they assume that candidates cannot commit themselves to particular policies. The main difference is in the timing: Elections come after the policy game rather than before it.[27]

---

[26] A more complicated adaptation would introduce elements of retrospective voting, discussed below, in order to determine equilibrium rents.

[27] See Barro (1973) and Ferejohn (1986). Another difference is that candidates' preferences need not be common knowledge. In models (like the one presented here) that assume all candidates are alike, the goal of retrospective voting is to motivate incumbents to limit their rent extraction. Because the candidates are identical, the voters' threat to punish high rent extraction by voting out the incumbent is credible. In versions in which candidates

In the typical formulation, a candidate first implements a policy and then voters choose whether or not to reelect him. If he is not reelected, a new candidate is chosen from a pool. All candidates are usually assumed to be *ex ante* identical. It is common to assume that incumbent politicians are motivated just by rents and that voters can coordinate on a common threshold, χ, for reelecting the incumbent. The question is how high that threshold will be.

The answer is that voters must set it sufficiently high that the incumbent will not strictly prefer to consume the whole budget in one period and get voted out of office. In other words, voters must permit incumbents to take a level of rents each period such that they are indifferent between, on the one hand, getting reelected indefinitely and, on the other, grabbing the whole budget in a single period and getting voted out.

Consider first a simple model with no uncertainty. Suppose the M voters all have the same income, y_t, where the subscript t indexes time, and share the same preferences: $U_t = h(g_t) + (1 - \tau_t)y_t$, where I have assumed a proportional income tax, $\tau_t \in [0, 1]$. For ease of exposition, I will relax here the assumption that officials' payoffs are strictly concave in their consumption of the budget and instead suppose that they increase linearly: $q(c) \equiv c$.[28] Voters reelect the incumbent if their utility at the time of the election is greater than or equal to the threshold level, χ (to be determined below). If the incumbent is not reelected, another candidate identical to him takes his place. The incumbent politician's payoff at time t if he is reelected is simply: $V_t = c_t + \delta V_{t+1}$, where V_{t+1} is the value of the game to him in period $t + 1$ assuming he is reelected, δ is his discount rate, and his budget constraint is $c_t + g_t = \tau_t y_t M$. He will choose each period between (a) setting g_t and τ_t such that $U_t = \chi$, and getting reelected, or (b) setting $\tau_t = 1$ and $c_t = y_t M$, and being voted out of office.

It is customary to focus on stationary equilibria of the game – that is, those in which the players' equilibrium actions in any round are independent of the history of play. In a stationary equilibrium in which the incumbent is reelected, $V_t^* = V_{t+1}^*$ (where asterisks indicate equilibrium values), and

---

differ in (non-observable) competence, the goal of retrospective voting is to vote out those who reveal themselves to have lower than average competence. There will often be both separating equilibria, in which the more competent incumbents set lower rents, and pooling equilibria, in which both incompetent and competent incumbents act as if they are competent.

[28] Similar results could be derived given strict concavity, but they are complicated by the additional effects of the officials' risk aversion.

so from $V_t = c_t + \delta V_{t+1}$, $V_t^* = c_t^*/(1 - \delta)$. For the incumbent to (weakly) prefer reelection, the voters must set χ such that this utility level is at least as great as that obtained by maximizing rent extraction in a given period: $c_t^*/(1 - \delta) \geq y_t M$. This determines a minimum level of c_t that the voters must allow the incumbent ($c_t^* = (1 - \delta)y_t M$). The voters will set χ at the level that maximizes their utility subject to the constraint that $c_t = c_t^*$. The incumbent extracts his c_t^* and maximizes the voters' payoff, $U_t = h(g_t) + (1 - \tau_t)y_t$, subject to the budget constraint $c_t^* + g_t = \tau_t y_t M$. It is as though he maximizes Equation (2.2) with $b = 0$, $M_F = M$, after taking a fixed payment of c_t^*.

Allowing for uncertainty complicates the model slightly. Suppose voters still reelect the incumbent if and only if $U_t \geq \chi$, but now voters' utility contains a stochastic element: $U_t = h(g_t) + (1 - \tau_t)y_t + \varepsilon_t$, where ε_t is a random variable with mean zero and known cumulative distribution function $F(\varepsilon_t)$. Now $V_t = c_t + p\delta V_{t+1}$, where $p = 1 - F(\chi - (h(g_t) + (1 - \tau_t)y_t))$ is the probability that the incumbent is reelected.

As before, in a stationary equilibrium, $V_t^* = V_{t+1}^*$, so $V_t^* = c_t^*/(1 - p\delta)$. To keep the incumbent from taking all income in a single round, the voters must set χ such that

$$\frac{c_t^*}{1 - p\delta} = \frac{c_t^*}{1 - [1 - F(\chi - [h(g_t^*) + (1 - \tau_t^*)y_t])]\delta} \geq y_t M \qquad (2.3)$$

where g_t^* and τ_t^* are the values that maximize $E(U_t) = h(g_t) + (1 - \tau_t)y_t$ subject to (2.3) and the budget constraint. This defines the level of c_t^*.

Comparing this with the certainty case, it is clear that equilibrium rents must be higher under uncertainty. (From (2.3), $c_t^* \geq (1 - p\delta)y_t M$, compared to $c_t^* \geq (1 - \delta)y_t M$ for the certainty case. Because $p < 1$, the right-hand side is larger under uncertainty, which means the constraint on rents is looser.) Because an incumbent risks losing office even if she sets policy as required, she has to be paid more to take this risk. In some applications, I will model the retrospective voting game explicitly (see the treatment of accountability in Chapter 7). But if we want to bracket the leadership selection game and focus on what happens afterward, we can think of the incumbent as maximizing $E(U_t) = h(g_t) + (1 - \tau_t)y_t$, which is (2.2) with $b = 0$, $M_F = M$, after taking a fixed fee of c^*. In both the certainty and uncertainty versions, the models reduce to a version of (2.2) with a tighter budget constraint ($g = \tau y_t M - c^*$, instead of $g = \tau y_t M$).

The three basic models of elections – Downsian, "citizen–candidate," and retrospective voting – make different assumptions and lend themselves to examination of different problems. Sometimes I will explicitly apply one or other version to formalize the leadership selection game. But in other cases, it will make sense to start by assuming that policy makers maximize a constrained quasilinear objective function and to leave the political economy foundations in the background.

2.2.3.4 Bureaucratic Slack

So far, I have treated the government of our isolated unit as a single decision maker. Of course, all governments – even absolute dictatorships – rely on more than one individual to implement their decisions, if not to make them. In the simplest terms, we can think of a president who is authorized to make all decisions and a single bureaucrat who implements them. If the bureaucrat's objectives differ from those of the president and his actions are not fully observable and verifiable, the bureaucrat may reshape the objective of policy during its implementation.

Suppose the bureaucrat can steal some public funds for his own private consumption, from which he derives linear utility. Call the amount of such consumption, c_b, where the subscript b stands for bureaucrat. Suppose that the probability of detection, $p(c_b)$, increases with c_b. If detected, the bureaucrat suffers a fixed punishment of magnitude $-\Pi$ (in utility terms). The bureaucrat and politician place the same value on citizen welfare, $a(b(g) + (1 - \tau)\hat{y})$, where $\hat{y}$ could be either the average or the median income, and the tax is an income tax. Even in a Downsian model in which the winning politician is motivated to maximize $a(b(g) + (1 - \tau)\hat{y})$, the bureaucrat will, when implementing his instructions, actually maximize: $a(b(g) + (1 - \tau)\hat{y}) + c_b - p(c_b)\Pi$. If the probability of detection rises at an increasing rate with c_b, then $c_b - p(c_b)\Pi$ is concave. We can rewrite the objective function of the bureaucrat as: $a(b(g) + (1 - \tau)\hat{y}) + q(c_b)$, which is just a variation on (2.2).[29] In Chapter 3, I will discuss how the problem of political control over bureaucrats affects the choice between administrative and political decentralization. But throughout the book, models that use quasilinear government objective functions like that in (2.2) can, where desired, be interpreted as implicitly assuming some degree of agency slack.

2.2.3.5 Distributive Policies

The possibility of distributive policies complicates analysis of voting. Within a Downsian framework, if one assumes that candidates cannot change their position on one "ideological"

---

[29] $q(c_b) = c_b - p(c_b)\Pi$ is only increasing at relatively low levels of c_b, but any interior equilibrium will have c_b on the increasing part of $q(c_b)$.

dimension, the approach of Dixit and Londregan (1996) and others discussed in section 2.2.3.1 can be used. Incumbents and challengers both target redistributive benefits disproportionately to groups that contain more "moderate" voters (i.e., groups with higher density around the equilibrium point on the "ideological" dimension) and more "swing" voters (i.e., those more sensitive to material benefits). As discussed in section 2.2.3.1, we can think of politicians maximizing a payoff function that is a weighted average of the payoffs of all groups.[30]

Within a retrospective voting setup, distributive policies interfere with the ability of voters to coordinate on voting strategies. If the incumbent can adopt different policies for different subgroups of voters, she will exploit competition among groups of voters to limit their control. Under certainty, the incumbent will target benefits to a minimum winning coalition of voters that contains the groups that are cheapest to "buy." Anticipating this, groups will bid their voting thresholds down to their default payoffs in order to get into the coalition. Under uncertainty, the incumbent may seek to insure herself by targeting a larger majority and providing groups with more than their default payoff. I develop some models along these lines in Chapter 7.

2.2.3.6 Authoritarian States
Of course, not all policy makers are elected. A number of political economists have considered how one might model the choices of authoritarian leaders (e.g., Wintrobe 1990; Grossman 1991; Olson 1993; Acemoglu and Robinson 2001, 2006; Gandhi and Przeworski 2006). I will argue that, perhaps surprisingly, the logic of authoritarian rule can often be assimilated to that formalized by the models of democratic elections already discussed.

One view of authoritarian regimes is that they are absolute dictatorships: The policy maker is unconstrained by any institutional pressure to respect the preferences of citizens. The dictator simply imposes whatever policy he likes, limited only by the laws of physics and economics. In other

---

[30] Another way to ensure equilibrium in a model of political redistribution is to assume that the candidates for office must simultaneously commit to policies, independently and without knowing the campaign promises of their opponents. Myerson (1993) shows that in a model of this type with two candidates and identical voters there is a unique symmetric equilibrium in which each candidate offers voters a random draw from the same uniform distribution. Lizzeri and Persico (2001) use this model to examine electoral competition under different voting rules, wherein candidates can promise either redistributive transfers or a public good. I do not use models of this type in the book because the assumption that candidates must commit to policies without knowing anything about their rivals' policies seems to me extreme.

words, given our assumption about policy makers' basic preferences, he imposes some version of (2.2). Dictatorial regimes might seem radically different from electoral democracies. Still, if candidates cannot commit to policies and are free to lie during the campaign, the constraining effect of elections is sure to be weak at best. The adapted citizen–candidate model makes exactly the same prediction: The winning candidate imposes her own preferences.

A second view of authoritarian rulers sees them as constrained, although in different ways than democratic politicians. To quote V. O. Key: "even in the least democratic regime opinion may influence the direction or tempo of substantive policy. Although a government may be erected on tyranny, to endure it needs the ungrudging support of substantial numbers of its people."[31] Authoritarian rulers may seek to forestall uprisings against their rule. Or they may need the support of factions within the military, security services, or a ruling party. These constraints can be formalized in ways that resemble the retrospective voting model. Instead of a probability of reelection, one might reinterpret p to represent the probability of surviving in office for some discrete period.

For instance, Grossman (1991) presents a model of an authoritarian ruler constrained by fear of peasant revolt. The larger the share of peasants' output a ruler extracts in taxes and land rents, the more attractive insurrection becomes to them. In equilibrium, the ruler trades off the benefit of higher tax revenues (which among other things go to pay soldiers) against the cost of radicalizing the peasantry. The fear of insurrection constrains the ruler in the way that fear of being voted out of office does in a retrospective voting model. Similarly, Acemoglu and Robinson (2001, 2006) view authoritarian regimes as cartels of the rich which, during recessions, seek to redistribute just enough income to the disenfranchised masses to prevent them from revolting.

Wintrobe (1990) also assumes that dictators are deposed if the population's loyalty falls below a threshold level. Loyalty is an increasing function of the inefficient public spending the dictator provides to the population and a decreasing function of the tax rate. The dictator maximizes his objective – rent extraction for "tin-pot" dictators and power over the population for "totalitarian" dictators – subject to the loyalty constraint. Again, this has the flavor of a retrospective voting model. So does a model developed by Gandhi and Przeworski (2006), in which weak dictators must provide

---

[31] Key (1961), quoted in Weingast (1997).

some subset of citizens with some combination of public goods and rents if they wish to avoid rebellion.

Finally, if authoritarian rulers are representatives of elite interest groups, we might think of their selection as analogous to a Downsian election – albeit with the franchise sharply restricted. Generals may compete for support among factions of the armed forces by promising, after a coup, to provide their preferred levels of taxation and military resources. One could construct a model similar to those of Dixit and Londregan (1996) in which incumbent dictators target resources to the "swing" elite factions – those most responsive to material benefits. Such factional popularity contests might be thought of as weakly institutionalized versions of a Downsian election, with uncertainty and very narrow participation.

Bueno de Mesquita et al. (2003) present a model of this type. Politics, whether under democracy or autocracy, is conceived as a competition for support within the country's elite (called the "selectorate"). An incumbent and a challenger propose packages of public goods and redistributive transfers to subsets of the elite. Members of the elite choose between the two, and whoever gets the necessary number of votes is elected and implements his proposal. The authors solve for a Markov perfect equilibrium of the repeated game. Autocracies differ from democracies in the model in that the number of elite voters needed to win the election is assumed to be smaller.

Thus, in each of these conceptualizations, authoritarian politics can be modeled in ways that look familiar. The constrained utility functions that emerge are similar in form to those derived from the models of democratic politics already discussed. Of course, the interesting variation among dictatorships merits exploration using more complicated models. But for the present purpose – comparing centralization with decentralization – a quasi-linear preference function may sometimes serve as a reasonable reduced form starting point.

2.2.4 The Policy Game

In the policy game, incumbent officials choose policies to maximize their objective functions, determined in the political game, subject to the constraints imposed by the economic game. There are two key issues here.

First, what policy instruments are available? In most of the arguments I discuss, these consist of tax rates and types of spending. Taxes may be lump sum or proportional to income or some other base. Income may be taxed at its source or in the jurisdiction where the recipient resides. Besides taxing income earned, governments may tax output sold. They may tax sales of different commodities at different rates. Finally, they may levy taxes on particular factors of production or assets – labor, capital, land, or real estate. Different types of taxes have different effects on economic behavior, as will be seen in the discussion of the economic game. Sometimes officials may also set negative tax rates – that is, pay positive cash transfers – to individuals or members of particular groups.

There are at least as many types of spending as there are varieties of taxes. Officials may supply a range of different goods and services. Their purchases may have characteristics of Samuelsonian public goods (non-excludability, nonrivalness), or of private goods. In the latter case, goods may be provided in different amounts to different groups or individuals. Such goods may be public inputs, or "infrastructure," which increase firms' productivity. Or they may be public outputs, which increase citizens' utility directly. Finally, as already noted, officials may consume part or all of the budget themselves.

The second key issue concerns the institutions that shape how policy makers' preferences translate into policy outcomes. (I continue to focus on a single, isolated political jurisdiction.) Although it is sometimes useful to treat one or other government as a single unit, in fact almost all governments are compound. They consist of multiple players, who interact according to procedures defined by laws, constitutions, or customs. Sometimes the key divisions are among executive, legislative, and judicial officials. Sometimes, divisions within one branch are relevant – such as those between the U.S. House of Representatives and the U.S. Senate. As a result, to predict outcomes one needs to go beyond the objective functions of individual players to consider the games they play with one another.

Even within a governmental body, there may be numerous players. The typical legislature contains many individuals, often divided into parties or factions. As is well known, what policies the legislature chooses will depend on the procedures and norms by which legislators interact. This will be relevant to some of the arguments discussed later in this book (see for instance section 5.2.4). If legislators can vote only on one-dimensional policies, a version of the median-voter theorem may apply: The most-preferred policy of the median legislator will be chosen. If policies are multidimensional, permitting redistribution among legislators or their constituencies, the outcome is far less clear. Assuming majority rule, some procedures may yield no pure strategy equilibrium, because any majority coalition can be defeated by another that is preferred by a majority of the voters.[32] If an agenda setter is first chosen (at random or by history) and can propose policies, the usual prediction in models with certainty (see, e.g., Baron 1991) is the formation of a minimum winning coalition: Exactly half the members get a benefit just slightly greater than their default payoff, and the agenda setter extracts maximally from all other members. Other analyses of the same problem derive equilibria in which benefits are distributed across all members' constituencies because of "log rolling" (Tullock 1970) or a norm of universalism (Weingast, Shepsle, and Johnsen 1981). Thus, the equilibrium outcome depends on the procedures for decision making in the legislature.

The policy game may feed back into the leadership selection game. In choosing officials, voters may look ahead to the bargaining games these officials will then have to play. They may select leaders with preferences different from their own because that will help them win in the subsequent policy bargaining. For instance, voters might choose a representative whose preferences make her cheaper for the agenda setter to co-opt – and therefore more likely to be included in the winning coalition (see Besley and Coate 1997, Chari et al. 1997).

Another important aspect of the policy game, about which I will have very little to say in this book, concerns lobbying by private individuals or groups for or against particular policies or government services.[33] I include this at time 1.5 in Figure 2.1 – after officials are selected and before they choose policies. Scholars differ in their understanding of just what it is lobbyists do. Some see them as buying policy decisions by promising private payments to officials contingent on the policy implemented (e.g., Grossman and Helpman 2001). Another view is that lobbyists help candidates win votes by offering endorsements in return for policies (e.g., Grossman and Helpman 1999). Still others see them as providing information that changes officials' beliefs about various aspects of the game (e.g., Potters and Van Winden 1992). I have only two rather unsatisfying excuses for leaving lobbying out of most analysis in this book. First, lobbying is not

---

[32] If, in a population of M voters, a coalition contains $X > M/2 + 1$ voters, it could be beaten by one that takes the benefits from $X - (M/2 + 1)$ members of the coalition and divides them among the remaining $M/2 + 1$ members. Any coalition, A, containing $M/2 + 1$ members can be beaten by another that takes all benefits away from one member of A and divides them among the remaining members of A and two voters outside A. Uncertainty can sometimes lead incumbents to seek coalitions larger than the "minimum winning coalition" (i.e., one with $M/2 + 1$ members).

[33] For a review of the extensive literature, see Austen-Smith (1997).

central to most of the arguments I set out to examine. Second, one cannot do everything.

2.2.5 The Economic Game

Once policies have been set, citizens make their economic decisions. At their simplest, these consist of allocating their endowments of labor and capital. Much of the analysis in later chapters concerns how the economic decisions citizens make are affected by the tax rates that different governments set.[34]

I will usually assume that the country contains a fixed amount of each factor – labor and capital – that can be allocated in different ways. To take labor first, each citizen has a stock of hours, $\bar{l}$, in each period that she can divide freely between work and leisure. She supplies l hours of labor and consumes $\bar{l} - l$ hours of leisure. I often assume that all citizens are equally productive, although this can easily be relaxed. Total hours of labor supplied by the M citizens is $\sum_m l_m \equiv L$. Some citizens own capital, which they invest wherever the return is highest. All capital must be invested each period. Total capital invested within the country is $\sum_m k_m \equiv K$. Some citizens also own land, which can be an input in production, a consumption good, or a store of value. As an input in production, land differs from mobile capital in that it can be used in only one location. It will be mentioned in passing when relevant to certain arguments, but it will not be central to most of the analysis.

I will often assume that output within the state, Y, is an increasing, strictly concave function of labor supplied and capital invested: $Y = f(L, K)$, with $f_L > 0$, $f_{LL} < 0$, $f_K > 0$, $f_{KK} < 0$, and $f_{LL}f_{KK} - f_{LK}^2 > 0$. Under perfect competition in capital and labor markets, investments earn a pre-tax rate of return equal to the marginal productivity of capital, $r = f_K(L, K)$, and labor is paid a wage equal to its marginal productivity, $w = f_L(L, K)$.

Policy can affect economic outcomes in several ways. First, taxes may influence the supply of labor. This is usually assumed not to be true of lump sum taxes.[35] But proportional taxes will often be distortionary. If labor income is subject to a proportional tax, τ, a higher tax rate decreases the

---

[34] As noted already, the "economic game" is not really a game at all in the standard economic sense because I will usually assume that citizens are nonstrategic when making labor supply and investment decisions.

[35] However, even lump sum taxes can have general equilibrium effects that reduce labor supply.

after-tax return to labor (to $(1 - \tau)w$), which may cause citizens to substitute leisure for work, thereby decreasing labor supply and output. For instance, suppose that a representative citizen sets l to maximize: $(1 - \tau)wl + v(\bar{l} - l)$, where $v(\cdot)$ is an increasing, concave function measuring the payoff to leisure. Suppose citizens do not coordinate their labor decisions and each neglects the effect of his labor supply on the wage rate. Differentiating the first order condition $((1 - \tau)w = v'(\bar{l} - l^*))$, we get $\frac{\partial l^*}{\partial \tau} = \frac{w}{v''(\bar{l} - l^*)} < 0$. In words, the representative citizen reduces his equilibrium labor supply, l^*, when the income tax rate rises. Thus, total equilibrium output, $f(L^*, K)$ (where $L^* = \sum_m l_m{}^*$), also falls as τ rises.

High proportional tax rates may also stimulate tax evasion. Suppose that the representative citizen conceals a share $a \in [0, 1]$ of her total income from the tax collectors and reports a share $(1 - a)$. There must be costs to concealing income, or all citizens would conceal all their income. Suppose that the cost of concealing income, $\phi(a)$, rises at an increasing rate with the share of income concealed (i.e., $\phi' > 0$, $\phi'' > 0$). This might be because the risk of getting caught and punished increases nonlinearly with the share of one's income concealed. Citizen m sets a to maximize $U_m = (1 - a)(1 - \tau)y_m + ay_m - \phi(a)$, which implies $\phi'(a^*) = \tau y_m$.[36] Again, this implies that officially reported income, $(1 - a^*)y_m$, will fall with increases in τ: $\frac{\partial a^*}{\partial \tau} = \frac{y_m}{\phi''(a^*)} > 0$, given $y_m > 0$, $a < 1$. Thus, a higher income tax rate might cause citizens both to work less (and consume more leisure) and to report a smaller proportion of their income. This would lead to both lower total income (including both official and unofficial parts), and a larger share of unofficial income in the total.

If higher tax rates cause citizens to work less – or report less income – then increasing the tax rate above a certain point may also cause tax revenues to decline. In his famous essay on the tax state, Joseph Schumpeter argued that tax revenues might be maximized at some intermediate rate. Before that, the idea can be traced to Ibn Kalduhn.[37] More recently, the notion has become associated with the economist Arthur Laffer. In a

---

[36] Again, because there are many citizens, the tax that any one individual pays will have a negligible effect on the quantity of the public goods provided to all; I leave public goods out of the citizen's objective function.

[37] See the discussion in Olson (1993, p. 569). Alexander Hamilton (2001 [1769–1804]) also noted the principle in Federalist No. 21: "It is a signal advantage of taxes on articles of consumption, that they contain in their own nature a security against excess...If duties are too high, they lessen the consumption; the collection is eluded; and the product to the treasury is not so great as when they are confined within proper and moderate bounds."

number of the arguments in this book, I will assume a "Laffer curve" with total tax revenues at first increasing and then decreasing with the tax rate as in Figure 2.2.

Empirical studies do not always have an easy time identifying a Laffer curve in revenue data (Goolsbee 1999). And there are problems with the theoretical argument too (for instance, in a general equilibrium model, the curve will slope downward at high tax rates only given certain production technologies; see Malcomson [1986]). Still, even highly predatory governments rarely attempt to tax away all income of citizens. And some version of the Laffer curve is a central assumption of various arguments about the consequences of decentralization. I therefore incorporate it into the models I use to examine these arguments.

Most simply, one can write official output as a function of the tax rate: $Y = Y(\tau); Y'(\tau) < 0$. Then, if there is an interior maximum, government revenue, $\tau Y(\tau)$, is maximized at a tax rate implicitly defined by:

$$\tau^* = -\frac{Y(\tau^*)}{Y'(\tau^*)} \tag{2.4}$$

For this to be a maximum, the second order condition, $2Y'(\tau^*) + \tau^* Y''(\tau^*) < 0$, must be satisfied. Combining the first and second order conditions, this means that at the equilibrium, $2(Y')^2 - YY'' > 0$. (This inequality will return in various applications.) For this to identify a unique maximum, we need the second order condition to hold for all tax rates, $\tau \in (0, 1)$. This will be true if output declines ever faster as the tax rate rises: $Y''(\tau) < 0, \forall \tau \in (0, 1)$. Figure 2.2 graphs an example, in which $Y = (1 - \tau)^{4/5}$.

Besides allocating their time between work and leisure and deciding what share of their income to declare, citizens decide where to invest their endowments of capital. (In the example of the single, isolated unit, they do not face a choice, but this will become important once we consider a larger state.) Output – and the return to capital – may be affected by the level of provision of publicly supplied inputs, or "infrastructure." Denoting the supply of infrastructure "I," I will sometimes write the production function as $f(L, K, I)$ (for instance, in section 4.2.4 I explore how infrastructure investments affect the location of capital investments). It is standard to assume that output is concave in infrastructure and that infrastructure increases the productivity of both labor and capital: $f_I > 0$, $f_{II} < 0$, $f_{LI} > 0$, $f_{KI} > 0$.

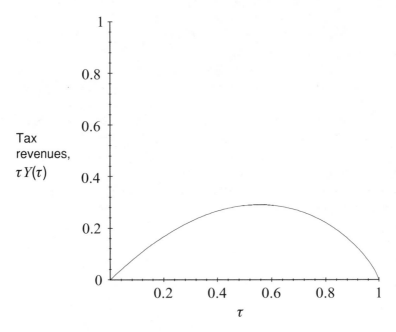

Figure 2.2. The revenue (Laffer) curve

2.2.6 Introducing Multiple Tiers

I have sketched a stylized portrait of politics in a single, isolated political unit. First, the leadership selection game determines what officials serve and what objectives they pursue. It selects candidates with particular preference functions or reshapes the winning candidates' objectives. Then the policy game transforms officials' objectives into policy choices. It determines tax rates and levels and types of public spending. Finally, in the economic game these policy outputs combine with citizens' objective functions to determine citizens' economic choices. Citizens make labor supply and investment decisions. In the aggregate, these choices determine economic output and other economic variables.

To analyze decentralization, we need to adapt this simple view to fit more complex, multilayered states. Suppose now that government is divided into J tiers, indexed $j = 1, 2, \ldots, J$. At each tier, the jurisdictions partition the country's territory. Each of the country's M citizens resides within one or other of the bottom tier jurisdictions. We can think of the three games – leadership selection, policy, and economic – being played within each jurisdiction during each period. But there are three important new elements:

actors from outside a given jurisdiction may now play a part in its policy game[38]; external actors may also play a part in its economic game (investing or working within the locality); and the governments of different tiers will themselves interact in a new set of games. I adapt the previously developed notation and concepts to this multi-tier setting as follows.

First, I index jurisdictions at a given subnational tier by $n = 1, 2, \ldots,$ N. Governments at any tier may, in theory, be authorized to levy taxes and spend revenues. Let G denote spending by the first tier or "central" government on public goods or services, and g_{jn} refer to spending by the government of the nth jurisdiction at tier j. Many arguments focus on just two tiers – "central" and "local" – and in such cases I will drop the j and denote public spending by the nth local government as g_n. Similarly, let T refer to the level of a nationwide lump sum tax set by the central government, while t_{jn} denotes the tax level set by the nth government at the jth tier; again, if only one local tier is considered, t_n denotes the tax set by the nth local government.

Adapting (2.1), the payoff for the mth resident of the nth local jurisdiction (again assuming only one local tier and still setting $\theta_m = 1$ for all m) becomes:

$$U_{nm} = H(G) + h(g_n) + \gamma(g_{-n}) + s_{nm} \qquad (2.1')$$

where $H(\cdot)$ measures the citizen's utility from central public spending, assumed here the same for all; $h(\cdot)$ now measures her utility from spending by her own local government; $\gamma(g_{-n})$ measures her utility from local public spending in all localities *other* than n (assumed the same for all residents of n); and s_{nm} is her private consumption. Under lump sum taxation, $s_{nm} \equiv y_{nm} - T - t_n + r_{nm} + R_{nm}$, where r_{nm} now denotes transfers to the mth resident of the nth local jurisdiction by her own local government and R_{nm} denotes transfers to her by the central government. (I assume that local governments do not make cash transfers to residents of other localities.) Under proportional taxation, $s_{nm} \equiv (1 - T - \tau_n)y_{nm} + r_{nm} + R_{nm}$. I assume $H', h' > 0, H'', h'' < 0$, $H(0) = h(0) = 0$, and $\underset{G \to 0}{Lim} H'(G) = \underset{g \to 0}{Lim} h'(g) = \infty$. In cases in which cross-jurisdiction externalities are not important, I will assume that $\gamma(g_{-n}) = 0$ for all n.

---

[38] Indeed, within some of the jurisdictions, there may be no policy game. Instead, policies are chosen by higher-level governments and merely implemented by the officials at lower levels.

Denoting consumption of the budget by local officials of jurisdiction n (in tier j) as c_{jn}, or c_n if there is only one local tier, we can adapt (2.2) to write the objective function for each local government as:

$$V_n = H(G) + h(g_n) + \gamma(g_{-n}) + \bar{s}_{F(n)} + bq(c_n) \qquad (2.2')$$

where $F(n)$ denotes the subset of residents of n favored by n's local government, and $\bar{x}_{F(n)}$ denotes the average value of variable x for members of $F(n)$. ($\bar{s}_{F(n)} = \bar{y}_{F(n)} + \bar{r}_{F(n)} + \bar{R}_{F(n)} - T - t_n$ under lump sum taxation, and $\bar{s}_{F(n)} = (1 - T - \tau_n)\bar{y}_{F(n)} + \bar{r}_{F(n)} + \bar{R}_{F(n)}$ under proportional income taxation.) In cases where each local government neglects the impact of other governments' spending, we can simplify this to: $V_n = h(g_n) + \bar{s}_{F(n)} + bq(c_n)$.

Central officials will have an objective function that is similar in form but more complicated because they may care about residents of multiple localities. Denoting by $\Phi(n)$ the set of residents of locality n that *central* officials care about, we can suppose that the central government maximizes: $V_c = a \sum_n \sum_{m \in \Phi(n)} U_{nm} + dq(C)$, where U_{nm} is as defined in (2.1'), and C measures consumption of the budget by central officials.

In a multi-tier setting, policies chosen by one government may influence economic behavior – and policy choices – in other jurisdictions. One government's action creates externalities for governments and residents of other areas. Indeed, this will be important in many of the arguments that follow. We can divide such externalities into "horizontal" and "vertical" ones. Horizontal externalities occur when the policies of one government at a given subnational tier affect the payoffs – and behavior – of residents of other jurisdictions at the same tier. I have already included a term, $\gamma(g_{-n})$, in the utility functions to capture external effects of local public good provision. But external effects may also be associated with local tax rates or provision of infrastructure. In Chapter 4, I consider how local governments may compete to attract mobile factors. Focusing on investment capital, I model complete mobility as an "arbitrage condition" which requires that in equilibrium the marginal, after-tax return to capital in any two jurisdictions be equal. Assuming that all types of income are taxed at a rate T nationwide and τ_n in local jurisdiction n (and that there is no deductibility of taxes), we can write this condition for any two localities $n = 1, 2$ as: $(1 - T - \tau_1)f_k(L_1, K_1) = (1 - T - \tau_2)f_k(L_2, K_2)$. Assuming the production function is concave and total capital nationwide is fixed, I show in Chapter 4 that this implies that, starting from equilibrium, an uncompensated increase in one locality's tax rate will lead to an outflow of capital from that locality. One important argument supposes that fear of losing mobile capital in this way disciplines local tax setting under decentralization.

A "vertical externality" occurs when the policies set by governments at one tier affect the payoff to – and choices of – governments at other tiers. In Chapter 6, I examine how, when the tax bases of different-tier governments overlap, a higher tax rate at one level affects the revenues of, and preferred tax rates set by, governments at other tiers. For instance, if output in a given locality is a decreasing function of the sum of the local and central income tax rates, $Y_n = Y(T + \tau_n)$; $Y' < 0$, then (2.4) becomes:

$$T^* + \tau_n^* = -\frac{Y(T^* + \tau_n^*)}{Y'(T^* + \tau_n^*)} \tag{2.4'}$$

Clearly the equilibrium levels of T^* and τ_n^* depend on each other.

Many arguments about decentralization concern interactions between the policy choices of local and central governments when their payoffs are interdependent. To analyze such arguments, I will often define games played between governments at the different levels. In order to do so, one must specify the order of moves and the equilibrium concept. In some cases, results are different if one level of government moves first (as in a Stackelberg game) than if they move simultaneously (as in a Cournot game). For instance, by assigning one government an early move in the game (and no chance to move again later), one implicitly assumes that the government can credibly commit itself to a policy. Some arguments (for instance, some models of the "soft budget constraint" examined in Chapter 5) assume a particular order of moves. In analyzing them, one should consider whether players in the real world are constrained to move in the order assumed.

Whether one prefers centralization or decentralization will depend in an obvious way on the nature of the policy games and the participants at the different levels. For instance, if local governments are better structured than central ones, or if local leaders are more honest and public-spirited than their central counterparts, that creates a presumption in favor of decentralization. If, by contrast, central leaders are more honest and public-spirited or central government institutions are more efficient, the presumption should be for centralization. It is quite legitimate to argue that higher-quality candidates will be attracted to public office at one level than at the other, or that local and central governments tend to be structured in different ways. But such arguments require a convincing logical or empirical foundation. In modeling, it is easy to beg the question inadvertently by assuming different policy-making and leadership selection games at the different levels. For instance, the central government might be modeled as a council of legislators – with associated coordination problems – while the local governments are modeled as individuals. In reality, councils usually exist at local and regional as well as at central levels. In the analysis, I will expect arguments to provide justification for any such tipping of the scales. Unless there is reason to do otherwise, I will assume that local and central governments have the same structure and quality of officials.

In the next chapter, I begin to put the notation and definitions developed here to work, examining arguments about the costs and benefits of administrative decentralization.

3

Administrative Efficiency

How could the general of an army be instantaneously obeyed by all its soldiers if the army were not divided into regiments, the regiments into companies, the companies into squadrons? This being so, the general's commandment is conveyed at once to the colonels, then by them to the captains, by the captains to the corporals, and by them to the plain soldiers, so that the lowest soldier in the army is very soon told of it. But the effect of order is still more admirable in a state than in an army. For while the army is crowded together in a small space, the state ordinarily embraces extensive territory; and while the army as a whole does not last very long, the state endures almost for ever. All this happens by virtue of order. For the sovereign lord has his general officers near him, and they send his directives to the provincial magistrates, they to the municipal magistrates, and these last see to it that the people carry them out.

Charles Loyseau (1994 [1610], p. 6)

In the first place, administration becomes more difficult over great distances, just as a weight becomes heavier at the end of a long lever. It also becomes more burdensome as the chain of command is lengthened. For to begin with, each town has its own administration, for which the people pays; each district has one, for which the people again pays; next each province, and then the larger governmental units, satrapies or vice-royalties, for which it is necessary to pay ever more dearly the higher up the scale we mount, and always at the expense of the unfortunate people; finally comes the supreme administration, which crushes everything. All these surcharges constantly exhaust the subjects; far from being better governed by all these various agencies, they are less well served than would be the case if they were subject to one only.

Jean-Jacques Rousseau (1986 [1762], pp. 48–9)

What is the best way to organize a team of bureaucratic agents to administer a country? In most of this book, I will focus on *political* decentralization – the devolution of rights to make policy decisions or choose leaders to residents of local communities. But in this chapter I suppose all political authority is concentrated in a central government and ask how that government should implement its policies. Should it keep all its officers close at hand in bureaus in the nation's capital? Should it assign agents to local districts, stationing them throughout the territory? If so, should it arrange agents in a hierarchy of tiers, as Loyseau recommends, with provincial magistrates supervising their municipal counterparts? Or will this just exhaust and burden the citizens, as Rousseau warns? If the government chooses to order its agents in tiers, how many should it create and how large should their jurisdictions be?

Economists faced an analogous problem when they sought to explain the boundaries of the firm. Why would a rational entrepreneur choose to produce some inputs "in house," while buying others on the open market? Ronald Coase (1937) suggested an answer in his famous article "The Nature of the Firm." In his view, it came down to a simple comparison of costs: The rational entrepreneur would produce inputs in house if the marginal cost of doing so were less than the marginal cost of contracting for them on the market. The balance of costs would vary from one setting to another, depending on the production technology and the contracting environment. Adapting Coase's argument, one might relate the efficient structure of government administration to a similar cost comparison. A rational central government will administer via locally based agents so long as the marginal cost of supervising and communicating with these agents is lower than the marginal cost of providing the same services using agents based in the capital. And it will choose the number of tiers and dimensions of jurisdictions to minimize such costs.

Administrative costs come in several forms. There are the direct costs of producing particular public goods or services – the expense of purchasing materials, renting equipment, paying employees, and so on. Such costs will exist whether administration is centralized or decentralized, but technology may make it cheaper to produce at one scale than at another. Several additional costs occur only in decentralized administrative structures. First, there is the cost of operating field offices to supervise agents. Second, the government must pay the cost of communicating with its agents. And third, public resources may leak away or be used inappropriately because the center cannot monitor and discipline its local agents perfectly. The center's loss of control implies some "agency costs."

These costs will vary with the internal organization of government. If different public goods have different production technologies, it may be cheapest to produce them in different-sized jurisdictions, located at different tiers. If tastes for certain goods are highly heterogeneous (and cluster geographically), it may make sense to provide them in small local units. Structuring multi-tier hierarchies in particular ways may reduce the costs of communication and information processing. On the other hand, if the fixed costs of setting up administrative bureaus are large, governments will wish to limit the number of tiers. And agency costs might get worse, the more tiers of bureaucrats a central government must control.

The simple conclusion about administrative decentralization is that – as with the boundaries of the firm – there is no simple conclusion. The optimal size and internal organization of private firms depend on the particular demand conditions, production and transport technologies, and contracting environment of the given industry. Depending on such factors, anything from a unitary structure to a multi-tier hierarchy may be optimal. The optimal degree of administrative decentralization is even more complicated to discover because almost all governments provide multiple goods and services. Given this, one can sometimes determine whether a specific government function should be administratively decentralized, but even this is difficult given the clash of mutually offsetting effects.

3.1 Optimal Scale

Different public goods and services can be provided most efficiently by units of different size. Some, such as defense from military attack, are most cost-effective to provide for large territories and populations. They exhibit economies of scale. Others, such as fire fighting, can be organized cost-effectively for small communities and may even exhibit diseconomies of scale. (Suppose that routing all emergency calls through a central telephone exchange results in a higher rate of errors than routing each locality's calls through a local exchange.) In a multi-tier structure, particular responsibilities can each be assigned to the most efficient level. If the system is well designed, each government, "rather than attempting to perform all the functions of the public sector, does what it can do best" (Oates 1972, p. 14).

Some version of this thinking can be traced back as far as Aristotle, who saw a functional logic in the three-tiered structure of household, village, and polis (see section 1.1). Aristotle's language is not that of public goods, cost minimization, and efficiency, and the roles of household and village are not political at all. Still, he identifies the advantage of a nested hierarchy of communities, in which each unit performs a different function appropriate to its scale. Much later, Montesquieu saw in the "federal republic" – by which he meant something closer to a confederation – a way to combine the benefits of size with those of smallness (Montesquieu 1989 [1748], Part I, Book 9, ch.1, p. 131). While large political units were necessary for military defense, civic virtue could best be cultivated in small republics.[1]

This insight can be formalized simply. Suppose a single official wishes to provide a certain amount, g, of a single local public good to $M > 1$ citizens. Suppose the cost per resident of providing this amount of the good falls at first as additional residents are added, perhaps because of nonrivalness; after a certain point, however, the per capita cost rises with community size, μ. For example, suppose the good provided is a radio broadcast. At first, the cost per listener decreases as the number of listeners increases. But eventually new residents must live beyond the reach of the original radio transmitter, and providing them with access to the broadcasts requires laying cables to their houses, which are farther and farther away as the community size rises. The per capita cost curve is U-shaped, as pictured in Figure 3.1, with a minimum at μ^*.

Now suppose the official wishes to provide citizens with two local public goods, indexed $w = \{1, 2\}$. For simplicity, suppose the amount of each provided is still g (one can define units so as to make this the case). Suppose the per capita cost curves for the two goods are both U-shaped, as before, but that they differ in the location of their minimum point, as in Figure 3.2. The cost per resident to provide g units of public good 1 is minimized in a community of size μ_1, while the cost per resident to provide g units of public good 2 is minimized when the community is of size $\mu_2 \neq \mu_1$. Clearly, the cost cannot be minimized for both these goods if they are both produced in a single community of a given size. In that case, the optimal size of community would be between μ_1 and μ_2, and the per capita cost of provision of each good would be greater than if each were provided in a separate unit at its minimum per capita cost.

---

[1] For a modern rediscovery, see Lowrie (1922), who asserts that "Governmental power should be as broad as the problems with which it must deal" and discusses the appropriate division of functions between U.S. state and federal governments.

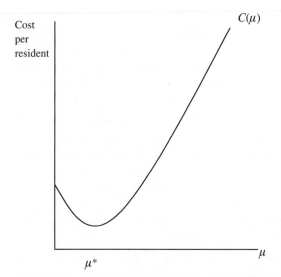

Figure 3.1. Cost per resident of providing g units of a local public good to μ residents

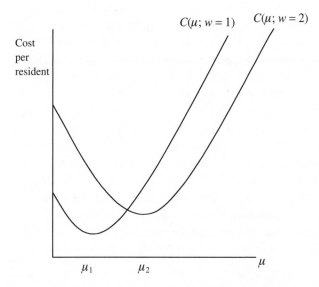

Figure 3.2. Cost per resident of providing g units of local public good $w = \{1, 2\}$ to μ residents

To see this algebraically for the more general case in which there are $W > 1$ local public goods, consider the following example. Suppose that the cost per resident of producing g units of good $w \in \{1, \ldots, W\}$ is $C(\mu; w) = w/\mu + \mu$. (I have ordered the goods so that those with higher w have higher optimal scale of production.) Differentiating with regard to μ and setting the derivative equal to zero, $C(\mu; w)$ is minimized when $\mu = w^{1/2}$, which I denote μ_w, in which case $C(\mu; w) = 2w^{1/2}$. The total cost of producing g units of each of the W goods at their minimum per capita cost levels is simply $\sum_{w=1}^{W} 2w^{1/2} M$.[2] If, on the other hand, all goods must be provided by a single government at a single tier, then at most one of the goods can be produced at its optimal scale, μ_w, and the per capita cost for each of the other goods will be greater than $2w^{1/2}$.

In short, when public goods and services have different optimal scales of provision, increasing the number of tiers and creating units of different size at the different levels make it possible to provide a diverse portfolio of public goods more cost-effectively. Note, however, that if one is concerned with just technical costs, only administrative – and not political – decentralization is required. A central government could set up separate fire stations in each municipality, subordinated to a central headquarters, and route local emergency calls through the local operators. And increasing the number of tiers may increase costs in an offsetting way, as I discuss in section 3.3. At the same time, administrative decentralization only makes cost savings *possible*; it does not guarantee them. Officials might choose a highly inefficient allocation of responsibilities across levels, costing more than if all functions had been centralized. Consider the odd possibility that a state might centralize fire fighting but decentralize defense to municipal militias.

Finally, the argument implies that local units which provide the same public goods should all be equal in size, which is certainly not true in practice. In the United States, municipalities range from New York, with a population of more than eight million, to townships with just a few hundred inhabitants. Perhaps these units "should" all be the same size, but Donahue (1997) seems right in arguing that their actual size and organization have "more to do with the accidents of a capricious history than with the shifting dictates of economic rationality."

---

[2] Note for future reference that the number of communities needed to produce good w at optimal scale for the M citizens is $M/\mu_w = M/w^{1/2}$. (For simplicity, I assume that M is divisible by each μ_w.) If a separate tier of government exists to provide each of the W goods, the total number of governments is $\sum_{w=1}^{W} (M/w^{1/2})$.

3.2 Heterogeneous Tastes and Policy Differentiation

Another argument for administrative decentralization is that it permits differentiation of policies among heterogeneous local communities. If citizens' tastes for public services vary and those with similar tastes tend to cluster geographically, providing different packages of public services in different local units may leave some better off than if all had to consume a nationally uniform package. Suppose all residents of Chicago prefer to have more snowplows than lifeguards, but all residents of Miami prefer more lifeguards than snowplows. Obviously, providing more snowplows in Chicago and more lifeguards in Miami will leave residents of both cities more satisfied.

Alesina and Spolaore (2003) pay particular attention to such preference heterogeneity. In their view, both the size of countries and the degree of centralization within them are determined by a basic tradeoff between economies of scale (which favor large size or central provision) and heterogeneity (which favors small size or decentralized provision). Higher levels of government "should provide public goods and policies for which economies of scale are large and heterogeneity of preferences low. For instance, defense and foreign policy clearly 'belong' to the national government, while education and school policy seem to have a more local nature" (ibid., p. 140).

If citizens with similar preferences cluster geographically, citizens may clearly benefit if policies are spatially differentiated. Some go further and contend that geographical differentiation of policies requires not just administrative but *political* decentralization: Locally selected officials must have the right to decide on policy for their own districts. There is a hard and a soft version of this argument. The hard version contends that it is technically impossible for a central government to implement different public policies in different local units. Tocqueville (1969 [1835], p. 161) seems to be arguing this when he writes that:

In large centralized nations the lawgiver is bound to give the laws a uniform character which does not fit the diversity of places and of mores; having never studied particular cases, he can only proceed by general rules; so men must bend to the needs of legislation, for the legislation has no skill to adapt itself to the needs and mores of men; and from this, much trouble and unhappiness results.

It is possible that Tocqueville meant this as a sociological generalization. But the wording makes it sound more like a statement of necessity: A central legislator *cannot* modulate his policies to fit local circumstances.

As a statement of necessity, the claim is certainly false. Central governments in heterogeneous countries both can and do differentiate their policies geographically (Brennan and Buchanan 1980, p. 174; Breton 1996; Seabright 1996, p. 63; Besley and Coate 2003).[3] This occurs even in countries generally considered to be extremely centralized politically. The Soviet Union in its totalitarian period did not allow local officials much autonomy. Yet even under Stalin, children were offered schooling in their native languages in each of the fourteen non-Russian republics (Bilinsky 1968). Under Brezhnev, Moscow authorized local experiments in economic policy in a number of regions (see section 9.2). Nor is this a recent phenomenon: One can read of similar policy differentiation within autocracies as far back as the Persian Empire of Darius. Although the shah's authority was absolute and he administered by means of appointed satraps, he nevertheless allowed subject communities to keep their legal traditions, political structures, and local cults and even to coin their own currencies (Finer 1997, vol. 1, pp. 292–8). Dante (1904 [c.1314–20], ch. 14) thought it obvious that "The Scythians, living beyond the seventh clime, suffering great inequality of days and nights, and oppressed by a degree of cold almost intolerable, need laws other than the Garamantes, dwelling under the equinoctial circle, who have their days always of equal length with their nights, and because of the unbearable heat of the air cannot endure the useless burden of clothing." But he thought they could observe their different laws under the rule of a single universal emperor.

Among democracies, the United Kingdom and France are often thought to be among the most centralized. But within the unitary British state, England and Scotland have for centuries operated under separate legal systems. Lawmakers in the U.K. are not bound to give the laws a uniform character at all. In France, even in the 1960s heyday of *dirigisme*, the national economic plan broke down into varied regional plans (MacLennan 1965). In short, it is perfectly possible as a technical matter for central governments to provide different educational, cultural, religious, or other policies to fit the desires of local populations.

Indeed, centralization may permit the national government of a large country to exploit economies of scale *in the satisfaction of heterogeneous*

---

[3] On examination, Tocqueville's claim is quite peculiar. Why must the lawmaker have "never studied particular cases"? What does it mean to say "the legislation has no skill to adapt itself"? What is to stop the legislator from adapting the law to "the needs and mores of men"?

preferences. Imagine a country divided into thirty districts. In ten districts, most citizens speak English; in ten, the majority speak French; and in ten, the majority language is Spanish. Respecting diverse preferences will require separate English, French, and Spanish language primary school curricula. But there are economies of scale in curriculum design: The same Spanish language curriculum can be used in each of the ten Spanish-speaking districts, and so on. Under decentralization, the ten Spanish-speaking districts might band together to fund the development of a single curriculum if they manage to overcome coordination problems. But under centralization, the central government will automatically capture the economies of scale.

The soft version of the argument claims that although central governments in a centralized state are perhaps technically able to differentiate policies in a Pareto optimal way, they are less likely to do so than local governments in a decentralized state. This might be so for several reasons. Some argue that local governments tend to be better informed about local tastes or conditions (see, e.g., Oates 1999, p. 1123).[4] I examine this claim in section 9.1 and find no reason to believe it would generally be true. Others contend that legal constraints may prevent the central government in a centralized state from differentiating policy. The constitution or other laws might prohibit central officials from treating local units differently without the consent of their governments (Strumpf 2002).[5] However, because we are discussing differentiating policies in ways that leave each locality at least as well off, there is no reason why the locals would not consent. Any differentiation that local governments would themselves generate under decentralization could be reproduced precisely under centralization – with local agreement. Again, there is no reason to expect greater geographical differentiation under decentralization.

Finally, a central government might not be motivated to provide citizens with Pareto optimal policies. Here, political issues arise that go beyond this chapter's focus on the technical efficiency of administration. In section 7.2,

---

[4] This might, in part, be what Tocqueville meant in the passage quoted. He goes on to describe how in the United States "[t]he central government of each state, being close to the governed, is continually informed of the needs that arise" (1969 [1835], p. 161).

[5] Strumpf argues that "the 10th Amendment to the U.S. Constitution is typically interpreted as reserving certain policies to the states." However, this does not imply that the central government cannot differentiate the policies that are constitutionally assigned to it, only that not all policy areas fall within its jurisdiction. In any case, the United States is a highly *decentralized* state, so the example does not tell us much about what limits there are on central governments in centralized states.

I discuss arguments that local governments will be more accountable to their voters than central governments. In general, I find this not to be the case. The problem for voters of controlling their local government is a microcosm of the problem voters face in controlling a central government. Unless we assume some arbitrary difference – for instance, that local policies cannot differentiate among groups of citizens, but central policies can – governments at local and central levels will be equally able to evade voter control. Although different voters may do better under centralization and decentralization, I have not found any convincing reason why policies under one would generally be Pareto superior to those under the other. Chapter 4 examines arguments that interregional competition will motivate local governments to satisfy citizen demands more precisely than a central government would. Again, I find little reason to believe the argument will hold in general.

In sum, when citizens' tastes vary with geography (or when citizens are mobile and so can sort themselves by taste), there will often be efficiency gains from differentiating policies geographically. Such differentiation may improve the match between policies provided and citizens' preferences. Differentiation may require some administrative decentralization. But it is possible under both politically decentralized and centralized regimes, and there is no compelling reason to think that policies will in general be more efficiently differentiated under one than under the other.

3.3 Costs of Organization

Suppose the central government wishes to provide differentiated packages of public goods to different parts of the country, and that some public goods are most efficiently provided in small units. This would seem to favor administrative decentralization. But how much? To determine how many subordinate tiers of administrators a central authority should create, one must consider certain organizational costs.

3.3.1 Costs of Operating Government Offices

Suppose first that besides the direct costs of providing public goods discussed in section 3.1, there are fixed costs associated with operating each additional government office. Rousseau seems to have something like this in mind when he writes about the numerous surcharges burdening the citizens of a state with many levels. Returning to the example of section 3.1, suppose that besides the cost of producing public outputs, each administrative body must pay a fixed cost of operating, S. Then the minimum cost of providing g units of each public good in a single community ("centralization") becomes $C_C = M \sum_{w=1}^{W} (w/\hat{\mu} + \hat{\mu}) + S = 2^{1/2} MW(W+1)^{1/2} + S$, where $\hat{\mu} = ((W+1)/2)^{1/2}$ is chosen to minimize the total cost. By contrast, the total cost of providing g units of each public good in a system with W tiers of government, in which each good is produced at the optimal scale ("decentralization"), becomes not $\sum_{w=1}^{W} 2w^{1/2} M$ but $C_D = \sum_{w=1}^{W} 2w^{1/2} M + S \sum_{w=1}^{W} (M/w^{1/2})$. (There are $\sum_{w=1}^{W} (M/w^{1/2})$ governments, $M/w^{1/2}$ at each tier, w [see footnote 2]. Each has a fixed cost of S.) Now there is a tradeoff in increasing the number of tiers, and governments within them. A system of multiple tiers means that all but one good can be provided at lower variable cost because for each w, $2w^{1/2} \le w/\hat{\mu} + \hat{\mu}$, and the inequality is strict for all but one good.[6] But such a system also means a larger total fixed cost of maintaining so many governments: $S \sum_{w=1}^{W} (M/w^{1/2}) > S$. If the fixed costs are high, it may be more efficient to restrict the number of tiers.[7] Thus, limits are introduced on the argument for administrative decentralization. Given sufficiently high fixed costs, a unitary government will be more cost-effective than a decentralized one.

3.3.2 Communication Costs

If a central government administers via local field agents, it will have to communicate with them. If communication costs increase with the physical distance that messages must travel, one way to reduce such costs is to reduce the territory of the state. But how can one minimize communication costs for a given territory? In general, as Loyseau sensed in the seventeenth century and various theoretical analyses have since confirmed, the optimal network for communication will be some kind of multi-tier hierarchy.[8]

---

[6] Note that $2w^{1/2} \le w/\hat{\mu} + \hat{\mu} \Leftrightarrow 2w^{1/2}\hat{\mu} - w - \hat{\mu}^2 \le 0 \Leftrightarrow -(w^{1/2} - \hat{\mu})^2 \le 0$, which is always true. The inequality holds strictly – implying that the variable cost is lower under decentralization – except when $w^{1/2} = \hat{\mu}$. For this good (the one for which the national jurisdiction is the optimal size), the variable cost is the same under centralization and decentralization.

[7] It is easy to see that this would still be true even if – as Rousseau suggests – the fixed costs are lower for lower-level governments.

[8] This section makes a few quick and simple points about a subject on which there is a large, sophisticated literature. See, for instance, Radner (1992), Marschak (1968), and Arrow (1991). For an early analysis, see Kochen and Deutsch (1969), which however considers only the optimal number of field offices in a local tier, not the number and organization of tiers.

One might think about the costs of communicating in several ways. Consider the task of a single central government, C, communicating with M citizens located at different points in a "periphery." By "communicating," I mean sending and receiving messages, which can be of different sizes. The center can send messages directly and separately to each recipient. Or, if messages can be bundled, it may make sense to send a package of messages first to one or more intermediate agents, who disaggregate them and forward them to other agents or final recipients. Communicating in the other direction, citizens might either send messages directly to C or via agents, who bundle them before relaying them upward.

Costs might accrue in several ways. First, there might be costs proportional to the distance that a given message or bundle must travel. Such costs might be fixed and independent of the number of messages (perhaps the cost of building a road or laying a telephone cable), or they might vary with the number of messages (perhaps the cost of sending a mail truck along a given road, or a call along a given phone line). Second, if a given agent can send or receive only so many messages per period, there might be a cost proportional to the delay before each message in a given set reaches its target recipient.

If there are no economies of scale in transmitting messages (if sending messages individually takes no longer than sending a bundle), then one cannot do better than to minimize the cost of each separate message's transmission. The optimal system will be to send each message separately along the most direct path, using no intermediate agents. However, at least some economies of scale will almost always exist. Roads or telephone lines, once built at some fixed cost, can be used repeatedly, resulting in diminishing average costs. If the same message is to be sent to multiple recipients, then just one copy can be sent part of the way before it is multiplied into copies for all recipients. Or the economies of scale might be in time saved. If messages can be sent simultaneously to several recipients, then the total time required to send messages to M recipients may be less than M times the time required to send it to one recipient.

Suppose there are economies of scale. If costs proportional to distance or to delay exist, it will often be cost-effective to communicate through a hierarchy of agents rather than directly with each recipient. I will consider the two cases in turn.

In the first case, suppose the cost of sending z messages between two points d units apart is $(\lambda + az)d$, where $\lambda d > 0$ is the fixed cost of communicating between these points (say, running a telephone line between them), and a is a positive constant.[9] This assumes that costs increase with distance, but that there are increasing returns to scale, because the per-message cost of communicating, $(\lambda/z + a)d$, decreases in z. Take a simple example in which N localities in the periphery are equally spaced on the circumference of a circle, centered at C, with radius r. If the center communicates directly with each locality, the total cost of sending one message to each is $Nr(\lambda + a)$. Suppose, instead, that the center creates an intermediate tier of $N/3$ "regional officials," equally spaced on a circle centered at C with radius $r/2$, and communicates directly only with these (see Figure 3.3).[10] Each regional official passes on the central message to each of the three nearest localities – call this "administrative decentralization." Now the total cost is: $(N/3)(\lambda r + 2\lambda x + 2ar + 2ax) = r(N/3)(\lambda + 2a + (\lambda + a)\sqrt{5 - 4\cos(360°/N)})$.[11] The total communication cost under administrative decentralization is less than that under direct communication if and only if: $r(N/3)(\lambda + 2a + (\lambda + a)\sqrt{5 - 4\cos(360°/N)}) < Nr(\lambda + a)$ or, more simply, if:

$$5 - 4\cos(360°/N) < [1 + \lambda/(\lambda + a)]^2 \qquad (3.1)$$

If the economies of scale are large (i.e., the fixed cost, λ, is large relative to the variable cost, a), then as the number of localities becomes large, administrative decentralization becomes more cost-effective. To see this, note that when $N > 2$, the left-hand side of (3.1) decreases from 9 toward 1. The right-hand side is always greater than 1. Therefore, for any given (λ, a), there will be a level of N above which administrative decentralization is more cost-effective than direct communication. The right-hand side increases in λ and decreases in a, so the greater are the economies of scale (the higher is λ and the smaller a), the lower will be the threshold number of localities above which administrative decentralization is more efficient. For instance, if $N = 5$, administrative decentralization is more efficient so long as $\lambda > 15.7a$. If $N = 6$, the threshold falls to $\lambda > 2.8a$, and if $N = 10$, the threshold is $\lambda > .5a$.

All of this assumes a particular way of structuring the hierarchy, with three messages relayed through each office, but the ideas are general. If there

---

[9] This is close to the formulation in Bolton and Dewatripont (1994).

[10] I assume for simplicity that N is divisible by 3.

[11] From Figure 3.3, we know: $\alpha + \beta + 360/N = 180$. Using the Sine Law, we also know that $\sin(360/N)/x = \sin\alpha/(r/2) = \sin\beta/r$. Solving these simultaneously yields: $x = (r/2)[5 - 4\cos(360°/N)]^{1/2}$.

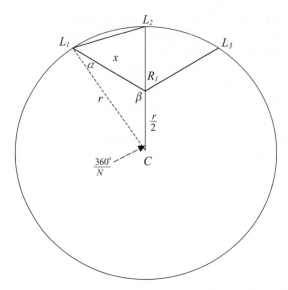

Figure 3.3. Communication costs and the number of tiers. Note: $x = (r/2)[5 - 4 \cos(360°/N)]^{1/2}$

are economies of scale in communicating between two points, this creates an incentive to economize on the number of paths messages go down. This can be done by bundling messages along certain parts of their route. There is a tradeoff between reducing the fixed costs (by bundling messages and sending them down common paths) and reducing the variable costs (which increase when messages are not sent along the most direct route). If, in addition, costs increase with the number of agents in the chain, this will raise the threshold number of localities at which administrative decentralization becomes efficient.

The second type of cost – that of delay caused by the limited capacity of agents to communicate many messages simultaneously – is the one most frequently considered in computer science and economic analyses.[12] Minimizing delay requires that agents be arranged so that they can operate simultaneously at close to their maximum rate for as much of the time as possible, rather than operate consecutively, with idle time in between. The cost-minimizing arrangement will generally be some form of multi-tiered hierarchy. Such a hierarchy can exploit the possibility of parallel – and therefore simultaneous – communication.

[12] See, for example, Radner (1992, 1993) and Bolton and Dewatripont (1994).

For instance, suppose that one bundle of messages can be transmitted between a given sender and a given recipient in each period. Each bundle can contain from one to one million messages. (For purposes of illustration, I assume an extreme form of economies of scale.) Suppose also that it takes a negligible amount of time for the sender to split a given bundle of messages into smaller bundles, or for a recipient to combine previously received bundles into a larger bundle.

It would take the central decision maker one million periods to send one message separately and directly to each of one million citizens. All the work of transmission would have to be done consecutively rather than simultaneously. If, on the other hand, the central decision maker sent half the original bundle of messages to each of two deputies, each of whom then relayed half to each of two deputies, and so on, then the government could reach the whole population within just forty periods. (This would require 20 tiers of deputies – $2^{20} \approx 1,000,000$; agents at each tier would take two periods to complete the transmission of their messages.)[13] To make this concrete, imagine a central decision maker with one million letters, each of which must be stamped. For him to stamp each consecutively will take far longer than to split up the letters in the way described and have them stamped by the bottom-level deputies. This seems to be what Loyseau had in mind when describing how the king could communicate via a hierarchy in "a very short time."

A central decision maker could choose to appoint any number of deputies. What would be the optimal number if the only delay or cost is the one already discussed? If we restrict attention to hierarchies in which each agent communicates with the same number of deputies (or, at the bottom tier, citizens), then it turns out that the delay-minimizing number of messages sent by each agent is $e \approx 2.72$. In practice, because messages cannot be split in fractions, the optimal number will be 3. To see this, suppose that the number of messages each sender sends is a. To reach all M citizens will require j tiers where $a^j = M$. Each tier of senders will require a periods to send its messages. So total delay is $aj = a(\ln M)/(\ln a)$,[14] which is minimized when $a = e$. The delay-minimizing number of tiers is $j^* = \ln M / \ln e = \ln M$, and the minimum total delay is $e \ln M$ – or, because

---

[13] As Radner (1992) shows, one could reduce the delay still further by giving some transmission tasks to higher-level agents after they have completed their main task (when they would otherwise be idle).

[14] From $a^j = M$, $j = \ln M / \ln a$.

messages cannot be split in fractions, $3(\ln M)/(\ln 3) \approx 2.73 \ln M$. The delay-minimizing number of tiers, $\ln M$, increases with the number of citizens, but at a decreasing rate.

If messages are to be communicated not from the top down but from the bottom up, minimizing delay presents essentially the same problem. (Here the constraint is that each recipient can receive only one bundle per period, rather than each sender's being able to send only one bundle.) Each recipient receives a bundles of messages and combines them into a single bundle. There are j tiers of recipients such that $M(1/a)^j = 1$. So, again, delay is $aj = a(\ln M)/(\ln a)$, which is minimized when $a = e$.

Both of the previous types of costs can be reduced by transmitting messages through a hierarchical network. However, expanding a communications chain may generate a third type of cost: Each time a given message is transferred from one agent to another, the message may get lost or garbled. According to Downs (1965, p. 443): "Officials inevitably distort information which they relay upwards to their superiors or downwards to their subordinates. Moreover, under many frequently-encountered conditions, these distortions tend to become cumulative rather than self-correcting as the number of hierarchical levels rises." The risk of such distortions, familiar to anyone who has played the party game "Chinese Whispers," was demonstrated by Bartlett (1932), who tried to transmit a line drawing of an owl along a chain of eighteen individuals, having each one copy his predecessor's sketch. The eighteenth produced a recognizable image of a cat.[15] If these distortions do cumulate, as Downs feared, this will tend to limit the number of tiers that is optimal for communication (Williamson 1967).

To sum up, the costs of communication between a "sender" and M "recipients" – or between M "senders" and a "recipient" – will often be lower when the messages are relayed through some sort of multi-tier hierarchy of agents. Such hierarchies will also often reduce costs of information processing.[16] The benefits of hierarchy typically require that there be economies of scale in transmitting (or processing) messages. Hierarchy can reduce the total distance messages must travel to reach all recipients and facilitate the parallel transmission of messages to cut down delay. These advantages must be traded off against possible pathologies of complex transmission

[15] This is discussed in Williamson (1967).

[16] In fact, the distinction between these is not as sharp as it might seem, because bundling and unbundling messages is itself a type of data processing.

chains, which may increase the chance a message will get lost or distorted en route.

So far in this section, I have asked what is the most cost-effective way to organize transmission of a given set of messages between a central government and local agents. Another question is, given a particular number of government tiers, how many messages should be sent to begin with. The central government could delegate responsibility for particular projects to its local agents and require only limited auditing rather than detailed operational reporting and extensive decision making on local issues from the national capital. So long as the local agents are still appointed from above and higher governments have the right to overrule their agents' decisions, this would still qualify as "administrative" rather than "political" decentralization, as defined in Chapter 2.

Delegation of this kind would economize on the costs of center–locality communication. These economies would have to be balanced against some drawbacks of delegation. John Stuart Mill, although enthusiastic about political decentralization for other reasons, argued forcefully for some centralization of information about local policies and their results so that general knowledge could be derived: "Power may be localized, but knowledge, to be most useful, must be centralized; there must be somewhere a focus at which all its scattered rays are collected, that the broken and colored lights which exist elsewhere may find there what is necessary to complete and purify them" (Mill 1991 [1861], ch. 15). Nevertheless, the information transmitted to the center could be limited to audits and reports rather than all the raw data. Thus, within an administratively decentralized state, some degree of delegation may be beneficial.

3.3.3 Agency Costs and Loss of Control

Instructions may not just get distorted every time they are transmitted from one agent to the next. If agents have different interests from those of the political leadership and are not perfectly monitored, they may deliberately disobey or change orders en route. One might expect such loss of control to snowball as the chain of command gets longer, turning the logic of Loyseau's army on its head.[17]

---

[17] In this section, I focus on models of hierarchies of supervisors, because this seems to best match the realities of administrative decentralization. Another literature considers possible loss of control when a central principal contracts with an agent to obtain a particular good, and the agent then subcontracts with producers. For a recent review, see Mookherjee (2006).

That, at least, was the expectation of Downs (1965) and Williamson (1967). Williamson presented a model of a hierarchical firm in which each subordinate implemented only a fixed fraction $0 < \overline{\alpha} < 1$ of the instructions given to him by his superior. As a result, the lowest-tier employees in a firm of $n + 1$ tiers would be faithfully performing only a fraction $\overline{\alpha}^n$ of their instructions. This captured a common intuition. But is it plausible that control losses would cumulate in this way? Subsequent papers criticized this assumption as ad hoc.[18]

Of course, the firm's director would not simply ignore insubordination. There are two main mechanisms by which a "principal" could control his "agents": He could monitor their actions and punish shirking or disobedience, or he could pay them based on their output (Stiglitz 1991). Either of these can prevent control losses from cumulating. Calvo and Wellisz (1978) studied supervision. They modeled a firm producing a good with a constant returns to scale production technology, in which each worker faced a fixed probability, P, that she would be monitored and penalized for any shirking or deliberate misimplementation. The supervisors, in turn, faced a fixed probability of being monitored by agents at the next highest level, and so on up to the top of the pyramid. Calvo and Wellisz showed that if agents could not tell exactly when they were being watched, then there was no cumulative loss of control as the number of tiers increased. By this logic, loss of control in public-sector agencies as well need not increase as the hierarchy grows taller.

Managers can achieve similar results using incentive pay schemes. Suppose all supervisors in a vertical chain are paid a wage that depends on the output of the worker at the bottom (Datta 1996). Under plausible conditions, this too can motivate employees to limit their opportunism. Because all that need be observable is the chain's final output, this avoids the tricky questions of how supervisory effort can be measured and how workers know whether their supervisor is watching. In effect, the vertical chain becomes a team. This raises some additional issues. A collective action problem may weaken motivation, because each agent is paid based on how hard all the others work. Each agent may also face greater wage variability, because stochastic shocks that affect any worker in the chain will affect everyone's

---

[18] For a review, see Datta (1996). Note that this section discusses only whether agency costs increase *as the chain of agents gets longer*. Some advocates of decentralization seem to assume that it can avoid agency costs entirely. But the problem of supervising agents exists in all governments. Even in the smallest villages, the mayor does not teach school, sweep streets, and build roads herself.

payment (Laffont 1990). Both these effects reduce the incentive for agents to exert effort, so the marginal payment rate around the equilibrium must be very high to compensate. If there are no stochastic shocks, a step function that rewards all members of the chain if output is above a threshold level can achieve the first-best outcome. If there are stochastic shocks, this outcome can be approximated under certain conditions (Holmström 1982, Dixit 2002 pp. 707–8).

In fact, there are probably better payment schemes that reduce these problems. Supervisors at intermediate tiers will typically have multiple bottom tier agents beneath them in the hierarchy. If the central government pays supervisors based on the average performance of all the bottom tier units in their jurisdiction, and stochastic shocks to the different agents are independent, this will reduce the variability in their pay. In addition, the central government can compare the average performance in each supervisor's bottom tier units with the average for other supervisors at the same level, exploiting yardstick competition to distinguish their effort from (common) stochastic shocks. These mechanisms will be most effective for agents higher up in the administrative hierarchy. A central government can motivate those lower down with the prospect of a career rising through the hierarchy, with higher wages paid at the higher levels.

The principal (in our case, central government) may not be able to use these mechanisms effectively if agents can collude to deceive their superiors (Laffont and Martimort 1998). Above a certain number of tiers, it may become simply too expensive for the central government to pay its direct subordinates enough to make them prefer to perform honestly rather than collude with their subordinates to defraud the government. This might imply an increase in control losses above a certain level of administrative decentralization, although where exactly this limit would lie would vary with the model's parameters.

However, there are possible solutions. Shareholders, worried about collusion within a company, can employ private auditors from outside to inspect the books. By changing auditors every year or two, they can make it difficult – though, of course, not impossible – for the auditors to collude with the company executives. In a similar way, a central government eager to discover how effectively its local agents are providing local public services could contract with a private survey firm either to measure local provision of public services directly or to poll local residents. Such surveys could be used to determine the rewards or punishment of all agents in the chain supervising the given district. This should be possible regardless of how many intermediate tiers of bureaucrats lie between the grass roots and the center.

Whether or not a central government will commission such surveys and supervise its agents actively is likely to depend on the degree of competition in central elections. If competition is more intense at the central than at local levels, the central government may tend to be better informed and more responsive to local wishes than the local government. Where incumbents are secure in office, whether at the central or local level, they will pay less attention to supervision.

Bureaucracies with many tiers have an extremely bad reputation. In part, this probably reflects the fact that most many-tiered bureaucracies have occurred in autocratic states, where low accountability may result from the lack of constraints on rulers rather than from overcentralization. Until recently, there have been few politically centralized democracies. McAfee and McMillan (1995) illustrate the "costs of hierarchical organization" by discussing the dysfunctional hierarchies of Soviet and Chinese industry. Milgrom and Roberts (1990, pp. 78–89) point to the "costs of central- ized authority" in medieval Europe, imperial China, feudal Japan, and Islamic theocracies. In such cases, unresponsive government seems overde- termined. A better thought experiment would be to compare the effective- ness of bureaucracies in politically centralized democracies like Britain's and France's with that in decentralized democracies such as the United States' or Canada's.

In sum, the loss of central control caused by moral hazard might increase with the number of administrative tiers. But it also might not. Or loss of control might increase only above a certain level that is hard to pin down. And if the central government can get accurate measures of local public service provision, for instance by commissioning surveys of residents, it can use these to motivate high levels of administrative effort regardless of how many tiers there are.

3.4 Conclusion

What is the most efficient size for a firm? How many subdivisions and tiers of supervisors should it employ? Most economists would view the search for a precise, general answer to these questions as misguided. The optimal size of a firm in a particular industry and country will depend on a com- plicated mix of factors – the production technology, demand conditions, communication costs, incentives in the tax and financial systems, and the contracting environment, to name a few. Each of these has been studied in depth, and one can say something about the influence of each. But generalizations about the optimal size and internal structure of firms within a given industry and country – let alone firms in general – are usually controversial.

So too with the size and technical efficiency of government. Even if one could assume away the politics analyzed in later chapters, it would be hard to say in general how many administrative tiers a government should employ. Choosing how to organize administration requires one to trade off many factors – economies of scale in producing public goods and services, the costs of organizing supervisory bureaus, economies and diseconomies of scale in communication, and the risk of central loss of control. Depending on demand conditions and various technological and social factors, anything from a unitary to a multi-tier structure could be most efficient in a given country at a given time.

The questions that have most interested political thinkers over the centuries, however, concern political decentralization. Whatever the technical efficiency of different structures of administration, are there advantages to letting local communities choose their own political leaders and policies? Do they outweigh the costs? I turn to these questions in the chapters that follow.

4

Competition among Governments

> Just as market competition pressures firm managers to reflect the interests of
> shareholders, competition among local governments helps to limit govern-
> ment's predatory behavior. Mobile resources can quickly leave jurisdictions
> with inappropriate behavior. Competition for mobile sources of revenue pre-
> vents local political leaders from imposing debilitating taxes or regulation.
>
> Yingyi Qian and Barry R. Weingast (1997, p. 88)

> Unlike competition in goods markets, there can be no presumption that com-
> petition for investment is efficiency enhancing (on the contrary, it directs
> capital to less efficient locations), and it clearly has the potential to result
> in "races to the bottom" in terms of wages, social protections, environmen-
> tal standards, and tax base degradation via subsidies and lower tax rates on
> mobile actors. Conscious intervention in markets is necessary to prevent these
> negative outcomes.
>
> Kenneth Thomas (2000, p. 271)

Political decentralization is often thought to induce a beneficial kind of
competition between subnational governments. Competition among firms
in a market motivates them to cut costs, please consumers, and innovate.
By a similar logic, competition among subnational governments to attract
mobile residents or capital might render them more efficient, honest, and
responsive to the demands of constituents. As Friedrich Hayek (1939) put
it, when states must compete against one another, major interference in
economic life becomes "altogether impracticable." Such competition forces
governments to "avoid all sorts of taxation which would drive capital or labor
elsewhere."

Do such arguments add up to a general reason to favor political decentralization over centralization? Before accepting this conclusion, one must

answer three questions. First, will competition actually occur under political decentralization? Second, if it does, will such competition have the presumed beneficial effects? And third, if competition occurs and is beneficial under decentralization, would a politically centralized government achieve equally desirable results? I first consider arguments about competition to attract mobile residents, in section 4.1, and then turn to arguments about competition to attract mobile capital, in section 4.2. In both cases, the claim that local competition implies a general advantage for decentralization appears very weak.

4.1 Competing for Mobile Residents

4.1.1 Tiebout's Argument

In a famous 1956 article, Charles Tiebout (1956) argued that political decentralization can motivate local governments to compete with one another in ways that benefit their constituents. When individuals can move from one locality to another, the choice of where to live becomes a kind of consumer decision – in Tiebout's words, the "local public-goods counterpart to the private market's shopping trip" (ibid., p. 422). Assuming that local officials benefit from having more constituents, they will compete to attract residents by offering packages of local public goods and services at the lowest feasible tax cost. Individuals will pick and choose among the available bundles, "buying" that which most closely matches their preferences. Such competition, Tiebout argued, could have three positive effects. It could reveal otherwise secret information about citizens' tastes, prompt efficient sorting, and enhance government accountability.[1]

First, competition among local governments could solve the information revelation problem that Samuelson identified for the case of national public goods. For private goods, individuals' purchases reveal their preferences. But this mechanism breaks down when a good can be supplied only collectively. Discovering a given individual's willingness to pay for such goods is much harder because, in Samuelson's words, "it is in the selfish interest of each person to give *false* signals, to pretend to have less interest in a given collective consumption activity than he really has" (Samuelson 1954,

---

[1] The literature inspired by Tiebout's article is enormous, but for a good, brief discussion see Rubinfeld (1987).

pp. 388–9). In Tiebout's geographical marketplace, individuals would reveal their preferences for local public goods by their residential choices.

Second, competition among localities to attract residents would induce a process of efficient sorting. Each individual would migrate to the locality with the package of public goods and taxes that most closely matched her own tastes. As a result, spending on public goods would reflect "the preferences of the population more adequately than they can be reflected at the national level" (Tiebout 1956, p. 416). Implicitly, Tiebout assumed that if local public goods were provided "at the national level," then a uniform package of public services and taxes would be chosen for the whole country. Decentralization to local governments would introduce variety. "The greater the number of communities and the greater the variance among them, the closer the consumer will come to fully realizing his preference position" (ibid., p. 418).

Third, Tiebout hinted – and others have since argued more explicitly – that local competition would motivate public officials to satisfy constituents' demands more cost-effectively. He assumed that under decentralization, "communities are forced to keep production costs at a minimum either through the efficiency of city managers or through competition from other communities.... In this model and in reality, the city manager or elected official who is not able to keep his costs (taxes) low compared with those of similar communities will find himself out of a job" (ibid., p. 422). The fear of voter exit will keep local officials accountable.[2]

The argument has been rightly recognized as brilliant. But does it provide reason to expect that in general, decentralized systems of government will perform better than more centralized ones? I will argue that it does not. First, as a range of scholars have noted, the argument requires a series of demanding assumptions, many of which are unlikely ever to hold. The failure of some assumptions is not fatal to the argument: It will merely result in weaker competition or less beneficial results. But the failure of others is more serious. In some cases, no equilibrium will exist, which makes it impossible to say how performance under decentralization compares with that under centralization. Second, even if the necessary assumptions all hold and a Pareto optimal equilibrium is achieved under decentralization, an equally efficient result should almost always obtain under centralization.

---

[2] In the paraphrase of Brennan and Buchanan (1980, p. 172): "Freedom of trade and migration among separate governmental units acts as a substitute for overt fiscal constraints."

4.1.2 Restrictive Assumptions and Problems of Equilibrium

Tiebout's argument requires a large number of highly restrictive assumptions, as many scholars have pointed out.[3] The first to comment on this was Tiebout himself. His article identified the following eight necessary conditions.[4]

1. Individuals can move costlessly between communities.
2. In deciding where to live, individuals care only about differences in local public policies.

This implies that:

    2.1. They do not work in a particular location. (All income is investment income.)

    2.2. There is no land and no housing (so tax differentials across localities are not capitalized into real estate prices.)[5]

    2.3. Individuals do not care who their neighbors are.

    2.4. They have no historical, cultural, or aesthetic attachments to particular localities.

3. Individuals have fixed preference patterns.
4. Individuals have perfect information about the public policies of all localities.
5. There are many localities (at least as many as there are types of individual preferences).[6]
6. There are no public policy externalities across communities.
7. There is a finite optimal community size for any level of provision of local public goods.
8. Communities below the optimal size seek to attract new residents. Those above the optimal size seek to lose residents.

Other scholars have suggested additional necessary assumptions.

9. Public goods are financed by lump sum taxes (Oates 1972, pp. 131–40; Rubinfeld 1987, p. 575).

---

[3] See, for instance, Bewley (1981) and Oates (1981).

[4] I have slightly rearranged the presentation.

[5] For discussion of this, see Rubinfeld (1987, p. 575) and Epple and Zelenitz (1981).

[6] Breton (1996, pp. 191–2) notes a complication in countries with more than two tiers of government. If competition among governments at tier 1 (higher) coincides with competition at tier 2 (lower), efficiency is harder to achieve. To make possible perfect matching, it would seem that there must be as many tier-1 jurisdictions as there are preference-types over tier-1 policies *and* as many tier-2 localities *within each tier-1 jurisdiction* as there are preference-types over tier-2 policies.

10. The identity of residents does not affect the cost of providing public goods (i.e., all are equally costly to educate or deter from committing crimes) (Bewley 1981, p. 728; Oates 1981).
11. New communities can be established costlessly (Rubinfeld 1987, p. 575).

We can add to these a critical assumption that Tiebout makes implicitly:

    2.5. The central government does not discriminate among localities in its policies (e.g., by charging different tax rates or providing different levels of benefits).

Of course, all models impose assumptions that will not always be met in reality. So we need to think whether they will hold in at least a significant number of important cases. And when the assumptions are not met in full, is there reason to think the model's predictions will still hold "more-or-less"? The most convincing way to answer this would be to formulate a general model of Tiebout competition and see what happens when each assumption is relaxed.[7] A second-best approach, which I pursue here, is to exploit intuitions about the role each assumption plays.[8] From this perspective, the assumptions fall into several groups.

Some – assumptions 3, 7, and 8 – seem quite innocuous. Positing fixed preferences is a standard simplification needed to analyze most political economy questions. It also seems pretty intuitive that the optimally sized community is neither empty nor infinitely large. And various objective functions might motivate local officials to prefer an optimally sized community.

For some other assumptions, partial failure would probably weaken the effects without changing the underlying logic. Competition might be less intense, permitting some waste or inefficiency; information might be revealed with noise; and sorting might be imperfect. But weak competition might still be better than none at all. For instance, if we relax assumption 1

---

[7] Note that one cannot adopt the Friedman (1953) line that if the predictions of the theory are borne out by evidence, then the "plausibility" or "realism" of the assumptions is beside the point. The Tiebout argument – as presented here – is essentially *evaluative*: It claims that given certain assumptions the outcome will be Pareto-optimal. But there is no way of directly observing whether a Pareto-optimal outcome has been reached, so we cannot judge its predictive power by observing "real world" cases.

[8] Because I will argue below that the argument for decentralization based on Tieboutian competition fails *even if* all assumptions are met, a rigorous demonstration of the consequences of relaxing each assumption is somewhat superfluous. In examining the role of each assumption, the major contributions of Bewley (1981) and Rubinfeld (1987) are extremely helpful.

slightly and suppose there are small costs of relocating, then residents will move only if public policies in their home districts differ significantly from their preferences. The discipline on local officials will be correspondingly softer, but it will still exist.

Violations of 2.1 and 2.4 also seem likely to reduce the impact of competition by weakening the link between policies and location decisions. If individuals prefer to live near their workplace or in particular localities, their local governments need not try so hard to provide those individuals with their most-preferred public policies. Assumption 4 (perfect information) will never be met fully – residents will never know exactly what policies are available in all other localities. However, if local governments gain by attracting new residents, as assumed, they may advertise their policies, enabling citizens to sort themselves reasonably well. Again, small violations of these assumptions would probably weaken competition rather than eliminate it completely.

However, other assumptions are likely to fail in more significant ways. If so, the Tiebout argument will not apply at all. If assumption 2.2 fails, and public service differentials are capitalized into property prices, then the pressure on governments may disappear completely. Consider two individuals with identical tastes – A, who owns a house in locality 1, and B, who owns a house in locality 2. Suppose that locality 1 does a much worse job of providing public services than locality 2. The Tiebout logic suggests that A should move (or threaten to move) to locality 2, thus pressuring 1 to improve its public service provision. But another way equilibrium might be achieved would be by a drop in the price of housing in locality 1 relative to that in locality 2 just sufficient to make it too expensive for A to want to move (i.e., capitalization). If house prices react like this (faster than residents are able to move), residents will not leave districts that provide public services poorly, so mobility will not discipline local officials.[9] Nor will citizens necessarily sort themselves according to taste for public goods. Under plausible conditions, one might indeed expect real estate markets to capitalize local policy differences into property prices.[10]

One can rediscover a source of discipline by supposing that local governments are run by real estate developers or cartels of local homeowners

[9] For a model that makes this point, see Caplan (2001).

[10] Rubinfeld argues that capitalization will be more complete when individuals have similar tastes for public goods (1987, p. 592). There is evidence that some degree of capitalization does occur in practice in the United States. See Oates (1981, p. 94), Palmon and Smith (1998), and Bogart and Cromwell (1997).

who aim to maximize their property values and thus have a strong private interest in local policies that drive up such values (Pauly 1976, Brueckner 1983). Or suppose that politics are democratic, but homeowners outnumber renters in each locality. Local voters may then pressure government to provide local public goods and services in a way that increases real estate prices. However, notice several things about this recasting of the problem. First, it renders Tiebout competition redundant. Even without any effects of mobility on land prices, local voters should favor efficient provision of local public services simply because they value the services and dislike paying taxes. Second, the point has changed from one about "exit" (as in the standard Tiebout model) to one about "voice"; local governments provide "good" policies not because they fear outflows of residents but in order to win votes or elite support.[11] The Tiebout argument was traditionally presented as a way of assuring responsive government even when electoral mechanisms of accountability failed. Third, for various reasons local homeowners may not be able to impose their demands on local government. Contrary to the assumption, renters may outnumber homeowners, and some (who use few public services) may prefer low house prices and rents. Alternatively, homeowners may be in the local majority but fail to coordinate their voting strategies. The incumbent may play off different property owners against one another. Building a school in the Northeast of the district may not affect property values much in the Southwest, and vice versa. In many models, competition between different voters to get into the incumbent's coalition drives benefits provided down toward zero (see Chapter 7).

Assumption 6 (no externalities) will almost never hold. This may either blunt competition or redirect it into harmful channels. The immediate effect of externalities will be to weaken the link between a local government's policies and its ability to retain residents.[12] The quality of life in locality A will depend not just on its policies but on those of its neighbors. Besides blunting the force of competition, externalities may also render

---

[11] Of course, a main reason land prices are sensitive to local public policies is that residents can move.

[12] If one assumes a benevolent central government, it might provide regulations or Pigovian grants to eliminate such externalities. But if one assumes a benevolent central government and the Tiebout argument is correct, then the benevolent central government would itself choose contracts with its agents that would reproduce the Pareto-optimal Tiebout equilibrium, without the need for any decentralization of authority (see section 4.1.3).

competition undesirable. One way to attract residents is by exploiting negative externalities – for instance, reducing local business costs by allowing firms to export pollution to neighboring regions. Competition in the presence of policy externalities may generate equilibria that are far from Pareto optimal.[13]

Assumption 2.5 (no geographically differentiated central policies) is both critical and unlikely to hold. This may be the most fundamental weakness of arguments about local competition. As argued elsewhere in the book (recall section 3.2), central governments can and almost always do intervene in ways that affect different regions differently. Such interventions will distort the impact of local government choices. Residents will decide whether to move based not just on local policies but also on how central policies affect particular districts. Again, this will weaken – and possibly undermine – the discipline imposed on local governments. And it will impair the sorting and information revelation functions of the Tiebout mechanism.[14] As attractive as the analogy to economic markets may be, one must apply it appropriately. To ignore the central government when studying competition among municipalities is like analyzing retail markets by focusing on a town's corner stores while ignoring the Wal-Mart megastore in their midst.

If certain other assumptions fail – as they will in most real cases – an equilibrium may not exist. And if no equilibrium exists under decentralization, we cannot compare its consequences with those of centralization; the Tiebout argument, which assumes a Pareto optimal equilibrium, then provides no useful insight. Consider first assumption 9 (lump sum taxes). Head taxes are rare in most developed countries. But the use of other, distortionary taxes may rule out any equilibrium. For instance, if local governments rely on an income tax, when income inequality within the country is large there may be no allocation of rich and poor residents across localities that will leave both types happy. Poor individuals will wish to cluster together with the rich (and benefit from higher average tax revenues and public good provision), but the rich would prefer to live apart from the poor (to avoid financing the free- or "easy"-riders). The poor will "chase" the rich, and the rich will continually be running away (Wheaton 1975; Rubinfeld 1987,

---

[13] See, for instance, Cumberland (1981) and Gordon (1983). I discuss this point in greater detail in the section on capital competition.

[14] One might argue, in response, that this makes it all the more important to deny a central government the ability to differentiate its taxes and policies geographically. But, short of eliminating the central government entirely, no one has found a reliable way to do this.

pp. 587–9; Kessler and Lülfesmann 2005). Local governments will have no idea what tax rate will attract more residents. One might encounter similar problems with a residential property tax: Each individual would want to live in a community with houses that were mostly larger than his (and so benefit from the higher taxes they pay).

The latter case might not be as serious as it sounds. In Western countries, local governments commonly rely on residential property taxes and often impose zoning regulations. If, within each community, zoning regulations require a minimum house size, the property tax becomes similar to a head tax (Hamilton 1976). The poor will no longer want to live in the same districts as the rich because they cannot afford the larger houses that are required there. Communities can still compete to attract individuals from among those who demand a certain amount of housing. An equilibrium may, once again, exist. But this puts additional strain on assumption 5: There must now be enough localities to satisfy every combination of demand for housing with demand for local public policy.

Violations of assumption 10 also threaten the existence of equilibrium. Equilibrium may not exist because of something like the "lemons" or adverse selection problem in insurance markets (Rothschild and Stiglitz 1976). Criminals may prefer to live in communities with many rich people. But rich people would prefer to live in communities without many criminals. Parents of children who are expensive to educate may prefer to live in localities where most children are cheap to school. But parents with children who are cheap to educate would prefer to pool with similar parents. Again, communities will seek to avoid such problems by limiting mobility.

Clearly, there are significant costs to establishing new communities – even in countries with an open frontier. And there will never be as many communities available as there are preference types. So assumption 5 can be met only approximately, which may again mean that no equilibrium exists (Pauly 1970, Bewley 1981).

In brief, it is unlikely that all the critical assumptions will hold even approximately. Competition will often be weak or non-existent, distorted by numerous intervening or offsetting factors. If competition exists, it may lead to undesirable rather than desirable behaviors (e.g., the exploitation of negative externalities). And even if competition is intense and focused on desirable behaviors, there will often be no equilibrium. A country in which the Tiebout model did apply would have rather unusual features: a population of rootless cosmopolitans, without personal or geographical attachments, all of whom are equally costly to educate, keep healthy, and deter from crime; a large number of local governments, whose policies are widely known and do not affect residents of neighboring jurisdictions; a central government that treats each locality identically; and a real estate market that does not capitalize on policy differences and in which moving houses is cheap or costless.

These problems seem bad enough, but there is another. Even if all the assumptions are met, there may be multiple equilibria, only some of which are Pareto optimal. For instance, as Bewley (1981) points out, if there are economies of scale in community size (at some level), these may not be captured in some equilibria. Given an existing set of inefficiently small localities, each individual may not have an incentive to move, even though all might be made better off by a coordinated relocation into a smaller number of larger units.[15]

This is particularly important when comparing centralization with decentralization. One potential advantage of centralization is precisely that a central government can avoid the type of "bad" equilibrium, in which local governments acting separately are prone to get stuck (Bolton and Farrell 1990). In Bewley's example with economies of community size, a powerful central government could, if it chose, consolidate the inefficiently small localities into more efficient larger ones, leaving all citizens better off. This is not to say that central governments *will* always choose the most efficient of multiple equilibria. The question is whether norms, expectations, or some other coordinating device under decentralization will be more likely to avoid Pareto inferior outcomes than will the deliberate choices of a central government under centralization. This question is not likely to have a general answer.

4.1.3 Mobility under Centralization

But suppose for a moment that the world of Tiebout did exist. Suppose the assumptions were, in fact, met, and there was a unique, Pareto optimal equilibrium under decentralization. Suppose that under decentralized provision of local public goods, citizens would sort themselves into homogeneous, optimally sized communities and that local governments would provide the public service packages that maximized local citizens' preferences. Would the Tiebout logic then imply the superiority of decentralized over centralized systems of government?

[15] This is Bewley's Example 5.1 (1981, p. 722).

Here another problem arises. What Tiebout identified was not an argument about political decentralization and centralization per se, but a mechanism that can be deployed under either. If the Tiebout mechanism "works" under decentralization, it can also work under centralization. The all-powerful central government of a unitary state could, if it wished, offer a variety of public policy packages in different localities and let citizens sort themselves among them. If the central government chose local policies *as if* to maximize the profits of local managers, that would lead it to precisely the same unique Pareto optimal outcome as under decentralized competition (Bewley 1981). By observing how residents move around, revealing information about their preferences, the center could adapt local policies just as local officials would do in a decentralized state. As Paul Seabright points out, this does not require any local autonomy at all: "Tiebout's model is best seen as a pioneering contribution to the theory of mechanism design, rather than as saying anything about the decentralization of power in government" (1996, p. 63).

One might object to this that, even if the central government in a centralized state could replicate local competition, decentralization is still better because under centralization the center might extract rents from citizens. But this is simply wrong. Nothing in the Tiebout argument constrains the central government from extracting rents under decentralization as well. To claim that decentralization constrains central government predation, one needs another argument.[16]

Similarly, one cannot argue that the Tiebout logic shows decentralization to be better because under centralization politically motivated income redistribution may occur. Redistribution may occur under decentralization as well. Under both systems, a central government will be able to reallocate income among groups of citizens by means of targeted tax breaks and transfers. The Tiebout argument does not affect this. (Tiebout, as already noted, leaves the central government very far in the background.) The extent and pattern of income redistribution might well be different under centralization and decentralization, although there do not seem to be general results about how these would differ (see Chapter 5). But given the results of income redistribution, whatever these are, local competition – or

---

[16] See the discussions of accountability in Chapter 7 and of limited government in Chapter 8. It is not enough simply to assume that political decentralization limits the discretion of central government without describing the mechanism that would – in general – enforce such limits.

some centrally designed replica of it – can achieve Pareto optimal local public policies under both constitutional arrangements.[17]

Given that the Tiebout mechanism is available to central governments, the real question is whether a central government would want to employ this mechanism. There might still be grounds to favor decentralization if central governments would typically choose not to replicate the results of local competition. Is there reason to think they would do so?

Note, first, that for a central government under centralization, using some equivalent of the Tiebout mechanism to achieve Pareto optimal local public policies is completely costless. The central government can do no better than to first extract any rents it desires, redistribute income among citizens however it wishes, and then implement some replica of local competition to take care of local public good provision. Given the results of the center's initial redistribution, local taxpayers then pay all the costs of providing the local public goods and services they receive. Local citizens benefit from the efficient mechanism for local public good provision, and the central government has lost nothing.

But even if providing an efficient mechanism is costless to the central government, would it choose to do so? It probably would, for various reasons. First, if the central incumbent places even a vanishingly small value on local welfare, this should overcome its indifference. Second, if the central incumbent must run for reelection, efficient local public policies may help win over voters. (Think of a Downsian setting in which two otherwise identical candidates, committed to the same redistributive strategies and national public goods programs, compete by committing to particular local public policies. If one candidate does not promise to provide local public goods efficiently in a given district, the rival candidate can win votes from those who anticipate living in that district by promising to do so. There is one caveat, which I discuss below.) Third, if the central government fears that local discontent might spark unrest, it can costlessly increase local welfare by improving local public good provision.

The logic might seem to fail if citizens care what policies are implemented in localities where they do not live, perhaps for ideological reasons. In Chapter 7, I discuss an example in which a nationwide majority believes

---

[17] One might worry that the center's redistribution of income might create such inequalities that a Tiebout equilibrium would no longer exist. But if this is a problem under centralization, exactly the same problem should arise as a result of central income redistribution under decentralization.

abortion should be legal in all localities, while local majorities in one-third of the localities would prefer to ban abortion. Under centralization, the central government might not wish to entrust policy making on this issue to some replica of the Tiebout mechanism because this would lead to bans on abortion in some localities – contrary to the preferences of the national majority.[18] But this is actually a case of strong public policy externalities – policies chosen in one locality affect the utility of those in other localities – and so violates a key assumption of Tiebout's argument. Even under decentralization, we could not assume in the presence of such externalities that equilibrium policies would be Pareto optimal.

A more valid, although somewhat contrived, objection focuses on the following case. Suppose that: (1) a central government (under either system) can redistribute only geographically and not to individuals or nongeographical groups, (2) citizens are perfectly mobile, and (3) the central government cannot provide local public goods under decentralization. Now, under centralization the center may deliberately offer inefficient packages of public goods in some localities in order to accomplish a redistribution of income that would otherwise be undermined by mobility. Suppose, for instance, that the center wishes to redistribute from members of one group ("A"), who have a high preference for a local public good, to members of a second group ("B"), who have a lower preference for the public good. The center might set public policies in two localities, 1 and 2, such that members of groups A and B would segregate themselves, clustering in respectively 1 and 2. In order to keep members of A from migrating into locality 2, the center might deliberately "underprovide" the public good to the members of B clustered in 2. That is, for members of B in 2, the marginal benefit from the public good would in equilibrium exceed the marginal cost of taxation to them.[19] Inefficient provision would make it possible to exploit the differences in tastes of the groups and transfer monetary benefits from one to the other.

One can, thus, construct cases in which the central government under centralization would not provide local public goods as efficiently as we have assumed would occur under decentralization. The example is somewhat artificial, however, for the following reasons. First, central governments typically have many ways of redistributing income among citizens and do not need to rely on just geographical redistribution. Second, central

---

[18] This possibility turns up again in section 9.2, on policy experimentation.

[19] I assume that utility for both groups is concave in the public good.

governments under decentralization can often provide local public goods if they so choose (and so the same issue might arise under decentralization). And third, in the example sketched above, all parties – members of A, members of B, and the central government itself – could be made better off by restricting citizen mobility. Decentralization – if it solves the problem – is certainly not the only solution.

In sum, the restrictive assumptions necessary for the Tiebout result are unlikely to hold even approximately in most real world applications. But even if they do, a central government in a centralized system would also achieve the same level of efficiency in almost all cases – if necessary, by replicating the Tiebout mechanism. Only if we make some implausible and arbitrary assumptions does an advantage for decentralization appear. And even in this case, all parties would prefer centralization to decentralization if they could commit to a deal that would restrict citizen mobility. Tiebout, at best, establishes that local decision making along with citizen mobility *might* – given a long list of unlikely conditions – leave citizens better off than centralization. But there is no reason to think it will do so in general.

4.2 Competing for Mobile Capital

In 1993, the Mercedes Benz company began scouting out locations in the United States for a new plant at which to build sport utility vehicles. The plant, providing 1,500 jobs, promised to provide a major economic boost to the surrounding community. A bidding war broke out among the leading contenders – Alabama, North Carolina, and South Carolina. Alabama's governor, James Folsom, flew to Mercedes headquarters in Stuttgart three times and put together a package of incentives worth more than $170 million. The state promised to buy and develop the land itself, ugrade local utilities, purchase 2,500 vehicles from the plant, and even pay the workers' salaries for the first year. After winning, Folsom deployed the National Guard to clear the site and tried to raid the state's education fund to finance the corporate incentives he had promised. When that failed, Alabama was forced to borrow $98 million at near junk bond rates from its own pension fund.[20]

Residents are not the only mobile factor that local governments compete to attract in decentralized systems. As the previous example shows, the contest to lure footloose capital can be even more intense. Although Alabama's

---

[20] For these and other details, see Myerson (1996), Thomas (2000), and Buchholz (2002).

largesse toward Mercedes may have set records, similar courtships of corporate investors by American states and cities are common. A survey in 1993 discovered that half the state governments had recently offered fiscal incentives to convince businesses to move to or stay in their jurisdictions (Burstein and Rolnick 1994). In the 1990s, New York City paid $30 million each to the investment banks Morgan Stanley and Kidder Peabody and Co. to persuade them not to leave town. Massachusetts awarded a $20 million tax break to Raytheon when it threatened to move jobs to Arizona and Tennessee (Myerson 1996). In the early 1990s, the city of Amarillo, Texas, hit on the ploy of sending checks for $8 million to some 1,300 companies. The only condition for cashing the checks was that the company create 700 new jobs in the city (Burstein and Rolnick 1994).[21]

How does competition for mobile capital affect public policies in decentralized systems? Many scholars have tried to answer this question.[22] One might view such competition as just a variation on the Tiebout models already discussed.[23] But some different questions arise. While the Tiebout argument supposes citizens have different tastes for public goods and so sort themselves by type, investment capital is usually thought of as homogeneous. Investors seek only the highest risk-adjusted returns rather than a particular combination of public policies.

If governments are purely benevolent and can use benefit taxes – charging each firm the marginal cost of the local services it uses – capital competition can be perfectly efficient. In equilibrium, each investor pays the marginal cost of the local public services she receives.[24] However, if governments are purely benevolent and can use benefit taxes, under plausible assumptions *centralization* should also result in efficiency. The central government would then sell local public services to firms using marginal cost pricing.

It is only when governments are not entirely benevolent or are limited to distortionary taxes that the results under decentralization and

---

[21] Nor is such cutthroat competition a recent invention. According to Benson (1941, p. 37), in the 1930s "A town in New Hampshire offered to dismantle, move, and set up all the machinery and equipment of a Lynn (Massachusetts) shoe factory. In addition it offered a building of twenty-four thousand square feet rent-free and a guarantee of $5,000 against labor troubles."

[22] For excellent recent reviews, see Wildasin and Wilson (2004) and Wilson (1999).

[23] Some scholars have adapted Tiebout models to the study of competition for mobile capital (e.g., Fischel 1975, White 1975).

[24] See, for example, Richter and Wellisch (1996).

centralization might differ. I will focus on such cases in this section. In particular, suppose that governments are partly self-interested and imperfectly controlled by voters. Some argue that under decentralization the fear of losing mobile capital will motivate local governments to reduce their corruption, waste, and inefficiency and to provide growth-promoting infrastructure. Such competition might also keep local tax rates low and reduce the burden of government. According to Geoffrey Brennan and James Buchanan, "Total government intrusion into the economy should be smaller, *ceteris paribus*, the greater the extent to which taxes and expenditures are decentralized" (Brennan and Buchanan 1980, p. 185).[25] Indeed, Brennan and Buchanan see one motive for centralization in the desire of local governments to avoid such mutually constraining competition: The central government becomes the enforcer of a cartel that keeps tax rates high.[26]

As in the previous section, there are three questions to consider when examining this argument. First, will competition among local governments occur? Second, if it does, will it induce "good" behavior? Third, if beneficial competition occurs under political decentralization, would equally attractive outcomes occur under centralization? The traditional arguments about mobile capital fail to establish general positive answers to the first two questions. But even if they did, a politically all-powerful central government could – and most probably would – use a similar mechanism to discipline its local agents, achieving similar efficiencies.

4.2.1 Constraining Leviathan

First, let us formalize the argument that competition to attract mobile capital disciplines local governments. Local governments could compete on various dimensions, but I will start by supposing that they compete by setting low tax rates. Imagine a country divided into two identical localities, $n = 1, 2$. Investors own a total amount of capital, normalized to one, that they invest in either or both of the two districts. All capital must be employed

---

[25] For similar arguments, see Qian and Roland (1998), Montinola, Qian, and Weingast (1995), and Qian and Weingast (1997), quoted in the epigraph to this chapter. In China, competition to attract foreign investment is said to have led provinces, cities, and townships to adopt pro-business laws, regulations, and tax systems (Montinola, Qian, and Weingast 1995, p. 77).

[26] For a similar argument, see Blankart (2000).

each period, and it can flow freely and costlessly between the localities. The amount of capital invested in district n is k_n. Output and income in each district is an increasing, strictly concave function of capital employed in that district, $f(k_n)$, where $f' > 0$, $f'' < 0$, $f(0) = 0$.

I compare two decision rules. Under *centralization*, a single, central government decides on the tax rates on output in localities 1 and 2, $\tau_1, \tau_2 \in [0, \overline{\tau}]$, where $\overline{\tau} \leq 1$ is the maximum feasible tax rate. Under *decentralization*, each local government sets the tax rate, $\tau_n \in [0, \overline{\tau}]$, on output produced in its jurisdiction. I suppose that the local governments move simultaneously and so play a Cournot game against each other.

Assume to begin with that governments do not care at all about private consumption and maximize their own revenues: $R_c = \tau_1 f(k_1) + \tau_2 f(k_2)$ for the central government under centralization, and $R_n = \tau_n f(k_n)$ for each local government under decentralization. This matches Brennan and Buchanan's Leviathan assumption. In both cases, because capital is costlessly mobile, the governments are subject to an arbitrage constraint: If the after-tax return to capital is higher in the other locality, capital will flow into it. So, in an interior equilibrium the marginal after-tax rates of return to capital in the two localities must be the same: $(1 - \tau_1)f'(k_1) = (1 - \tau_2)f'(k_2)$, which implies that in equilibrium:

$$\frac{\partial k_1^*}{\partial \tau_1} = \frac{f'(k_1^*)}{(1 - \tau_1)f''(k_1^*) + (1 - \tau_2)f''(k_2^*)} \tag{4.1}$$

which is less than zero given strict concavity of f. So a higher tax rate in one locality, holding constant the tax rate in the other, causes capital to flow out of the first into the second.

Under centralization, the central government will maximize its revenues by setting the maximum feasible tax rate in both localities: $\tau_1 = \tau_2 = \overline{\tau}$.[27] Capital mobility does not constrain the government because it can tax capital wherever it is invested. Because the tax rate is the same for both regions, capital must all be employed each period, and returns to capital are decreasing, it follows that $k_1 = k_2 = 1/2$. Under decentralization, the government of n sets τ_n to maximize $\tau_n f(k_n^*)$, where k_n^* is a function of τ_1 and τ_2, as defined implicitly by the arbitrage condition. The first order conditions

---

[27] If we assumed no maximum τ but that f declined with τ sufficiently fast, creating a Laffer curve, the central government would set both local tax rates at the peak of the Laffer curve.

represent the government of n's best response to the other government's tax rate:

$$1. f(k_1{}^*) + \tau_1 \frac{df(k_1{}^*)}{dk_1} \frac{\partial k_1{}^*}{\partial \tau_1} = 0$$

$$2. f(k_2{}^*) + \tau_2 \frac{df(k_2{}^*)}{dk_2} \frac{\partial k_2{}^*}{\partial \tau_2} = 0$$

(4.2)

The first term (which is positive) represents the direct increase in revenue for locality n from raising its tax rate marginally if $k_n{}^*$ and the tax rate in the other locality, τ_{-n}, remained unchanged. The second term (which is negative) adjusts for the fact that raising the tax rate causes capital to flow out of locality n (at a rate of $\partial k_n{}^*/\partial \tau_n$), thus reducing n's tax base. In this case, unlike that of centralization, each government is constrained by the knowledge that it will lose capital if it increases the tax rate. Thus, capital mobility imposes fiscal discipline. The Nash equilibrium is derived by solving the first order conditions simultaneously (thus identifying the intersection of the two localities' reaction curves).

Suppose, to illustrate, that the local production function takes a simple quadratic form:

$$f(k_n) = \alpha k_n - \beta k_n{}^2 \quad \text{for } n = 1, 2 \tag{4.3}$$

where α and β are positive constants and $\alpha \geq 2\beta$ (which ensures that the marginal productivity is never negative even if all capital is invested in one locality). Given this, the solution is at $\tau_1{}^* = \tau_2{}^* = (2\alpha\beta - \beta^2)/\alpha^2$, so long as $(2\alpha\beta - \beta^2)/\alpha^2 < \bar{\tau}$. Assuming $(2\alpha\beta - \beta^2)/\alpha^2 < \bar{\tau}$, the equilibrium tax rate under decentralization with capital mobility is lower than the tax rate under centralization. This is the argument that capital competition in a decentralized state can constrain Leviathan.

4.2.2 Heterogeneous Regions and Uneven Competition

Competition in a simple model places downward pressure on the tax rate. But how general is this result? We assumed in the previous example that the production functions in the two localities were identical. Suppose now that capital is more productive in one locality than in the other, perhaps because of exogenous differences in resource endowments, location, or inherited human capital. Using the production function in (4.3), we can incorporate this by supposing that the parameter α is higher for locality 1 than locality 2:

$$f(k_n) = \alpha_n k_n - \beta k_n{}^2 \text{ for } n = 1, 2; \alpha_1 > \alpha_2 \tag{4.3'}$$

The arbitrage condition now implies that in an equilibrium in which each locality gets some capital:

$$k_1{}^*(\tau_1, \tau_2) = \frac{\alpha_1(1 - \tau_1) - (\alpha_2 - 2\beta)(1 - \tau_2)}{2\beta(2 - \tau_1 - \tau_2)} \tag{4.4}$$

If α_1 and α_2 are not too far apart, one might still get the same qualitative result as in the previous section: Competition for capital under decentralization would lead to lower tax rates than under centralization. But if locality 1 is much more exogenously productive than 2(α_1 is large relative to α_2), the government of 1 will be able to set a tax rate such that it receives all the capital. To see this, note that from (4.4) and the analogous condition for $k_2{}^*(\tau_1, \tau_2)$:

$$k_1{}^* - k_2{}^* = \frac{\alpha_1(1 - \tau_1) - \alpha_2(1 - \tau_2) + \beta(\tau_1 - \tau_2)}{\beta(2 - \tau_1 - \tau_2)} \tag{4.5}$$

This will be greater than or equal to one – that is, all capital will flow into locality 1 – if $\tau_1 \le 1 - \alpha_2(1 - \tau_2)/(\alpha_1 - 2\beta)$. For a large enough disparity in productivity between the two localities, $\alpha_1 - \alpha_2 \ge \bar{\tau} + 2\beta$, the more productive locality will be able to set the maximum tax rate, $\tau = \bar{\tau}$, and still attract all the capital even if the less productive locality sets a tax rate of zero.[28] Decentralization will not reduce the tax rate at all relative to centralization. The less productive locality cannot compete because even if it sets a tax rate of zero, all capital will flow into the more productive one.

The complete segregation of all capital into one locality is a consequence of the simple quadratic production function and obviously represents an extreme case. But the idea is quite general. One can show with other production functions that the intensity of competition will fall with increases in the disparity in exogenous productivity.[29]

Thus, if one region starts out substantially more productive than the other – because of greater human capital, natural resources, or some other factor – decentralization with capital mobility will not lead to a lower tax rate than centralization. In such cases, capital mobility under either centralization or decentralization accentuates inequalities in the distribution of capital across regions without necessarily reducing the tax rate in the region that absorbs most or all of the capital. And regions that know they will lose

---

[28] This requires, in addition, that $\bar{\tau} < 1$.

[29] For instance, suppose $f(k_n) = \alpha_n k_n{}^\beta$ for $n = 1, 2; \alpha_1 > \alpha_2; 0 < \beta < 1$. The arbitrage condition: $(1 - t_1)f'(k_1) = (1 - t_2)f'(k_2)$ can now be solved to yield: $k_1{}^* = 1/[1 + (\alpha_2/\alpha_1)^{1/(1-\beta)}((1 - \tau_2)/(1 - \tau_1))^{1/(1-\beta)}]$. As α_2/α_1 approaches zero – that is, as locality 1's relative productivity increases – locality 1's share of the capital, $k_1{}^*$, goes to one.

all their mobile capital to more productive rivals have even less incentive to improve their governments than if capital mobility were lower.[30]

This is not just an artificial example. In many countries, some districts or regions start out so disadvantaged that they cannot hope to win the contest for mobile capital – and so do not even try. Greater capital mobility in these settings often leads to clustering of capital in the most attractive regions. Cai and Treisman (2005a) looked at the pattern of investment flows in Russia after market reforms in the early 1990s liberated private capital to flow relatively unimpeded among the country's eighty-nine regions. We found that those regions which started out with better initial endowments (natural resources, proximity to Europe, transport infrastructure, education level, etc.) competed harder to attract investment by spending on market development and improving their business climates. And investment flowed disproportionately to regions with more business-friendly policies. Major urban or industrial centers like Moscow or Samara improved their business environment to lure domestic and foreign capital and succeeded in attracting it. More underdeveloped, resource-poor, or isolated regions such as Tyva or Kalmykia gave up on winning the race, let their physical infrastructure run down, and did almost nothing to upgrade market institutions. Net savings were flowing out of these regions.

In China, private investment inflows – and business-friendly reforms – have concentrated on the coastal provinces, which have better access to port facilities and infrastructure. (In fact, some of the coastal provinces – for example, Guangdong and Fujian – started out with less developed infrastructure but got a major early boost from *central* government decisions to site special economic zones in their territory.) Inland provinces have found it hard to compete. Although differences in initial endowments among localities in the United States are generally smaller, some observers of the urban scene have noticed a similar phenomenon there. According to Yates (1978, pp. 186–7):

Tiebout's argument makes some sense if we are talking about a set of relatively affluent suburbs that differ largely in their amenities and life-style characteristics. But viewed from the perspective of the city, Tiebout's argument is a recipe for certain disaster because most cities simply cannot compete with most suburbs for fiscally profitable residents and industries. ... Because of their fiscal structures and service obligations, cities cannot compete (or even survive) in a system of free market federalism.

---

[30] For a development of this idea, see Cai and Treisman (2005a).

While capital competition may impose discipline on governments within clubs of similar regions or states, it may be ineffective or even counterproductive when the units are too heterogeneous.

4.2.3 Introducing a Central Government

The previous models are well suited to analyze relations between countries. But they are an odd framework within which to study decentralized states. Something essential is missing – a central government.[31] The comparison in section 4.2.1 does not, in fact, compare centralization with decentralization; rather, it compares a unitary state with two separate states. When a central government is included, an additional game exists between center and localities, and the results of decentralized competition for capital are no longer so clear. Vertical competition may then lead to an excessively high aggregate tax burden, as the different-level governments compete against one another to extract income from the same taxpayers (see Chapter 6). Horizontal competition – among local governments to attract mobile capital – may reduce such "over-grazing."[32] But, in simple models, complete centralization would reduce it still more.

I now adapt the model of section 4.2.1 to incorporate two levels of government. To keep the structure of the game as similar as possible, suppose that under *centralization*, a single, central government decides on a common tax rate, $T \in [0, \bar{\tau}]$, on output for the whole country. (Local governments make no independent decisions and may be thought of as just implementing central directives.) Under *decentralization*, each local government sets its own tax rate, $\tau_n \in [0, \bar{\tau}]$, on output produced in the locality. As before, the local governments move simultaneously and so play Cournot-Nash against one another. But, unlike in section 4.2.1, the central government can also impose its own tax, with rate $T_n \in [0, \bar{\tau}]$, on output in locality n. The two taxes together cannot exceed the maximum feasible level: $T_n + \tau_n \leq \bar{\tau}, \forall n$.

Under centralization, the results are as before. The central government sets the maximum feasible tax rate: $T = \bar{\tau}$. Under decentralization, one must specify in what order the local and central governments set their tax rates. However, whether one assumes the central government or the local

---

[31] Michael Keen (1998, p. 454) expresses surprise that "until recently almost all of the formal literature on fiscal federalism dealt with just one level of government, the federal government being notable by its absence." See also Flowers (1988).

[32] Keen and Kotsogiannis (2002) analyze a model including both effects.

governments move first, it is easy to see that the aggregate tax rate at the end of play will always be $T_n + \tau_n = \overline{\tau}$ in all localities. If the central government moves first, it will set $T_n = \overline{\tau}$ in all localities, exhausting all available tax revenues, and forcing the local governments to set $\tau_n = 0$. If the central government moves second, then it will set $T_n = \overline{\tau} - \tau_n$ in each locality, bringing the aggregate tax rate up to $\overline{\tau}$. Either way, the equilibrium total tax rate will be exactly the same as under centralization.

It might seem artificial to assume a fixed maximum feasible tax rate, $\overline{\tau}$. So, instead, suppose there is a Laffer curve: Total revenues at first increase and then decrease as the aggregate tax rate rises. One simple way to model this is to adapt the production function to write "taxable" output as:

$$f^t(k_n, \tau_n, T) = (1 - \tau_n - T)\left(\alpha k_n - \beta k_n^2\right) \quad \text{for } n = 1, 2 \qquad (4.3'')$$

Thus, taxable output decreases linearly with the aggregate tax rate, $(\tau_n + T)$.[33]

Under centralization, there are no local taxes. The central government sets T to maximize: $T(1 - T)(\alpha k_1 - \beta k_1^2 + \alpha k_2 - \beta k_2^2)$. Because the tax rate is the same nationwide and local returns to capital are decreasing, capital will distribute itself evenly across the two localities. In equilibrium, $k_1^* = k_2^* = 1/2$ and $T^* = 1/2$.

Under decentralization, the aggregate equilibrium tax rate, in this example, is higher.[34] One could model the central government moving first, the local government moving first, or both moving simultaneously. In each case $T^* + \tau^* > 1/2$. To illustrate, suppose that all governments set their tax rates simultaneously, playing Cournot-Nash. Each local government maximizes: $\tau_n(1 - \tau_n - T)(\alpha k_n^* - \beta k_n^{*2})$ subject to the mobility constraint $(1 - \tau_1 - T)f_k(k_1^*, \tau_1 + T) = (1 - \tau_2 - T)f_k(k_2^*, \tau_2 + T)$. Focusing on the symmetric equilibrium, in which $\tau_1^* = \tau_2^* = \tau$ and $k_1^* = k_2^* = 1/2$,

---

[33] One might motivate this taxable output function in the following way. Suppose first that, as in section 2.2.5, firms conceal a proportion of their output, $a \in [0, 1]$, and report the remaining share, $1 - a$; and second that the cost of concealing output increases with the share concealed according to the formula: $C = (a^2/2)f(k_n)$. Suppose, for simplicity, there is just one firm in each locality. We can write its total net output (after paying tax on reported output and concealment costs on the unofficial portion) as: $y_n^N = (1 - a)(1 - \tau_n - T)f(k_n) + af(k_n) - (a^2/2)f(k_n)$. It makes sense to expect costs of concealment to increase in the share of output concealed because enforcement efforts are likely to increase as the scale of evasion rises. Setting a to maximize y_n^N, we get: $1 - a = 1 - \tau_n - T$.

[34] At least, this is true assuming as I do below that the symmetric equilibrium in which both localities set the same tax rate occurs.

the first order conditions for the local governments simplify to: $\tau^* = (1 - T)(2\alpha\beta - \beta^2)/2\alpha^2$. (This parallels the result in 4.2.1 when no central government existed: $\tau^* = (2\alpha\beta - \beta^2)/2\alpha^2$.) The central government maximizes $T_1 f(k_1^*, \tau_1 + T_1) + T_2 f(k_2^*, \tau_2 + T_2)$. In the symmetric equilibrium, the central government sets the same tax rate in both localities, and the first order condition reduces to: $T^* = (1 - \tau)/2$. From this alone, we can see that so long as $\tau^* > 0$, which it will be, the aggregate tax rate, $T^* + \tau^* = (1 + \tau^*)/2$, will be greater than one-half, the rate chosen under centralization. Solving the two reaction functions simultaneously, we get $\tau^* = (2\alpha\beta - \beta^2)/(\beta^2 - 2\alpha\beta + 4\alpha^2)$, $T^* = (2\alpha^2 - 2\alpha\beta + \beta^2)/(\beta^2 - 2\alpha\beta + 4\alpha^2)$, and $T^* + \tau^* = 2\alpha^2/(\beta^2 - 2\alpha\beta + 4\alpha^2) > 1/2$. The aggregate tax rate under decentralization, in this example, is greater than that under centralization.[35]

This analysis stands the common intuition on its head. Under decentralization, capital mobility may – as supposed – reduce the level of predation by noncooperative tiers of government. But, at least in some cases, predation could be reduced even more by complete centralization, even centralization to a purely predatory unitary government. The problems created by decentralization may be alleviated by capital mobility. But if controlling rent extraction is the priority, complete centralization would sometimes be more effective.[36]

Capital mobility may also have a surprising impact on the size of government, as demonstrated elegantly by Keen (1998). If, as is to be expected, the aggregate tax rate without capital mobility is on the far side of the Laffer curve, then if capital mobility reduces the aggregate tax rate this will actually *increase* total tax revenues. Keen discusses the interaction of two levels' tax-rate setting in a model with capital mobility and concludes – as I do – that

[35] If the center moves first, it sets a tax rate of 1/2 and the local governments sets $\tau^* = (1 - T)$ $[(2\alpha\beta - \beta^2)/(2\alpha^2)] = (1/2)[(2\alpha\beta - \beta^2)/(2\alpha^2)]$. Thus, the center acts as though it were a unitary government, and the aggregate tax rate is greater than 1/2. If the local governments move first, the aggregate tax rate $T^* + \tau^* = (4\alpha^2 - 2\alpha\beta + \beta^2)/(8\alpha^2 - 8\alpha\beta + 4\beta^2) > 1/2$.

[36] One might argue that another way to eliminate this problem would be to prevent the central government from taxing the same tax base as the local governments. But it is not clear what mechanism would prevent a predatory central government from stepping in to take advantage of the lower local tax rates induced by horizontal competition. If some other mechanism restrains a predatory central government, presumably some version of it could have been used to restrain predatory local governments. For instance, if constitutional proscriptions keep the central government from taxing a "local" tax base, why could constitutional proscriptions not limit the tax rate the local governments can set? The mechanism of interregional competition is supposed to be useful in precisely the cases in which words on paper will not do the trick.

"theory admits no unambiguous answer to the question of whether federal structure creates an inherent tendency toward excessively high tax rates" (Keen 1998, p. 470).

4.2.4 Competing by Building Infrastructure

Subnational governments can compete for mobile capital in many ways besides setting low tax rates. They may appeal to investors by building infrastructure that reduces businesses' costs or increases their productivity. In its bid for Mercedes' business, Alabama promised to spend more than $75 million improving water, sewers, and other utilities at the proposed plant site (Myerson 1996). China's economic reforms in the 1980s generated a boom in airport construction as local governments competed for investment. As a result, there are now five airports within a 100-mile radius in the Pearl River Delta.[37] Of China's 143 aiports, almost 90 percent were losing money as of 2003.[38] One can model such competition quite simply, and – again assuming localities are identical and ignoring the central government – one can derive the standard disciplining effect of capital competition. However, when heterogeneity or a central government is reintroduced, again no general result survives.

To see this, adapt the aggregate output function to include a term for public infrastructure investments, I_n. Output in each of two identical localities, indexed $n = 1, 2$, is $f(k_n, I_n)$, where f is increasing and concave in both k_n and I_n. To capture the notion that public infrastructure increases businesses' productivity, suppose that infrastructure and capital are complements: $f_{kI} > 0$. Suppose now that the tax rate (for the central government under centralization, for each local government under decentralization) is fixed at τ, and as before total capital is normalized to one. For simplicity, suppose here too that all governments are revenue-maximizing Leviathans. Under *centralization*, the central government sets I_1 and I_2 for the two localities to maximize $R_c = \tau[f(k_1, I_1) + f(1 - k_1, I_2)] - I_1 - I_2$. Under *decentralization*, each local government n maximizes $R_n = \tau f(k_n, I_n) - I_n$. In both cases, because capital is mobile, the governments are subject to an arbitrage condition: $(1 - \tau)f_k(k_1, I_1) = (1 - \tau)f_k(k_2, I_2)$.

---

[37] Joseph Lo, "Pearl Delta airspace faces traffic jam," *South China Morning Post*, May 10, 2002, p. 10.

[38] Mark O'Neill, "Airports reflect edifice complexes of their backers," *South China Morning Post*, May 7, 2003, p. 16.

If there is a symmetric interior equilibrium, in which $I_1 = I_2 > 0$ and $k_1 = k_2 = 1/2$, then the first order conditions reduce to:

Centralization: $\tau f_I(k_n, I^c) = 1 \quad n = 1, 2$ (4.6a)

Decentralization: $\tau \left[f_k(k_n, I^d)\dfrac{\partial k_n{}^*}{\partial I_n} + f_I(k_n, I^d) \right] = 1 \quad n = 1, 2$ (4.6b)

where I^c and I^d denote respectively the level of infrastructure investment in each locality in the symmetric interior equilibrium under centralization and decentralization.[39]

Comparing (4.6a) and (4.6b), it is easy to see that the local governments set a higher rate of infrastructure investment in the equilibrium under decentralization than that set by the central government in the centralization equilibrium. In both (4.6a) and (4.6b), the right-hand side measures the opportunity cost to the government of investing a dollar in infrastructure. The left-hand sides measure the marginal benefit to the government of a marginal dollar invested in infrastructure. The condition for decentralization contains an additional term, $f_k(k_n, I^d)(\partial k_n{}^*/\partial I_n)$, which represents the marginal increment to output in n caused by capital attracted into the locality by a higher level of infrastructure investment. (This must be positive, because by assumption $f_k(k_n, I^d) > 0$ and from the arbitrage condition, given concavity of f, $\partial k_n{}^*/\partial I_n > 0$.) Knowing that higher infrastructure investment not only increases output directly but also attracts additional capital, the local governments have an added incentive to invest. Because $f_k(k_n, I^d)(\partial k_n{}^*/\partial I_n) > 0$, to maintain the equalities $f_I(1/2, I^d)$ must be less than $f_I(1/2, I^c)$, which given the concavity of f means that $I^d > I^c$.

Thus, by a logic analogous to that of section 4.2.1, competition for mobile capital may lead to a higher level of infrastructure investment under decentralization than under centralization. However, several assumptions are necessary to ensure that such competition occurs. First, capital and infrastructure cannot be too complementary – otherwise no interior equilibrium will exist under centralization or decentralization.[40] Second, if localities are heterogeneous, as in section 4.2.2, the less exogenously productive locality may have such a low chance of winning the competition for capital

---

[39] More generally, under centralization the first order conditions are: $[f_k(k_1, I_1) - f_k(1 - k_1, I_2)](\partial k_1{}^*/\partial I_1) + f_I(k_1, I_1) = 1/\tau$, and $[f_k(k_1, I_1) - f_k(1 - k_1, I_2)](\partial k_1{}^*/\partial I_2) + f_I(1 - k_1, I_2) = 1/\tau$. In the symmetric equilibrium, the first terms equal zero and these reduce to (4.6a).

[40] In this case, the first order conditions in (4.6a) and (4.6b) would represent minima, not maxima.

that it hardly invests in infrastructure at all. In such cases, under either centralization or decentralization, all or almost all mobile capital would cluster in the more productive locality.[41]

Third, if central and local governments can both provide infrastructure under decentralization, then aggregate infrastructure in equilibrium may be either higher or lower than under centralization. There are two possibilities. If both levels of government make positive infrastructure investments in equilibrium under decentralization, then the aggregate level must be lower than under centralization. To see this, note that each level of government gets only part of the benefit (in higher tax revenues) from a marginal dollar invested in infrastructure. (If one level got the whole benefit, then the other would not make a positive infrastructure investment.) Given this, the central government will invest only if the marginal productivity of infrastructure is higher (and therefore the total amount of infrastructure investment lower) than in the equilibrium under centralization (in which the central government gets all the benefit). If only the local governments build infrastructure in equilibrium, they may provide either less or more than is provided under centralization. Several effects pull in opposite directions. First, each local government receives only a fraction of the benefits of its investment because the center gets some share of tax revenues. Second, the local governments ignore any positive externalities from their infrastructure investments on the other locality. Both these effects tend to reduce infrastructure investment relative to centralization. However, they may be offset by the standard disciplining effect: Local governments will lose capital to their neighbors if they do not provide enough infrastructure. If capital is sufficiently productive and complementary with infrastructure – that is, $f_k(k_n^*, I_n^*)(\partial k_n^*/\partial I_n)$ is large – this effect may overwhelm the first two.

4.2.5 If Competition Does Occur, Is It Beneficial?

Even if local governments do compete to attract capital, this may not be a good thing. There are at least five possible reasons why it might not.

First, competition may distort the allocation of the public budget. If governments divide revenues between business-attracting infrastructure and other valuable public goods, the latter may be underprovided because of the need to appeal to investors. As Keen and Marchand (1997) put it, the pressures to provide "business centers and airports" may lead to underprovision

---

[41] See Cai and Treisman (2005a).

of "parks and libraries." As Alabama bid desperately for the Mercedes plant, the governor tried to dip into the state's education fund. "It used to be we taxed industry and gave it to education," one state representative reportedly complained. "Now we're taxing education and giving it to business" (Buchholz 2002).

Competition that reduces waste and corruption is obviously beneficial. But competition that distorts the allocation of public goods may not be. Many writers have expressed fears of a "race to the bottom" in provision of benefits to less mobile factors, such as labor.[42] If such benefits are valuable, centralization might be preferable to decentralization for this reason. At the same time, competition will focus on those who decide the location of investments – usually company managers – at the expense of those who just put up the cash. Bebchuk and Ferrell (1999) argue that interstate competition has led U.S. state legislatures to pass laws on mergers and takeovers that favor company managers at the expense of their shareholders. Associated with this criticism, competition among local governments over tax rates may lead to equilibrium rates too low to finance the desired level of non–business-promoting public services. The "race to the bottom" may be in subnational tax rates.[43]

Second, as noted in the section on competition for residents, local governments can play a strategy of "beggar your neighbor," competing in ways that impose costs on other districts. For instance, local governments may attract polluting firms to their jurisdiction by weakening environmental regulations, knowing that the costs of the pollution will be borne largely by nearby regions (Cumberland 1981, Wilson 1996).[44] After the 1970 Clean Air Act established strict limits on emissions in the American states, factories started building much taller smokestacks, which cause winds to carry the pollutants farther away. In the 1970s, only two stacks in the United States were higher than 500 feet; by 1985, more than 180 were (Revesz 1997, p. 111). Or local governments might set low product quality standards given that some local goods are sold outside the locality (Sinn 1997).

---

[42] One of the first to suggest this possibility was Oates (1972, p. 143): "In an attempt to keep taxes low to attract business investment, local officials may hold spending below those levels for which marginal benefits equal marginal costs, particularly for those programs that do not offer direct benefits to local business." Rom, Peterson, and Scheve (1998) discuss the "race-to-the-bottom" in U.S. welfare policies and social services.

[43] For example, see Break (1967), or the discussion in Oates (1999).

[44] Oates and Schwab (1988) show that competition to attract capital may not induce suboptimal levels of pollution – but only in a world without interregional spillovers.

Third, governments may try to compete by "exporting taxes," for instance by imposing high sales taxes on goods or services purchased in part by nonresidents. For instance, many cities impose a tax on hotel rooms. These three points go beyond the standard argument that central intervention is needed because local governments will ignore interregional spillovers. Local governments will not just ignore interregional negative externalities; they will deliberately exploit them.

Fourth, resources may be wasted in the competition itself. Here, I refer not to transfers from a government to an investor, which affect distribution but need not be inefficient. But suppose local governments employ public relations departments whose only goal is to persuade corporations to locate in their district rather than in their neighbors'. Assuming such lobbyists do something more than just provide useful, unbiased information to investors, the resources they expend in a purely distributive battle do not lead to greater output or income. While local governments have an incentive to spend money in this way, a central government would not.

Fifth, subnational governments sometimes compete to attract mobile capital by methods that undermine the central government's ability to provide public benefits. Rather than playing "beggar your neighbor," they may try to "beggar" their superior. For instance, local governments may make it harder to enforce national regulations that impose costs on businesses, or obstruct the central government's attempts to collect tax from local firms.[45] Such tactics are not a problem if one assumes (along with Brennan and Buchanan 1980) that governments act as pure Leviathans. Then constraining the central government from any taxation or regulation would be optimal. But if the central government provides some valuable goods or services – such as, perhaps, corrective subsidies to offset interregional externalities, or a framework of economic law and order – undermining its ability to fund these may have real costs.

Consider, for example, the case of the Russian oil company Tatneft, located in Tatarstan, a Muslim republic on the Volga River (Cai and Treisman 2004). In the mid-1990s, the Russian federal government was struggling to avert a financial crisis. An epidemic of tax nonpayments by major companies was alarming holders of the country's treasury bonds. By October 1996, Tatneft, then Russia's fifth-largest oil company, had run up federal arrears of $75 million, despite earning pre-tax profits the previous year of

---

[45] See Cai and Treisman (2004) for a model that demonstrates this result. See also Sonin (2003).

about $470 million.[46] Attempts by federal authorities to collect on these were met by resistance and lobbying by the republic's president, Mintimer Shaimiev, whose close relations with the local courts would have made it hard to enforce a bankruptcy order. When the federal government threatened to cut Tatneft's access to the export pipeline, Shaimiev quickly flew to Moscow, met with the prime minister, and announced that export restrictions had been "taken off the agenda."

In between such trips to Moscow, Shaimiev and his aides were wooing foreign investors on behalf of Tatneft. In December 1996, just months after the company was threatened with bankruptcy, Tatneft was the second Russian firm to float ADRs on the London Stock Exchange. Its share price increased by more than three times during 1997, and Western banks signed up for multi-million-dollar loans. According to one Western business columnist, the dramatic rise in Tatneft's share price "was achieved in no small part due to the full faith and support with which the Tatarstan government blessed its top enterprise. State officials went out of their way to participate in the company's road show and give assurances to investors."[47] By co-opting local courts and lobbying fiercely, the Tatar president helped enterprises such as Tatneft reduce their tax costs, and this in turn attracted a large inflow of foreign investment. The hunger in regional capitals for such investment prompted governors to shield local companies from the central government. But the cost of undermining the federal budget was significant. In 1998, in the wake of the Asian financial crisis, the ruble crashed, bankrupting many of the country's leading banks and pushing the poverty rate up sharply.

Or consider the West Virginia state government's efforts in the late 1990s to keep big coal companies investing in the state. In 1998, a group of environmentalists sued the state government, claiming it was simply not enforcing federal regulations designed to protect streams from the acid runoff and sludge that mountaintop removal mining produced (Cai and Treisman 2004). West Virginia was in competition with other states for the coal companies' business, and ignoring the federal regulations was an effective way to compete. When the lawsuit disrupted the Arch Coal company's

---

[46] Aleksandr Bekker, "Dunning Letter Sent to Biggest Budget Debtors," *Segodnya*, October 16, 1996, p. 1, translated in *Current Digest of the Post-Soviet Press*, 1996, Vol. 48, No. 42, p. 17; Peter Henderson, "Tatar Oil Firm Bucks Downward Trend," *Moscow Times*, July 31, 1996.

[47] Gary Peach, "Tatarstan Pulls into Lead in Regions' Bid for Cash," *The Moscow Times*, July 15, 1997.

operations, it immediately began dismantling equipment in West Viriginia to ship to another mine it owned in Wyoming – an extreme illustration of how mobile capital can be. The state lost 900 coal industry jobs in 1998–9, most of which moved to Wyoming (Vollers 1999). The West Virginia government fought back with a team of outside lawyers and a vigorous public relations campaign. Such lax enforcement or non-enforcement of federal environmental regulations by state governments may be quite common. According to a report by the National Wildlife Federation, as of the late 1990s, 38 of 50 states were failing to enforce a provision of the Clean Water Act limiting water pollution caused by runoffs from forests and farms (Nugent 2000).

4.2.6 Conclusion

Under some quite demanding assumptions, and in particular special cases, the competition to attract capital that political decentralization makes possible may "constrain Leviathan," reducing equilibrium tax rates and bureaucratic corruption and inducing more business-friendly spending. But such effects do not appear to be at all general. If units are sufficiently heterogeneous or if different tiers of government compete for the same tax base, the effects become ambiguous. Competition among subnational governments to attract capital can then lead to *higher* tax rates or *less* business-friendly spending than under centralization. Even if decentralization leads to more intense competition for mobile capital, this may have undesirable consequences as well as desirable ones.

Finally – although I have not discussed this here – if competition for capital among local governments is beneficial, a central government could replicate such competition without giving up ultimate control of decision making or the right to select local officials. Just as in the discussion of Tiebout models of mobile labor, the central government could appoint local agents and give them contracts that reward the pursuit of mobile capital. It would have to allow them some discretion over the allocation of local spending or the level of local taxes. But it could do so in a conditional way that could be immediately reversed by central order. If capital competition is a useful mechanism, it can be used to discipline local officials under centralization as well as decentralization.

5

Fiscal Policy and Redistribution

Does decentralization . . . make it more difficult to adjust fiscal accounts once a structural deficit has developed? The experience of many countries suggests that under the circumstances often found in developing countries subnational governments are likely to contribute – sometimes significantly – to the aggravation of macroeconomic problems.

Vito Tanzi (1996, p. 305)

[C]ontrary to a common misconception, decentralized fiscal systems offer a greater potential for improved macroeconomic governance and regional fiscal equity than centralized fiscal systems. While empirical evidence on these questions is quite weak, nevertheless it further supports the conclusion that fiscal decentralization is associated with improved fiscal performance and better functioning of the internal common market. This is to be expected as decentralized fiscal systems require greater clarity in the roles of various players (centers of decision making), transparency in rules and greater care in the design of institutions that govern interactions to ensure fair play and limit opportunities for rent seeking.

Anwar Shah (2005, p. 3)

Governments take money from some and give it to others.[1] They impose taxes that fall more heavily on certain individuals and corporations, and they use the revenues to provide public goods, services, and cash transfers that benefit other groups. Some types of redistribution discriminate among citizens based on where they live or work – "geographical redistribution"; others use ascriptive, economic, or social criteria – "intergroup redistribution." Most governments use both types. Officials may redistribute for many

---

[1] An enormous literature examines the political economy of distributive and redistributive policies. For references, see Persson and Tabellini (2000, chs. 6–7). One early classic is Lowi (1964). Collie (1988) surveys the formal literature on distributive politics in legislatures.

reasons, including commitments to social justice. But a common motive is to co-opt constituencies whose support is needed to stay in power. In a democracy, that usually means redistributing in favor of particular groups of voters. In an authoritarian system, it might mean seeking to placate powerful interests such as the military, security forces, or regional warlords.

How might political decentralization affect the extent and pattern of central government redistribution and the fiscal policies that result? A first argument notes that local officials, unless unusually altruistic, tend to favor generous central transfers to their own districts. They view the central budget as a "common pool" and seek to catch all the fish before their neighbors do. I argue below that local governments' demands are irrelevant unless they can persuade the central government to satisfy them. A second argument contends that decentralization not only whets local actors' appetites for central grants, it also gives them leverage to obtain them. By commiting to policies the central government dislikes, they may be able to extort central aid, thus "softening" their budget constraints and undermining macroeconomic discipline. I will show, however, that the implications of such precommitment games for fiscal outcomes are ambiguous. In some cases, they may indeed soften local government budget constraints, but in other cases they will harden them. Even if these arguments established that decentralization tends to increase central geographical redistribution, the effect on total redistribution would remain unclear. For a central incumbent seeking votes, geographical and intergroup redistribution may be substitutes. If the incumbent is not wooing voters with geographically targeted transfers, he is probably promising to redistribute to particular income or occupational groups.

A second set of questions concerns not the effect of decentralization on redistribution but the effect of decentralizing redistribution. If the exclusive right to redistribute were assigned to subnational governments, would they redistribute more or less in the aggregate than a central government? The answer depends in part on how costly it is for people and capital to move from one locality to another. I discuss several treatments of the question. Without resolving the issue, I argue that it is largely irrelevant. In practice, all levels of government wish to redistribute, and no reliable way of limiting redistribution to just one level has been discovered. In the real world, central governments redistribute under both centralization and decentralization, while under decentralization local governments do so as well. This may alter the final pattern of winners and losers, but it is not clear what effect it will have on the amount of redistribution.

5.1 The "Common Pool"

For each local government, some have argued, the central budget is a "common pool" or "common property" resource. Each local community bears only a fraction of the cost of paying for spending from the central budget. But the community gets the full benefit of any money it spends. Like fishermen, who might collectively favor limits on overfishing but who individually race to fish the declining stocks, local officials set irresponsibly high levels of centrally financed spending, continuing until the marginal benefit is far lower than the marginal cost.[2]

The idea is easy to formalize. Imagine a country divided into $n = 1, 2, \ldots, N$ localities, each containing one citizen with income y. Public spending in locality n, denoted g_n, is entirely funded by a central transfer to that region, r_n. These transfers are, in turn, financed by a uniform, central lump sum tax on each citizen, T. Each local government maximizes a version of Equation 2.2 in Chapter 2: $V_n = h(g_n) + y - T$, where $h' > 0$, $h'' < 0$, $h(0) = 0$, and $\underset{g \to 0}{Lim} h'(g) = \infty$.[3] By the central budget constraint, $\sum_n g_n = \sum_n r_n = TN$. The first order condition:

$$h_g(g_n{}^*) = \frac{1}{N} \tag{5.1}$$

defines equilibrium spending in each locality.[4] To derive the efficient level of spending, one can solve the same problem assuming instead that each locality must finance its spending with a lump sum tax on its own citizen; the equilibrium condition is then:

$$h_g(g_n{}^*) = 1 \tag{5.2}$$

Comparing (5.1) and (5.2), the level of spending in (5.1) is higher than that in (5.2), given $N > 1$. Because each locality bears only $1/N$ of the cost of a marginal dollar it spends, it will spend more than if its taxpayers had to bear the whole cost.

This simple idea is invoked broadly in political economy and public finance. The common pool problem is often said to explain cases of fiscal indiscipline in decentralized states. However, by itself, it is hard to see how it could. What leads to the inefficiency is the assumption that local

---

[2] See, for instance, Jones, Sanguinetti, and Tommasi (2000).

[3] I leave out the official's utility from consumption, $hq(c)$, supposing for simplicity that officials are perfectly constrained to maximize the citizen's payoff.

[4] I assume, as is standard here, that an interior equilibrium exists – that is, $h_g{}^{-1}(1/N) \le y$.

governments can spend without limit from the national budget.[5] Taken literally, this assumption seems absurd. Theoretically, it implies either that the central government is irrational, or that it can raise tax revenues costlessly. Empirically, no country in the world gives subnational governments unlimited authority to write checks on the central budget.

There are two ways that such an assumption is sometimes rationalized. First, some suggest that the central government – modeled as a legislature – is itself subject to the common pool problem. Weingast and Shepsle, in a celebrated series of papers, argued that in a central legislature an equilibrium could exist in which all members vote in favor of a package that includes inefficiently large spending allocations for each member's constituency (Weingast 1979; Shepsle and Weingast 1981; Weingast, Shepsle, and Johnsen 1981). If each member expects the others to vote for the bill and against any alternative, then it is a Nash equilibrium for each member to vote for the bill.[6] Deviating will make no difference to the outcome, so no member has an incentive to deviate. The sociological manifestation of this equilibrium is a norm called "universalism" (Mayhew 1974).

Universalism in a central legislature might explain high central spending. But this has nothing to do with decentralization.[7] Alesina and Perotti (1995, p. 21), referring to this literature, write that they "can think of an analogy" between issues of fiscal federalism and the common pool problem in a central legislature. However, where such an analogy leads is unclear. If the central government itself suffers from a common pool problem that causes it to overspend, then one would get overspending even in a unitary state with no local governments at all. The preferences of local governments are irrelevant. Furthermore, one would get the same problem if there were

---

[5] For some authors, this is an explicit assumption. For instance, Velasco, in a dynamic model of the common pool problem, assumes that "the central fiscal authority is weak, and that group i itself can determine the sequence" of central transfers to it (1997, p. 6). Others instead use "if . . . then . . . " constructions but are vague about why one should ever expect the "if" clause to hold. Bordignon and Turati (2002, p. 83) note that "if local governments perceive they can externalize the cost of providing local services to other jurisdictions or higher levels of government, they will have an incentive to do so, expecting others to foot the bill."

[6] This shows only that common pool problems are *possible* within a central legislature. There are infinitely many equilibria, in many of which the legislature underspends. If all members expect all others to vote against any bill that has positive spending for any constituency and for a bill with zero spending, each cannot do better than to do the same.

[7] As Weingast, Shepsle, and Johnsen (1981) discuss and subsequent work has confirmed, whether or not overspending occurs depends crucially on the rules of procedure in the legislature. Under certain procedures, one gets no overspending.

multiple nongeographic interest groups with supporters in the central legislature, motivated by a nongeographic norm of universalism.

The second way of rationalizing the assumption is to argue that decentralization does not just give local governments common pool preferences; it also provides them with levers to pressure the central government to provide aid. I analyze such arguments in section 5.2 on the "soft budget constraint" and agree that they will sometimes be valid. But such reasoning renders the common pool argument irrelevant. If decentralization empowers subnational governments to pressure the central government for cash, subnational governments will use such levers whether or not central spending is financed from a common pool. In fact, they might press even harder if the central budget were funded from an external source such as foreign aid. In that case, each locality would bear no part of the cost of financing the central transfers they receive.[8]

5.2 The "Soft Budget Constraint"

When central and local governments' objectives overlap and the central government can pay fiscal transfers to the localities, a problem of moral hazard arises. Local governments may try to manipulate the center into providing aid. If such manipulation succeeds, the local governments that extract more funds face a "soft budget constraint." The term, first coined by Kornai (1979, 1980) to describe a pathological interaction between enterprises and bureaucrats in a socialist economy, has since been applied to many other contexts, including interactions between levels of government.[9]

---

[8] Similarly, for arguments about lobbying (see Persson and Tabellini 1994). One might suppose that local governments sign contingent contribution contracts with the center, motivating it to finance overspending. But if such lobbying provides net benefits to the local governments, this is sufficient to explain why local governments engage in it, whether or not funds come from a "common pool." And the local governments will lobby at least as hard if the central budget is financed from external sources. Moreover, there is no reason to think that geographical lobbies in a decentralized political system will generally be more powerful or well funded than sectoral, business, or geographical lobbies in a centralized one.

[9] For recent reviews of literature on the soft budget constraint, see Maskin (1999) and Maskin and Xu (2001). In Maskin's definition: "A soft budget-constraint arises whenever a funding source finds it impossible to keep an enterprise to a fixed budget, i.e., whenever the enterprise can extract ex post a bigger subsidy or loan than would have been considered efficient ex ante" (1996, p. 125). In the present context, replace "enterprise" with "local government."

Along with the common pool argument, the soft budget constraint idea has led many to associate political decentralization with overspending and macroeconomic imbalances.[10] The more autonomous are subnational governments, the more scope they have to blackmail the central government into providing bailouts. According to Pisauro (2001, p. 24), a "wide consensus" exists among economists "that a centralized budget process is more conducive to fiscal restraint" and that "decentralization of revenue and expenditure responsibilities is likely to entail a bias toward higher public expenses and deficits." The perceived link between political decentralization and soft budget constraints has motivated both empirical work and policy advice, especially that given to developing countries, which are often warned of the macroeconomic dangers of decentralization.[11]

There are two ways that giving local governments greater autonomy might soften their budget constraints. First, this might allow them to exploit asymmetric information. Suppose the central government wants to finance profitable local public investment projects, but that only the local governments directly observe which projects are profitable. Suppose, in addition, that local governments benefit from unprofitable as well as profitable investments. The local governments may then trick the center into funding unprofitable projects by claiming that they are profitable. Moreover, it may be in the center's interest to refinance an unprofitable project even after discovering it has been tricked because by that point the losses are sunk and the rate of return to refinancing is positive (Dewatripont and Maksin 1995).

Such information asymmetries may lead to an inefficient allocation of resources and enable local governments to earn informational rents.[12]

---

[10] See, for example, Pisauro (2001); Burki et al. (1999, p. 36); Jin and Zou (2002); Rodden, Eskeland, and Litvack (2003, p. 4); Hausmann (1998, p. 26); and Rodden (2002).

[11] Empirical work looking for evidence of such a link includes Fornasari, Webb, and Zou (1998); Dillinger and Webb (1999); Saiegh and Tomassi (1999); De Mello (2000); Rodden (2002); Rodden and Wibbels (2002); Rodden, Eskeland, and Litvack (2003); and Webb (2003). For a skeptical view, see Shah (2005), quoted in the epigraph. I discuss the empirical evidence in Chapter 11. For an example of policy advice, see Ter-Minassian (1997b).

[12] Similar problems might also arise in a centralized system if local agents of the central government enjoy comparable informational advantages. However, it may be easier for the central government to motivate its agents to act honestly than to do so for locally elected officials, whose constituents may benefit from over-investment. One can think of various solutions – the central government might send its auditors to acquire the necessary information or might make local officials legally liable for misrepresenting profitability – but these are not likely to work in all cases. Dewatripont and Maskin (1995) propose a solution based on even more decentralization. However, their solution – dividing creditors into units so cash-poor that they cannot independently refinance any projects – seems (in

However, it is not clear that they would lead to fiscal or macroeconomic imbalances. Unless local investment projects are *ex ante* profitable *on average* – that is, the expected value of investing in a set of projects is higher than the opportunity cost – the central government will not invest at all. If projects are profitable on average, funding these should not – on average – lead to central or local deficits.

The second, more common argument associating decentralization with soft budget constraints has to do with strategic pre-commitment. If a local government can commit to a policy the center does not like, the center may be pressured into providing additional funds to change the policy. For instance, if local governments commit to overspend, the central government may prefer to send emergency cash rather than watch local citizens suffer under an onerous tax burden. If local governments borrow to the point of insolvency, the center might bail them out to preempt a financial crisis that would damage the center's own credit rating. Decentralization may enable local governments to commit to policies in a way that local agents of a centralized state could not. It may also give them more locally focused objectives. The result will be inefficiently high public spending and deficits under decentralization, so the argument goes.

Recent experience in several countries seems to fit this logic, as Vito Tanzi quite accurately noted in his 1996 summary of the dangers of decentralization. Russia after the fall of communism offers one example. In the mid-1990s, regional governments in Russia went on a hiring binge. Despite staffing rates in public education and health care that were among the highest in the world, governors chose to hire large numbers of additional doctors and teachers. The number of teachers in state schools increased by 291,000 (or 20 percent) between 1991 and 2000, and the number of university professors grew by 45,000 (also a 20 percent increase). In the middle of the decade, with output falling and the tax system in crisis, regional governments announced that they could not pay their employees in full and started running up massive wage arrears. This prompted strikes and protests, which often ended when the central government sent emergency infusions of cash (Gimpelson and Treisman 2002).

In January 2002, for instance, seven teachers in the Far Eastern region of Primore went on a hunger strike. They had not been paid for four months

---

this application) to require local governments that are unrealistically tiny. They also need to introduce an additional distortion to explain why outside creditors could not buy out unprofitable projects for their (positive) continuation value.

and said they did not have money to buy firewood. When local governors flew to Moscow to plead for aid, the finance minister, Alexei Kudrin, accused them of being "blackmailers" and "deliberately exaggerating" their problems. President Vladimir Putin also complained of being blackmailed. But the central authorities gave in and provided an additional 3.5 billion rubles ($114 million) to help cover arrears to state workers.[13] By hiring more public employees than they could afford to pay, the regional governments committed themselves to high spending, forcing the central government either to sit by as teachers starved themselves or to hand out additional cash.

A similar game appeared in Argentina around the same time, after provincial governments became responsible for paying teachers. By 1999, some provinces had run up arrears to teachers worth six months' salary. This prompted a wave of strikes and protests, including picketing outside the National Congress in Buenos Aires. President Carlos Menem, after some initial tough talk, sent an additional six million pesos to help.

The argument that local government commitments can pressure the center to increase funding, driving up public spending levels, seems plausible. As I show below in a simple model, the logic can hold under certain circumstances. However, it is far from general. First, it turns out that such interactions may lead to either overspending or *under* spending, depending on whether local governments can commit to spending levels or tax rates. Second, for local governments to blackmail the central government in this way, the latter must be sensitive to the costs that the local governments can impose, which will not always be the case. Third, if the central government needs support from only a majority of localities or voters, competition to get into the winning coalition can undermine local governments' bargaining power. Fourth, even if decentralization enhances local governments' ability to demand central transfers, there is also a supply side in this "market." Decentralization may tighten the supply of cash the center could use for bailouts, rendering the net effect unclear. And fifth, if the central government has a long enough time horizon, it may deliberately ignore such local pleas for aid in order to establish a reputation for toughness in future interactions.

To be fair, some scholars make a more qualified argument about the relationship between decentralization and fiscal imbalance. Decentralization is

---

[13] See *Radio Free Europe/Radio Liberty Daily Reports* for January 15, 28, and 29 and February 13, 2002.

destabilizing only, they argue, "if done wrong."[14] To avoid softening budget constraints, governments that decentralize should assign local governments sufficiently large tax bases, reduce the role of intergovernmental transfers, clarify the formal division of spending responsibilities, and limit or prohibit local government borrowing. I will return to these points to see whether, in light of the analysis, these remedies are likely to work.

5.2.1 A Simple Model of Soft Budget Constraints on Local Governments

Suppose a state is divided into three local units, indexed $n = 1, 2, 3$.[15] Suppose also, to begin with, that all units are identical. Population size in each is normalized to one, and there is no mobility across units. A local government in each unit levies a local income tax, at rate τ_n. A central government sets a nationally uniform rate of income tax, T. The preferences of citizens in region n are given by:

$$U_n = H(g_n) + (1 - \tau_n - T)y_n \tag{5.3}$$

where g_n is spending on local public goods and services in locality n, y_n is average (and total) income in locality n, and $H' > 0$, $H'' < 0$, $H(0) = 0$, $\underset{g \to 0}{Lim} H'(g) = \infty$.

To orient the analysis, suppose to begin with that the objectives of the local and central governments correspond perfectly and match those of the citizens. Suppose that each local government's payoff is given by (5.3) and that the central government's payoff is $U_1 + U_2 + U_3$. The central government can allocate transfers, $\{r_n\}$, to local government budgets to help finance local public spending. I assume in addition that output is a decreasing function of the aggregate tax rate in the locality: $y_n = y(\tau_n + T)$, where $y' < 0$, and that no one works when the tax rate is 1: $y(1) = 0$. As discussed in Chapter 2, higher tax rates are assumed to induce distortions in economic activity. I assume that nondistortionary taxes are not available.

---

[14] For instance, the World Bank's *World Development Report 1999–2000* (1999, p. 111) claims that "Decentralization, *if handled poorly*, can threaten macroeconomic stability" (italics added). Rodden, Eskeland, and Litvack (2003, p. 5) define their task as to study not just whether decentralization is good or bad for macroeconomic management but "how to improve management in decentralized settings."

[15] The model developed here is based on Bordignon, Manasse, and Tabellini (2001). Other approaches to modeling the soft budget constraint on local governments include Wildasin (1997), Inman (2003), and Goodspeed (2002).

The "Soft Budget Constraint"

Under centralization, the central government makes all policy decisions for the country, setting $\{g_n, \tau_n, r_n, T\}$ for all n to maximize $U_1 + U_2 + U_3$, subject to the budget constraint: $g_1 + g_2 + g_3 = (T + \tau_1)y_1 + (T + \tau_2)y_2 + (T + \tau_3)y_3$. The first order conditions imply that $g_1{}^c = g_2{}^c = g_3{}^c$, where the superscript stands for equilibrium under centralization, and that

$$H_g\left(g_n{}^c\right) = \frac{y_n - \left(1 - \tau_n{}^c - T^c\right)y_n'}{y_n + \left(\tau_n{}^c + T^c\right)y_n'} \quad \text{for } n = 1, 2, 3 \tag{5.4}$$

If we rewrite this as:

$$H_g\left(g_n{}^c\right)\frac{\partial\left(\tau_n{}^c + T^c\right)y_n}{\partial(\tau_n + T)} = -\frac{\partial\left(1 - \tau_n{}^c - T^c\right)y_n}{\partial(\tau_n + T)} \tag{5.5}$$

the left-hand side measures the marginal benefit from increased public spending financed by raising the aggregate tax rate marginally, while the right-hand side measures the marginal loss from decreased private consumption caused by a marginal increase in the tax rate. The government trades off the marginal benefit against the marginal cost of raising taxes, taking into account the distortionary effect on output.

I now make the additional assumption that everywhere $2(y_n')^2 > y_n y_n''$ for all n. This ensures that there is a unique $0 < \tau_n + T < 1$ at which tax revenues are maximized: The Laffer curve has a unique maximum.[16] Given this, $H_g(g_n)[y_n + (\tau_n + T)y_n']/[y_n - (1 - \tau_n - T)y_n']$ decreases monotonically in $(\tau_n + T)$, so there is at most one solution to the first order condition. Thus, assuming there is a solution, it must be true that $\tau_1{}^c = \tau_2{}^c = \tau_3{}^c \equiv \tau^c$. In equilibrium, each locality has the same level of public spending, the same tax rate, and the same level of private consumption. Public spending in each is given by: $g_n{}^c = (\tau^c + T^c)y(\tau^c + T^c)$.

Now consider what happens under decentralization. The essence of the pre-commitment soft budget constraint argument is that local governments are able to commit to some policy variable. To model this, we must give the local governments the first move. Which policy lever local governments can pre-commit to turns out to determine the result. To show the conventional effect, suppose that at time 1 each of the local governments

---

[16] To see this, maximize $(\tau + T)y(\tau + T)$. Using the first order condition, $y + (\tau + T)y' = 0$, to eliminate $(\tau + T)$ from the second order condition, $2y' + (\tau + T)y'' < 0$, and multiplying both sides by y', we get $2(y')^2 > yy''$. If this holds everywhere, then any tax rate that satisfies the first order condition must identify a maximum. Because at $\tau + T = 0$, $(\tau + T)y = 0$, and at $\tau + T = 1$, $(\tau + T)y = 0$, and there are no local minima, assuming tax revenues are not always zero, there must be a unique maximum in the range $0 < \tau + T < 1$.

sets its level of spending, g_n. They move simultaneously and so play a Cournot game against one another. At time 2, the central government sets levels of transfers, $\{r_n\}$, to each of the localities and a central tax rate, T, subject to its budget constraint: $r_1 + r_2 + r_3 = T(y_1 + y_2 + y_3)$. The local tax rates are residually determined by the local budget constraints: $g_n = \tau_n y_n + r_n$ for $n = 1, 2, 3$.

Proceeding by backward induction, at time 2 the central government will set $\{r_n, T\}$ to maximize: $U_1 + U_2 + U_3 = \sum_{n=1}^{3}(H(g_n) + (1 - \tau_n(r_n) - T)$ $y(\tau_n(r_n) + T))$, subject to $g_n = \tau_n y_n + r_n, n = 1, 2, 3$ and $r_1 + r_2 + r_3 = T(y_1 + y_2 + y_3)$. The first order conditions simplify to:

$$\frac{y_1 - \left(1 - \tau_1{}^d - T^d\right)y_1'}{y_1 + \left(\tau_1{}^d + T^d\right)y_1'} = \frac{y_2 - \left(1 - \tau_2{}^d - T^d\right)y_2'}{y_2 + \left(\tau_2{}^d + T^d\right)y_2'}$$

$$= \frac{y_3 - \left(1 - \tau_3{}^d - T^d\right)y_3'}{y_3 + \left(\tau_3{}^d + T^d\right)y_3'} = \lambda \tag{5.6}$$

where λ is the Lagrange multiplier on the central government's budget constraint, and the superscript indicates equilibrium under decentralization. This implies that in equilibrium each locality has the same local tax rate, $\tau_n{}^d \equiv \tau^d$, and therefore also the same output level, $y_1 = y_2 = y_3 = y(\tau^d + T^d)$. In words, the central government observes the spending levels set by each of the localities at time 1 and allocates transfers to equalize the end-of-game tax rates – and thus the tax-induced distortion – across the localities. Clearly, it will allocate larger transfers to localities that set higher spending levels. Combining the central and local budget constraints, given that $\tau_n{}^d \equiv \tau^d$ for all n, we get:

$$g_1 + g_2 + g_3 = 3(\tau^d + T^d)y(\tau^d + T^d) \tag{5.7}$$

Each local government views this as the central government's reaction function.

At time 1, the local governments set their spending levels to maximize (5.3), subject to (5.7), in Cournot competition with one another. Given the spending levels of the other localities, each views itself as determining $(\tau^d + T^d)$ with its choice of g_n. Thus, each local government sets its g_n to maximize:

$$U_n = H\left(3(\tau^d + T^d)y(\tau^d + T^d) - \sum_{j \neq n} g_j\right) + (1 - (\tau^d + T^d))y(\tau^d + T^d) \tag{5.8}$$

The "Soft Budget Constraint"

The first order conditions are:

$$H_g(g_n^d) = \frac{1}{3}\frac{y - (1 - \tau^d - T^d)y'}{y + (\tau^d + T^d)y'} \text{ for } n = 1, 2, 3 \tag{5.9}$$

which imply that $g_1^d = g_2^d = g_3^d = (\tau^d + T^d)y(\tau^d + T^d)$. Comparing (5.9) and (5.4), and recalling that $H_g(g_n)[y_n + (\tau_n + T)y_n']/[y_n - (1 - \tau_n - T)y_n']$ decreases monotonically in $(\tau_n + T)$, we see that the aggregate tax rate under decentralization, $(\tau^d + T^d)$, is higher than that under centralization, $(\tau^c + T^c)$. And, because equilibrium public spending is increasing in the aggregate tax rate,[17] this means that spending is higher under decentralization.

In short, the central government is sensitive to the hardship that high local tax rates impose on local consumers. By committing to high levels of spending, local governments pressure the center to bail them out. They ignore the costs that other localities suffer when forced to help finance transfers to them. Rewriting (5.9) as

$$H_g(g_n^d)\frac{\partial(\tau_n^d + T^d)y_n}{\partial(\tau_n + T)} = -\frac{1}{3}\frac{\partial(1 - \tau_n^d - T^d)y_n}{\partial(\tau_n + T)} \tag{5.9'}$$

we see that local government n sets the marginal benefit of raising the tax rate to finance its spending (the left-hand side) equal to just one-third of the marginal cost in lower private consumption $(-\partial(1 - \tau_n^d - T^d)y_n/\partial(\tau_n + T))$. The other two-thirds of the cost are borne by the other two localities.

Thus, the local governments pre-commit to inefficiently high spending levels, resulting in excessive spending. But note a paradoxical aspect of the result. Given the symmetry (identical localities), no locality actually receives a net transfer (i.e., a $r_n > Ty_n$). Given $g_1^d = g_2^d = g_3^d = (\tau^d + T^d)y(\tau^d + T^d)$, spending in each locality is exactly equal to the revenues collected in that locality. And the transfer to each exactly equals the central tax that locality pays.[18] The demands of the localities precisely offset one another. Local governments, of course, anticipate this. In fact, they do not overspend in the illusion that doing so will lead to greater net transfers to their locality. They overspend because if they did not, the center would tax them more

---

[17] We must be on the upward sloping part of the Laffer curve because the denominator of the right-hand side of (5.9), which equals $\partial(\tau^d + T^d)y/\partial(\tau + T)$, must be positive; so revenues – and hence spending – are increasing with $(\tau^d + T^d)$.

[18] Substituting $g_1^d = g_2^d = g_3^d = (\tau^d + T^d)y(\tau^d + T^d)$ into $g_n = \tau_n y_n + r_n$, we see that $r^d = T^d y(\tau^d + T^d)$. The actual transfer is indeterminate, but the net transfer, $r^d - T^d y$, must be zero.

heavily in order to finance transfers to their more profligate neighbors. The real goal is just to prevent local income from being redistributed out of the locality.[19]

Still, the result is a higher level of spending and taxation than under centralization. Some version of this logic underlies the common arguments about soft budget constraints under decentralization leading to fiscal excesses and macroeconomic instability. But how general are such arguments? In the following sections, I suggest a series of considerations that would weaken or even reverse the conclusion.

5.2.2 Local Governments Commit to a Tax Rate, Not a Spending Level

The distortion operates in the opposite direction if local governments pre-commit not to a level of spending but to a local tax rate (Bordignon, Manasse, and Tabellini 2001). Then, local governments will deliberately undertax themselves, pressuring the central government to intervene to increase provision of the local public good. To analyze this case, suppose that under decentralization the order of moves is as follows. At time 1, each local government, playing a Cournot game against the others, sets its tax rate, τ_n. At time 2, the central government sets transfers and its own tax rate, subject to its budget constraint $r_1 + r_2 + r_3 = T(y_1 + y_2 + y_3)$. Local public spending levels, $\{g_n\}$, are then residually determined by the local budget constraints: $g_n = \tau_n y_n + r_n$ for all n.

The result under centralization is unchanged, as in (5.4). Under decentralization, at time 2, the central government maximizes its Benthamite social welfare function: $U_1 + U_2 + U_3 = \sum_{n=1}^{3} (H(g_n(r_n)) + (1 - \tau_n - T)y(\tau_n + T))$ subject to the budget constraints. The first order conditions now imply:

$$H_g(g_1{}^d) = H_g(g_2{}^d) = H_g(g_3{}^d) = \lambda \tag{5.10}$$

where λ is, as before, the multiplier on the center's budget constraint. These imply that $g_1{}^d = g_2{}^d = g_3{}^d \equiv g^d$ and so $g^d = [(\tau_1 + T)y_1 + (\tau_2 + T)y_2 + (\tau_3 + T)y_3]/3$. At time 1, the local governments take this as the center's

---

[19] In fact, given the definition in footnote 9, the local budget constraints are not soft. Local governments do not "extract ex post a bigger subsidy or loan than would have been considered efficient ex ante." Net transfers are zero.

reaction function and set their tax levels to maximize (5.3) subject to it. The first order conditions are now:

$$H_g\left(g_n{}^d\right) = 3\frac{y_n - (1 - \tau^d - \mathrm{T}^d)y_n{}'}{y_n + (\tau^d + \mathrm{T}^d)y_n{}'} \quad \text{for } n = 1, 2, 3 \tag{5.11}$$

Clearly, given that (5.9) defines an equilibrium level of spending higher than under centralization, (5.11) defines a level that is *lower* than under centralization. In this case, the attempt to extort benefits from the central government leads to equilibrium underspending rather than overspending.

Is it more plausible that local governments can commit to a spending level or a tax rate? One can make arguments for either of these. Bordignon et al. (2001, p. 714) suggest that the former is more realistic because "spending decisions are more irreversible than decisions over taxes." But this is likely to depend upon the particular budgeting procedures and political conditions in a given country or region. For instance, in California, increases in municipal property tax rates are quite strictly limited by Proposition 13, and many local bond issues must be directly approved by voters. By contrast, local governments face few legal hurdles to reducing particular categories of spending mid-year. In most settings, changing either the tax rate or the level of spending would require a similar mid-year amendment to local legislation. Perhaps the idea is that once the local government signs contracts to spend more than its budget, the legal system will enforce these contracts against it. But a local government could also contract to compensate taxpayers if it raised taxes within a certain period of time. If the legal system enforces the commitment, there is no reason it could enforce only one type of commitment. Governments in many countries *do* delay or cancel spending projects, from time to time, just as they do pass temporary changes to the tax rate or – more frequently – authorize additional borrowing. They may also do both at the same time – say, commiting to pay public employees higher wages while lowering taxes or failing to collect as much as they had budgeted (recall the Russian example in section 5.2). Thus, either of these assumptions seems quite plausible.

5.2.3 Central Government Cares More About Public Spending, or Less About Private Consumption, Than Local Governments

Suppose local governments under decentralization commit to a level of local spending, as in section 5.2.1. But suppose the payoff function for the central government is no longer just the sum of the local governments' payoffs. In particular, suppose the central government values public spending more (or private consumption less) than their local counterparts. The local governments' objectives are still given by (5.3). But the central government's objective is now:

$$\sum_{n=1}^{3} (a\,H(g_n) + (1 - \tau_n - T)y_n) \tag{5.12}$$

where $a > 1$ is a constant. Now under centralization the first order conditions simplify to:

$$H_g\left(g_n^c\right) = \frac{1}{a} \frac{y - (1 - \tau^c - T^c)y'}{y + (\tau^c + T^c)y'} \quad \text{for } n = 1, 2, 3 \tag{5.13}$$

Those under decentralization are as before in (5.9). Thus, spending will be higher under decentralization than under centralization if and only if $a < 3$. If $a > 3$, or more generally if a is greater than the number of localities, equilibrium spending will be higher under centralization. In such cases, despite the counterproductive competition between local governments under decentralization, they still set spending lower than the central government would under centralization. Local governments' budget constraints are soft – they spend more than they would if there were no prospect of external financing. But the central government's lack of concern for the costs borne by taxpayers prompts it to spend even more.

Would central governments ever have such a strong preference for public spending – or, put another way, so little concern for the effect of taxation on private consumption? Although probably not common, such cases could certainly occur. If a central government were staffed by corrupt officials, able to embezzle a cut from public projects, they might indeed value public spending much more highly than private consumption. If local officials were more honest or accountable, they might choose to spend less.[20] In such cases, decentralization would reduce local spending.

---

[20] In section 2.2.6, I criticized models which assume – in ways that are convenient for the argument – that leaders at one level are more honest or public spirited than those at another level. Note here that I am doing the opposite. I am not advancing general conclusions, derived from assumptions about actors' motivations that are of dubious generality. I am showing that a particular, supposedly general argument is vulnerable to failure of its motivational assumption.

The "Soft Budget Constraint"

5.2.4 Central Government Cares More About Some Localities

So far, I have assumed the central government wishes to maximize a Benthamite social welfare function that sums the payoffs of citizens in all the localities. But what if central officials are less impartial, or are constrained by voters to pursue other objectives?

A natural alternative would be to suppose that the central decision maker must obtain the support of a majority of voters, or of a majority of the local governments, to pass any measure. As is well known, in a game of distributing a fixed budget among three or more players, there is no Condorcet winner – that is, no proposed division of the budget among the players would defeat all other possible divisions under majority rule. To see how an equilibrium could exist, one must introduce more structure into the problem. There are two ways this is often done.

First, suppose that the competition over policies takes place during national elections. Consider a version of the Downsian voting model in which two parties compete for central office by committing themselves to policies that they will implement if elected. Suppose that, as in the models of Lindbeck and Weibull (1987) and Dixit and Londregan (1996), the parties cannot change their position on one "ideological" dimension (see Chapter 2). Suppose that the only groups of citizens among which they can redistribute income are geographical districts. Parties care only about winning office. They propose balanced-budget allocations of net transfers across the districts: $\{r_n, T\}$ where $r_1 + r_2 + r_3 = T(y_1 + y_2 + y_3)$. The presence of the nonmanipulable "ideological" dimension provides the structure necessary to ensure an equilibrium.[21] The main result in such models is that the parties converge on a redistributive program that targets benefits disproportionately to those groups (in this case localities) that have a higher density of voters around the equilibrium point on the fixed issue (more "swing" voters) and whose voters are more sensitive to redistributive appeals relative to ideology. In the present context, assuming localities are *ex ante* identical, we can think of the parties as maximizing a weighted average of the local utilities, where the weights are greater for localities with more centrist and *ex ante* non-ideological voters. Denoting the weight the parties place on locality n by a_n, the parties converge on proposals that maximize: $\sum_{n=1}^{3} a_n (H(g_n) + (1 - \tau_n - T)y_n)$.

---

[21] One must assume also that the cumulative distribution function for the ideological preferences of voters in each locality is quasiconcave.

Adapting the analysis in sections 5.2.1 and 5.2.2, we get that in a centralized system the parties will promise policies that satisfy:

$$a_1 H_g(g_1^c) = a_2 H_g(g_2^c) = a_3 H_g(g_3^c)$$

$$= a_1 \frac{y_1 - (1 - \tau_1^c - T^c)y_1'}{y_1 + (\tau_1^c + T^c)y_1'} = a_2 \frac{y_2 - (1 - \tau_2^c - T^c)y_2'}{y_2 + (\tau_2^c + T^c)y_2'}$$

$$= a_3 \frac{y_3 - (1 - \tau_3^c - T^c)y_3'}{y_3 + (\tau_3^c + T^c)y_3'} \tag{5.14}$$

From this, spending will be lower and the tax rate higher in localities that have lower a_n. Under decentralization, suppose local governments commit to either g_n or τ_n before the central parties make their election promises. The central parties now offer programs that satisfy:

$$a_1 \frac{y_1 - (1 - \tau_1^d - T^d)y_1'}{y_1 + (\tau_1^d + T^d)y_1'} = a_2 \frac{y_2 - (1 - \tau_2^d - T^d)y_2'}{y_2 + (\tau_2^d + T^d)y_2'}$$

$$= a_3 \frac{y_3 - (1 - \tau_3^d - T^d)y_3'}{y_3 + (\tau_3^d + T^d)y_3'} = \lambda \tag{5.6'}$$

if the local governments commit to g_n, or

$$a_1 H_g(g_1^d) = a_2 H_g(g_2^d) = a_3 H_g(g_3^d) = \lambda \tag{5.10'}$$

if the local governments commit to τ_n. Now, the local governments will take into account at time 1 that the center will be more responsive to attempts at extortion made by the localities with high weights. This will affect the extent to which each plays such games, inducing some to distort more and others less. One would still see soft budget constraint effects leading to either higher or lower spending than under centralization, as in sections 5.2.1 and 5.2.2.

A second way to impose structure on the problem of central redistribution is to suppose central policy is set in a legislature, operating with particular procedural rules.[22] Suppose each of N localities has one representative in the central legislature, and this representative has a payoff identical to that of his local constituents (as in Equation (5.3)).[23] Suppose that decision-making procedures are as follows. An "agenda setter" is selected at random

---

[22] Classic papers analyzing this problem include Shepsle (1979), Shepsle and Weingast (1981), Romer and Rosenthal (1978), Baron and Ferejohn (1989), and Baron (1991).

[23] This assumes no cross-locality externalities. If there were externalities, the analysis would be more similar to that in sections 5.2.1 and 5.2.2.

from among the legislators and makes a policy proposal. Under a "closed rule," the legislators then vote on this proposal. Under an "open rule," others can then propose amendments, and only after a majority vote to end the amendment process do legislators vote on the proposal itself. If a majority votes for the (possibly amended) proposal, it passes and is implemented. If it does not pass, the legislators get some "default" payoff. The default payoff might be zero. It might be that derived from renewing the previous period's policies. Or the failure of a proposal might trigger selection of another agenda setter and a repeat of the procedure. In this case, the default payoff is the legislator's "continuation value" of the subgame that starts at that point.

Under a closed rule, with perfect information, the agenda setter will typically tailor her proposal to receive support from a narrow majority containing $(N-1)/2$ of the other legislators – Riker's "minimum winning coalition."[24] In the simplest case, the subgame perfect equilibrium will divide the legislators into three subgroups. First, $(N-1)/2$ legislators will be in the agenda setter's support coalition, receiving slightly more than their default payoffs – call this payoff "D." Second, $(N-1)/2$ legislators will be excluded from the coalition; the agenda setter will maximally extract revenues from them and provide no benefits. Call this payoff "L." Third, the agenda setter herself will receive a payoff derived from maximizing her utility subject to the constraint of providing D to $(N-1)/2$ legislators and L to the other $(N-1)/2$. Call the agenda setter's equilibrium payoff "A." It is natural to assume that $A > D > L$. If different legislators have different values of D, the agenda setter will choose to buy the support of the "cheapest" $(N-1)/2$. If all legislators have the same D, the agenda setter chooses randomly among them.

Within this setup, what difference would decentralization make? Suppose that under decentralization, the local governments, in Cournot competition against one another, set some policy variable (g_n or τ_n) at time 1, and then at time 2 the game of the previous paragraph is played in the central legislature, taking the local policies as given. Suppose that local policies affect the values of L, D, and A. (For instance, a locality might be able to increase its L by setting a positive τ_n; even though this would drive up the aggregate tax rate in the locality, the benefit from positive g_n might outweigh the cost of lower private consumption. Or if the default rule were

---

[24] See, for instance, Baron (1991). Under an "open rule," the legislator may sometimes spread benefits more widely, to reduce the incentive for others to try to amend the proposal.

that $T = r_n = 0$, for all n, localities could increase D by setting positive g_n and τ_n.) How would local governments set their policies, anticipating the distributive game in the central legislature?

Several effects come into play. First, competition to be included in the winning coalition (and receive $D > L$) will motivate the localities to lower their value of D – thus making themselves cheaper for the agenda setter to "buy." In direct contrast to the soft budget constraint logic, localities use their policy leverage to *reduce* their demands for transfers. Competition wipes out the local bargaining power that is central to the soft budget constraint story. Second, if they can, localities may seek to protect themselves against central government exploitation, increasing L. By preemptively setting positive τ_n, they may guarantee themselves positive g_n even if they end up in the losing coalition. But this will drive up total taxation in the losing localities.

In short, local governments' attempts to blackmail the central government into providing greater benefits are undermined by the competition among localities to get into the winning coalition. However, decentralization may enable local governments to protect themselves against central revenue extraction. Given the Laffer curve, this may lead to higher taxation and spending than under centralization, although because of a mechanism quite different from that of the soft budget constraint.

5.2.5 Local Governments Constrain the Center's Supply of Funds

As the previous section suggested, and as many scholars have noted, certain central institutions and procedures can protect the central government against manipulation by the local governments. But there are ways in which decentralization might *itself* limit central redistribution. The soft budget constraint argument claims that decentralization exacerbates demands on the central government to redistribute income. But in this "market," there is a "supply side" as well. Even if decentralization gives local governments the ability and motive to lobby for bailouts, it may also constrain the supply of funds available to finance them.[25]

An extreme form of decentralization is the formation of a confederation in which each local government can veto central taxation within its jurisdiction. All central funds must be raised as voluntary contributions from

---

[25] Wildasin (1996) argued in this vein that in South Africa "strengthening provincial and local institutions may create a credible institutional constraint on the exercise of the redistributive powers of the public sector."

the local governments. Now if all central funds are used to finance transfers between localities and there is no uncertainty or altruism on the part of local communities, no central redistributive proposal will get funded. Any communities that anticipate ending up net donors will choose not to contribute, so there will be nothing to redistribute. (One might get some minimal voluntary contributions if the central government also provided some public good. But the usual problems with voluntary contribution to public goods would be exacerbated still further by the prospect of redistributive leakages.)

What about less extreme possibilities? One way in which local rights are protected in some decentralized systems is by the explicit representation of local governments in central policy-making bodies. (In Chapter 2, I called this "constitutional decentralization." I discuss how such institutional features could entrench status quo policies in Chapter 8.) The upper houses of the German and Russian parliaments both contain appointees of the regional governments, for instance.[26] In some circumstances, this may act as an additional check on redistributive proposals that make it past the legislative games described in the previous section. However, it is not clear that this would reduce the total amount redistributed, rather than just requiring the lower-house agenda setter, on occasion, to co-opt a broader coalition.

Lohmann (1998) presents a related argument about Germany, where the policy-making body of the central Bundesbank is composed in part of representatives of the country's Länder. Monetary policy before the country's entry into the European Monetary Union had to get the support of a majority of regional governments. This narrowed the central government's ability to inflate the economy before elections, at least in periods when the same party did not control both the central parliament and a majority of the Land governments. This constraint was more binding than a similar limitation on *fiscal* policy because monetary policy cannot discriminate geographically in a fine-grained way. The Bundesbank could not target lower inflation rates at favored parts of the country in order to build a coalition, and so the central government could not exploit interregional competition as easily as it could by, say, targeting federal spending to particular Länder.

Decentralization might also limit the central government's access to funds to redistribute if decentralization empowers regional governments

---

[26] Although, from 2005, the regional governors who appoint some of these in Russia are themselves nominated by the country's president.

to block tax payments to the central budget or threaten credibly to secede. Both of these are easier if the regional government has its own autonomous political and economomic institutions. In some decentralized systems, the constitution even guarantees regions the right to secede. More important, if decentralization means that local leaders are elected rather than centrally appointed, separatists may win and claim a mandate. Such separatists can use the resources and prestige of office to mobilize and coordinate the local population. Competitive electoral campaigns may publicize and highlight the issue of secession and prompt accusations of central exploitation. And if the advocates of secession already control the local administration, they will not have to storm the statehouse in order to declare independence (see Chapter 10 for more on this).

Suppose that under centralization the cost of seceding is virtually infinite, and the game is the same as in section 5.2.1, but under decentralization the cost of seceding is significantly lower. (Costs of secession might include the risk of military sanctions, civil war, and inexperienced, illegitimate leadership in the new state.) Suppose that the central government strongly wishes to avoid secession. Now there may be a maximum tax level, $\overline{T}$, that the center can impose under decentralization without prompting rich regions to secede (i.e., one at which the benefits to a region of not having to pay taxes to finance interregional redistribution – or not having to overspend in order to preempt such taxation, as in section 5.2.1 – just equal the cost to the region of secession). This imposes an additional condition $T \leq \overline{T}$ on the center's choice of strategy in the game of section 5.2.1. If $\overline{T}$ is high, then even if the condition binds, the equilibrium may be similar to that in section 5.2.1, with competing demands for redistribution prompting the localities to overspend. But if $\overline{T}$ is low, localities may prefer to give up on competing over the small central pie and instead choose not to distort their local spending levels.

For example, if we assume the particular functional forms $H(g_n) = \ln(1 + g_n)$ and $y_n = 1 - \tau_n - T$, solving for equilibrium under decentralization given the constraint $T \leq \overline{T}$ yields the solution: $\tau^d \approx .188 - T; g^d \approx .153$ and $U_n \approx .802$. However, if locality n gives up on central transfers completely, assumes it will pay the maximum central tax, and sets its policy optimally subject to $T = \overline{T}$, $r_n = 0$, and $g_n = \tau_n y(\tau_n + \overline{T})$, it will choose to set $\tau_n = g_n = 0$, and anticipate receiving a payoff of $U_n = (1 - \overline{T})^2$. If $\overline{T} < .111$, this payoff will be greater than that of optimally competing for transfers, $U_n \approx .802$. Thus, if decentralization constrains the central government to set an income tax rate below 11 percent to avoid secession, then in this example the soft budget constraint problem disappears: Local governments no longer overspend in order to attract transfers.

If the ability to threaten credibly to secede is distributed asymmetrically across regions, then the central government may redistribute from less credible to more credible seceders. Treisman (1999a) argued that in Russia after the Soviet collapse, the Yeltsin administration used fiscal transfers and tax breaks to appease most of the country's ethnic regions that had the most vociferous and determined autonomy movements. This included tolerating sharp drops in tax remittances from relatively rich ethnic republics such as Tatarstan and Bashkortostan. The budget squeeze caused by such nonpayments forced reductions in redistribution to some poorer regions with overwhelmingly Russian populations. Treisman (1999b) modeled a game in which local leaders with a greater ability to exploit public hostility toward the central government are able to extract larger transfers from it. Such political dynamics, exacerbated by the local electoral competitions that come with political decentralization, can lead either to greater taxation and redistribution (if the credible separatists are poor) or to less taxation and redistribution (if the credible separatist are rich).

5.2.6 Transfers in a Repeated Game

Even if in a one-shot game the central government is vulnerable to the blackmail of local governments, this may not be true when the central government faces the prospect of many similar interactions in the future (Inman 2003). Suppose that central governments are of different types. At least some of them are extremely insensitive to local recessions caused by high local tax rates. One can construct models, along the lines of Kreps and Wilson (1982) and Milgrom and Roberts (1982), in which even central governments that care about local economic performance refuse, in order to preserve a reputation for "toughness," to bail out profligate localities. Such central governments suffer short-term losses in order to deter similar challenges in future rounds of the game. For this to make sense, the central government must anticipate staying in power for at least a few more budget cycles.[27]

---

[27] There is an additional subtlety: The equilibrium cannot be symmetric if the central government is going to signal toughness. Recall that in section 5.2.1, the overspending equilibrium is quite consistent with the central government's setting zero transfers all around, in which case no toughness would be revealed by doing so. However, in a version of the game with

Weingast (1997) provides another example of how central redistribution might be restrained in a repeated game (see also section 8.1). Building on a tradition that dates to Montesquieu and Alexander Hamilton, he argues that politically independent subnational governments might coordinate among themselves to punish any central attempt to redistribute among them. One can adapt the example to the soft budget constraint models discussed in this chapter. Consider the subgame perfect equilibrium of the one-round game under decentralization in section 5.2.1. In this equilibrium, the localities set their spending levels inefficiently high, but because they counteract one another, none actually gets a net transfer. Each locality and the center would prefer the outcome under centralization, in which the marginal benefit of raising taxes equals the marginal cost, as in Equation (5.4). In an indefinitely repeated game, they could use trigger strategies to enforce this efficient equilibrium. Each local government could play a strategy that called for it to punish any deviation from the efficient spending levels by any locality by setting spending at the inefficiently high rate of the one-shot decentralization equilibrium for a number of periods. Any deviation would prompt a reversion to the inefficient decentralization equilibrium sufficiently long to make the initial deviation unattractive.

Such coordinated punishment strategies do represent one equilibrium in an indefinitely repeated game. It is not the only equilibrium, and there is no reason to think localities would generally coordinate upon it. But if decentralization does lead to stronger local demands for central transfers, these demands may nevertheless be trumped by interregional coordination to prevent central redistribution.[28]

5.2.7 Conditional Arguments and Proposed Remedies

Some scholars argue that decentralization does not always lead to soft budget constraints on local governments: It is fiscally destabilizing only when

more and less productive localities, positive transfers to the less productive localities do occur in equilibrium (Bordignon et al. 2001). In such a game, the center's refusal to provide such transfers to the less productive localities could be taken as a sign of toughness (or a decision to pretend to be tough) and could harden local budget constraints until late in the game.

[28] It might seem like having it both ways to argue in Chapter 8, on freedom, that this mechanism cannot be relied upon to restrain the central government, and to argue here that it may do so. But both claims are true. The point in both cases is that, given the multiple equilibria, this model does not support general conclusions.

combined with certain other conditions. A number of risk factors have been suggested, with associated recommendations for reform.

First, many argue that subnational governments are more likely to exploit soft budget constraints when they receive a large share of their revenues as transfers from higher-level budgets.[29] This is sometimes referred to as having a large "vertical imbalance." Several intuitions inform this claim. If local communities bear only a small fraction of the cost of their public spending, their demands will be lavish because they are, in large part, spending other people's money (Fornasari, Webb, and Zou 1998, p. 1; De Mello, Jr. 2000, pp. 374–6; Saiegh and Tommasi 2001). At the same time, if local governments have meager revenue sources of their own, they can claim more credibly to be unable to finance local spending themselves.[30] Second, some expect the soft budget constraint problem to be worse when local governments are free to borrow. They can pile up debt to the point of default and pressure the central government to bail them out. Third, it is often argued that an unclear division of spending responsibilities between levels of government exacerbates the moral hazard problem (Rodden and Eskeland 2003, p. 444).

These arguments motivate a number of common policy recommendations: reduce vertical imbalances, limit local borrowing, specify spending responsibilities clearly. But each is problematic. Consider the claims about vertical fiscal imbalance first. That local communities with high vertical imbalances would like to spend other people's money is really beside the point (recall the discussion in section 5.1). Even regions *without* large vertical imbalances would like to do this too. Those with imbalances are those that have managed to get the central government to provide large transfers. The question is how. If these local governments have obtained lavish transfers by playing the sort of commitment games that generate soft budget constraints, then the vertical imbalance is an effect, not a cause. In this

---

[29] See, for example, Ter-Minassian (1997b, p. 5), Rodden and Wibbels (2002), and Rodden (2002).

[30] For instance, Von Hagen and Eichengreen (1996, p. 135) argue that if a local government's own resources are scarce, "it may face bankruptcy due to even a small shock to its economy. The only choices left to the central government will then be to allow the subcentral government to go bankrupt or to bail it out. Under many circumstances, the first alternative will not be palatable, leaving the central government to opt for the second. Anticipating this, subcentral governments have an incentive to engage in riskier fiscal and financial policies than if there were no prospect of a bailout. In contrast, when subcentral governments possess tax resources of their own, a third alternative exists: The central government can demand that they use these to service and restructure their debts."

case, to say one can harden budget constraints by reducing vertical fiscal imbalance is like saying one can eliminate theft by reducing the extent to which criminals possess stolen items – true, but not very useful.

If local governments obtain central transfers in ways that do not involve soft budget constraints, then reducing vertical fiscal imbalance will not solve that problem. In reality, high vertical fiscal imbalance can coincide with very hard budget constraints at the margin. Central authorities may provide a large block grant but insist that the recipient locality fund all additional spending itself. Having provided a large grant, central officials may even be more resolved to deny future requests. The extent of vertical imbalance would then correlate negatively – rather than positively – with the tightness of budget constraints at the margin.

Empirically, soft budget constraints could coincide with vertical imbalance even if no causal relationship runs between them in either direction. Common factors might well explain both. For instance, poor regions may depend more on central transfers aimed at reducing inequality. At the same time, in some countries regional poverty may make it easier for the local government to threaten central officials with social upheaval. And in poor regions, a larger share of the workforce is often made up of public-sector workers, who can usually be relied upon to strike and protest if their wages are not paid.

Based on the vertical imbalance argument, one might think that one could harden budget constraints by assigning local governments their own nondistortionary tax bases. If they asked for central transfers, the central government could then tell them to tax their own bases. Unfortunately, the model in section 5.2.1 suggests that this could be counterproductive, actually *increasing* local overspending. In equilibrium, local governments would first exhaust their own nondistortionary bases and *then* play the same game as before to pressure the center for transfers. This might seem to require an unrealistic amount of overspending. But recall that local governments act in this way in equilibrium not because they greatly desire such high spending but because otherwise the center will tax their income to redistribute to other localities. (If they do not exhaust their nondistortionary bases, the center will cut their transfers to zero and set high taxes on their distortionary bases to obtain funds to redistribute to other districts committed to very high overspending.) Thus, assigning larger tax bases to local governments may have the opposite effect of that expected, causing even greater overspending rather than stricter fiscal discipline.

What about local borrowing? This does not feature explicitly in the models examined so far. It might seem possible to prevent local governments from committing to overspend by prohibiting them from borrowing. But so long as the local government does not have to pay cash in advance to its suppliers, it can use nonpayment to create pressure for central aid. If the center provides a transfer in equilibrium, public contractors will realize this and be willing to wait for payment. Recall also that in equilibrium in the model in section 5.2.1, transfers might actually be zero: Local overspending may in fact be financed entirely from local taxes.[31] Local borrowing would not change anything important about the previous models if such borrowing would, in the absence of central transfers, be repaid by means of high local taxes. If local overborrowing is resolved through default, this can have different consequences. First, if the central government cares more about owners of local bonds than about local taxpayers, overborrowing may be a more effective instrument for pressuring the center than just overspending. Second, if a local default undermines the credit ratings of neighboring localities – or the central government itself – this may increase the central government's sensitivity to local overspending. Thus, local borrowing autonomy might complicate macroeconomic management. However, restricting it may just cause local governments to focus on different ways of pressuring the center, rather than force them to give up such games.

In practice, local governments that are banned from credit markets – or that have lost the confidence of creditors – often find ingenious ways of accruing debts. Both Argentine provincial and Russian regional governments have paid their employees in coupons or IOUs or have simply run up arrears on wage or pension payments. The Argentine province of Rio Negro had eight months' worth of pension arrears as of 1995 (Nicolini et al. 2000, p. 11). In Uruguay, the constitution requires subnational governments to pass balanced budgets. But deficits arise nevertheless. Local governments often finance them by running up arrears to state-owned electric, telephone, and water utilities or by failing to make payments to the national social security system. By 1989, the country's eighteen departments had run up debts to the social security system equal on average to about half a year's required contribution. The central government restructured these

---

[31] This is not true in nonsymmetrical cases, in which some localities do get net transfers. But then contractors should fully anticipate these.

debts and provided additional transfers to help departments pay (Filgueira et al. 2002).

Finally, the clarity or vagueness of the formal division of expenditure responsibilities does not seem likely to affect the extent of soft budget constraints very much. What matters is less what the laws say than what politicians believe their constituents will hold them accountable for. Local constituents are grateful to central incumbents who provide large transfers to their regions, regardless of whether laws or constitutions say they should. The blurring of such responsibilities occurs endogenously in a variety of countries.[32]

In short, campaigns to reduce vertical fiscal imbalance, proscribe local borrowing, and clarify spending responsibilities do not seem likely to have a major effect on the softness of local budget constraints. What might make a difference? The models in previous sections suggest a number of possibilities. First, any measures that make it harder for local governments to pre-commit themselves might help. Requiring all local government spending contracts to include an escape clause permitting the government to cancel the contract for a small fee might accomplish this, although at the cost of making it harder for them to raise funding for desirable projects. Second, measures that enhance the ability of regional governments to veto central government tax increases might help, although – again – at the cost of slowing down tax increases for necessary and popular projects. Third, the incentive for central governments to preserve a reputation for "toughness" will be greater in countries where incumbent governments – or parties – expect to face many similar challenges in the future.[33]

---

[32] See those surveyed in Rodden et al. (2003). This might seem like an extreme claim. I do not mean to suggest that laws never matter. But they are endogenous to the political process, and expenditure assignments are relatively easy either to change, to bend at the margins, or to mischaracterize to the voters. The problem is that all levels of government will often have an interest in obscuring the assignment of responsibilities (blaming other levels for failures, taking unearned credit for successes, performing functions that are demanded but neglected by other levels, etc.). There is no obvious short-term victim of such actions with power to prevent it.

[33] A fourth point that is plausible, although not discussed here, concerns inter-locality spillovers. Wildasin (1997) argues that the negative external effect of a local government's debt default will be greater for large than for small localities. Budget constraints might therefore be softer, the larger are the local units. On the other hand, the smaller are the units – or, more precisely, the more units there are – the less each will internalize the cost of its own bailout. This would lead to a stronger demand for bailouts (see also, on this, Pisauro 2001, pp. 14–15). Thus, the size of localities may have different, offsetting effects.

5.2.8 Conclusion

If local governments can pre-commit themselves, but the central government cannot; if the local governments pre-commit to spending levels rather than tax rates; if local governments are not much more sensitive to the wishes of local taxpayers than the central government; if central policy is not made in a majority-rule legislature in which the agenda setter can play localities off against one another; if local governments cannot veto or significantly limit central tax increases; and if the central government does not have a long enough time horizon to care about reputation, then local governments in a decentralized state may face soft budget constraints, leading to higher spending than under centralization.

However, if some of these conditions do not hold, then spending may actually be lower in a decentralized system. For instance, if local governments pre-commit to particular tax rates rather than spending levels, then their equilibrium spending will be lower than under centralization. If decentralization empowers rich regions to resist central taxation, this may harden the central government's budget constraint in a way that offsets decentralization-induced increases in the demand for bailouts. If a given local government cares much more than the central government about the taxpayers in its jurisdiction, then, again, local government spending could be lower under decentralization than under centralization.

As various scholars (Wildasin 1997, Bordignon et al. 2001) have correctly shown, soft budget constraints can arise in decentralized systems. However, decentralization can also harden local government budget constraints. There is no clear reason to think one effect will generally be more powerful than the other. Some decentralized countries – Russia and Argentina in the 1990s – have suffered from serious macroeconomic imbalances, prompted in part by opportunistic behavior of regional governments. Other decentralized countries – the United States, Switzerland – have experienced enviable macroeconomic stability in recent decades. And some unitary states – for example, Uruguay – have suffered from classic soft budget constraint problems, despite strict formal limits on local government borrowing and limited vertical imbalance.

5.3 Decentralizing Redistribution

Decentralizing some policy authority to local governments does not have clear, general effects on the level of central geographical redistribution.

Even if it did, such effects might be offset by central *intergroup* redistribution. But what if one could decentralize redistribution itself – that is, assign authority to redistribute exclusively to local governments? How would this affect the overall level and pattern of redistribution?

One common argument contends that because redistribution is limited by mobility of the tax base, there will be less of it if authority to redistribute is held only by lower tier governments. As Musgrave (1997, p. 67) puts it:

> In practice, decentralized redistribution policy can only operate within narrow limits. Any jurisdiction which unilaterally imposes higher taxes at the upper end of the scale invites the loss of mobile resources, including both capital and high-income residents. Conversely, jurisdictions which unilaterally offer greater benefits to the poor will attract outsiders to share in the benefits. Movement between jurisdictions now assumes a perverse function. For this reason, distribution policy must be a matter of national concern.

It is usually cheaper for rich citizens to move from one city or region to another than for them to emigrate to another country, and this imposes a tighter constraint on local than on national policy. Some empirical evidence supports this contention. For instance, Feldstein and Wrobel (1998) find that in the United States, state attempts to redistribute from skilled to nonskilled workers via progressive income taxes have been largely ineffective because of mobility. However, mobility protects owners of only certain factors. Land and buildings cannot migrate, so local governments can tax real estate owners in order to redistribute to local house renters (Epple and Romer 1991).[34]

If one assumes, by contrast, that citizens and capital are not mobile, then local governments might choose to redistribute *more* than a central government. Several economists have explored the politics of redistribution assuming that voters cannot move and that redistribution can be done on only one dimension (e.g., from poor to rich or rich to poor). Governments are restricted to setting a linear tax on income and allocating the revenues as equal lump sum transfers to each citizen in their jurisdiction. This simplification makes it possible to apply the median-voter theorem and focus on the level of redistribution favored by the median voter.

For instance, Persson and Tabellini (1994) extend Meltzer and Richard's (1981) model of redistribution to a decentralized setting. Citizens differ on one dimension, productivity (or income), and have quasilinear preferences

---

[34] Of course, taxation – by any level of government – of immobile factors such as land and buildings can distort investment in them (see, e.g., Chamley 1986).

over consumption of a private good and a public good. Governments set a proportional income tax and a fixed lump sum transfer that is the same for each citizen. Thus, the net transfer to an individual decreases linearly in his productivity. In this setting, citizen preferences are single-peaked. The voter with the median income gets to pick the level of redistribution. The extent of equilibrium redistribution increases monotonically with the gap between the mean and median productivity (or income) levels in the jurisdiction.

Suppose the country is divided into two regions that differ only in their average incomes. That is, each has an income distribution with the same shape, just a different mean. And suppose that in this distribution, the median is below the mean (it is skewed to the right, as is typical of most countries' pre-tax income distributions). Persson and Tabellini show that the median income will be closer to the mean nationwide than is the case in the two regions. As a result, there will be more redistribution if only the regional governments redistribute than if only the central government can redistribute. Decentralizing redistribution under these conditions leads to greater redistribution.

This holds if redistribution aims to increase equality by transferring income from rich to poor citizens. The opposite is likely to be the case for redistribution that serves a social insurance function, insuring people against unemployment or disabilities. In this case, the distribution is usually skewed to the left (more people are healthy and employed than are disabled or unemployed), and consequently the median will be above the mean, implying that redistribution will be greater when the program is run centrally than when it is run regionally. Social insurance schemes should be more generous when they are national than when they are local.[35]

Persson and Tabellini assumed that the distributions of income or productivity in the two regions had the same shape. But what if the distributions – and levels of inequality – vary from place to place? Bolton and

[35] Centrally run social insurance schemes could also insure against region-specific shocks. Alesina and Perotti (1998) examine the likely costs and benefits of such central programs. They find that such redistribution may reduce the risk to individuals from economic shocks. But such insurance comes at a cost: It increases the variance of regional tax rates over time because the regions that are "lucky" in a given year must raise their tax rates to finance aid to the "unlucky" regions. Thus, there is a tradeoff between economic risk and what Alesina and Perotti call "political risk" – the cost of variation in tax rates. However, such costs seem easily avoidable. Rational governments will smooth tax rates across years as implied by optimal taxation theory. In reality, countries do not usually increase social security taxes in years with a lot of claims and reduce them in years with fewer claims.

Roland (1997) examine this case, again assuming that only one-dimensional redistribution is possible. The level of income redistribution preferred by the nationwide median voter may differ greatly from that preferred by the median voter in a particular region. If local dissatisfaction with central income redistribution is strong enough, it may overshadow the benefits of integration and prompt local leaders to seek secession. But, as Bolton and Roland note, the regions would not need to secede if the country adopted a federal structure and assigned income redistribution to regional governments rather than to the center. Such decentralization would make it possible to satisfy the median voters within all regions simultaneously, pre-empting their demands for independence.

Boix (2003, p. 155) suggests another way decentralization might affect the politics of redistribution. Again restricting redistribution to one dimension as in the Meltzer and Richard (1981) model, Boix argues that, other things equal, greater inequality is likely to provoke rich elites to stage authoritarian coups in order to prevent expropriation at the hands of the median voter. Decentralizing authority to redistribute from the central government to the regions will transfer the class war down to smaller arenas. If some regions have a more equal income distribution than the country as a whole, they will have better odds of remaining democratic. By the same logic, regions with greater inequality will be more likely to turn authoritarian. Rather than being all democratic or all authoritarian, the country may evolve into a patchwork of democratic regions and authoritarian fiefdoms. Adsera and Boix (2004) consider what happens when what differs across regions is not the income distribution but average wealth. A small, rich region might not wish to integrate with a large, poor region on a democratic basis because the national median voter would be poor and would favor redistribution from the rich region to the poor region. In such cases, a credible transfer of redistribution authority to regional governments would remove this danger and make democracy acceptable to all.

To recap, these analyses predict that if factor mobility is high, decentralizing redistribution will lead to less of it. If factor mobility is low and regional income distributions are similar, decentralizing redistribution will lead to more of it (at least of the kind aimed at equalization rather than social insurance). If factor mobility is low and regional income distributions differ, decentralizing redistribution (a) will reduce the odds of secession and (b) may decentralize class warfare and regime choice to the regional level. If factor mobility is low and average regional wealth or income differs, decentralizing redistribution will make democracy less dangerous to small, rich regions.

However, several considerations cast doubt on the relevance of these arguments. First, the assumption that governments can redistribute on only one dimension is highly unrealistic. Of course governments can and do tax and spend in more complicated ways. They can tax both poor and rich to benefit the middle class, or tax the middle class to benefit the poor and the rich. They can target benefits at particular regions or particular occupational or age groups. Given this, the median-voter theorem will almost never apply, and the simple relationship between inequality and redistribution on which the Persson and Tabellini, Bolton and Roland, and Boix arguments depend disappears.

Second, the Bolton and Roland argument and the Boix argument assume an oddly passive, myopic, or constrained central government. The median voter is not only restricted to redistribute in a crude way, he is also assumed to be naïvely unaware of the consequences of different policies. In reality, central governments rarely sit on their hands as their country disintegrates or the rich stage a coup. The advantage of federalism, according to Bolton and Roland, is that it allows for different redistributive policies within each of the country's regions. But central governments in centralized states can also implement different redistributive policies in different regions. If the alternative is civil war or disintegration of the state, surely the central government or national median voter will make some policy concessions to avoid this.[36] And because most voters would suffer under authoritarian rule, surely they would prefer a tax rate below the threshold that would trigger a coup.

Third, the premise of this section – that one can limit redistribution to just the local level – is hard to accept. In practice, in even the most decentralized states both central and local governments usually redistribute income among their constituents to some extent, sometimes overtly, sometimes indirectly. Equilibrium emerges from the interaction between their redistributive strategies.[37]

---

[36] Buchanan and Faith's (1987) model takes this into account.

[37] As noted in section 5.2.6, Weingast (1997) suggests one way that, in an indefinitely repeated game, central redistribution might be eliminated, leaving room for only local redistribution. But, as noted already, the mechanism relies on a particular equilibrium in a setting of multiple equilibria and so cannot be taken as a general guide to what to expect under decentralization.

If one assumes that both central and local governments can redistribute, on multiple dimensions, the math becomes more complicated and the outcomes become less determinate. Dixit and Londregan (1998) study this problem, using the kind of adapted Downsian voting model discussed in sections 5.2.4 and 2.2.3.1. They find no general results about whether total redistribution is greater when both levels redistribute or when just the central government does so. But the pattern will usually be different in the two cases. Redistribution will create different winners and losers in a unitary and a decentralized state. Under decentralization, there may also be multiple equilibria, which complicates any comparison.

In short, if only local governments could redistribute, they might be constrained by factor mobility to redistribute less than a similar central government, although they might wish to redistribute more. But this is immaterial because central governments can always redistribute as well to some degree. Analyzing the interaction between central and local redistributive programs is complicated, but to date no one has given a convincing, general reason to think decentralization would result in either more or less redistribution than centralization.

6

Fiscal Coordination and Incentives

> The benefits of federalism derive from the operation of vertical competition... politicians at a given jurisdictional level will assess the performance of governments inhabiting other tiers. If they come to the conclusion that they can do better than these governments, they will act on that conviction.
>
> Albert Breton (2000, pp. 6–7)

> When tax rights over a tax base are divided among more than one government, the tax base becomes a common property resource... as more independent tax agencies share the same tax base, the standard tragedy of the commons problem emerges and the commons – the tax base – is "over-grazed," leading to an equilibrium with an excessively high aggregate tax rate, meager aggregate tax collections, deficient provision of public goods, low investment and low output.
>
> Daniel Berkowitz and Wei Li (2000, p. 371)

Competition between local and central governments can take many forms. In Chapter 5, I explored how local governments may blackmail central officials into playing Santa Claus, pressuring them to make unplanned fiscal transfers. But even if no such transfers were possible, the two levels would still try to outmaneuver each other in various ways. An element of competition arises inevitably from the fact that the two levels are governing the same citizens. Depending on whether they are benevolent or predatory, the governments may compete to please their common beneficiaries or exploit their common victims. Some scholars – such as Albert Breton in the quotation at the start of this chapter – focus on desirable aspects of vertical competition: Incumbents seeking electoral support will try to outperform one another in the voters' eyes.

But most – including Berkowitz and Li – focus on the downside. If central and local governments tax the same distortionary base, more revenues for one means less for the other. The tax base becomes a kind of common property that both overgraze, driving the aggregate tax rate prohibitively high. If the two levels share responsibility for a given public service – or even if the electorate just *thinks* they do – both may shirk and free ride on the other's contribution. If the two levels supply different but complementary services, acting independently they will again provide too little. In any of these cases, devolving fiscal powers could lead to serious inefficiencies.

Such inefficiencies result from a lack of coordination. Recognizing the danger, governments at different tiers might try to cooperate. They might agree to set a fixed rate of tax on each base and share the revenues in some pre-agreed proportion. (Such arrangements also protect each level against idiosyncratic declines in particular tax bases.) Similarly, they might contract to provide defined amounts of the joint public services. Tax-sharing schemes exist in many countries, and many decentralized states assign some functions concurrently to two or more levels. Yet even if the governments sign agreements, the signatories will have incentives to cheat or implement them in self-serving ways. Officials who retain only a share of tax revenues can do better by extracting bribes or other informal payments from the same base, all the proceeds of which go into their own pockets. If they coordinate tax rates but do not coordinate complementary infrastructure investments, these will still be underprovided. Tax-sharing systems, rather than eliminating harmful vertical competition, may just drive it underground.

Recently, some scholars have proposed a solution. Building on a widespread intuition, they argue that giving local governments a large share in marginal tax revenues should motivate them to support business activity, which should improve economic performance. When local officials have a strong, direct interest in local economic growth – which increases local revenues – they will change from corrupt opponents to eager facilitators of development.

In this chapter, I examine both the argument that coordination failures in decentralized systems lead to excessive taxation and the claim that fiscal decentralization in a tax-sharing system improves incentives and promotes economic activity. I conclude that the first argument is valid, although the inefficiencies may be reduced by either horizontal or vertical competition for capital or votes. However, even when it holds, the argument's implications are unclear, at least for governments that are not entirely predatory. While uncoordinated taxation may result in excessive tax rates, uncoordinated public service provision will tend to lead to underspending.

If these effects occur together, they will pull in opposite directions, making it hard to say in general whether more autonomous tiers will increase or decrease the aggregate tax rate and size of the budget. The second argument makes an invalid leap from the conclusion that fiscal decentralization improves local incentives to the claim that it improves performance overall. There is also a central government to consider. Giving local governments a larger share in marginal revenues means giving the central government a smaller share, worsening *its* incentives. Because both levels can either assist or hinder economic activity, there is no way to know in general which effect will dominate.

6.1 Vertical "Overgrazing"

In March 2004, the former Indonesian President Mohamed Suharto received an unusual honor. The anti-corruption group Transparency International awarded the ailing ex-dictator the title of the world's most corrupt leader. It estimated that during his three decades in office Suharto and his family had amassed a fortune of more than $15 billion, outdoing even such seasoned kleptocrats as the Philippines' Ferdinand Marcos and Zaire's Mobutu Sese Seko.[1] After Suharto's fall from power in 1998, Indonesians naturally hoped that political reforms – such as the fiscal and political decentralization programs introduced by the dictator's successors – would reduce the extent of graft in the bureaucracy.

To judge from surveys and newspaper reports, they have been disappointed. Whereas before bribes flowed primarily to a coterie of Suharto's cronies, now businesses seeking privileges or just permission to operate have to pay off officials at multiple levels of the state. As the *Wall Street Journal* reported in 2003:

One Jakarta-based executive of a gold-mining company in Indonesian Borneo, who says he never had to bribe local officials during the Suharto days, now pays off scores of them. It is a continuous, confusing and discouraging process, he says, because local laws and regulations keep changing. "Before, you paid a lump sum in Jakarta and could be certain you had smoothed things out," the businessman says. "Now you pay a lot of small amounts locally, and you can't be sure things will be smooth." (Borsuck 2003)

---

[1] *The New York Times*, "World Briefing: Asia: Indonesia: Suharto Tops List of Embezzling Leaders," March 26, 2004.

Besides the unpredictability of the system, some believed the total amount of bribes extorted from businesses had increased substantially. Such accounts match results from a recent World Bank survey of Indonesian firms, which found that almost 50 percent of respondents thought decentralization had made policy uncertainty and corruption worse. More than one-third reported that informal payments had increased since decentralization, compared with only 15 percent who thought they had decreased. Regional governments had reportedly used their new powers to impose many new nuisance taxes and fees on small businesses (Campos and Hellman 2005).

One theory predicts exactly such a flowering of bribery as authority is decentralized. Suppose two levels of government can independently set tax – or, in the Indonesian case, bribe – rates on a common, distortionary base or on distortionary bases that overlap. The rate that government at one level sets will affect the size of the base available to the other. In the terminology of public finance, there is a "vertical externality." If the two governments do not coordinate, they will ignore the costs they impose on each other, and the aggregate tax rate that results will be higher than the efficient level – sometimes even higher than would be set by a predatory, unitary government.

The basic problem is that identified by Spengler (1950) in his analysis of double marginalization under linked monopolies. The idea was developed by Shleifer and Vishny (1993), who discussed how coordination problems could lead independent government agencies to set tax or bribe rates higher than a unitary government would choose. Treatments of the vertical externality in public finance include Hansson and Stuart (1987), Dahlby (1996), Boadway, Marchand, and Vigneault (1998), Flowers (1988), Keen (1998), Wrede (1999), Berkowitz and Li (2000), Dahlby and Wilson (2003), and Volden (2005). Similar arguments have been made regarding regulation. For instance, Tanzi (2001) suggests that a larger number of layers of government may be associated with a greater burden of economically damaging zoning ordinances, rent controls, limits on store opening hours, and other regulations.[2] A parallel problem arises if multiple levels of government benefit from a particular type of public spending. They will together spend less than the efficient level, because each neglects the benefits that other levels receive from its spending (Wrede 2000).

---

[2] See also Kreimer (2001, pp. 68–9).

It might seem easy enough to separate tax bases and spending responsibilities by a simple act of constitutional engineering. But separating tax bases and policy responsibilities is in practice extremely difficult. For a start, constitutions always leave something to interpretation: "Although in theory a multi-tiered system may have been intended to create a regime of dual sovereignty, the ambiguous definition of exclusive spheres means that areas of separateness often collapse" (Gillette 1997, p. 1359). Many taxes, although formally distinct, have effects on the same tax bases. For instance, a general sales tax and a proportional tax on wage income are known to have similar effects if capital markets work efficiently (Keen 1998, p. 460). Or if one factor is internationally mobile and another is not, the impact of a tax on the mobile factor may be largely borne by the owners of the immobile factor. On the expenditure side, if voters choose to hold both levels of government responsible for a given policy issue – as they might rationally do if they lack information – then this policy will feature in the objective functions of officials at both levels, whatever the fine legal distinctions in the constitution. In reality, policy assignments and tax bases are both perceived to overlap in many countries, which suggests the need to take issues raised by such overlap seriously.

Below, I show formally how such vertical competition could lead to an aggregate tax rate that is inefficiently high from all governments' perspectives. I also develop a model in which shared responsibility for provision of some public good creates an increasing incentive to shirk as the number of tiers increases. I abstract here from the issues that arise when financial transfers are possible between levels of government (as analyzed in Chapter 5). (If the center could pre-commit to a level of transfers, it could eliminate the fiscal externality by setting transfers to offset the distortionary effects of local taxation [Boadway and Keen 1996].) I also assume throughout this chapter that the tax bases are completely immobile (for analysis of mobile tax bases, see Chapter 4). I start out assuming that governments are completely predatory – the Leviathans of Hobbes and Brennan and Buchanan (1980) – and move on to see how results change if they are partly benevolent.

Consider a state with J tiers, and where the bottom tier jurisdictions are indexed by $n = 1, 2, \ldots, N$. Governments levy a tax on incomes earned within their jurisdictions, for simplicity assumed to equal output produced there. To start, suppose governments are completely predatory and maximize revenue. Citizens in each bottom tier jurisdiction pay tax to governments at each of the J tiers. Denote the rate of tax paid by citizens of bottom tier jurisdiction n to their government at tier j by τ_{jn}; the aggregate tax rate for citizens of n is $\sum_{j=1}^{J} (\tau_{jn})$, which to save space I will abbreviate to simply: $\sum \tau_{jn}$.

The governments can be thought of as playing games against one another over each of the N bottom tier jurisdictions. (I implicitly assume here that higher-level governments can set different tax rates and spending levels for different bottom tier units within their jurisdictions. I also assume no horizontal externalities.) Assume for now that the governments play Cournot-Nash, moving simultaneously and supposing that what tax rate they set within jurisdiction n will not affect what rate other governments set there. That is, all governments, at tiers $j = 1, 2, \ldots, J$, simultaneously announce their tax rates for each bottom tier unit within their jurisdiction. Reported income decreases with increases in the tax rate, because citizens substitute leisure for labor and conceal a larger share of earnings, so governments face a Laffer curve like that discussed in section 2.2.5. Because taxes are not deductible and what matters to citizens is the aggregate tax rate rather than which government gets the revenues, we can assume simply that output decreases in $\sum \tau_{jn}$; I also assume output is positive when the tax rate is zero: $Y_n = Y\left(\sum \tau_{jn}\right); Y(0) > 0; Y' < 0.$[3]

An identical game is played to determine the aggregate tax rate in each bottom tier jurisdiction. Focusing on a single bottom tier jurisdiction, and suppressing the n subscripts, the government at tier j sets its tax rate, τ_j, for that jurisdiction to maximize: $\tau_j Y(\sum \tau_j)$, taking the tax rates of the other tiers as given. The first order condition implicitly defines the j-tier government's equilibrium tax rate:

$$\tau_j^* = -\frac{Y\left(\sum \tau_j^*\right)}{Y'\left(\sum \tau_j^*\right)} \tag{6.1}$$

(I assume there is a unique, interior equilibrium – that is, the second order condition $2Y' + \tau_j^* Y'' < 0$ or $2(Y')^2 - YY'' > 0$ holds everywhere. This ensures that the Laffer curve has a unique maximum.) If we focus on the symmetric equilibrium, in which $\tau_j^* = \tau^*$ for all j, we can write this as:

$$\tau^* = -\frac{Y(J\tau^*)}{Y'(J\tau^*)} \qquad \text{or equivalently} \sum \tau_j^* = -J\frac{Y\left(\sum \tau_j^*\right)}{Y'\left(\sum \tau_j^*\right)} \tag{6.1'}$$

How does the aggregate equilibrium tax rate, $\sum \tau_j^*$, change with the number of tiers, J? Note first that given our assumptions $-J[Y(0)/Y'(0)] > 0$,

---

[3] I assume also that $Y(\cdot)$ is continuous.

so for there to be a unique solution to (6.1'), the $-\mathcal{J}[Y(\sum \tau_j{}^*)/Y'(\sum \tau_j{}^*)]$ curve must cross the $\sum \tau_j{}^*$ curve from above, with a slope of less than one. This is equivalent to the condition that in equilibrium $(\mathcal{J} + 1)Y'^2 - \mathcal{J}YY'' > 0$. Totally differentiating (6.1') with regard to $\mathcal{J}$, we get: $d\sum \tau_j{}^*/d\mathcal{J} = -YY'/[(\mathcal{J} + 1)Y'^2 - \mathcal{J}YY'']$, which, given our assumption of a unique equilibrium, must be positive. In words, the aggregate equilibrium tax rate must increase with the number of tiers of government.

This is the standard argument about uncoordinated taxation and "overgrazing" of the fiscal commons. If we allowed for multiple equilibria, it is possible that in some of them the $-\mathcal{J}[Y(\sum \tau_j{}^*)/Y'(\sum \tau_j{}^*)]$ curve would intersect the $\sum \tau_j{}^*$ curve from below, and increasing $\mathcal{J}$ could lead to a *drop* in the aggregate tax rate. But it would take quite an unusual output function (with a Y'' that is positive and very large relative to Y'). In most cases, the standard argument seems likely to hold.

What happens if governments are allowed to be partially benevolent? Suppose now that each government, j, has a payoff function similar to (2.2) in Chapter 2: $V_j = h(g_j) + (1 - \sum \tau_j)Y(\sum \tau_j) + bq(c_j)$, where g_j is now spending by the j-tier government in locality n, and c_j is consumption of the budget by the j-tier government financed by taxes on locality n, and $h(\cdot)$ and $q(\cdot)$ are both increasing and concave. The government maximizes this payoff, taking the tax rates of the other levels as given. To simplify, suppose there is only one citizen in the bottom tier jurisdiction in question, whose income is given by $Y(\sum \tau_j)$, $Y' < 0$. The budget constraint, which is met at equality, is $c_j + g_j \leq \tau_j Y(\sum \tau_j)$. I suppose also for simplicity that each level of government disregards utility that citizens get from provision of public goods by other levels. As before, I assume there is a unique, symmetric equilibrium.

The first order conditions are now:

$$h_g(g_j{}^*)\frac{\partial(\tau_j{}^* Y)}{\partial \tau_j} = bq_c(c_j{}^*)\frac{\partial(\tau_j{}^* Y)}{\partial \tau_j} = -\frac{\partial\left((1 - \sum \tau_j{}^*)\, Y\right)}{\partial \tau_j} \text{ or}$$

$$h_g(g_j{}^*)(Y + \tau_j{}^* Y') = bq_c(c_j{}^*)(Y + \tau_j{}^* Y') = Y - \left(1 - \sum \tau_j{}^*\right) Y' \quad (6.2)$$

where the partial derivatives are taken holding the other governments' tax rates constant. The left-hand element is the marginal utility the government gets from raising the tax rate marginally to increase spending on the public service, g. The middle term is the marginal utility the government gets from a marginal tax increase to increase its own consumption. The term on the right represents the disutility for the government from the reduction in private consumption caused by a marginally higher tax rate. In equilibrium, the benefit and cost to the government of marginally increasing its tax rate are equated.

Note first that because $Y - (1 - \sum \tau_j^*)Y'$, h_g, and q_c are all positive, $Y + \tau_j^*Y' = \partial(\tau_j^*Y)/\partial\tau_j$ must also be positive. Graphically, equilibrium occurs to the left of the peak of government j's Laffer curve. Given this, both $h_g(g_j^*)\partial(\tau_j^*Y)/\partial\tau_j$ and $bq_c(c_j^*)\partial(\tau_j^*Y)/\partial\tau_j$ must be decreasing in τ_j. Note also that at the level of τ_j at which $\sum \tau_j = 1$, $h_g(g_j^*)\partial(\tau_j^*Y)/\partial\tau_j$ and $bq_c(c_j^*)\partial(\tau_j^*Y)/\partial\tau_j$ must both be less than zero ($\partial(\tau_j^*Y)/\partial\tau_j < 0$ when τ_j^* is to the right of the peak of the Laffer curve, $h_g, q_c > 0$); but at this level of τ_j – as at all others – $Y - (1 - \sum \tau_j)Y' \geq 0$. Given that $Y - (1 - \sum \tau_j)Y' > h_g(g_j^*)\partial(\tau_j^*Y)/\partial\tau_j$ at $\sum \tau_j = 1$, and that for there to be a unique equilibrium these curves must intersect exactly once, the former must cut the latter at equilibrium from below. ($Y - (1 - \sum \tau_j)Y'$ must also cut $bq_c(c_j^*)\partial(\tau_j^*Y)/\partial\tau_j$ from below.) In the symmetric equilibrium, $\sum \tau_j = J\tau^*$, so the right-hand term of (6.2) can be written: $Y - (1 - J\tau^*)Y'$. For a given $\sum \tau_j^*$ and τ^*, and therefore Y, $Y - (1 - J\tau^*)Y'$ decreases in J, so the $Y - (1 - J\tau)Y'$ curve (plotted against τ) shifts down when the number of tiers increases. As a result, τ^* must increase with J, and so $J\tau^* = \sum \tau_j^*$ also increases with J. The aggregate tax rate still increases with the number of tiers even when governments are partly (or completely) benevolent.

Similar externalities may occur when different levels of government have the right to regulate the same citizens or businesses. They may then use their regulations to extract bribes in ways that discourage economic activity, ignoring the effect on the other levels' bribe revenues. Indonesia's local authorities, liberated from hierarchical control by political decentralization, showed great talent in devising new hoops for private firms to jump through. Some levied an advertising tax on the hanging of "No Smoking" and "Fire Exit" signs, while others introduced special licensing requirements for women to work a night shift (World Bank 2005).

Vertical externalities can also occur over government spending if the responsibilities of different levels overlap. In Norway the national government pays for hospitals, while local governments are responsible for primary care. The municipalities have an obvious incentive to shirk on preventive and outpatient services because seriously ill residents will be treated in centrally funded hospitals (Joumard and Suyker 2002, Joumard and Kongsrud 2003). To see this logic mathematically, we can adjust the previous model in a simple way. Suppose now that governments at all levels benefit from the provision of public services by all levels. Specifically, we can replace $h(g_j)$ in the expression for V_j by $h(\sum_j g_j/J)$: Each government j derives concavely increasing utility from the *average* provision of public services by all the relevant governments.

This might be because voters lack the information to attribute credit for public spending across the levels of government and so give an equal share of the credit to each level.

Now government j's first order condition becomes:

$$\frac{1}{\mathcal{J}}b_g\left(\frac{1}{\mathcal{J}}\sum_j g_j\right)(Y+\tau_j{}^*Y') = bq_c(c_j)(Y+\tau_j{}^*Y') = Y-\left(1-\sum_j \tau_j\right)Y' \tag{6.2'}$$

and in symmetric equilibrium:

$$\frac{1}{\mathcal{J}}b_g(g^*)(Y+\tau^*Y') = bq_c(c^*)(Y+\tau^*Y') = Y-(1-\mathcal{J}\tau^*)Y' \tag{6.2''}$$

As before, the left-hand and middle terms must be downward sloping when plotted against τ, and the $Y-(1-\sum \tau_j)Y'$ curve must cut the others from below. As before, increasing $\mathcal{J}$ shifts the $Y-(1-\mathcal{J}\tau^*)Y'$ curve down, tending to increase τ^* and $\sum \tau_j{}^* = \mathcal{J}\tau^*$. But now increasing $\mathcal{J}$ also shifts the $(1/\mathcal{J})b_g(g^*)(Y+\tau^*Y')$ curve down, which tends to reduce τ^* and $\sum \tau_j{}^* = \mathcal{J}\tau^*$. As the marginal utility to the government of public spending goes down, the marginal benefit of tax revenues also goes down. The government also shifts some of its public spending, g, into its own consumption, c, decreasing the marginal utility of c until it equals the lower marginal benefit of taxation.

Thus, vertical externalities in taxation increase governments' marginal demand for tax revenues, but vertical externalities in public spending decrease their marginal demand for tax revenues. It is not clear how these opposing effects will net out. Depending on the relative elasticities, increasing the number of tiers could either increase or decrease the equilibrium aggregate tax rate. Either way, though, in this simple model it will cause substitution from public spending into consumption by government officials.

So far I have assumed that the interactions between the local government of locality n and higher-tier governments are not affected by the behavior of other local governments. In Chapter 4, however, I discussed the possibility that competition among localities to attract mobile capital or voters could place downward pressure on the local tax rate. Although it was not clear that this would generally happen, or if it did that it would generally reduce the aggregate tax rate rather than just result in a larger share for the center, such horizontal competition could offset the tendency for vertical competition to increase the tax rate.[4]

This pessimistic view of vertical competition is probably the most widespread. But there is also a more optimistic view. If multiple tiers of government provide the same public good or service, voters can use the performance of each as a benchmark to judge the efficiency of the other. The resulting yardstick competition can be used to discipline governments at all levels. While yardstick competition is often said to occur among governments at the same tier (Besley and Case 1995), Salmon (1987) and Breton (1996) extended the concept to the vertical dimension.[5] A government that provides the common good or service inefficiently will be punished by the voters. By this logic, so long as governments at all levels are subject to electoral accountability and the particular contributions of each government are clear to the voters, the effectiveness and honesty of government should be *greater* when several governments provide the same public good. One might expect this to reduce $c_j{}^*$ – and therefore also τ_j – for all j.

In short, given one technical condition (the existence of a unique, symmetric equilibrium), increasing the number of tiers may lead to overgrazing of the fiscal commons by governments, resulting in a higher aggregate tax rate. But it may also lead to free riding on other levels' public spending, resulting in a lower aggregate tax rate, albeit accompanied by a shift of spending from public services into officials' own consumption. The net effects on the tax rate, on tax revenues, and on output are unclear. Moreover, if governments compete against one another horizontally for mobile capital or residents, or vertically for electoral support, such competition may reduce or even eliminate overgrazing and shirking. Although increasing the number of interdependent but autonomous tiers may sometimes lead to pathological outcomes, in many other cases it will not. It seems hard to reach a more general conclusion.

6.2 *Fiscal Decentralization and Incentives*

One apparent solution to the coordination problems discussed in the previous section might be for the different levels of government to cooperate. Instead of each independently setting its tax rate, the governments might

[4] On this, see Keen and Kotsogiannis (2002).
[5] I return to the question of horizontal yardstick competition in section 7.2.1.

together levy a single tax on a given base at an agreed rate and then share the revenues among themselves in predetermined proportions. We might expect the governments then to set the tax rate at the jointly optimal level. A system of this type goes by the name of "tax sharing."[6]

Tax-sharing systems are extremely common. A very partial list of countries where at least one level of subnational government got more than half its tax revenues from interlevel tax sharing as of the late 1990s would include Albania, Armenia, Austria, Belarus, Belgium, Bolivia, Bulgaria, Croatia, the Czech Republic, Estonia, Georgia, Germany, Hungary, Kazakhstan, Latvia, Lithuania, Mexico, Moldova, Nigeria, Norway, Poland, Romania, Russia, Spain, Tajikistan, Turkey, and Ukraine.[7] In many other countries, tax sharing exists in a less pronounced form. Even where tax sharing does not occur *de jure*, if central governments provide fiscal transfers to local budgets that vary with local performance, then a kind of tax sharing often exists *de facto*.

Although tax sharing can be used to keep the governments from setting an inefficiently high official tax rate, it will not eliminate all potentially harmful vertical interactions. First, it may merely push tax competition underground. If governments can extract bribes, they may do so from the shared base and from bases assigned exclusively to other levels. This will generate the same sort of overgrazing modeled in the previous section. Second, even if the governments manage to cooperate on taxation, that does not mean they will coordinate efficiently their provision of public services and infrastructure construction. They may still face incentives to shirk on public service provision and underexploit the complementarities of their investments.

In this context, some scholars have argued that assigning a large share of marginal tax revenues to local governments will improve performance. The larger the local governments' share of marginal revenues, the stronger should be their incentive to assist local business, leading to higher economic output. Local officials who know they will get to keep the lion's share of any additional revenues generated should be more eager to invest in business-promoting infrastructure, to limit costly regulations, and to curb their appetite for bribes. On the other hand, if most of the marginal

---

[6] This section draws on Treisman (2006). I am grateful to Blackwell Publishing for permission to reuse the material.

[7] See OECD (1999), Dabla-Norris and Wade (2002, p. 28), Ebel and Yilmaz (2002, p. 8), Ter-Minassian (1997a), and Turkish State Institute of Statistics (1999, p. 624).

dollar of locally generated revenues is siphoned off to higher-level budgets, local officials will place lower priority on stimulating economic activity and more on other objectives such as lining their own pockets.

This argument has been applied to a variety of countries. For instance, some think China's vigorous development in the 1980s and 1990s can be at least partly explained by the high – and increasingly secure – share of revenues retained by subnational governments (Jin, Qian, and Weingast 2005). According to Roland (2000, p. 281), China's "fiscal decentraliza-tion has helped to align the incentives of government authorities with eco-nomic efficiency." By contrast, Russia's stagnation in the 1990s is sometimes attributed to the low *ex post* share of revenue that city governments retained (Blanchard and Shleifer 2000; Zhuravskaya 2000). Some scholars have seen a similar logic at work in Uganda and Pakistan (Shah 1998, p. 141; Kisubi 1999, p. 123; Ahmad and Wasti 2003, pp. 196–8). *The Economist* magazine even pointed to inadequate revenue decentralization in Britain as a reason why municipalities there refuse planning permission to firms that wish to expand: "The state of the local economy...makes little difference to local government coffers, so in the balance between growth and beauty, growth does not get much of a say" (*The Economist* 2001, p. 20).

Decentralizing revenues may, indeed, improve incentives for local gov-ernments. However, it does not follow that government as a whole will be more business-friendly or that economic performance will be better. The common intuition ignores one important actor in the game. If decentral-izing revenues strengthens incentives for local governments, it simultane-ously weakens them for the *central* government by reducing its stake in economic development. Any improvement in local government behavior will likely be accompanied by a worsening of central government behavior. If equilibrium output is much more sensitive to local than to central inter-ventions, the local effect might dominate. But in most cases interventions by both levels of government influence economic activity, and there is no reason to think one effect will generally be stronger than the other. Indeed, in certain plausible formulations, the two effects exactly cancel each other out. Predatory behavior is merely shifted from one level to the other, while output is unchanged.

6.2.1 The Standard Argument

To see the logic at its simplest, consider a two-level state and focus on a single locality, containing a single citizen with a productive business.

Output – and income – in the locality is Y.[8] A single tax is levied on output, at rate $\tau \in [0, 1]$, for now assumed fixed. The revenue from this tax is divided between the local and central governments; the local government receives a share $r \in (0, 1)$, and the central government receives a share $1 - r$. The goal of the analysis is to see how government behavior and output change as r changes.

Various types of government intervention might affect economic performance. Suppose first that governments extract bribes from business, proportional to output. The local government chooses a bribe rate $b_l \in [0, 1 - \tau]$.[9] One might imagine that local officials demand a share of the firm's revenue in return for waiving some costly regulation.[10] To model the argument that decentralization reduces output-depleting government interventions, we must assume that at least some interventions deplete output. Thus, I suppose that output in this locality, Y, decreases in b_l: $Y = f(\tau, b_l)$ where $f_2 < 0$ if $b_l > 0$ and $f(0, 0) > 0$ (subscripts on functions denote derivatives). It also seems reasonable to assume that if the sum of the tax and bribe rates equaled 100 percent, output would cease: if $\tau + b_l = 1$, $f(\tau, b_l) = 0$.

Suppose, for now, that governments maximize their revenues from taxation and bribery. Given τ and r, the local government sets b_l to maximize $R_l = (\tau r + b_l) f(\tau, b_l)$. Its first order condition is:

$$b_l^* = -\frac{f(\tau, b_l^*)}{f_2(\tau, b_l^*)} - \tau r \tag{6.3}$$

where asterisks indicate equilibrium values. For the standard argument to go through, we need to assume that this represents a maximum. The second order condition, combined with the first, reduces to $2 f_2^2 - f f_{22} > 0$, which is a version of the standard condition for the Laffer curve to have an interior maximum (see Chapter 2). We can guarantee this by assuming f is concave in the bribe rate – and I assume this.[11] Then, (6.3) implicitly defines a function $b_l^*(\tau, r)$.

---

[8] There is no interregional trade or investment, so all income accrues to the citizen in the locality.

[9] I assume throughout that bribe rates are set *after* the tax rate is fixed. This seems reasonable because tax rates are usually set by government in an annual law, whereas the bribe rate can be altered by local government officials at their discretion.

[10] Although strict proportionality may not occur, it seems reasonable to think that the size of the bribe demanded might change with the size of the business.

[11] If the second order condition did not hold, the first order condition would identify a minimum. But then the only possible equilibrium would be at $b_l^* = 0$, and bribery would not be a problem to begin with. (There could not be an equilibrium at $b_l^* = 1 - \tau$, because

From (6.3), it is clear that increasing r reduces the equilibrium local bribe rate, $b_l^*(\tau, r)$, and increases equilibrium output. Totally differentiating (6.3) with regard to r, we get:

$$\frac{\partial b_l^*(\tau, r)}{\partial r} = -\tau \frac{f_2^2}{2f_2^2 - ff_{22}} < 0 \tag{6.4}$$

So the impact of increases in r on output, $(\partial f/\partial b_l)(\partial b_l^*/\partial r) > 0$. This is the standard argument in a nutshell. Increasing r decreases the local government's equilibrium bribe rate, which increases equilibrium output. Fiscal decentralization, by strengthening the incentives for local governments to support local business, improves economic performance.

6.2.2 Adding a Central Government

However, the model makes one key omission: It does not include a strategic central government. Suppose instead that the central government can also extract a rate of bribes, $b_c \in [0, 1 - \tau]$, from local business and that it acts strategically. To maintain the parallel as strictly as possible, suppose output in the locality, $Y = f(\tau, b_l, b_c)$, decreases concavely in both the central and local bribe rates, and that the central government also seeks to maximize its total revenues, $R_c = (\tau(1 - r) + b_c)f(\tau, b_l, b_c)$. The local government's maximand is now $R_l = (\tau r + b_l)f(\tau, b_l, b_c)$. It is most realistic to suppose that the two governments set their bribe rates simultaneously – otherwise we would have to believe one could commit to a particular bribe rate, which given the verification difficulties seems unlikely – and so the appropriate solution concept is Cournot-Nash. It seems reasonable to suppose that if $b_c + b_l + \tau \geq 1$, $f = 0$ (i.e., if governments together extract 100 percent of output, no one will produce), so this will never be the case in equilibrium. The first order conditions become

$$b_l^* = -\frac{f(\tau, b_l^*, b_c)}{f_2(\tau, b_l^*, b_c)} - \tau r \text{ and } b_c^* = -\frac{f(\tau, b_l, b_c^*)}{f_3(\tau, b_l, b_c^*)} - \tau(1 - r) \tag{6.5}$$

These define the reaction functions of the two governments, $b_l^*(b_c; \tau, r)$ and $b_c^*(b_l; \tau, r)$.[12] To avoid trivial cases in which one government's

---

then output, and the government's revenue, would be zero.) If bribery did not exist in equilibrium, then increasing r could not reduce bribery.

[12] Because f is concavely decreasing in both b_l and b_c, the second order conditions, $2f_2 + (\tau r + b_l^*)f_{22} \leq 0$ and $2f_3 + (\tau(1 - r) + b_c^*)f_{33} \leq 0$, are also met.

intervention drives the other completely out of the bribe "market" or in which both wish to increase their interventions without bound, I make a few technical assumptions common in similar problems in industrial organization: $0 < b_l^*(0; \tau, r) < b_c^{*-1}(0; \tau, r); \ 0 < b_c^*(0; \tau, r) < b_l^{*-1}(0; \tau, r); |f_2 f_3 - ff_{23}| < 2 f_2^2 - ff_{22};$ and $|f_2 f_3 - ff_{23}| < 2 f_3^2 - ff_{33}.$ The first two state that the bribe rate one government would set if its rival set a rate of zero is positive and lower than the rate it would have to set to drive its rival down to a zero bribe rate. The second two require that the slopes (in absolute value) of the two reaction curves are less than one.[13] These also ensure that the interior Nash equilibrium defined by the intersection of the reaction curves is unique.

How do the equilibrium bribe rates, b_l^* and b_c^*, respond to changes in r? Differentiating the conditions in (6.5) with respect to r, we see that an increase in r will shift the local government's reaction curve, $b_l^*(b_c; \tau, r)$, down, and the central government's reaction curve, $b_c^*(b_l; \tau, r)$, up.[14] The effect on equilibrium bribery then depends on whether central and local bribery are strategic substitutes or complements, as well as on the curvature of f.

If central and local bribery are strategic substitutes (i.e., the reaction curves slope down), increasing r has opposite effects on b_l^* and b_c^* (see Figure 6.1a). It reduces the equilibrium local bribe rate but simultaneously *increases* the central bribe rate. The net effect on output is indeterminate. If local and central bribery are strategic complements (upward-sloping reaction curves), the equilibrium levels of the central and local bribe rates may change in a variety of ways in response to an increase in r (see Figure 6.1b). In fact, the only combination of changes that is ruled out is an increase in b_l^* and a decrease in b_c^*. Output might increase, decrease, or remain the same.[15]

---

[13] This also rules out unstable equililbria. If the absolute value slopes of the reaction curves are greater than one, unstable equilibria may still exist. I discuss these in Treisman (2005) and argue there that the net effect of changing r will still be indeterminate.

[14] Differentiating (6.5) with respect to r, we get $\partial b_l^*(b_c; \tau, r)/\partial r = -\tau f_2^2/(2 f_2^2 - ff_{22}) < 0$ and $\partial b_c^*(b_l; \tau, r)/\partial r = \tau f_3^2/(2 f_3^2 - ff_{33}) > 0.$

[15] The two governments' actions are likely to be strategic substitutes when, as in this example, the governments intervene by extracting bribes. An increase in b_c will decrease f for a given b_l, which one would expect to increase $|\partial f/\partial b_l|$, implying $f_{23} < 0$, and therefore $f_2 f_3 - ff_{23} > 0$, the condition for downward-sloping reaction curves. However, if governments intervene by providing infrastructure, the governments' actions are likely to be strategic complements if central and local infrastructure are complementary.

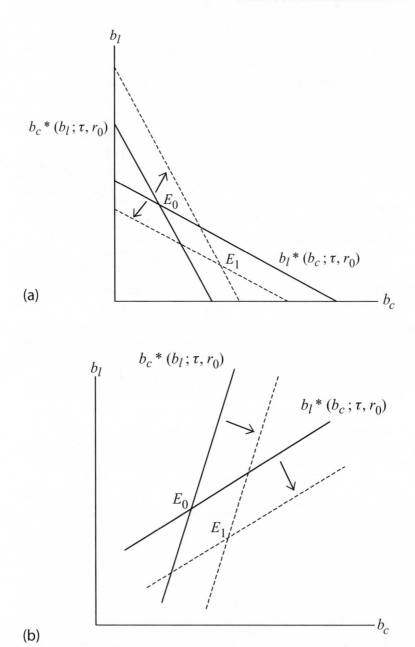

Figure 6.1. Effects of fiscal decentralization on local and central bribe rates. (a) Strategic substitutes: b_l^* decreases, b_c^* increases; (b) strategic complements: b_l^*, b_c^* may increase, decrease, or stay the same.

152

In short, without specifying more about the output function, there is no reason to think the incentive effects of fiscal decentralization would generally decrease – rather than increase – the aggregate burden. Indeed, in one interesting and quite plausible special case, the effects of fiscal decentralization on central government behavior precisely offset the effects on local governments. So far I have assumed the reduced form output function $Y = f(\tau, b_l, b_c)$. However, consider an example in which output is a concavely increasing function of the labor supplied by the locality's resident: $Y = f(l)$; $f' > 0$, $f'' < 0$. As before, the governments share revenues from a tax on output with fixed rate, τ, and each can extract bribes proportional to output. The remaining revenue is consumed by the resident. Taking the tax and bribe rates as given, the resident allocates a fixed time budget, normalized to one, between labor and leisure to maximize his utility: $U = (1 - (\tau + b_l + b_c)) f(l) + v(1 - l)$, where $(1 - (\tau + b_l + b_c)) f(l)$ is the resident's consumption and $v(\cdot)$ is a concavely increasing function measuring the value he places on leisure. The first order condition $(1 - (\tau + b_l + b_c)) f'(l^*) - v'(1 - l^*) = 0$ implicitly defines equilibrium labor supply, $l^*(\Sigma)$, as a decreasing function of the sum of the bribe and tax rates, $\Sigma \equiv \tau + b_l + b_c$.[16] The respective governments simultaneously choose bribe rates to maximize $R_c = (\tau(1 - r) + b_c) f(l^*(\Sigma))$ and $R_l = (\tau r + b_l) f(l^*(\Sigma))$. Their first order conditions are: $f(l^*) + (\tau r + b_l) f'(l^*) l^{*\prime}(\Sigma) = 0$ and $f(l^*) + (\tau(1 - r) + b_c) f'(l^*) l^{*\prime}(\Sigma) = 0$, which when combined define the equilibrium total tax and bribe rate, Σ^*, in a way that is independent of r: $\Sigma^* l'(\Sigma^*) = -2 f(l(\Sigma^*)) / f'(l(\Sigma^*))$. Thus equilibrium labor supply and output are also independent of r. The effect of r on the local government's bribe rate is precisely offset by its opposite effect on the central government's rate.

In general, increasing the local tax share will reduce the aggregate bribe burden and increase output only if $\left| \partial b_l^*(b_c; \tau, r) / \partial r \right| = \tau f_2^2 / (2 f_2^2 - ff_{22})$ is large relative to $\partial b_c^*(b_l; \tau, r) / \partial r = \tau f_3^2 / (2 f_3^2 - ff_{33})$, which implies that $-f_{22} / f_2^2$ must be small relative to $-f_{33} / f_3^2$. So if in the initial equilibrium output is more sensitive to local than to central bribery and less concave in the local than in the central bribe rate, increasing the local tax share will increase output.

The effect of fiscal decentralization on output remains indeterminate even when the model is reformulated in various respects (Treisman 2005).

---

[16] It is easy to see that the second order condition will always be met.

Governments might intervene to extract bribes from firms (discouraging production) or to provide business infrastructure (encouraging it). They might demand lump sum bribes, the same for all, or payments proportional to the firm's revenues.[17] They might be predatory, consuming all tax revenues themselves; benevolent, providing public goods that residents demand; or self-interested but accountable to the voters. Governments might get a higher payoff from bribes (which can be spent without oversight) or taxes (which need not be collected in secret). Local governments might be able to invest in infrastructure more productively than central government. None of these changes would remove the basic indeterminacy of decentralization. One can also derive similar results in models in which the tax rate is endogenous or in which the local governments compete to attract mobile capital (as in Chapter 4).

Finally, I considered a model in which instead of sharing taxes, each level of governmment had the right to set the tax rate on its own separate tax base. If collection and enforcement are perfect, and each government's policies can affect only its own tax base, this will eliminate the externalities examined here. However, if the effects of different levels' policies spill over even a little, the implication for output is uncertain, and formally separating the tax bases might make things even worse than under tax sharing.

In practice, such overlap seems hard to eliminate. Export duties may accrue to the federal budget. But regional regulations – on labor conditions, the environment, minimum wages, and so on – will affect the profitability of exports, so exporters will have an incentive to bribe regional governments to waive them. Residential real estate taxes may belong entirely to local governments. But federal laws – on everything from discrimination to mortgages – will affect house prices. While overlapping taxation and bribery may mostly affect developing countries, overlapping effects of infrastructure investments may loom large in developed ones. Central and local government infrastructure investments will tend to increase many tax bases in parallel. In short, it is hard to separate the fiscal interests of central and local governments neatly enough to eliminate the incentive for opportunism at the other level's expense.

---

[17] One must assume lump sum bribes are distortionary or the argument that reducing bribery increases output makes no sense. Although lump sum levies are often thought to be nondistortionary, paying a lump sum bribe might impose indirect costs if it requires firms to engage in secretive behavior (Shleifer and Vishny 1993).

6.2.3 Summing Up

Increasing subnational officials' stake in tax revenues may reduce their appetite for bribes and embezzled funds and motivate them to invest more in public infrastructure. In countries with tax-sharing systems, the larger the share of revenues retained by local governments, the more they should care about stimulating economic performance. Better fiscal incentives have been said to explain why China grew faster than Russia in the 1990s.

However, even decentralized states have central as well as local governments. If fiscal decentralization motivates local governments to become less predatory, by the same logic it should render the central government *more* predatory. There is no reason to think the net effect will in general be to improve the business climate. In a variety of models, the effect can go either way, depending on the output function. Once again, the impact of decentralization turns out to be indeterminate.

7

Citizens and Government

> In a town-meeting, the great secret of political science was uncovered, and the problem solved, how to give every individual his fair weight in the government, without any disorder from numbers. . . . In this open democracy, every opinion had utterance; every objection, every fact, every acre of land, every bushel of rye, its entire weight. . . . A general contentment is the result. And the people truly feel that they are lords of the soil.
>
> Ralph Waldo Emerson (1903 [1835])

> I wish only to stress a significant, and frequently misconceived, point: decentralization is one thing, democracy is another. The government of Sweden is far more decentralized than the government of New York City, but it is not thereby more democratic.
>
> Irving Kristol (1968, p. 22)

This chapter examines two claims about the way decentralization influences the relationship between citizens and their governments. Since the days of the Greek polis, involvement in public affairs has been thought to develop citizens' political capacities and to cultivate civic spirit. Decentralization has been seen as a way to increase the opportunities for citizens to participate even within large states. A second set of arguments focuses on cases in which, rather than take part in government themselves, citizens control their representatives indirectly by means of the ballot box. Decentralized institutions are said to render officials more accountable to the voters.

7.1 Civic Virtue

An ancient argument contends that human beings realize their true nature, or acquire important values and skills, by helping to govern their communities. Such direct involvement is inevitably limited in most modern states, which contain hundreds of thousands or millions of inhabitants. Political decentralization is seen as a way to make participation possible for as large a share of the population as possible.

The first part of this argument dates to Aristotle. The capacities for practical and theoretical reasoning, according to Aristotle, are what distinguish humans from other animals. To exercise these capacities – and live a life of excellence – requires that one take active part in the processes of government. The notion that involvement in public life develops or liberates the individual was revived during the Enlightenment. In the republic of Rousseau, freedom is exercised by participating in the legislature. The nineteenth-century Prussian reformer Baron vom Stein thought an inclusive political system could awaken the "sleeping energy of passive subjects":

> Entrusting power and responsibility to a man develops his ability: continuous tutelage hampers his development. Participation in public affairs confers a sense of political significance, and the stronger this sense becomes, the greater also grows his interest in the common good and the fascination of taking part in public activities, both of which contribute to a nation's spirit.[1]

In a similar vein, John Stuart Mill argued that allowing the lower middle class a role in government would inculcate a sense of civic responsibility and develop the intelligence of those who had "done nothing in their lives but drive a quill, or sell goods over a counter" (Mill 1991 [1861], pp. 255, 412).

Obviously, in large states not all individuals can find a place in the central organs of decision making. So in the era of the nation-state, the argument evolved into one about decentralization. Devolving authority to local governments would enable more citizens to participate meaningfully at the local – if not the national – level. Thomas Jefferson (1999 [1774–1826], p. 205) saw in this a way to nurture patriotism in the young American republic:

> Where every man is a sharer in the direction of his ward-republic, or of some of the higher ones, and feels that he is a participator in the government of affairs, not merely at an election one day in the year, but every day; when there shall not be a man in the State who will not be a member of some one of its councils, great or small, he will let the heart be torn out of his body sooner than his power be wrested from him by a Caesar or a Bonaparte.

Tocqueville (1969 [1835], p. 70) observed evidence of such effects during his famous North American tour: "With much care and skill power

---

[1] Quoted in Norton (1994, p. 238).

has been broken into fragments in the American township, so that the maximum possible number of people have some concern with public affairs...The New Englander is attached to his township because it is strong and independent...in the restricted sphere within his scope, he learns to rule society." Mill, too, viewed decentralization as a way to extend the opportunities for participation that he thought so important. Local government was, he wrote, "a school of political capacity and general intelligence" (Mill 1991 [1861], p. 417).

This is an attractive argument, eloquently supported by some of the great political thinkers. Still, it merits close examination. Note that the original arguments focused on enabling individuals to serve as local officials or legislators themselves. Modern discussions of political participation sometimes invoke a broader set of activities – petitioning or meeting with public officials, joining political parties, demonstrating, voting, and so on.[2] I will focus on such modes of *indirect* participation first and then return to arguments about direct service in government.

Are there reasons to think citizens would participate indirectly more frequently in a decentralized than in a centralized state? It might seem that local governments would hold more public meetings than a central government, providing greater opportunities for citizens to interact with officials. But there is no clear reason why this would be so. Members of national parliaments are often active in constituency work, visiting local events and meeting their voters. Local field agents of a central government might also hold frequent meetings to discuss administration with those affected. An intelligent central government would instruct its agents to do just this in order to stay informed about local conditions and get advance notice of problems. Even if local governments do not hold more meetings with constituents, one might think that if both local and central governments exist, there will be more officials in total – and so more officials for citizens to contact. But, again, there is no reason to think this would be the case. The center's local agents under centralization may be as numerous as the locally selected officials under decentralization. In any case, citizens' demand for contacts would surely depend on the number and importance of the policy decisions a given government makes, not on the number of officials it employs.

Third, one might argue that citizens care more about the issues of local politics and so will contact local officials or go to local public meetings

---

[2] See, e.g., Page (1991, p. 80).

more frequently than they would involve themselves in aspects of central policy. There are two problems with this. First, it is not clear that citizens do care more about local than national issues. Defense against invasion may obviously seem more urgent at times than, say, the quality of street lighting. Second, the point is irrelevant in any case. Local issues will exist regardless of the system of government. If people mobilize to lobby about local issues under decentralization, they will mobilize to lobby about the same issues under centralization.

A fourth argument is that smaller communities tend to be more cohesive, inspiring greater loyalty and activism on the part of their members. In Rousseau's words: "The more the social bond is stretched, the weaker it becomes" (Rousseau 1986 [1762], Book II, ch. 9). So the desire to participate may be greater in small units because of a more intense sense of belonging. However, this says nothing about the structure of government. Strong bonds of community at the local level may inspire local groups to become politically active, whether in a centralized or decentralized state. This last point gets at a common confusion. Arguments for political decentralization are often really arguments about the value of strong communities, social groups, and self-governing associations – in a phrase, civil society. But a vibrant civil society can exist alongside – and in interaction with – a centralized state. One can believe in the need for autonomous spheres of self-organization and social interaction without insisting that these must occur inside a city hall. Indeed, the autonomy of civil society from government, whether at the central or local level, might be something important to protect.

Finally, certain arguments about indirect participation focus on the act of voting. Some expect voters to turn out to vote in larger numbers in local elections because the chance of any given voter's being pivotal is greater in smaller units (Borck 2002, p. 155). I discuss this argument in section 7.2.2.1 and argue there that: (a) if the stakes in central politics are perceived to be higher – for example, war and peace versus fixing potholes – turnout may still be higher in national elections despite the lower chance of any individual voter's being pivotal; (b) a voter's subjective probability of being pivotal will depend on how evenly split she expects the other voters will be; this may or may not vary with the size of the unit, but it is quite possible voters expect national elections to be more competitive than local ones; and (c) empirically, voter turnout is lower, not higher, at the local level in many countries. Even if local elections have lower turnout, one might still contend that participation is greater in decentralized countries because voters get to vote for local officials as well as for central ones. They get two votes, rather than one. However, especially if these votes are administered together, it is hard to imagine that punching two holes in the ballot instead of one provides a significant boost to civic virtue. Furthermore, if a central government in a centralized state wants to stimulate citizen participation, it can do so in many ways – holding referenda, encouraging nongovernmental organizations to consult with government, or creating incentives for the growth of mass parties.

In short, there does not seem to be a clear, general reason to think citizens would attend political meetings, petition officials, demonstrate for or against government decisions, or turn out to vote more in a decentralized than in a centralized state. I focus, therefore, on the stricter definition of participation as serving as a subnational official or legislator, or taking part in institutions of direct democracy such as the town meeting.

At this point, advocates of decentralized participation run into the problem of numbers. To enable all adults to take part in their own government would require shrinking the units to microscopic size. Imagine a town meeting in which each adult is allowed to speak for ten minutes (Dahl 1998, pp. 106–7). In a village of one hundred adult residents, the meeting would need to last more than sixteen hours to let all participate. To give all Chicago's adult residents a chance to speak, the meeting would need to run for more than forty years without a break. So to allow participation for all, assemblies must become tiny. Dahl and Tufte (1973, p. 70) put the maximum size of a group in which all can participate directly in decision making at around twenty-five to thirty persons. But as one scales down the assembly's size, the issues appropriate for it to decide also become smaller. The dilemma, in Dahl's rendition, is that "for most citizens, participation in very large units becomes minimal and in very small units it becomes trivial" (1967, p. 960). No one has yet found a way to square this circle.[3]

Of course, even in small town meetings, not everyone participates. In fact, most eligible citizens do not. In ancient Athens, probably no more than about 6,000 of some 40,000 eligible male adults usually attended meetings of the assembly, even though attendees were paid for their time. From the sixth to the fourth centuries B.C., the Pnyx, where the assembly usually

---

[3] Dahl (1961) expresses the hope that medium-sized cities (of 50,000–200,000) can provide a setting small enough for citizens to participate but large enough for them to care about the outcomes of politics. This sounds like a search for the elusive golden mean. Dahl's own previous discussion suggests that even in units this small only a small fraction of the citizens could participate meaningfully.

met, could probably have accommodated no more than around 6,000 (Saxonhouse 1993, p. 486). Bryan (1995, quoted in Dahl 1998, p. 111) studied the records of annual meetings in 210 Vermont towns with populations below 4,500 between 1970 and 1994. He found that on average 19 percent of the eligible voters attended, and only 7 percent spoke. This was fortunate because the average meeting lasted only long enough "to give each of its attenders two minutes and 14 seconds of time to talk." Unlike in the seventeenth-century town meeting Emerson imagined, it seems that not *every* opinion had utterance.

Why do more citizens not participate in small groups such as these? Perhaps they find the issues at stake too trivial to be worth many lost evenings. Some are probably alienated by their sense of *in*efficacy in such settings. Jane Mansbridge studied the town meetings in a Vermont town of about 350 adult residents in the 1970s. Although she remained convinced of the value of deliberative assemblies, she uncovered a good deal of evidence that the meetings affected citizens in negative as well as positive ways. She asked town residents in interviews why participation was not higher. People were reticent, her respondents told her, because of fears of being laughed at, ridiculed, gossiped about, or ostracized:

"They're just scared," "scared to death...petrified," "afraid to open up," "afraid...fear or something...no courage." "Some people are afraid to get up and say anything." "They're afraid that others won't like it." Or as Lena Thresher has it, "Everybody's pussy!" (Mansbridge 1983, p. 64)

The inarticulate, the working class, women, and other groups of lower status were particularly intimidated. Some believed that town business was prearranged in any case by powerful members of the community and then merely pushed through the meeting for the sake of appearances. As one respondent complained to Mansbridge: "This small group had gotten together first, and everyone had learned their part, what they were supposed to say, and they swept the budget through the meeting." Another thought insiders deliberately tried to confuse ordinary town members about what it was they were voting for. Others just expressed distaste for the "arguing," "bickering," "petty quarrels," and "fights."[4]

Even if only a minority takes part in such governing assemblies and some of them go home disillusioned or cynical, one might still contend that some

---

[4] Yates (1973, p. 160) also found in his study of city decentralization that "Widespread internal conflict was the dominant characteristic of neighborhood governance."

local participation is better than none. But even this is open to question. It is very possible the three-quarters or more who choose not to participate in town meetings might be better served by – and might prefer – some version of representative democracy. At present, the interests of those too nervous to speak or too overworked to attend are defended by no one.

The alternative to representative government is not decision making by consensus within a circle of friends; the alternative to representative government is *un*representative government (Dahl and Tufte 1973, p. 72). In court cases, the civic competence and public speaking skill of defendants would develop if they were obliged to represent themselves rather than hire a lawyer. But it would seem unreasonable to require this. Is it more just to require that townspeople – even the most inarticulate, overworked, and inexperienced – represent their own interests in the game of local politics? Defenders of direct democracy such as Mansbridge recognize this problem and argue that deliberative assemblies should focus just on those issues where interests are genuinely aligned. They can then help to identify the common interest and how best to pursue it. But because common and particular interests are intertwined in almost every aspect of politics – local and national – it is hard to see how this separation could be achieved in practice.[5]

Another question that advocates of decentralized participation must confront is whether it is true in general that participation in local government – town meetings, councils, or executive bodies – cultivates the civic virtue of citizens. Is public service inherently ennobling? In fact, it seems almost self-evident that the effect of participation will depend on what one participates *in*.

Aristotle did not believe that involvement in just any kind of government developed the virtues natural to human beings. What served this purpose was participation in a particular type of government, the polis. In *The Politics*, he offers no discussion of decentralization within the polis because the ideal polis was to be small enough that all citizens could participate directly in the central organs. As noted in Chapter 1, Aristotle has very little to say (at least in surviving works) about the *demes*, smaller political units that existed within the actual Athenian polity, and he certainly did not advocate decentralizing political authority to them. Nor did he advocate building larger states, with polises embedded in them.

---

[5] For a systematic critique of arguments for popular deliberation, see Sanders (1997).

Mill ties himself in knots on this score. On the one hand, he is enthusiastic about local government's role as a "school of political capacity." On the other, he recognizes that "a school supposes teachers as well as scholars . . . The school, moreover, is worthless, and a school of evil instead of good, if . . . the body is allowed, as it often is, to degenerate into an equally unscrupulous and stupid pursuit of the self-interest of its members" (1991 [1861], p. 417). He accuses local representative bodies of having "a perpetual tendency to become joint-stock associations for carrying into effect the private jobs of their various members" (ibid., p. 419). His remedy is for each local body to contain some of the "very best minds of the locality" who can inspire the lowlier types with their own "more enlarged ideas, and higher and more enlightened purposes" (ibid., p. 418). Where these intelligent and public-spirited individuals will come from, how they will be persuaded to serve, and how they will transform their dimwitted and venal fellow councilors is left to the reader's imagination.

Discussions of local government in the United States have traditionally had a strangely bifurcated character. On the one hand, one finds exuberant praise for the rural townships, on the other almost paranoid gloom about the "shame of the cities." For Jefferson (1999 [1774–1826], p. 214) the townships were "the wisest invention ever devised by the wit of man for the perfect exercise of self-government, and for its preservation." By contrast, the "mobs of great cities add just so much to the support of pure government, as sores do to the strength of the human body" (1998 [1785]). Jefferson even saw a silver lining in the outbreak of yellow fever because this would discourage the growth of large cities that were "pestilential to the morals, the health and the liberties of man" (1999 [1774–1826], p. 28). To Tocqueville, admirer of the New England local governments, America's cities contained "a rabble more dangerous even than that of European towns," which posed "a real danger threatening the future of the democratic republics of the New World" (Tocqueville 1969 [1835], p. 278). Almost a century later, James Bryce drew an equally dramatic contrast between the cooperative democracy of the New England towns and the embezzlement, bribery, cronyism, police corruption, fraud, and violence associated with the city bosses (Bryce 1924, pp. 98–111). Rather than participatory institutions for the cities, Tocqueville recommended "creating an armed force capable of suppressing their excesses" (Tocqueville 1969 [1835], p. 278). One senses that Jefferson would have preferred to raze them.

If Mill is right that local governments differ in quality and that some are "schools of evil" rather than "schools of good," then expanding the role of local governments might either increase or decrease civic virtue. How citizens' characters are shaped by public service will depend on whether the governments in which they serve are, on balance, legitimate, honest, and effective or illegitimate, corrupt, and inefficient. Those who have "done nothing in their lives but drive a quill, or sell goods over a counter" may learn in government to value the public interest and to respect opinions of others. Or they may learn to solicit gifts in brown envelopes and to secure sinecures for their nephews.

Perhaps the best way to interpret Mill's argument, and the argument about decentralization and civic virtue in general, is that in settings in which most citizens are already virtuous, local government service may help train and indoctrinate new generations – at least a few members of them. In states where corruption is common and politics unruly, giving power to local governments will probably just spread these vices to other levels. Within limits and in particular countries, decentralization may cultivate desirable qualities. But we should not assume this will generally be true.

One additional caveat is worth considering. The traditional arguments about decentralization and participation assume that virtues learned in the local arena render the citizen virtuous also in national politics. By participating in his local ward-republic, Jefferson's American citizen is supposed to develop an intense attachment to the freedoms and independence of his country. But what if acts of participation at different levels of the state are not complements but substitutes? What if a citizen's sense of belonging to the national community is actually weakened by a more intense sense of belonging to his city or region? Such phenomena are certainly possible and have been observed in various states (see section 10.1). They constitute one more reason to doubt the general claim that political decentralization increases civic virtue.

7.2 *Accountability*

Political decentralization is often said to increase the accountability of government. Governments are "accountable" if "citizens can discern whether governments are acting in their best interest and sanction them appropriately," rewarding officials who perform well and punishing or replacing those who do not (Cheibub and Przeworski 1999, p. 225). By a politically decentralized system, I mean here one in which local officials are chosen in local elections (appointment decentralization) and can make policy on at least one question without fear of being overruled from above (decision-making decentralization). I contrast this with "centralized" systems, in which there is only a nationally elected central government (perhaps with administrative agents in local districts).

To hold incumbent officials accountable at the ballot box, voters must be able to do two things. They must be able to get accurate information about the government's performance and to coordinate their voting strategies. Both of these are problematic. Decentralization might help in two ways. First, some argue that information or coordination problems are easier to solve in small units, so the more responsibilities are devolved to local governments, the more accountable the system will be overall. Second, others focus not on the size of units but on the number of tiers. When multiple tiers of government exist, different tasks can be assigned to different levels in ways that enable voters to attribute responsibility more precisely.[6]

7.2.1 Informational Advantages

The purported informational advantages of decentralization are the subject of section 9.1, but it is worth considering here several that bear directly on the question of accountability. One common argument holds that local electorates are generally better informed about what their local government is doing than national electorates are about their national government. Why would this be the case? A first version of the argument simply assumes that voters absorb information about local government performance as a byproduct of living in the local community. Voters observe how quickly snow is plowed on their streets and learn about the quality of local schools from their children's experience. A first problem with this is that such inadvertently acquired information may be highly misleading. Each voter will know when his street is plowed but may have no idea how quickly snow is removed on the *average* street. He will learn something about the quality of his children's school, but not necessarily about other schools in the district. Only if the local unit is minuscule will such means of acquiring information

---

[6] Various scholars have argued that the nature of the electoral system – single-member district or proportional representation – will affect the accountability of incumbents (e.g., Persson and Tabellini 2000, Chang 2005, Kunicová and Rose-Ackerman 2005). Because electoral systems at any tier may be of either type, I treat this as orthogonal to the comparison between centralization and decentralization.

be at all reliable.[7] A second problem is that voters can observe central government performance in exactly the same way: They learn from their daily experience whether foreign armies are invading, whether the currency is stable, and whether their Social Security check arrives on time.

In most real political units – both local and national – acquiring accurate information about government performance requires an investment in more systematic monitoring. For voters, such monitoring has qualities of a public good. If monitoring must be financed by voluntary contributions, individual citizens will tend to undercontribute, seeking to free ride on the efforts of others. So the effectiveness of monitoring will generally depend mostly on the efforts of those with some extrinsic motivation, such as investigative reporters or nongovernmental watchdog groups.[8] Monitoring will be more intense where such actors are more numerous and determined. Because more is usually at stake at the central level, or perhaps because national reporters have a larger potential readership, one might expect the media and watchdog groups to be more active in monitoring the *central* than local governments.[9] If so, electorates in national elections should be

[7] And it is not enough for voters to be right "on average," because in the retrospective voting models that capture intuitions about accountability, voters have to agree on the quality of government performance in order to coordinate their strategies.

[8] It might seem that free-riding would be worse in national than in local units because of the larger scale. Olson (1965) argued that the incentive to free-ride in a game of this type increases with the number of players. Subsequent research has shown, however, that there is no general association between group size and public-good provision (see, e.g., Chamberlin 1974). For instance, if players vary in their tastes for the public good, only the one with the highest marginal valuation of the public good will contribute at all in some simple models, regardless of how many other players there are (see Mas-Colel et al. 1995, ch. 12). Even in games where the level of provision does fall with the number of players, contributions often drop to a negligible level when the number rises above just a few hundred. Thus, the difference in contribution level between a national unit and all but the tiniest local units is likely to be insignificant – and monitoring by those with some extrinsic motivation will be most important.

[9] John Stuart Mill argues along these lines that "Far less interference is exercised by the press and by public discussion, and that which is exercised may with much more impunity be disregarded, in the proceedings of local, than in those of national authorities" (1991 [1861], p. 422). He also notes that "the comparative smallness of the interests involved" in local politics leads the public to pay less attention. However, he argues that these defects are outweighed by the direct, personal interest locally elected officials have in the results of local policy and by the problems for central officials of monitoring their local agents. I contend in Chapter 9 that centrally appointed administrators may also have a personal interest in the locality they administer if the center appoints its agents from among local residents (as occurs in many countries). And, except in the tiniest communities, local governments also employ agents and have similar – and not necessarily less extreme – problems monitoring them (recall the discussion in section 3.3.3).

better informed about the incumbent's performance than electorates in local elections.[10] As Riker (1975, p. 157) writes: "In general, one would expect that the greatest interest of the citizens would be centered on that level of government that does the most important things." Opposition political parties may also provide information to voters, although they have obvious incentives to bias their reports. Political competition, by attracting the attention of voters, may also motivate them to educate themselves about the candidates. If this is important, it suggests that the intensity of political competition should affect how informed the voters are. There is no obvious reason why competition would generally be more vigorous at the local or the central level, so this will likely vary from case to case.

A second, more sophisticated argument notes that there will usually be multiple jurisdictions at subnational tiers. In such cases, voters may get a more precise estimate of the competence or effort of their own subnational government by comparing its performance with that of its peers. The subnational governments are constrained by a kind of "yardstick competition." Note the conditions under which this will make voters better off. First, for voters to derive useful information from such comparisons, governments at the same tier must be responsible for the same (or similar) tasks. Second, government performance must depend in part on some attribute of the incumbent, such as competence or effort, that is not observable by the voters (if it were observable, they could simply reelect competent or hardworking incumbents without the need for cross-regional comparisons). Third, governments' performance must be subject to some random shock that is the same (or similar) for all units, but not observable by the voters. (If there were no shock, or if it were observable, voters could deduce their government's competence or effort directly from its performance without making any comparisons. If the shocks were not correlated across units, comparisons would reveal no information.) Fourth, there must be some cost to the voters of voting competent or diligent incumbents out of office – otherwise, the voters would lose nothing by simply rejecting officials whose performance was poor, whether this was caused by incompetence, low effort, or just bad luck.[11]

---

[10] Note that this does not imply one should shift local responsibilities to the central level. If the stakes for voters are typically higher for "central" issues, moving lower-stakes "local" issues to the central level will not make these suddenly more important to voters, prompting voters to become better informed about them.

[11] For the idea of using comparisons to elicit information when there are common shocks, see, for instance, Holmström (1982). On yardstick competition, see, for instance, Shleifer

Where these conditions hold, there may indeed be an informational advantage in assigning public service responsibilities to levels of government at which multiple units exist. The conditions, although quite demanding, do seem likely to be met in various cases. For instance, one might think of comparing the performance of local school boards in districts with similar social and economic characteristics. The "shock" might represent an across-the-board reduction in state-level financing of primary education (if we assume that such cuts are not observable by voters). The school boards where reading scores decline more in response to the funding cut might reasonably be thought to have less competent or diligent staff than those in which reading scores decline less.

Of course, exactly the same is true in a system with completely centralized decision-making authority (so long as there remains administrative decentralization). Suppose all local school boards were appointed by an elected national government. If citizens can compare the performance of school boards that are locally elected, they can also compare the performance of boards that are centrally appointed. So the informational advantage of yardstick competition requires only administrative – not political – decentralization. The real question is whether local electorates can coordinate more effectively to discipline locally elected school boards than to get a central government to discipline its local agents. Various arguments suggest they can. I discuss these in turn in section 7.2.2.

Summarizing, I have identified one argument which suggests that voters will be better informed about the performance of their central government than about that of their local governments (more highly motivated press and watchdog groups at the national level), and one that suggests an informational advantage of administrative decentralization but not necessarily political decentralization (yardstick competition). I have not found an informational advantage for political decentralization.

7.2.2 *Coordination*

Even if one thinks – contrary to the previous analysis – that political decentralization produces a better-informed electorate, this would imply greater

(1985). Besley and Case (1985) apply the idea to decentralized governments. Salmon (1987) and Breton (1996) suggest that voters may also discipline central governments by comparing their performance with that of lower level governments (see section 6.1).

accountability only if decentralization also solves the coordination problems of voters at least as effectively as centralization. Given their information about government performance, voters must be able to agree on a voting strategy that will motivate the incumbent to perform well. A number of arguments purport to show that voters will be better able to coordinate their voting strategies in local than in national elections.

7.2.2.1 Overcoming the "Voting Paradox"   In order to use elections to discipline incumbent officials, citizens must vote. A first argument contends that the incentive to vote is higher in small units, and so accountability will be greater at the local level.

The argument begins from the well-known "paradox of voting" (see, for instance, Mueller 1989). As the size of the electorate increases, the chance of any one voter's being pivotal – that is, determining the outcome – diminishes. Above a certain level, this probability becomes vanishingly small, and if there is any cost to voting (such as that of getting to the polls), the expected utility for a given individual of voting becomes negative. So from a purely self-interested, instrumental perspective, voters should not choose to vote. Of course, if voters do not vote, then elections will not discipline incumbent officials. Some have seen in this a reason to favor decentralization. If the probability of being pivotal decreases as the electorate grows larger, this probability should be highest in local units, which have the smallest electorates. In municipal elections, the chance of being pivotal – and, other things equal, the expected utility of voting – should be greater than in national elections (e.g., Borck 2002, p. 155). Thus, local elected governments should be more accountable than their central counterparts, and decentralized systems – which assign greater responsibilities to local governments – should be more accountable overall.

The argument is quite logical, but there are several reasons to doubt the conclusion. First, even if the probability of being pivotal is higher in local than in national elections, the stakes are often higher in the latter. Whether the country goes to war or suffers from hyperinflation may be more important to voters than how well parks are maintained. If so, the expected utility of voting (the probability of being pivotal times the stakes) may still be higher in the national elections. Second, the voter's probability of being pivotal actually depends not on the size of the electorate per se but on (a) how many others choose to vote, and (b) how evenly split between candidates the others are. In equilibrium, it cannot be that no one votes because then anyone who did would certainly be pivotal. Positive turnout can occur, and the level will depend in a complicated way on the beliefs of each voter about who else will vote (Ledyard 1984). Alternatively, if we suppose voters naïvely assume that a cross-section of the electorate will vote, then they should focus on how evenly divided they think the electorate is. If the national electorate is more evenly split between the two leading parties than the local electorate (for instance, if local populations tend to be more homogeneous in their political sympathies), one would expect higher turnout in national than in local elections.

Third, voters do, of course, participate in elections, in both small and large units, which suggests that some factors other than the atomistic expected utility calculation cause them to vote. And in many countries, turnout in local elections is *lower* than turnout in national elections. This appears to be true in the United States, where in recent decades "turnout in city elections may average half that of national elections, with turnout in some cities regularly falling below one-quarter of the voting age population" (Hajnal and Lewis 2003, p. 646). Milner (2001) found that turnout was lower on average in municipal than in national elections in the U.K., Canada, Ireland, the Netherlands, Denmark, Sweden, and Austria. (In Switzerland, however, municipal turnout was higher than the national level.) Morlan (1984, p. 462) found lower average turnout in municipal elections in Denmark, Finland, Ireland, the Netherlands, Norway, Sweden, the United States, and West Germany.[12] However, among municipalities, turnout increased as the size of the municipality fell in Denmark, Finland, Ireland, the Netherlands, and Germany – although not in the United States and Norway. In the United States, turnout can be extremely low even in very small units. Yates (1973) studied seven experiments in municipal decentralization in New York and New Haven in the 1960s and found that only in block associations of a few hundred members was participation widespread. In neighborhoods of 10,000 or more residents, "citizen participation rarely exceeded the 5–10 percent range in neighborhood elections" (1973, p. 159). In short, there is not much reason to think that decentralization – except, perhaps, to the tiniest of units – increases voter turnout, and in many cases it seems to decrease it.

7.2.2.2 *Clarity of Policy Responsibilities*

One problem for voters in coordinating to use their votes to discipline incumbents is that each

[12] The figures were for 1956–79.

government is typically responsible for many different policy areas. As Manin et al. (1999) put it: "Governments make thousands of decisions that affect individual welfare; citizens have only one instrument to control these decisions: the vote. One cannot control a thousand targets with one instrument." How can voters decide whether, in a given election, to punish a given government for its poor performance hiring school teachers, say, or to reward it for its efforts to protect the environment? This suggests another possible argument in favor of decentralization. By increasing the number of tiers of elected government to include subnational levels, one may be able to divide policy responsibilities more clearly among them.

This sounds reasonable, but again there are problems. To start with, if it is true that governments "make thousands of decisions," one cannot split them into thousands of tiers. Perhaps voters can coordinate on a system to aggregate the many actions of government into a few policy areas and vote based on their "average performance" in these. But unless one decomposes government into single-purpose authorities such as school boards, sanitary inspectorates, and dogcatchers, each government will still have multiple responsibilities. Confusion is likely to remain over which issue or issues the voters are focusing on, undermining their ability to discipline the incumbent. In fact, even if one replaces governments with single-purpose authorities, there will still be multiple dimensions on which voters might wish to evaluate them. Does a school board promote diversity? Improve reading, math, or science skills? Purchase supplies cheaply? Keep pupils safe? If voters disagree on the relative importance of these, it will be hard, using a single vote, to impose discipline on any of these dimensions.

Second, even if we suppose there are only as many dimensions of government performance as there are tiers of government in a decentralized state, this does not mean that accountability will necessarily be greater under decentralization than centralization. Increasing the number of tiers of government *might* help clarify policy assignments and reduce confusion. But it could also have the opposite effect. Suppose that in a completely centralized state the central government is responsible for health care and parks. If local governments were created, one could assign health care to the center and parks to the localities. However, it would also be possible to assign joint responsibility for both health care and parks to both levels of government, blurring rather than clarifying responsibilities and making it even harder for the voters to assign praise and blame. Both levels of government could now accuse the other of their own failures, as well as hide behind their multiple responsibilities.[13]

This should not seem fanciful. In a number of decentralized states, the constitution or governing legislation does assign certain policy areas to the joint or shared responsibility of central and local or regional governments.[14] For instance, Schedule VII of the Indian constitution lists a series of policy areas – including economic and social planning, trade unions, administration of justice, criminal law, social security, and education – over which state and national legislatures have "concurrent" authority.[15] Vernon Henderson (2003) examined how policy responsibility was divided up among tiers of government on three issues – primary education, infrastructure, and policing – in countries around the world. As of 1995, out of the forty-nine countries for which data were available, responsibility for primary education was shared between two or more levels in twenty-six; responsibility for infrastructure was shared in thirty-three; and responsibility for policing was shared in twenty-two.[16] Furthermore, the extent of sharing across levels increased during the 1980s and 1990s as the fashion for decentralization took off. As Rodden (2004, pp. 484–6) summarizes the evidence: "Very rarely do central governments fully cede autonomy to subnational governments. In the vast majority of cases, decentralization entails a move from complete central dominance to joint involvement of the center and one or more subnational tier . . . situations in which a single subnational tier is involved in policymaking . . . are extremely rare."

Even when the laws do not blur responsibility, voters often do so themselves, blaming both levels for poor performance on some dimension. Politicians respond by invading one anothers' policy space. The history of federalism in Canada, according to its former prime minister Pierre Trudeau, is one of "sometimes subtle, sometimes brazen, and usually tolerated

---

[13] Dividing policy responsibilities can also create incentives for both levels to shirk, as discussed in section 6.1. If all responsibilities were shared across levels, the state would not meet the definition of decision-making decentralization; but one can imagine a situation in which the local governments have exclusive authority for one policy area, while all others are shared.

[14] Recall sections 2.1 and 5.2.7.

[15] Article 74 of the German Constitution also identifies a list of areas on which the federation and the Länder have concurrent legislative power. For other examples of constitutions that assign policy areas concurrently to central and subnational legislatures, see Malaysia's (Schedule 9, List 3), Russia's (Article 72), and Brazil's (Article 24).

[16] See Henderson's data-set, available at http://www.econ.brown.edu/faculty/Henderson/papers.html (downloaded December 2, 2005).

172

encroachments by one government upon the jurisdiction of the other" (Trudeau 1968, p. 137). In the postwar period, the Canadian central government has become "active in most fields that constitutionally are the sole jurisdiction of the provinces: namely, manpower training and apprenticeship, social services, culture, housing, tourism, and sports and recreation" (Migue 1995–6). In the United States, Morton Grodzins famously compared the country's federal system not to a three-layer cake, in which responsibilities are neatly assigned to different levels, but to a "rainbow or marble cake, characterized by an inseparable mingling of differently colored ingredients, the colors appearing in vertical and diagonal strands and unexpected whirls . . . From abattoirs and accounting through zoning and zoo administration, any governmental activity is almost certain to involve the influence, if not the formal administration, of all three planes of the federal system" (Grodzins 1967, pp. 257–8). Other federal systems apparently employ the same pastry chef. According to German President Johannes Rau speaking in 2002: "The framers of the Basic Law actually wanted a clear delineation of responsibility between the federation and the Länder, one similar to a layer cake. Today, however, the federal system in Germany more closely resembles a marble cake" (Rau 2003, p. 530). In Argentina, Gélineau and Remmer (2005, p. 133) found that voters' assignments of responsibility across provincial and national levels were so unclear as to undermine electoral accountability: "Voters not only blame and reward subnational officials for national performance, but also attribute responsibility for subnational performance to national authorities." Bednar (2005) provides a formal analysis of why different-level governments may deliberately create confusion about their policy responsibilities.

Sometimes, even when full policy-setting authority is given to an elected local government, it remains financially dependent on higher-level governments, creating a *de facto* joint responsibility for the policy area. Or else the central government uses financial leverage to dictate policy. In the early 1980s, the U.S. Congress, recognizing it had no constitutional right to legislate a nationwide drinking age, simply required that states raise their drinking age to twenty-one in order to receive federal highway money. The Supreme Court upheld Washington's right to do so in 1987, and all the states quickly complied (Kincaid 1999, p. 215). It is not clear whom voters should blame in such cases if they disagree with the policy – the central government that applied pressure or the state governments that yielded to it. Complete centralization removes such ambiguities: The central government is responsible for everything. In short, decentralization can either clarify or confuse policy responsibilities, enhancing or reducing the prospect of accountability.[17]

7.2.2.3 Distributive Politics

One common argument contends that local elections control incumbents better than national elections because in the latter each local electorate must join forces with others to be effective. If an elected local official performs poorly, local voters can vote him out of office. But if a local community is dissatisfied with the *central* government, it can vote it out only if joined by voters from other communities.[18] Smart central incumbents will play the communities off against one another, preventing opposition coalitions from forming. If voters are better able to discipline local than central governments, a system that devolves authority to local units should be more accountable.

This argument depends on a particular trick of perspective. The local electorate is treated as a single unit, with a uniform interest to express at the ballot box, while the national electorate is viewed as a composite of many geographical subgroups. Central officials can therefore exploit competition between groups of voters to escape accountability, but local officials – by assumption – cannot. Distributive politics is possible for central governments but ruled out for local ones. It should not be surprising that, by assuming that local officials have a blunter instrument with which to manipulate voters, we constrain them to manipulate less.

This might be reasonable if the assumption were based on observable reality. But it is not. Local governments can always discriminate among their constituents to some degree. They spend more on building and equipping schools and libraries in some neighborhoods than in others. They repair some roads more frequently than others. They set taxes and fees in ways that distribute the burden unevenly. Local governments' ability to discriminate need not even be geographical for them to exploit the competition

---

[17] Powell and Whitten (1993) suggest that when responsibility for policy is shared across several institutions or political actors, voters are less likely to hold the incumbent government responsible for poor economic outcomes. They do not look at decentralization specifically, but they do find that voters punish incumbents less for bad economic performance in bicameral systems where an opposition party controls one house.

[18] See, for instance, Seabright (1996, p. 65): Under centralization "regions and localities no longer have the ability to determine re-election [of the government] individually but must do so in concert with others whose interests may not coincide with theirs"; and Kreimer (2001, p. 69): "there is certainly reason to believe that, for any individual citizen, ceteris paribus, her potential influence on government is likely to be greater at the local than the national level."

among voters. They can evade responsibility by playing off the competition between rich and poor, homeowners and renters, or old and young.

If both central and local governments can exploit competition among groups of voters to drive up their rents, what restrains such opportunism? A believer in decentralization might reply that, while both levels of government can discriminate among constituents, central incumbents will have more groups to choose between. They will be able to target policies to groups both larger and smaller than the local electorate. In itself, however, this should not matter. All that is required to drive the rents of office up to their maximal level is competition among at least three subgroups to get into the winning coalition.[19] So long as a local government can discriminate among at least three subgroups in allocating its budget, these groups will tend to compete their targeted benefits down toward zero.

Working out a model of retrospective voting in which distributive policy is possible suggests two limits on government rent extraction. I spell out the formal basis for the following claims in the appendix to this chapter. The first limit has to do with the nature of the public goods or services that the government provides. In a model that assumes certainty, limits on government rents are greatest when voters care a lot about public goods that are "non-excludable" within the relevant jurisdiction. A public good is "non-excludable" if the costs of preventing additional individuals from consuming the good are very high. If the good is provided for one resident, it is provided for all. Common examples are radio broadcasts – which can be picked up by anyone with a radio receiver – or fresh air, which can be breathed by anyone in the neighborhood. When government services are excludable, incumbents can exploit competition among voters to get into the favored coalition – they can offer benefits selectively to whichever groups sell their votes most cheaply. Under certainty, such competition drives provision of such benefits down toward zero. By contrast, if a publicly provided service is non-excludable, voters may be able to coordinate on a voting strategy that will enforce positive provision of this service.

The second possible limit on government opportunism relates to uncertainty. It might seem strange, given the previous argument, that governments would provide any distributive benefits at all. But of course, they do: Competition even in large units does not reduce such provision to zero. The best explanation is that this follows from uncertainty. If incumbents

---

[19] Assuming certainty; under uncertainty, other constraints on equilibrium rent extraction come into play, but these are not clearly tighter or looser at central than local levels.

are not sure how happy they need to make each group in order to get its vote (or if they are uncertain about how happy particular public services make the group's members), this softens the competition. The incumbents may provide more generous benefits to a broader set of groups in order to insure against the unexpected. The pattern and level of benefits they provide will then depend upon the pattern and extent of their uncertainty. I see no general reason why the pattern of such uncertainty should lead to greater provision of distributive benefits by elected local governments than by an elected central government.

Taking the first point first, the relative accountability of local and central governments may depend in part on whether each provides benefits that are non-excludable within its jurisdiction, and on how highly its electorate values these benefits. It is not hard to think of public goods typically provided by central governments that are non-excludable – or nearly so – for the whole country. Some of these are likely to be extremely important to voters. One example is national defense. If a government defends its border regions, it is simultaneously defending regions in the interior. It is difficult to defend a country's territory without committing to defend all parts of it.[20] Providing standard weights and measures and a common currency are also public goods that, if provided to any citizens, are available to all.

What about local governments? On reflection, most of the goods and services usually provided by local governments seem highly divisible and excludable. The use of schools, hospitals, garbage-collection services, utilities, law enforcement, and so on can all be restricted to certain citizens, or provided at different levels or cost in different neighborhoods. (Note, the question is not whether these services commonly *are* provided in different quantities to different groups but whether they *could be*.) [21] A main road in a city's center might seem valuable to all – except for those who live in the suburbs and rarely go downtown. Buses, trains, and airports obviously provide excludable public services, so governments could charge different

---

[20] It is possible, even here, to imagine a central government's exploiting competition between different border territories – think of a French government in the 1930s deciding whether to fortify its eastern front or its northern beaches. But the reality is that an attacker's goal is usually to occupy the whole country (or at least the capital), and a hostile army will storm whichever point on the border is most poorly defended.

[21] Higher level laws might require uniform provision within localities; but why would the central government wish to pay the cost of passing and enforcing such laws? In fact, the central enforcement of such laws could be seen as a type of distributive benefit provided by the central government to particular local communities – a benefit that theory suggests should be competed away.

access fees to different groups of residents (think of pensioner and student discount cards) or subsidize the fares on certain routes. Even if a local public hospital is prohibited from turning away patients, local government still gets to decide whether to fill it with arthritis specialists or pediatricians. Childless adults will derive no benefit from the latter; the young will get little benefit from the former. As soon as political benefits can be targeted in such ways, competition among groups of voters will weaken or undermine voters' ability to coordinate on holding incumbents accountable.

My sense is that very few of the public services typically provided by local and regional governments are non-excludable within their jurisdictions. Perhaps local weather reports, local public radio broadcasts, and mosquito abatement would fit the bill. Restrictions on airborne pollution may also be non-excludable within a locality, although the inflow of pollution from neighboring regions would complicate efforts to identify the local government's contribution. Other than this, almost all local public spending has a strong distributive component, which makes it very difficult for voters to coordinate to enforce provision. If I am right that the services provided by central government are more non-excludable in general than those provided by subnational governments, this would suggest that voters might be better able to coordinate to discipline central governments than to discipline their subnational counterparts.[22]

In section 7.2.1, I introduced an example of yardstick competition among local school boards. Because the same information could be derived from comparing performance of administratively decentralized units as from comparing performance of elected local governments, I argued that yardstick competition would imply greater accountability under political decentralization only if voters could coordinate better to motivate an elected local school board (to provide educational services in district A) than to motivate an elected central government (to provide educational services in district A). Is this the case? It is clear that under certainty a central government will be able to compete its provision of educational services to district A down to zero. However, if an elected local school board can allocate resources among three schools within locality A (where parents of children in any two add up to more than half of the local electorate), the school board will also be able to compete its provision down toward zero. So only in the tiniest of

[22] Again, this does not imply that one should centralize local responsibilities; the point is that on some issues, elections are an ineffective source of discipline, whether these issues are assigned to central or local government.

communities will the information provided by yardstick competition make greater accountability possible.

Does the analysis incorporating uncertainty suggest that voter coordination would be easier or harder at the local level? This depends on whether random shocks in the way public services translate into voter utility are greater – and less correlated across subgroups of voters – at one level than at the other (see the appendix). I see no reason to expect a relationship in either direction. Misperception or incompetence on the part of the policy-implementing bureaucracy might increase such random shocks. But no level of administration has a monopoly on incompetence.

In short, distributive politics greatly complicate the task for voters of coordinating on a strategy to discipline incumbent governments. But such politics occur at all levels of the state. And it does not appear that the effects would generally be worse at one level than at another.

7.2.2.4 *Assignment of Policy Responsibilities – Again*   However, the analysis in the previous section suggests a possible resurrection of the argument about clarity of assignments. In models that assume certainty, it is sometimes possible for voters to hold governments accountable when the relevant government provides a non-excludable public good that a majority of voters value highly. Different public services may be non-excludable at different scales of political unit. For instance, publicly provided weather reports may be non-excludable within a region but of little use to those outside the region, permitting the central government to exploit competition for its meteorological services. In this case, devolving responsibility for weather reports to the regional governments may enable voters to enforce their provision, whereas if the central government did the forecasting, it could play regions off against one another, reducing provision.

This is probably the most compelling argument that decentralization may increase accountability. However, many previously noted problems arise here too. First, as observed in section 7.2.2.2, the fact that in a multi-tiered structure public responsibilities *could* be more rationally assigned does not mean that they *will* be. The argument at best identifies a hopeful possibility. Second, it is in fact just a possibility of a possibility. As in all the previous arguments that involve retrospective voting, multiple equilibria exist. Even if responsibilities were assigned in the most desirable way, voters at each tier might or might not coordinate on the strategies that maximally discipline the incumbent. They might also coordinate on an equilibrium that does not discipline her at all. Third, assuming voters do coordinate on the "best" equilibrium and responsibilities are optimally assigned, the potential benefits are limited by the fact that – as discussed in section 7.2.2.3 – few local government responsibilities appear to be non-excludable. Decentralization might make it possible for voters to motivate local governments to provide local weather reports and local public radio broadcasts efficiently. But these are not the main activities that one thinks of in the context of government accountability. Most of the services governments provide have distributive elements that governments at any level can exploit.

7.2.2.5 Loss of Control and Agency Costs – Again

Motivating a government to please the voters is only the first half of the accountability equation. The government must also be able to implement the voters' wishes. At either the central or the local level, they must do so by means of subordinate agents. Not even in the smallest villages does the mayor teach the schoolchildren, operate the health clinic, repair the roads, and collect the garbage himself. In both cases, such relationships may be subject to agency problems: The agents may shirk, distort, or disobey the political official's instructions.

Some have argued that such loss of control tends to increase with the number of tiers of government involved in implementing a policy. As the chain of command lengthens, discipline weakens. I discussed such arguments in Chapter 3. Somewhat surprisingly, I found there was no theoretical consensus on this score. Longer chains of agents may or may not lead to greater shirking or disobedience. The intuition that they would seemed to be based largely on observation of authoritarian states, whose dysfunctional administrative hierarchies might be better explained by the lack of electoral accountability, inadequate transparency, and a lack of constitutional restraints. Under centralized democracy, central incumbents should fear ejection from office if they do not keep their local agents' rent seeking to an acceptable level. As a result, central incumbents should be motivated to obtain the necessary information (by using private survey firms if necessary) and discipline delinquent agents appropriately. Beyond this, one should not underestimate the agency problems that can arise between a city government and the police officers, firefighters, teachers, garbage collectors, and other agents who provide the services for which local governments are often responsible. If such municipal employees are unionized, they may have significant resources to fight the mayor's attempts to make them work as efficiently and cheaply as local voters might like. By contrast, a central

179

government might be able to bargain with such a union from a position of greater strength.

7.2.3 Accountability as Respecting Majority Preferences

So far, I have treated accountability as a matter of effective retrospective voting. Government is accountable to the extent that citizens can obtain accurate information about its performance and vote poorly performing incumbents out of office. Poor performance, in discussions of retrospective voting, is usually equated with the extraction of rents. Accountability is highest when officials' consumption of the budget is kept to a minimum.

This seems to me the most natural way to think about the subject, and the one that is closest to the definition given at the start of the chapter. But one might also take "accountability" to refer to the extent to which – for a given level of rent extraction – the policies enacted by incumbents reflect the preferences of the majority of voters. In this sense, a government that enacts the policies favored by a majority of the voters is accountable; one that enacts policies that the majority rejects is not.[23]

An obvious question, however, is *which* majority? The majority of voters nationwide? Or the majorities within each locality? If the preferences of local and national majorities conflict, it does not seem right to say that a government that favors one over the other is therefore more "accountable." For example, suppose that government policy must declare abortion either legal or illegal in a given jurisdiction, with no finer distinctions. Suppose that the majority nationwide favors legal abortion throughout the country, but in one-third of the local districts a majority favors a ban. Listening to the nationwide majority would mean legalizing abortion nationwide; listening to each local majority would mean banning abortion in one-third of the districts. These outcomes obviously make different sets of citizens happy. One might argue on moral grounds about which majority has a right to make decisions on this issue. But it seems reasonable to say that under centralization (which favors the nationwide majority) and decentralization (which favors the local majorities) government is equally accountable – just accountable to different majorities.

---

[23] For this way of thinking to make sense, there must be a single policy that is most preferred by a majority of the voters within the relevant unit. In the Downsian framework, we need to assume that there is a unique median-voter equilibrium.

Abraham Lincoln fixed on this point in countering the arguments of Senator Stephen Douglas in 1854. Douglas had proposed allowing the residents of Kansas and Nebraska to decide for themselves whether or not to permit slavery. Lincoln argued that this should be decided by the federal government. "What better moral right," asked Lincoln, "have thirty-one citizens of Nebraska to say that the thirty-second shall not hold slaves than the people of thirty-one states have to say that slavery shall not go into the thirty-second state at all?" (Nevins and Commager 1992, p. 205). If a majority of citizens may impose their views on a minority within their state, why may not a majority of states impose their view on a minority of states?

In the examples of abortion and slavery, voters cared about not just the policy in their locality but also what policy was implemented in other parts of the country. The logic is somewhat different if voters care only about what the policy is where they live.[24] Instead of the legality of abortion, the policy in question might be the amount of locally funded street cleaning in the district. In such cases, the majority relevant to the question of accountability is clearly the majority within the locality in question. We might say, then, that a government is accountable to the citizens of a given locality to the extent that it provides the level of locally financed street cleaning most preferred by the local median voter.[25]

Would decentralization lead to more accountable government in such cases? It seems reasonable to conjecture that competition at the center would drive candidates for central office to promise each district the level of locally financed street cleaning that the local median voter prefers. Consider the problem within a Downsian setting, and for simplicity assume certainty. Under both centralization and decentralization, the central government can redistribute income among local districts and provide national public goods. If there is a unique program of redistribution and national public good provision that maximizes a central candidate's probability of election, both central candidates will choose this program in equilibrium under either centralization or decentralization.[26] Given this program, candidates – whether local or central – are judged on how they promise to provide local public goods, which, given the center's income redistribution, must be paid for by taxes in the recipient locality.

---

[24] This distinction was already noted in section 4.1.3 and turns out to be important in the discussion of policy experimentation in Chapter 9.

[25] Of course, assuming there is a Condorcet winner.

[26] I must assume also that each voter's preferences over central public goods and private income are separable from their preferences over local public goods.

Under decentralization, in each locality two identical candidates compete for office by promising a balanced-budget vector of local public goods and tax rates. Assuming a median voter equilibrium exists, both candidates in each locality promise the vector most preferred by the local median voter. Government is fully accountable. Under centralization, the two identical candidates offer packages of balanced-budget vectors of local public goods and tax rates, one for each locality. (We have already fixed the income distribution, so budgets must balance.) In equilibrium, each will offer the program in each locality that is preferred by its median voter, resulting in the same outcome as under decentralization.

To see this, consider the following logic. Call the package of local policies consisting of those policies most preferred by the median voter in each locality "m." Suppose one candidate offered m, but the other offered a package that coincided with m in all but one locality – call it v – and offered some other policy in v. In all localities other than v, voters would be indifferent between the candidates, and the expected vote share for each would be 50 percent. In v, the candidate offering m would win at least a bare majority. His expected total nationwide would be greater than 50 percent. Thus, given that one candidate offers m, the other cannot do better by deviating from m in one locality. (The same can be shown for any number of localities.) It is easy to see, also, that if one candidate offers any policy other than m, the other candidate can always expect to defeat it by offering m.[27] Again, government is fully accountable.

In short, under some plausible conditions, electoral competition drives governments to choose the same local policies under centralization and decentralization – those most preferred by the local median voters. They are equally accountable.

7.2.4 Career Incentives for Officials

In a politically decentralized system, local elected officials may hope to run for national office later in their careers. This may motivate them to serve their local constituents effectively in order to acquire a reputation for probity and competence. In the United States, every second state governor harbors thoughts of running for president, and many past presidents learned the art of governing in one of the fifty state capitals. In other countries, the

---

[27] Laffont and Zantman (2002) develop a model along these lines, focusing on the motivation of governments to acquire information. I work out a version of this model in section 9.1.3.

job of mayor of the capital city is sometimes a springboard to higher office, as shown for instance by the late career of mayor Jacques Chirac of Paris. Even centrally appointed local administrators in a centralized state might acquire good or bad reputations for competence that could help or hinder bids for high elective office. But the incentives are likely to be strongest when local units have elected leaders with wide-ranging responsibilities comparable to those of a national leader. In the case of subordinate agents, responsibility for both administrative successes and failures will lie largely with the central decision makers rather than with local implementers, so voters will not give them so much credit.

Roger Myerson (2006) presents a model that captures this logic. Public office at the local level serves in part as a screening device and setting for officials to establish reputations that they can then exploit in national electoral competition. Public officials are of two types; most are self-interested and maximize their own utility subject to the constraint imposed by the voters' reelection strategy, but there is a small probability that a given official is inherently "virtuous" and maximizes the voters' payoff. Under unitary democracy, the only election held is for a national leader. Myerson shows that there are many equilibria, ranging from one in which the incumbent acts completely virtuously to one in which he acts completely corruptly. Myerson then analyzes a "federal" system, in which elections occur at both the central and provincial levels. There are equilibria in which voters correctly expect all officials at one level to act corruptly and all at the other level to act virtuously. However, Myerson proves that if there are self-interested incumbents at both central and provincial levels it will not be an equilibrium for the officials to act corruptly at both levels simultaneously. Federalism – by giving provincial officials a motive to build a good reputation – thus precludes the worst equilibrium possible under unitary democracy. Myerson argues that this feature of federal democracy will be particularly important in transitional democracies, where voters may start out pessimistic and few politicians will begin the game with reputations for honesty.

The argument is ingenious and captures a powerful intuition about how political careers progress in various multilevel democracies. But, as Myerson himself notes, there are reasons not to view the argument as too general. First, federal democracy excludes only the very worst equilibrium – perpetual corruption at both levels; some pretty bad ones are still possible. Which equilibrium occurs will depend on prevailing beliefs and the coordination of voting strategies. Second, if local identities are strong, serving the local electorate effectively may not always endear a local politician to the national electorate. Rather than see the candidate as "virtuous," those outside her province may see her as a narrow advocate of parochial interests. If, on the other hand, the local candidate tries to appeal to the national electorate through moderation and magnanimity, she may be punished at the polls by the local voters. Third, if national office usually arrives close to the end of a politician's career, this may create the problems of unraveling that afflict reputational models as the end of play approaches. In the last few rounds of an official's political life, the incentive to preserve a reputation may give way to the urge to "cash in." Thus, local performance may be a poor guide to behavior once the local politician makes it to the big leagues. Fourth, if local officials perform well, the central incumbent will have an incentive to try to claim credit, blurring the allocation of responsibility in voters' minds. Fifth, if a corrupt central incumbent is threatened by competition from local politicians with pristine reputations, this may motivate him to cancel elections. Rather than produce accountable government, this logic of federal reputation building and competition could actually lead to an authoritarian coup. As Myerson points out (2006, p. 22): "the effects of successful democracy, which should make voters want to defend a democratic system, could also make politicians want to undermine it."

7.2.5 Summing Up

On examination, the association between decentralization and accountability seems at best quite weak and contingent. Most of the arguments commonly invoked do not seem compelling. Decentralization could either increase or decrease voters' ability to get accurate information about government performance. Given the level of voter information, decentralization might enhance the ability of voters to coordinate to discipline government on a very limited number of policy areas. The ambition to rise from local to national politics might motivate local elected officials to serve responsibly. It is hard to say much more than this.

Appendix: Modeling Retrospective Voting with Distributive Politics

To explore the arguments made informally in section 7.2.2.3, consider the following simple model of retrospective voting in an indefinitely repeated game, similar to that sketched in Chapter 2. I develop the framework first without – and then with – distributive politics.

Appendix

A.1 No Distributive Politics; Certainty

A single elected official (either central or local) sets policy within a single jurisdiction, inhabited by M residents. He levies a uniform, lump sum tax, t, on all residents and allocates the budget, tM, between spending on a single public good, g, and his own consumption, c. (For simplicity, suppose that the incumbent official has no income other than c.) All residents have the same income, y, which is the same in each period, and there is a maximum tax that can be extracted from any resident, $\bar{t} \leq y$. Benefits of spending on the public good, g, accrue to all voters. The utility of each voter increases concavely in local public good provision and linearly in private consumption, $y - t$: $U = h(g) + y - t$, where $h(\cdot)$ is an increasing, concave function with $h(0) = 0$. For simplicity, suppose the official derives utility only from his own private consumption and is not subject to any tax: His current period utility is $V = c$.

In each period, after the official sets policy an election is held. The incumbent runs against another candidate, who is identical to him from the voters' perspective. To win, the official must get more than half the votes. If voted out, an official can never be elected again; his utility from being out of office is normalized to zero. The official seeks to maximize the sum of his utility from present and future rents, with future utility discounted by a discount rate, $\delta \in (0, 1)$. Thus, the official's task is:

$$\max_{t, c_t} V_t = c_t + p_t \delta V_{t+1} \tag{7.1}$$

subject to the budget constraint, $c_t + g_t = t_t M \leq \bar{t} M$, where the subscript t indexes time period, p_t is the probability of reelection in period t, and δV_{t+1} is the discounted present value of future consumption if the incumbent is reelected. I focus on stationary equilibria, in which both the official and the voters adopt the same strategy in each period, independent of history.

I assume that voters coordinate on a strategy to vote the incumbent out of office if and only if their utility, U, falls below a threshold level, χ.[28] Because the official will be replaced by another identical to him, the voters are indifferent between carrying out the punishment and not carrying it out, and so it is credible. The incumbent will either set $c_t = \bar{t} M$, consuming the whole of taxable income and giving up on reelection, or $c_t = c^*$ where c^* is the solution to (7.1) subject to $c_t + g_t = t_t M$ and $U_t = h(g_t) + y - t_t = \chi$.

---

[28] Banks and Sundaram (1998) show in a similar agency model that adopting a retrospective "cut-off rule" of this type is optimal for the principal (in this case, the voters).

To get the incumbent to choose $c_t = c^*$ and not $\bar{t}M$, voters must set χ such that $c^* + \delta V_{t+1} \geq \bar{t}M$. There will be multiple equilibria. But the voters do best when χ is such that this is met at equality, so

$$c^* + \delta V_{t+1} = \bar{t}M \tag{7.2}$$

Using (7.1), the definition of V_t, and the fact that in stationary equilibrium c^* and V^* are the same in each period, we get that in the stationary reelection equilibrium most preferred by voters:

$$c^* = (1 - \delta)\bar{t}M \tag{7.3}$$

This defines c^*. If taxable revenues are relatively high $-\bar{t}M \geq b_g^{-1}(1/M) + c^* = b_g^{-1}(1/M)/\delta$ – the voters set χ to induce the efficient level of the public good, $g^* = b_g^{-1}(1/M)$, and $t = (g^* + c^*)/M$. If taxable revenues are lower $-\bar{t}M < b_g^{-1}(1/M)/\delta$ – the voters set χ such that $g^* = \bar{t}M - c^* = \bar{t}M\delta$ and $t = \bar{t}$.

A.2 Distributive Politics; Certainty

Now suppose the government can engage in distributive politics. It still provides a non-excludable public good, g, that gives the same utility to all voters. But now it can set different, lump sum tax rates for different subgroups of voters. I normalize the number of voters in each subgroup to one, so the number of subgroups is M. (To keep things as simple as possible, suppose M is odd.) Denote by t_m the (identical) lump sum tax paid by the member of group $m = 1, 2, \ldots, M$. This tax can also be negative, in which case the government pays a net transfer to that group of voters. Thus, t_m stands for the effect of distributive policies on group m. The utility of the member of m is now $U_m = b(g) + y - t_m$. As before, the maximum size of the government budget is $\bar{t}M$.

Suppose, to parallel the previous analysis, that voters in group m set a threshold, χ_m, and vote for the incumbent if and only if $U_m \geq \chi_m$. If voted out, the incumbent is replaced by an identical candidate. Under certainty, the incumbent's equilibrium strategy will be to set policies that satisfy the minimum winning coalition of voters that can be bought most cheaply. This will require getting the support of $(M + 1)/2$ groups. The groups set their thresholds simultaneously, so I look for Nash equilibria in their strategies. As before, there will be multiple Nash equilibria. Suppose the voters are able to coordinate on the equilibrium that maximally restricts the incumbent's rent extraction.

Appendix

Where this "best" equilibrium lies – and how large are the rents it allows the incumbent – will now depend on how highly the voters value the public good relative to cash transfers. If the voters' taste for the public good is sufficiently high ($h_g(\delta \bar{t} M) \geq 2/(M+1)$), then the "best" equilibrium will be the same as in the case without redistribution: Voters restrict incumbent rents to $c^* = (1 - \delta)\bar{t}M$. In this case, voters all set $\chi_m = \chi = h(\delta \bar{t} M)$, and the incumbent sets $g = \delta \bar{t} M$. The voters prefer to receive only the public good and no private consumption. To see that this is an equilibrium, note that given this strategy on the part of voters the incumbent cannot do better than to set $g = \delta \bar{t} M$ and be reelected indefinitely. (His discounted stream of payoffs from reelection: $c^*/(1 - \delta) = \bar{t}M$ equals the payoff he would get if he consumed the whole budget this period and gave up on reelection, $\bar{t}M$.) Because when $g \leq \delta \bar{t} M$ it is at least as cheap for the incumbent to buy a winning coalition by increasing g as it is by lowering groups' net tax rates,[29] he sets the maximum tax rate for all groups in equilibrium. So, given $\chi = h(\delta \bar{t} M)$, it is a best response for the incumbent to set $g = \delta \bar{t} M$ and $c = (1 - \delta)\bar{t}M$. Given that all other voters set $\chi_m = h(\delta \bar{t} M)$, it is a best response for any given voter to do so because her vote will not change the outcome.

So if there is *some* public good that all voters value so highly that all would prefer to have all their income taxed away and spent on this public good, then maximal control over politicians is possible (although not guaranteed because there will be many other equilibria). In this case, the fact that voters compete against one another for distributive policies does not prevent them from coordinating on a strategy to hold the government accountable for efficient provision of the public good.

However, this sounds like a rather extreme case. If voters' taste for public goods is lower – $h_g(\delta \bar{t} M) < 2/(M+1)$ – then the equilibrium with lowest incumbent rents is one in which all voters set $\chi_m = \chi = h(h_g^{-1}(2/(M+1)))$. The incumbent sets $g = h_g^{-1}(2/(M+1))$ and still sets $t = \bar{t}$ for all groups. Rents are higher than when voters' taste for public goods is higher. To see that this is an equilibrium, note that given the voters' strategy, it is a best response for the incumbent to set $g = h_g^{-1}(2/(M+1))$

---

[29] The cost of buying a one-unit increase in utility of all voters via g is (approximately) $1/h_g(g)$; the cost of buying a one-unit increase in utility of a minimum winning coalition of voters by lowering their tax rates is $(M+1)/2$, because the tax paid by each member of the coalition must be lowered by one unit. Recall that the minimum winning coalition contains $(M+1)/2$ groups, each containing 1 voter. Given $h_g(\delta \bar{t} M) \geq 2/(M+1)$ and $g \leq \delta \bar{t} M$, it must be that $1/h_g(g) \leq (M+1)/2$.

and get reelected.[30] Because at $g < h_g^{-1}(2/(M+1))$ the marginal cost of satisfying voters with public spending, $1/h_g(g)$, is lower than the marginal cost of satisfying a minimum winning coalition by reducing its net tax, $(M+1)/2$, the incumbent will again set $t = \bar{t}$ for all groups. Given that all other voters set $\chi_m = h(h_g^{-1}(2/(M+1)))$, each voter cannot do better than to adopt the same strategy.

To see that there cannot be an equilibrium with coordination on a higher χ, suppose there were. The incumbent must prefer reelection, or the voters would prefer a lower χ. The incumbent will prefer to provide some of the utility for groups in his support coalition by reducing their tax rates, because the cost of doing this is lower at the margin than that of providing more of the public good. Thus, he will provide some positive amount of cash $\chi - h(h_g^{-1}(2/(M+1)))$ to each member of each of $(M+1)/2$ groups of voters. But, given this, those outside the support coalition would prefer to have set their threshold slightly lower than χ, thus winning a place in the coalition. This competition drives the value of the cash transfers to zero. So in equilibrium voters cannot coordinate on a χ higher than $\chi = h(h_g^{-1}(2/(M+1)))$. The incumbent sets the maximum tax rate for all.

In this case, voters' weaker taste for public goods works to their disadvantage. Their strong preference for distributive benefits enables the incumbent to exploit competition over such benefits to increase her own rents. Notice, however, that in all cases competition among the groups drives the net tax rate up to the maximum level. The only difference is in how the budget is divided between the public good and the incumbent's rents. Even though no distributive benefits are provided in equilibrium, the possibility of them may reduce the maximum level of public good provision that the groups can enforce.

In sum, when governments can provide distributive benefits as well as a non-excludable public good, the ability of voters to reduce the incumbent's rents (assuming they coordinate optimally) decreases with the voters' relative preference for distributive benefits.[31] The model just presented predicts

---

[30] Given concavity of h and $h_g(\delta\bar{t}M) < 2/(M+1)$, we know that $g = h_g^{-1}(2/(M+1)) < \delta\bar{t}M$. So meeting the voters' requirement leaves the incumbent greater rents than in the previous case, in which $g = \delta\bar{t}M$. But given the level of rents in the previous case, $c^* = (1-\delta)\bar{t}M$, the incumbent already could do no better than to meet the requirement and get reelected.

[31] This analysis differs slightly from that of Ferejohn (1986), which claims that in a model with distributive transfers voters can still constrain the incumbent if they vote sociotropically – that is, if they condition their vote on the statewide level of benefits

that all distributive benefits are competed down to zero. This is an extreme and somewhat unrealistic result. One reason why incumbents might provide some positive distributive benefits has to do with uncertainty (section A.3).[32]

A.3 Uncertainty

How do the results change if we assume some uncertainty? One way to think about this is to suppose that some "noise" interferes with political communications. Politicians are not sure exactly what level of χ voters are coordinating on. Or one might assume uncertainty in how policies are translated into voter utility. Either way, we might say voters in group m vote for the incumbent if and only if $U_m + \varepsilon_m \geq \chi_m$, where as before $U_m = h(g) + y - t_m$, and ε_m is a random shock to group m's payoff, with mean zero, cumulative distribution function $F(\varepsilon_m)$, and probability density function $f(\varepsilon_m)$.

Incorporating uncertainty of this type complicates the picture but does not provide any reason to think that local governments are more accountable than central ones. Such uncertainty has two effects. On the one hand, in a model with just a non-excludable public good, the voters must allow the incumbent greater rents to compensate her for the fact that even if she satisfies the voters' requirement, a negative shock could still get her voted out of office. This reduces the present value of staying in office and increases equilibrium rents. On the other hand, in a model with just distributive benefits – in which, under certainty, competition drives rents to the maximum level – uncertainty gives incumbents an incentive to limit their extraction. By setting $U_m > \chi_m$ for some groups, an incumbent can insure herself against being removed from office by a random shock. The way she insures herself will depend on whether the shocks to different subgroups of the electorate are related. If they are identical, she will still focus on a minimum winning coalition but reduce the level of extraction from its members. If the shocks are independent, she will insure herself better by reducing rents across a broader coalition.

To see the first effect (when distributive politics is ruled out), constrain t to be the same for all groups. The incumbent will either give up on

rather than on their particular benefits. I am not sure why such strategies would be individually rational for the voting groups unless their preference for the public good is extremely strong.

[32] If voters have different relative preferences for the public good, equilibria will depend on the distribution of these preferences. It is not easy to reach any general conclusions.

reelection and consume $\bar{t}M$, or maximize $V_t = c_t + \pi_t \delta V_{t+1}$, where π is the probability that a majority of groups vote for her. Each group, m, votes for the incumbent if and only if $U_m + \varepsilon_m \geq \chi_m$. For the incumbent to prefer reelection to consuming $\bar{t}M$, it must be that in stationary equilibrium $V = c^*/(1 - \pi\delta) \geq \bar{t}M$. Under certainty, it was necessary only that $c^*/(1 - \delta) \geq \bar{t}M$ (recall Equation (7.3)). Because $\pi \leq 1$, the voters must allow the incumbent as great or greater rents under uncertainty as were extracted in the lowest-rent equilibrium under certainty. The most interesting cases are those in which the support of $f(\varepsilon_m)$ is unbounded, so even if the incumbent provides very high utility to voters, there is still a chance she will be voted out: $\pi < 1, \forall g, t$. Given this, the minimum level of equilibrium rents under uncertainty is strictly greater than that under certainty. Thus, in the best equilibrium from the voters' perspective, voters have to allow the incumbent greater rents under uncertainty to compensate her for the risk of being "wrongly" voted out of office.

Consider now the effect of uncertainty when the government can provide only distributive benefits (set $g = 0$). I work out the results for three groups of voters ($m = 1, 2, 3$), because the general principles are the same regardless of the number. The incumbent maximizes $c + \pi\delta V_{t+1}$, subject to $t_1 + t_2 + t_3 = c$. In stationary equilibrium, the incumbent's task reduces to:

$$\underset{t_1, t_2, t_3}{\text{Max}} \frac{t_1 + t_2 + t_3}{1 - \pi\delta} \qquad (7.4)$$

Denote the event that voters in group m vote for the incumbent as "v_m." Now,

$$\pi = \Pr[v_1 \cap v_2] + \Pr[v_1 \cap v_3] + \Pr[v_2 \cap v_3] - 2\Pr[v_1 \cap v_2 \cap v_3] \qquad (7.5)$$

the value of which depends on the way in which the shocks of the different groups of voters are or are not related. Members of group m set a threshold χ_m and vote for the incumbent if and only if $y - t_m + \varepsilon_m \geq \chi_m$.

Suppose first that the shocks are identical, and label the common shock ε. As usual, there will be multiple equilibria; in some, the incumbent is elected, in others she is not. In equilibria with reelection, the incumbent will set $t_m < \bar{t}$ for at most two of the groups. To see this, note first that if the incumbent set $t_m < \bar{t}$ for all three groups, then it would have to be true that $\chi_1 + t_1 = \chi_2 + t_2 = \chi_3 + t_3$. If this were not true – say, $\chi_1 + t_1 > \chi_2 + t_2 > \chi_3 + t_3$ – then v_1 would occur only in cases in which v_2 and v_3 also occurred. Given this, setting $t_1 < \bar{t}$ would be a waste of the incumbent's money – this group's vote is given only when it is not needed. Given $\chi_1 + t_1 = \chi_2 + t_2 = \chi_3 + t_3$, v_1, v_2 and v_3 will all occur in precisely the same cases, so again setting $t_m < \bar{t}$ for all three is redundant. The incumbent can achieve the same probability of reelection by lowering the tax for just two groups. It will be cheapest to choose the two groups with the lowest χ_m. But this means the groups will compete their χ_m's down to the point at which they are indifferent between being in the winning coalition and being outside it. Given risk-neutral groups, they will each set $\chi_m = y - \bar{t} + E[\varepsilon_m] = y - \bar{t}$.

Unlike under certainty, however, this does not necessarily mean that the tax rate for the "winning" groups will be competed up to the maximum level, $\bar{t}$. Even given that $\chi_m = y - \bar{t}$ for the two groups in the winning coalition (call these 1 and 2), the incumbent can increase his probability of reelection by lowering t_1 and t_2 below $\bar{t}$.[33] The decrease in t_1 and t_2 reduces the denominator of (7.4); at the same time, it reduces the numerator. The incumbent trades off the benefit in higher odds of reelection against the reduction in rents received each period in office. As a result, even if the groups set their χ_m's at $y - \bar{t}$, the incumbent may choose not to extract the maximum tax so as to insure himself against a negative shock.

Suppose now that the groups' shocks are not perfectly positively correlated. Then competition among groups of voters is softened because the incumbent can insure herself by seeking to satisfy a larger coalition of groups whose shocks may balance one another out. To see the logic most clearly, suppose the shocks in the three groups are completely independent. As in the previous example, given the levels of the χ_m's, the incumbent trades off the benefit of lower tax rates – which increase the odds of reelection – against the cost in lower rents.[34]

In equilibrium, each group sets its χ_m just low enough to make the incumbent indifferent between, on the one hand, satisfying it and, on the

[33] The probability of reelection is $\pi = \Pr[v_1 \cap v_2] + \Pr[v_1 \cap v_3] + \Pr[v_2 \cap v_3] - 2\Pr[v_1 \cap v_2 \cap v_3]$. Reducing the tax on 1 and 2 does not affect the second, third, or fourth terms on the right-hand side because none of the events in the brackets can hold without v_3 being true, and as already discussed, given the identical shock, even with maximum tax set on 1 and 2, v_1 and v_2 already hold whenever v_3 holds. Starting from $\chi_1 = \chi_2 = y - \bar{t}$ and $t_1 = t_2 = \bar{t}$, and constraining the change in t_1 to equal the change in t_2, we get $\partial\pi/\partial t_1 = \partial[1 - F(t_1 - \bar{t})]/\partial t_1 = -f(t_1 - \bar{t}) < 0$. So lower t_1 leads to higher π.

[34] Given independence of the shocks, $\pi = \Pr[v_1]\Pr[v_2] + \Pr[v_1]\Pr[v_3] + \Pr[v_2]\Pr[v_3] - 2\Pr[v_1]\Pr[v_2]\Pr[v_3]$, and, focusing for example on t_3, $\partial\pi/\partial t_3 = -f(\chi_3 - y + t_3)(\Pr[v_1] + \Pr[v_2] - 2\Pr[v_1]\Pr[v_2]) < 0$.

other, focusing on just the other two groups. Given χ_1 and χ_2, locality 3 sets χ_3 so that:

$$\underset{t_1,t_2,t_3}{\arg\max} \frac{t_1 + t_2 + t_3}{1 - \pi\delta} = \underset{t_1,t_2}{\arg\max} \frac{t_1 + t_2 + \bar{t}}{1 - \Pr[v_1 \cap v_2]\delta} \tag{7.6}$$

and groups 2 and 3 solve analogous problems. The left-hand side is the incumbent's payoff from seeking the votes of all three groups. The right-hand side is her payoff from maximally extracting from group 3 and seeking the votes of 1 and 2. This determines equilibrium values $t_1^*(\chi_1, \chi_2, \chi_3)$, $t_2^*(\chi_1, \chi_2, \chi_3)$ and $t_3^*(\chi_1, \chi_2, \chi_3)$. (There may be more than one solution.) Note that in equilibrium it must be that $(t_1^* + t_2^* + t_3^*)/(1 - \pi\delta) \geq 3\bar{t}$, or else the government would prefer to give up on reelection altogether, in which case the groups would do better to set their χ_m's lower. Because the voters are not perfect substitutes (they insure against different shocks), the incumbent gives up something if she focuses on just a minimum winning coalition. In the equilibrium most favorable to the voters, each group, m, in effect charges the incumbent for the increase in the latter's probability of reelection that the incumbent gets by trying to satisfy the voters of m. And in this case, all three groups will set their χ_m's low enough that the incumbent does prefer to include them in the coalition. Total rents will be lower than under certainty.

I have analyzed retrospective voting with a non-excludable public good and with distributive benefits separately here, in order to identify two opposite effects. It is complicated to combine the two in a model with uncertainty. It appears that, compared with certainty, uncertainty reduces the level of a non-excludable public good that voters can demand from government. But it increases the amount of distributive benefits that governments will provide. We cannot say much more than this in general. The implications – if there are any – for the comparison between centralized and decentralized governments are unclear.

8

![black bar]

Checks, Balances, and Freedom

> But from the point of view of the real, the historical roots of liberal democracy, freedom has rested ... upon the *diversification* and the *decentralization* of power in society. In the division of authority and the multiplication of its sources lie the most enduring conditions of freedom.
>
> Robert Nisbet (1962, pp. 269–70)

> Clearly ... in the United States, the main effect of federalism since the Civil War has been to perpetuate racism ... the claim of the ideologists of federalism that the system strengthens freedom is ... false.
>
> William Riker (1975, pp. 154–7)

One common defense of decentralization is that it helps to protect individual freedom. Advocates make two main arguments to this effect. The first concerns misbehavior by the national government. Under decentralization, powerful local or regional governments can defend individuals against abuses by a central ruler. The second argument concerns misbehavior by local governments. If local officials persecute citizens, the latter can escape by moving to other localities. Because international migration is more costly or difficult, the corresponding safeguard against central government persecution is weaker. I examine both these arguments. The first seems less than compelling because, as Riker points out and as the second argument assumes, what local governments preserve may not be freedom. It may just as well be slavery, indentured servitude, or the abuse of women, children, or ethnic minorities. As for the mobility argument, it requires that local rulers allow their victims to leave. The refuge offered to escaped slaves by abolitionists in the American North was of little service to the vast majority of slaves, who remained in shackles. In any case, mobility solves a problem largely created by decentralization. Unless the central government is equally abusive – in which case crossing state lines will not help much – *centralization* would also constrain the local abusers.

If decentralizing power does not necessarily protect freedom, some argue that it does increase the stability of central government policies. By introducing additional veto players, political decentralization tends to entrench whatever policies are already in place. As a result, decentralized states are slower to innovate. I find this argument valid, although with certain caveats. But from the point of view of the institutional engineer, this does not offer much guidance. Because change can be either good or bad, it is not possible to say in general whether institutions that inhibit it are desirable or undesirable.

8.1 Freedom

8.1.1 Strong Subnational Governments Protect Against Central Abuses

That strong subnational governments can defend individuals from a tyrannical central government was forcefully argued by the American Federalists in the 1780s. In a federal government, Alexander Hamilton reassured his readers, the state governments would "afford complete security against invasions of the public liberty by the national authority" (2001 [1769–1804], p. 282). State legislatures would unmask central government abuses and rouse their citizens to resist, joining forces with the other states.[1]

Madison concurred. When threatened by "ambitious encroachments of the federal government," the state governments would unite to defend one another. Such encroachments "would be signals of general alarm. Every government would espouse the common cause. A correspondence would be opened. Plans of resistance would be concerted" (Madison 1999 [1772–1836], p. 270). Writing later, Madison saw the lack of political decentralization as a reason for the illiberal politics of France under the

---

[1] See also his "Speech on Representation," to the New York ratifying convention, in Hamilton (2001 [1769–1804], pp. 487–95): "The people have an obvious and powerful protection in their own State governments: Should any thing dangerous be attempted, these bodies of perpetual observation, will be capable of forming and conducting plans of regular opposition. Can we suppose the people's love of liberty will not, under the incitement of their legislative leaders, be roused into resistance, and the madness of tyranny be extinguished at a blow? Sire, the danger is too distant; it is beyond all rational calculations."

Directory, where "all power being collected into one government, the people cannot act, by any intermediate, local authorities in checking its excesses."[2]

The arguments were not original to Hamilton and Madison. Montesquieu had included towns along with the nobility and clergy among the "corps intermédiaires" that could prevent a monarch from destroying liberty (Montesquieu 1989 [1748], Part I, ch. 4). Later, Tocqueville also emphasized the importance of secondary associations and suggested that in democracies provincial institutions might play the role of aristocratic bodies in monarchies, holding central "abuses of power in check" (Tocqueville 1969 [1835], p. 192). The greatest danger of abuse in a democracy, he warned, came from the unfettered authority of a tyrannical majority. Municipal and county governments could act "like so many hidden reefs retarding or dividing the flood of the popular will" (ibid., p. 263). Montesquieu's and Tocqueville's association of freedom with the existence of a sturdy undergrowth of autonomous associations and local institutions inspired a tradition of thought represented recently in the work of Robert Nisbet.

American lawyers and judges have taken a liking to such arguments.[3] U.S. Supreme Court Justice Sandra Day O'Connor, for instance, quoted Hamilton's Federalist No. 28 in her opinion in *Gregory v. Ashcroft*.[4] In her words: "Perhaps the principal benefit of the federalist system is a check on abuses of government power ... In the tension between federal and state power lies the promise of liberty." Justice Lewis F. Powell, in his dissenting opinion in *Garcia v. San Antonio Metropolitan Transit Authority*, also argued that a balance of power between the states and federal government served to protect "fundamental liberties."[5]

In a pathbreaking series of articles, Barry Weingast recently cast these arguments in the language of game theory (1995, 1997). He showed that if local governments – or other actors – coordinate to rebel against the central government when it violates the individual liberties of their citizens, this

---

[2] "Political Reflections" (1799), in Madison (1999 [1772–1836], p. 606).

[3] See Kreimer (2001), and the cases he cites.

[4] No. 82–1913, 469 U.S. 528, at 572, 1985.

[5] 473 U.S. 234, 242, 87 L. Ed. 2d 171, 105 S. Ct. 3142 (1985). There is a hint of the veto-players argument in these quotations about the "tension" or "balance" between different-level governments. In section 8.2, I argue that such tensions tend to increase policy stability, but there is no reason to equate preserving the status quo with protecting liberty.

can deter central transgressions. In a repeated game, such strategies of coordinated rebellion may constitute a subgame perfect equilibrium.

The argument proceeds as follows. A set of economic and political rights is clearly defined at the start of the game. Society is divided into two groups. A central sovereign moves first and can either respect or violate the rights of all groups. If both rebel against the sovereign, they can depose him. But if only one rebels, its rebellion fails and it is punished severely. The game is a simple one of coordination. In a one-shot version, there are two pure strategy subgame perfect equilibria. In one, the sovereign transgresses and both groups acquiesce. In the other, which is the focus of Weingast's analysis, the sovereign is deterred from transgressing because he correctly believes that if he did, both groups would rebel. Which equilibrium occurs depends on what A and B think about how the other will react to a transgression.

Weingast develops his argument in a very general context. The groups might represent social factions, ethnic communities, economic interest groups, or political parties. But they could also stand for provincial or local governments, in which case the model captures the logic of Hamilton's and Madison's claims. Would "the State governments . . . afford complete security against invasions of the public liberty by the national authority," as Hamilton argued? Are powerful subnational governments, therefore, an effective bulwark of freedom?

They could be. But there are two reasons to think this need not be the case. First, even if all state governments agree about what constitutes an "invasion of the public liberty," in only one of the two equilibria do they manage to deter transgressions. As Weingast notes, coordination is crucial and depends upon a particular set of shared beliefs. Second, even if the states do coordinate, there is no guarantee they would do so in defense of liberty. I have arbitrarily assumed that all central "transgressions" represent invasions of freedom. But this is to beg the question. It may be subnational governments that are abusive and central government interventions that aim to defend individual liberties. In this case, the ability of states to repel central intervention would protect not freedom but local abuses.

The last point has occurred to various readers of the literature linking federalism to freedom. Kreimer (2001) detects "a peculiarly morbid variety of humor" in the association of "states' rights" with individual liberties in the U.S. context, given the use of "states' rights" arguments to defend slavery, limit Reconstruction, and oppose federal desegregation.

Riker (1975, pp. 154–7) also found this argument "absurd."[6] Historically, the federal courts – and sometimes Congress – have defended individual liberties against violations by the states much more often than the reverse, not just on racial issues but in the areas of "reproductive rights, criminal procedure, civil rights, free speech, and freedom of religion" (Moulton 1997, p. 135). Rather than the states holding back an illiberal center, the federal authorities have repeatedly acted "to limit the exercise of state power against unpopular individuals or groups" (Shapiro 1995, p. 55). In developing countries, too, the focus on checking the power of the central government may miss the point, where "the poor and the minorities, oppressed by the local power groups, may be looking to the central state for protection and relief" (Bardhan 2002, p. 188). In short, subnational governments may not be able to coordinate to defend freedom, and if they *are* able to coordinate, it may not be in defense of freedom.

But things get still more complicated. I have assumed so far that central transgressions harm all the groups. In reality, a central government can usually transgress against one without harming others – and may even share the spoils with the unharmed groups. In the context of decentralization, higher taxes collected from one region can be used to lower the tax on others or provide them with financial aid. This changes the game. Now, in a one-shot version, there are no equilibria in which the groups coordinate to prevent all transgressions. In the best case, one should expect to see asymmetric central exploitation: The central government transgresses against one region, but not the other.

If the game is repeated an indefinite number of times, then the groups may again be able to coordinate to deter transgressions. In a game of this type, the "Folk Theorem" applies, which means that many outcomes could occur in equilibrium (Fudenberg and Maskin 1986). For a sufficiently high discount factor, an equilibrium exists in which all groups rebel in response to a central transgression against any group.

---

[6] Late in life, Riker softened this view. While noting that "for well over half its history federalism in the United States actually meant freedom for some southern whites to oppress blacks, hardly the conventional picture of federalism as freedom," he still concluded, "Taking together all federations in the world at all times, I believe that federalism has been a significant force for limited government and hence for personal freedom" (Riker 1993, p. 26). However, he gives no account of *how* federalism protects freedom. In the previous paragraph, he eliminates the question with a definition: If a central government, such as that of the Soviet Union, ignores the constitutional rights of regions, "then federalism is itself destroyed." Because federal states cannot, by his definition, ignore the rights of regions, of course federal states must be limited governments in this sense.

However, this remains vulnerable to exactly the same criticisms as before. First, the no-transgression equilibrium is just one among many. In all other equilibria, the sovereign transgresses at least some of the time. For example, it remains an equilibrium for the sovereign to abuse both groups in all periods and for both groups always to acquiesce. (Because this is an equilibrium in the one-shot game, the repetition of it is an equilibrium in the repeated game.) Anything from full deterrence to zero deterrence could occur in equilibrium.

Second, as noted, even if the groups coordinated to deter "transgressions," this might defend local abuses rather than individual liberty. Unless we have reason to believe that local governments are generally more liberal than central governments, there is no reason to think an equilibrium in which the local governments "win" will favor liberty more than an equilibrium in which they always "lose." Hamilton's rhetorical claim that the U.S. state governments would "afford complete security against invasions of the public liberty by the national authority" was wrong in both theory and fact.

Finally, even if one did pin one's hopes on this mechanism for protecting liberty, political decentralization is neither necessary nor sufficient for it. It is not necessary because social factions could accomplish the same goal of constraining a central sovereign, as Weingast's interesting discussion of historical examples makes clear. It is not sufficient for the reasons already noted: Local governments might not coordinate on the particular equilibrium that deters central intervention, and if they did, this might deter a central intervention designed to protect – rather than one designed to violate – individual liberties. This mechanism may explain liberal politics in certain periods of U.S. history. But if it does, this is a fortunate accident without general implications. As Lipson (1965, p. 265, quoted in Duchacek 1975, p. 49) put it forty years ago:

Dictatorship can reign at the center; but so can freedom. There can be local tyrannies; or alternately local liberties. Local independence may defy a central dictator; and freedom, centrally-organized, can defeat a local autocrat.

In short, anything is possible.

8.1.2 Interjurisdictional Mobility and Freedom

A second argument focuses on threats to individual freedom that come from illiberal local governments. If local – rather than central – governments oppress their citizens, then it will be easier for the victims to escape by moving to other locations. In Kreimer's (2001, pp. 71–2) words:

A nationally applicable norm is unavoidable short of exile; a state law can be avoided with a moving van. . . . where states adopt different positions on issues of irreducible moral disagreement, the variety of local political regimes gives citizens a choice of the rules they live under that would be unavailable in a centralized system.

As examples, he mentions the Mormon exodus from Illinois to Utah as well as the migrations of African Americans from the Jim Crow South. Similarly, James Buchanan (1995–6) contends that: "The ability of persons to migrate and to shift investment and trade across boundaries serves to limit political exploitation."

The argument is a variation on Tiebout's (1956) notion that mobility can empower citizens in a decentralized state. For problems with such claims, see Chapter 4.[7] But whereas Tiebout, and most of the literature that followed, focused on efficiency, here the subject is protection of individual rights. This opens up additional reasons to question the claims made for mobility.

First, note that, unlike in the standard Tiebout argument, the threat of exit may not cause an abusive local elite to respect minority rights. Indeed, forcing the minority to exit – or eliminating it entirely – may be precisely the goal of the abusive elite. If so, the "ability of persons to migrate" may not serve "to limit political exploitation" any better than the ability of mice to hide may protect them from a cat. The beauty of the Tiebout logic is that citizens do not have to move in equilibrium to discipline their local leaders – the threat of moving should be sufficient. However, if a local leader aims not to maximize economic development but to ethnically purify his region or to enforce a religious orthodoxy, the fear of losing minority members will not impose any restraint.[8]

Even if exit is an option that must be exercised to have value, it may still be worth a great deal. If one can avoid persecution with a "moving van," that is surely better than having to take an airliner. But there are still

---

[7] A significant one in this case is that moving between localities or states is rarely costless. Perhaps migration protects lives and religious freedom, but it rarely protects property rights against determined assault.

[8] An elected leader might even seek to increase his majority by "persuading" supporters of his rivals to move out (Glaeser and Shleifer 2005).

problems. First, migration is not just an option available to individuals – it is also open to groups, including those that repress their members. Such groups can exploit the exit option to preserve their own illiberal practices. If religious dissenters can escape persecution by fleeing into virgin territory – as in the days of the Mormon exodus – the same open frontier will provide safe haven for criminal groups and violent cults. In less developed countries, parents can "move" into states that permit child marriage to marry off their children, before returning to those where such marriages are prohibited (Benson 1941, p. 26). The option for political dissenters to flee into the woods did not increase the liberty of Cambodians much in the late twentieth century. Second, as the example of slavery makes clear, outmigration will help persecuted individuals only if their persecutors permit them to leave. This is not always the case. Either private individuals (slaveowners) or repressive local governments (e.g., agricultural oligarchs with a need for cheap labor) may force individuals to stay because exploiting them provides benefits to the exploiters.

Third, even if individuals can migrate freely, it is only under quite restrictive conditions that the argument implies an advantage for decentralization. If the central government is liberal, one could prevent local abuses by *centralizing* authority. If the central government is illiberal and strong enough to commit abuses even if power is decentralized, then decentralization will not necessarily help. So it is only when the central government is both illiberal and weak (under decentralization) that the opportunities for migration implied by decentralization might protect victimized groups better than centralization.[9]

In short, the protections provided by interregional migration may either fail – if the center is illiberal and able to persecute minorities – or solve a problem that occurs only under decentralization – if the center is liberal but limited, and local governments are abusive. The argument does not establish much of a reason to decentralize. Rather, it suggests a partial remedy for one noted pathology of decentralization – powerful, abusive local governments. In the United States, arguing that African Americans benefited from federalism because of the option to migrate it provided seems a little perverse. Greater centralization would probably have meant that fewer African Americans *needed* to move to protect their basic rights.

---

[9] We must also assume there is at least one locality whose government would not abuse the victimized minority, or there is no point in moving to begin with.

8.2 Policy Stability

There is one aspect of decentralization on which both its critics and advocates often agree. By dividing and subdividing power, decentralization can make it difficult for government to do *anything*. The machinery of a decentralized state can be hard to set in motion; and policies, once in place, are hard to change. The result, some have argued, is an inherent tendency toward conservatism.

The claim that decentralization tends to entrench preexisting policies is an application of the theory of "veto players," formulated recently by George Tsebelis (2002). According to Tsebelis, the stability of central government policies is related to the number of actors "whose agreement is necessary for a change of the status quo," whom Tsebelis labels "veto players" (2002, p. 19; 1995). Other things equal, the more veto players there are, and the greater the divergence in their preferences, the less policies are likely to change in response to exogenous shocks.[10]

Various types of political decentralization may either increase the number of veto players or increase the likely divergence in their policy preferences. Some systems assign subnational governments or their representatives a formal role in central policy making. In Chapter 2, I called this "constitutional decentralization." For instance, in Germany the upper house of Parliament, the Bundesrat, is composed of representatives appointed by the sixteen Land governments. In Russia since 2001, the upper house, the Council of Federation, consists of representatives chosen by the country's regional legislatures or appointed by the regional chief executives. (From 1995 to 2001, the regional governors and speakers of regional legislatures themselves served in the Council.) The original U.S. Constitution assigned the state legislatures the role of appointing federal senators. In all these cases, the upper house could block certain bills passed by the lower house, or at least require that the lower house pass them with a supermajority. Thus, compared to a unicameral parliament, there was both an additional veto player (the upper house) and reason to expect it to have preferences different from those of the lower house (it was formed by subnational governments rather than elected nationwide).[11] Such constitutional

---

[10] The other things that must be equal include the number of policy dimensions and the rules of procedure for public decision making.

[11] I distinguish this type of "constitutional decentralization" – in which subnational governments choose representatives to serve in the central upper house – from "disproportionate geographical representation" – in which seats in the upper house are filled by regional

decentralization should, therefore, increase policy stability compared with systems in which the parliament consists of only one veto player or two with identical preferences.

Another example is also found in Germany (see the discussion in Chapter 5). Before Germany entered the European Monetary Union and adopted the Euro, its monetary policy was controlled by the country's central bank, the Bundesbank. From 1957 to 2002, the procedure for appointing officials to the Bundesbank entrenched regional rights: Nine of the seventeen members of the Bank's policymaking council were the presidents of the Land central banks, who had been nominated by Land governments. These regional representatives outnumbered the eight members nominated by the federal chancellor and ensured the Land governments considerable authority over monetary policy.[12] At least in cases in which the Land governments shared a preference at odds with that of the central government, one would expect greater difficulty changing from the status quo than if policy were made by just central government appointees.[13]

Decentralization may also increase the number of veto players in a second way – by permitting subnational governments to legislate on matters over which the central government also has legislative authority. As noted in Chapter 2, the constitutions of various countries – including India, Malaysia, Russia, Germany, and Brazil – assign authority to legislate on certain policy areas concurrently to both central and subnational governments. In such cases, subnational governments can often enact legislation that – in practice, if not explicitly – contradicts central laws. Depending on how such conflicts are resolved, this may increase the number of veto players. (If both can, in practice, cancel out the innovation of another level of power by passing conflicting law, then in cases of disagreement the status quo is entrenched.)

elections but are allocated to regions not in proportion to their populations. Disproportionate geographical representation is even more common than the type of constitutional decentralization I discuss. It will also tend to create a divergence in policy preferences between the two houses. However, it seems to me that even under disproportionate geographical representation all power could be concentrated at the central level; it does not seem appropriate to refer to this as a type of decentralization.

[12] Since 2002, the Bundesbank's Executive Board has consisted of four members, including the president and vice president, who are appointed by the federal government, and four nominated by the Bundesrat in consultation with the federal government. Information from the Bundesbank's web site, http://www.bundesbank.de/aufgaben/aufgaben_organisation.en.php, downloaded June 8, 2004.

[13] Lohmann (1998) finds evidence that this was the case.

Third, countries where lower-level governments have significant policy responsibilities and autonomy to legislate on certain matters often have more independent judiciaries, with the right to adjudicate between the levels of government and overturn central legislation. As Tsebelis discusses, such independent courts do not necessarily constitute an additional veto player. If the role of judges is just to interpret statutes, then they are not veto players because any ruling can be overturned by new legislation (Tsebelis 2002, p. 226). But if, as in the United States, the federal courts are responsible for interpreting the constitution and cannot be overruled on this except by a constitutional amendment, then they may be an additional veto player. In France, the Conseil Constitutionel can overrule bills on constitutional grounds before they are enacted (ibid.).

However, the procedures for appointing the top judges in many countries reduce the odds that they will have independent policy preferences. Often it is the existing veto players themselves who select the judges, rendering it likely that the median judge will have preferences somewhere in between those of the veto players. Nevertheless, constitutional courts do sometimes take positions that are extreme relative to those of the legislature and executive. This might be because new policy dimensions arise that were not considered when the judges were chosen; because judges' preferences on certain questions were not known; because judges were chosen for competence, not for particular policy preferences; or because the judges are expressing preferences on procedure rather than on the substance of policy (Ferejohn and Weingast 1992). In such cases, the judiciary's preferences will limit the extent of change from the status quo that is possible.

Fourth, a certain type of decentralization may increase the number of actors able to block policies in *implementation*, if not in enactment. Some central governments delegate enforcement of certain policies to subnational actors. In the United States, for example, the federal government often entrusts implementation of environmental laws to the states. In such cases, the subnational actors may be able to block implementation of the central policy, even if they lack the legal right to overturn it. Of course, there are limits to such arguments. If the center can easily reverse the delegation or can monitor and punish subnational actors who fail to implement its policies, then such failures will be – at most – transitory.[14] Such arguments

---

[14] In some cases, central actors may deliberately delegate enforcement of certain legislation to known opponents of the legislation at lower levels in order to sabotage its implementation. Some have suggested that Republican presidents have done so vis-à-vis environmental

apply also in centralized states if the central government has difficulty monitoring its subnational agents. The difference is that politically autonomous subnational governments may have preferences that are further from the central government's than those of the central government's paid agent. Thus, decentralization – in the sense of creating politically autonomous subnational governments – combined with delegation of enforcement by the center may help to entrench the status quo.

These arguments suggest that certain types of decentralization will be associated with a larger number of veto players and a greater divergence in policy preferences among them. Other things being equal, this should make established policies more resistant to change. As Tsebelis notes, the argument builds on ideas expressed informally by a variety of earlier thinkers.[15] There are hints of it in David Hume's blueprint for a "perfect commonwealth," in which "the parts are so distant and remote, that it is very difficult, either by intrigue, prejudice, or passion, to hurry them into any measures against the public interest."[16] Enlightenment political thinkers, from Montesquieu to Madison, sought protection from the politics of the mob in the institutional separation of powers and large country size, which should increase diversity of preferences.[17] Perhaps the most trenchant application to political decentralization came from the nineteenth-century anarchist Pierre Joseph Proudhon (1979 [1863], p. 62):

The federal system puts a stop to mass agitation, to the ambitions and tumults of the demagogues; it is the end of rule by the public square, of the triumphs of the tribunes, and of domination by the capital city. Let Paris make revolution within its own walls. What is the use, if Lyon, Marseilles, Toulouse, Bordeaux, Nantes, Rouen, Lille, Strasbourg, Dijon, and so on, if the Departments, masters of themselves, do not follow? Paris will have wasted its time. Federation is thus the salvation of the people, for by dividing them it saves them at once from the tyranny of their leaders and from their own folly.

regulations passed by Democratic-dominated congresses. Such cases, though, do not represent a case of additional veto players. They represent a surreptitious exercise by one central actor of its veto.

[15] Tsebelis (2002, p. 10) traces antecedents to Livy's *History of Rome*.

[16] Or to hurry them into any measures *for* the public interest, one might add. See "Idea of a Perfect Commonwealth," in Hume (1994 [1752]).

[17] To quote Madison in Federalist No. 51: "In the extended (and compound) republic of the United States, and among the great variety of interests, parties, and sects which it embraces, a coalition of a majority of the whole society could seldom take place on any other principles than those of justice and the general good" (1999 [1772–1836], p. 298). Replace "justice and the general good" with "the status quo," and one has an early statement of the veto players thesis.

Much as Jefferson had some years earlier recommended splitting the U.S. counties into wards, Proudhon (ibid., p. 49) advocates the division and subdivision of power:

Within each federated state organize government on the principle of organic separation; that is, separate all powers that can be separated, define everything that can be defined, distribute what has been separated and defined among distinct organs and functionaries; leave nothing undivided; subject public administration to all the constraints of publicity and control.

Whereas Jefferson's goal was to democratize the state, and Madison's to make it safe for democracy, Proudhon's was actually to dismember it.[18] By multiplying the number of veto players, one could in the end prevent the government from acting at all.

The veto players argument provides a unifying framework within which many aspects of comparative politics can be understood. Unlike most of the theories discussed in this book, it has found some empirical support (see Chapter 11). There are, nevertheless, a few issues to consider in using it to draw conclusions about political decentralization. As Tsebelis makes clear, the association of more veto players with greater policy stability holds *ceteris paribus*. Various other factors must be constant – or at least independent of the number of veto players – for the relationship to hold on average. These other factors include the number of policy dimensions, the preferences of the veto players, the identity of the agenda setter (who makes the proposal that the veto players consider), and the nature of the status quo. If these factors vary across countries, time, and policy contexts in a way that is independent of the number of veto players, then one should observe the predicted relationship statistically in large data sets. But one cannot use the theory to make predictions about particular settings (e.g., whether Britain or the United States will adopt environmental regulations faster to address global warming) unless one has a great deal of additional information about the specific context.

Would *ceteris* be *paribus*? Although it seems reasonable to assume that the other key factors would usually be independent of the number of veto players, one might worry about certain possibilities. Decentralization might introduce additional policy dimensions by focusing attention on geographical redistribution or local issues. For instance, Sabatini (2003, p. 149) argues that in Latin America political decentralization fueled the emergence of

---

[18] See the excellent discussion in Hoffmann (1959, p. 134).

regional parties "oriented primarily around limited agendas and electoral bases." Introducing additional policy dimensions could either increase or decrease the stability of policy, for a given number of veto players. Decentralization might also lead to more frequent changes in the identity of the veto players. Tsebelis (2002, p. 209) argues that, paradoxically, "policy stability leads to government instability." Precisely because governments constrained by many veto players are unable to respond adequately to shocks, they are frequently turned out of office. Thus, although increasing the number of veto players may prevent large changes in policy, it may increase the frequency of small changes, as alternating governments repeatedly adjust policy within the restricted range of what is feasible. We might expect to see such minor zigzags frequently in decentralized polities.

At the same time, only certain types of decentralization increase the number of veto players; others may not increase policy stability at all. Suppose unitary governments at the different levels are assigned non-overlapping policy responsibilities. In this case, the number of veto players on each issue would be one – the same as in a unitary state. (Of course, this leaves open how disputes over the boundaries of jurisdiction would be settled.) If decentralization *does* increase the number of veto players, other mechanisms may also increase the number in unitary states. Indeed, constitution makers might view decentralization and central separation of powers as alternative means to the same end. They might compensate for high centralization in unitary states by increasing the number of central veto players. Philip Williams argued that in the French Fourth Republic, without "local defenses, the wary provincial is the more inclined to insist on checks and balances at the center – achieved in France by subordinating the government to a parliament which, it is reasonably assumed, will be too divided to be capable of oppression."[19] The net effect might be to equalize the number of veto players across systems, making it difficult to sort out empirically the partial effect of decentralization.

In sum, the types of decentralization that (a) assign local governments authority to veto central policies, (b) enable local governments to legislate around central legislation, (c) empower independent judiciaries to adjudicate interlevel disputes, and (d) securely delegate implementation to local governments should – other things being equal – increase the stability of central policies. However, centralized states will also vary on the policy

[19] Williams (1957), quoted in Hoffmann (1959, p. 144).

stability dimension, and other factors may weaken the effect in some decentralized states.

Even if decentralization does reduce change in policies, this is in itself neither good nor bad. The desirability of policy stability depends on what policies are stabilized and what alternatives are precluded. It may prevent reckless mistakes, but it will also block urgent adjustments. To those who think central reforms imperative, the delays and immobilism of decentralized institutions have often seemed dangerous. Harold Laski (1939, p. 367), writing in the spring of 1939, thought the United States could no longer afford the "luxury" of federalism:

It is insufficiently positive in character; it does not provide for sufficient rapidity of action; it inhibits the emergence of necessary standards of uniformity; it relies upon compacts and compromises which take insufficient account of the urgent category of time; it leaves the backward areas a restraint, at once parasitic and poisonous, on those which seek to move forward; not least, its psychological results, especially in an age of crisis, are depressing to a democracy that needs the drama of positive achievement to retain its faith.

By contrast, those who, like Proudhon, start with a deep suspicion of the state tend to like the idea of trussing it up in a girdle of decentralized institutions and constitutional barriers. Even those who see a positive role for state action are sometimes willing to tolerate the delays caused by decentralization in order to prevent greater evils. About the same time as Laski lamented the failures of federalism, Walter Lippmann (1963 [1935], p. 221) took an opposite position:

It is true that if we maintain a limited central government and a federal system of states, progress in good works is slow in that it is necessary to convince each locality that the good works are good. There are many who think that takes too long. But they will do well to remember that if it is a slow business converting each state to good ideas, it is also a slow business converting each state to bad ones. For myself, I would rather wait till Mayor LaGuardia converted New York City to good housing if that means that men like Huey Long have to wait till they have converted forty-eight states to their ideas.

The reason no dictator could seize power in the United States as Mussolini had done in Italy, Lippmann argued, was that there was "no Rome against which an American dictator can march. He would need to march in forty-nine different directions at once" (ibid.).

It might seem that conservatives should therefore favor decentralization, while socialists and liberal activists should prefer centralization. In fact, it is somewhat more complicated. Recall Tsebelis's warning that "policy stability leads to governmental instability." Ultimately, an inability to adapt policy to changing circumstances can even lead to constitutional instability, as crises erode faith in the basic governing institutions. Whereas delays and ineffectiveness may be an inconvenience in peaceful times, they may generate support for revolutionary solutions at more extreme moments, hardly what conservatives would wish for. Or the blocked system may encourage cynical efforts to circumvent the rules. One cause of corruption throughout U.S. history, according to James Q. Wilson, has been "the need to exchange favors to overcome decentralized authority" (Wilson 1970, p. 304). In short, if political decentralization increases policy stability, it is difficult even given a particular set of political values to say – independent of context – whether this is good or bad.

9

Acquiring and Using Knowledge

> Locally elected leaders know their constituents better than authorities at the national level and so should be well positioned to provide the public services local residents want and need.
>
> The World Bank (1999, p. 108)

> I need not dwell on the deficiencies of the central authority in detailed knowledge of local persons and things... but in comprehension of the principles even of purely local management, the superiority of the central government, when rightly constituted, ought to be prodigious... the knowledge and experience of any local authority is but local knowledge and experience, confined to their own part of the country and its modes of management, whereas the central government has the means of knowing all that is to be learnt from the united experience of the whole kingdom, with the addition of easy access to that of foreign countries.
>
> John Stuart Mill (1991 [1861], p. 423)

Two common arguments concern how political decentralization affects the quality of the information on which policies are based. Some see in decentralization a means of incorporating into public decision making the "local knowledge" individuals glean from everyday experience. Others contend that decentralized political institutions stimulate policy experimentation. I consider both arguments in this chapter but find neither to be both general and convincing.

9.1 Information

To some of its advocates, the greatest virtue of decentralization is that it makes for policies that are informed by detailed and specific knowledge of local circumstances.[1] Arguments to this effect come in three forms. Some view information acquisition as essentially a technical problem and claim that local governments have a cost advantage. Others see it as a strategic problem – citizens can conceal facts about their preferences and incomes – and argue that decentralized institutions can better break through local subterfuges. Still others point out that, whatever the nature of the obstacles, governments require some motivation to overcome them. They expect local governments to be more motivated than their central counterparts to seek out information about local tastes or conditions.

9.1.1 Information Gathering as a Technical Problem

Information is often said to be "naturally" decentralized. Local communities know more about their own tastes and resources than a central government does. Therefore, decisions made by local policy makers will be better informed than those made by the proverbial "faceless bureaucrats" in the nation's capital.

Every step of this argument merits careful examination. First, not all types of information are naturally dispersed. John Stuart Mill distinguished between, on the one hand, the "detailed knowledge of local persons and things" and, on the other, the knowledge of "principles" of public management. The first type of information – raw data about local preferences and resources – may be found more often in the relevant local community. But the second – theoretical knowledge about how to *use* the raw data – can be derived only by comparing the record of different governments in a systematic way.[2] To acquire the second type of knowledge, the local data must be brought together so that patterns can be identified and inferences made. For precisely this reason, Mill favored a strong central government that could "collect the scattered rays" of local intelligence, ensure local record keeping and transparency, and derive general lessons from varied local outcomes.

In this section, I will therefore focus on the first type of information – facts about local communities.[3] In an obvious sense, knowledge of

---

[1] In section 7.1, on accountability, I discussed arguments about *citizens'* information about the quality of government performance. Here I focus on the information of *officials*.

[2] See Mill (1991 [1861], ch. 15), and the discussion in Chapter 3.

[3] Another type of "local knowledge" is the inarticulate skill of a pastry chef, cyclist, or concert pianist who cannot transcribe his capacities into written lists of facts or instructions (Polanyi 1967, Oakeshott 1991). One might suppose that local officials also acquire some of this type of nonverbal expertise in the course of their service. But it seems to me that a locally based

individuals' tastes and capacities is naturally decentralized to the individuals themselves. Others cannot directly observe what an individual herself knows from introspection. This insight lay behind Hayek's famous argument about the superiority of market coordination over central planning. Planning would require a great deal of "knowledge of particular circumstances of time and place," Hayek argued. But "the knowledge of the circumstances of which we must make use never exists in concentrated or integrated form, but solely as the dispersed bits of incomplete and frequently contradictory knowledge which all the separate individuals possess" (Hayek 1945).

It might seem tempting to extend Hayek's argument by analogy to posit the superiority of local over central government decision making. However, on inspection, the analogy does not make much sense. Local officials cannot discover the tastes and capacities of their constituents by introspection any more than can central officials. Even if they could, this would not solve the problem of coordination, which was Hayek's main concern: "the 'man on the spot' cannot decide solely on the basis of his limited but intimate knowledge of the facts of his immediate surroundings. There still remains the problem of communicating to him such further information as he needs to fit his decisions into the whole pattern of changes of the larger economic system" (ibid., pp. 524–5). Hayek's argument was not about the territorial scope of political units but about the superiority of the price system over political organization as a coordinating device (as his dismissive allusion in the article to the "states" of termites makes clear). In other writings, Hayek did sometimes seem to favor some decentralization of government, in part in the hope that local governments could be subjected to competition (see Chapter 4), but he was clearly concerned that state or local governments might also interfere with the free market in undesirable ways.[4]

---

field agent of the central government could acquire such proficiency in the art of governing a particular place just as well as a locally elected official in a decentralized order. This would depend on length of service and intensity of involvement.

[4] See, for instance, Hayek (1939), pp. 266–8. In *Law, Legislation, and Liberty*, he suggests that if a central legislature could somehow be limited to making general laws that ruled out favoritism toward special interests, then most "service activities now rendered by central government could be devolved to regional or local authorities." But this would transform "local and even regional governments into quasi-commercial corporations competing for citizens" – that is, something akin to clubs (Hayek 1982, Vol. 3, p. 146). He also has a sentence or two on the benefits of local government competition in *The Constitution of Liberty* (Hayek 1960, pp. 263–4).

Are there other reasons to believe that local governments are, by their nature, better informed about their citizens' tastes and resources than central governments? Many writers simply assume this to be the case.[5] One common intuition is that local officials pick up such information costlessly as a byproduct of living in the relevant community.[6] The mayor of Chicago is more likely to learn relevant facts about his city by accident or as the result of daily life than is an official based hundreds of miles away in the nation's capital. The mayor may notice potholes in the road on his drive to work or find the local public hospital overstaffed when he has his appendix removed.

But there are three problems with this intuition. First, although such accidental learning certainly occurs, it is unlikely to occur frequently enough to make much of a difference.[7] Even in a small town, the mayor will have to make dozens of decisions every day on matters that go beyond his personal daily experiences. Second, such accidental observations may be highly misleading. The potholes on the mayor's route may be smaller than those on other streets. The hospital may shift staff into the mayor's ward to ensure that such an important patient is well attended. Third, to the extent that such serendipitous learning *does* occur, it may also occur for the locally based agent of a central decision maker. If the central government can get the incentives right for its subordinates, it need not decentralize decision-making authority in order to exploit such accidental knowledge. All that is required is local assignment of agents (Tanzi 1996, p. 301). Bardhan (2002, p. 191) also wonders "why a central government cannot procure for itself the same information advantage of proximity through local agents" and notes the use of central *préfets* in France and Italy and *intendentes* in Chile in part for this purpose.[8]

---

[5] J. S. Mill, for one. Various formal models include the better information of the local official or agent among the assumptions (Gilbert and Picard 1996; Gautier and Paolini 2000).

[6] I examined the analogous assumption about *citizens* and local knowledge in Chapter 7.

[7] I am distinguishing between such serendipitous direct observations, on the one hand, and information that arises from communications with local residents, on the other. Local residents have an incentive to misrepresent the facts, and so we need to view the problem of extracting information from their communications as one of mechanism design. I discuss this in the next section.

[8] In Bardhan's discussion, the argument for superior local information reduces to the argument about local accountability: "the main reason why in practice the local government still retains the informational advantage has to do with political accountability. In democratic countries, the local politicians may have more incentive to use local information than national or

Information

If we view information not as something that descends like manna from heaven but as a product that must be generated through costly activity, then we need to ask whether local governments have some cost advantage in this over their central counterparts. Leaving aside for a moment the question of strategic obstacles, there seems little reason to expect that local governments will be able to collect information more cheaply. Both levels of government can contract with private survey firms or analysts to discover the necessary facts. If such firms are unavailable and the government must conduct research itself, the costs may actually be lower under centralization because of economies of scale in designing and organizing such surveys. According to Breton (1996, p. 223): "Casual observation . . . points to economies of scale in polling, canvassing, and consulting and to economies of size in interest groups or demand lobbies that convey information on the preferences of their members."

Some see decentralization as beneficial, even if neither level has a cost advantage in collecting information, because the information does not need to be communicated to the central government. Local governments can use the local information without having to transmit it upward, presumably at some cost. Some also anticipate possible savings in computational costs, because the data processing could be done at local levels.[9] However, if – as is usually the case even in small units – the information collector is not the same person as the decision maker, such communication is inevitable whether government is centralized or decentralized. In either case, the information gatherer must communicate with the decision maker. So the argument reduces to one about whether the cost of physically transmitting information increases with geographical distance.

This will depend on the technology of communication. If communication costs increase with distance, it might indeed be more cost-effective to keep locally gathered information in the localities. However, especially in an age of electronic communications, it is not clear that costs would vary significantly with distance. And keeping information local in this way would preclude the kind of analysis necessary to decipher principles of good government about which Mill is so concerned (there would be no "focus"

provincial politicians, since the former are answerable to the local electorate while the latter have wider constituencies, where the local issues may get diluted." I analyzed this and other arguments about accountability in Chapter 7, and I return to them in section 9.1.3.

[9] I discuss some related arguments in section 3.3.2.

for the "scattered rays of knowledge"). Still, if keeping local information local is more cost-effective, this could be accomplished to a considerable extent under a system of administrative rather than political decentralization. Much technical information necessary for program implementation could remain in the field offices. In making policy decisions, central officials – and local officials, for that matter – would tend to employ highly aggregated summaries of the data and analyses. It is, thus, hard to see transmission costs as a major reason for political decentralization. As for the greater computational costs of central analysis, the center is free to set up in the capital precisely the same information processing system for each locality that the locality would set up for itself (or to station its analysts *in* the relevant locality, if communication costs are a problem as in the previous argument). There may be economies of scale, reducing computational costs when it is done by the center; it is hard to see how there could be diseconomies.

9.1.2 Information Gathering as a Strategic Problem

Of course, acquiring information about citizens' incomes and preferences over public goods is not just a technical operation; it is a strategic problem. Individuals will try to mislead the government if by so doing they can get an outcome they prefer. Two arguments suggest that decentralized institutions help to solve this strategic problem. To see their logic, it helps to formalize the problem they aim to solve.

If public goods must be financed by taxing citizens, and citizens can conceal the size of their incomes or taxable assets, a free-rider problem arises. By underreporting their incomes, citizens pass on the burden to their peers. Imagine a country with $M > 2$ citizens and a single, central government. Each citizen, indexed $m = 1, 2, \ldots M$, has income, y_m, known only to herself. Suppose the government first sets a fixed, proportional income tax rate, $\tau \in [0, 1]$; then all citizens simultaneously announce an income level, $\hat{y}_m$, and pay a tax equal to $\tau \hat{y}_m$, the proceeds from which are used to fund an amount $g = \tau \sum_m \hat{y}_m$ of a single public good that benefits all citizens. Because the voters announce simultaneously, they play Cournot-Nash and take others' announcements as given. Voter m sets $\hat{y}_m$ to maximize her payoff, $U_m = h(g) + y_m - \tau \hat{y}_m$, subject to $g = \tau \sum_m \hat{y}_m$, where $h(\cdot)$ is concave and increasing.

The first order condition for an interior solution implies that in equilibrium $h_g(g) = 1$. In the aggregate, citizens pay tax sufficient to finance provision of the public good at the level that a single citizen acting alone would be willing to finance. This is far below the efficient level, at which $h_g(g) = 1/M$. Because of the free-rider problem, each citizen declares only a fraction of her real income, and the public good is underprovided.[10]

The announcement game is a simple version of a private contribution to public goods game (see, for example, Bergstrom, Hume, and Varian [1986]), with contributions set inefficiently low in equilibrium. Economists have suggested a number of mechanisms to elicit accurate self-reports (Clarke 1971, Groves 1973), although these do not usually get to the first best if budgets must be balanced. Two arguments suggest that political decentralization might help to solve the problem.

First, if local governments use tax dollars more effectively than their central counterparts to satisfy local demands, citizens might be willing to declare more income when subject to local control. This argument appears in a famous memorandum, written for Louis XVI's controller general, Anne-Robert-Jacques Turgot, on the eve of the French Revolution. Convinced that only a radical decentralization of decision-making authority could solve the information problems that were eroding the monarchy's control, Turgot instructed his secretary, Samuel Dupont de Nemours, to draft proposals for reform of France's provincial administration. The memorandum, never delivered to the king because Turgot fell from favor shortly thereafter, diagnosed a free-rider problem like the one just modeled, in which "everyone seeks to cheat the authorities and to pass social obligations on to his neighbors," and in which "[i]ncomes are concealed and can only be discovered very imperfectly by a kind of inquisition which would lead one to say that Your Majesty is at war with your people" (Turgot 1775).

Nemours' memorandum proposed a number of measures. Some of these had little to do with decentralization per se.[11] But it argued that giving local representative assemblies the right to spend some portion of local revenues would motivate taxpayers to cooperate with the authorities. Instead of representing a hostile central power, each local administration "would be on the side of its own fellow citizens" (ibid., p. 104). Consequently, "the tax

---

[10] This is the case whatever the level of τ. I have implicitly assumed that the equilibrium level of g, at which $h_g(g) = 1$, is smaller than the country's entire tax base: $\tau \sum_m y_m$.

[11] For instance, the memorandum suggested making voting power in subnational assemblies proportional to declared income. This mechanism might be effective at getting citizens to declare more of their income. But if so, it could work just as well in a central assembly as in a provincial one.

assessment will be carried out...by the inhabitants themselves, without any difficulty" (ibid., p. 108). As a result of voluntary revelations by the citizens, Nemours suggested, "the kingdom would be perfectly known" (ibid., p. 117).

Could such decentralization solve the problem of information revelation? The argument makes a large assumption that local governments satisfy citizen demands better than central government. In Chapter 7, I questioned whether one can assume this in general. Because Nemours was comparing elected, representative local assemblies with an ineffective and grasping French monarchy, it may have made sense in this context. Given the assumption, Nemours' strategy would attenuate – but not eliminate – the free-rider problem. And it would do this only if the king could find some way to commit himself not to exploit the information thus acquired.[12]

To see this, suppose now that when g and τ are determined in local units, the payoff of voter m is $U_m = \theta h(g) + y_m - \tau \hat{y}_m$, where $\theta > 1$ measures the greater effectiveness of local governments in satisfying voter demands, and the residents are now indexed by $m = 1, 2, \ldots L; L < M$. The first order condition for voters now becomes: $h_g(g) = 1/\theta$. Compared with the equilibrium level of public spending under centralization, $h_g(g) = 1$, g is higher. Because public funds are spent more effectively, citizens do reveal more of their income than under centralization. To a point, Nemours' conjecture is borne out. However, the free-rider problem remains, just to a lesser extent. The efficient level of provision in each district would now be at: $h_g(g) = 1/L\theta$, which implies higher g than that defined by $h_g(g) = 1/\theta$. If the number of citizens in each district is large, the remaining free-rider problem will still be significant.

At the same time, to elicit such information by decentralizing authority, the central government would need to be able to commit not to recentralize and use the knowledge thus acquired to increase taxation. Local residents could hardly be expected to share Turgot's eagerness to see the kingdom "perfectly known." By reporting higher incomes and paying more tax to finance local public good provision, citizens would lay themselves open to greater central government extraction in the future. Only if the central

---

[12] It is interesting that the European country which made the greatest advance in increasing tax revenues in the eighteenth century, England, did so not by decentralizing tax collection to local administrations but by creating a disciplined, effective central tax-collection bureaucracy (see Brewer 1989).

government were somehow precluded from taxing citizens at high rates would this mechanism work.[13]

A second way that decentralization might help elicit information focuses on the revelation of private tastes by location decisions. This is the well-known Tiebout mechanism, discussed in Chapter 4. Tiebout (1956) argued that, just as consumers reveal their preferences by making purchases in the market, citizens in a decentralized system might – under certain conditions – reveal their preferences for public goods and tax combinations by moving between municipalities (Tiebout 1956, p. 422).

In Chapter 4, I reached two conclusions about Tiebout's argument. First, it requires a long list of demanding assumptions that will rarely be met even approximately. Second, even if they are met, the central government in a centralized system could also replicate the mechanism, instructing its local agents to act as if they sought to maximize local property values and paying them accordingly. Some administrative decentralization might be needed (at least until the system reached a stable equilibrium), but no political decentralization is required. If political decentralization elicits information via the Tiebout mechanism, political centralization could do the same.

9.1.3 The Motivation of Governments

Decentralized systems do not have obvious technical or strategic advantages over centralized ones in eliciting information about citizen preferences or resources. But that raises another question. Even if governments under centralization and decentralization have the same tools to extract information and face the same costs of doing so, would local governments under decentralization be more strongly *motivated* to pay these costs?

If local governments were more accountable to local voters, they might care more than their central counterparts about obtaining accurate measures of local preferences. But in Chapter 7, I found there was no convincing reason to think local governments would in general be more accountable.

---

[13] At the time, Turgot seems to have believed the monarchy was already so weakened that creating such subnational legislatures would itself alter the power balance in a way that entrenched their autonomy. Turgot told his friend the Abbé de Véri that "Whatever restraints one might at first impose on these assemblies there is no doubt that, because of their being instituted in every province and of the communications that would be established between them, they would acquire in time a degree of power which would certainly alter the monarchical constitution presently existing." Turgot went on to say that he was "untroubled by this prospect," although he was not sure the young king would be as sanguine about it if he recognized the danger (Cavanaugh 1969, p. 50).

If we allow for multidimensional redistributive policies, a central government could exploit competition among localities to extract greater rents from them. It would not need to bother inquiring about local tastes for public goods. But local governments can also exploit competition among subgroups of local voters to extract greater rents from them. The two types of government are similar in this regard. If one excludes any redistribution, I argued that competition among candidates at the center would motivate them to offer the median voter's preferred local policy in each local district. If one candidate did not do this, a rival could sneak ahead at the ballot box. Similarly, in this context, one would expect the central candidates to compete in each local district to *find out* what policy the local median voter preferred.

To show the logic, I present here an adaptation of a Downsian model developed by Laffont and Zantman (2002) to explore the question of local governments' information gathering. I do not assume as they do that local governments are more effective at eliciting information, because the previous sections found no basis for this assumption. I also leave out externalities, which would give an advantage to centralization, and, like Laffont and Zantman, abstract from any multidimensional redistribution: Under either centralization or decentralization, each locality's local public goods must be financed by means of a proportional income tax that is uniform within that locality.[14]

A state consists of two localities, A and B, each of which contains the same number of voters, indexed $m = 1, 2, \ldots M$, who differ only in their taste for a single local public good (which is non-excludable within the locality). All citizens have the same income, y. Under *centralization*, a single nationally elected official decides levels of provision of this good for each local district, g^A and g^B. Provision in district $n \in \{A, B\}$ is funded by a uniform (nondistortionary) tax, with rate $\tau^n \in [0, 1]$, on income of voters in n. Thus, for each n, the budget constraint is $g^n = \tau^n My$. Under *decentralization*, a separate, locally elected official in each locality sets g^n and $\tau^n \in [0, 1]$ for her district, subject to $g^n = \tau^n My$. The preferences of citizen m in district n are given by: $U_{nm} = \theta_m h(g^n) + (1 - \tau^n)y$, where $h' > 0$, $h'' < 0$, $h(0) = 0$, and $\lim_{g \to 0} h'(g) = \infty$. The parameter $\theta_m \in \{\underline{\theta}, \overline{\theta}\}$, where $0 < \underline{\theta} < \overline{\theta}$, distinguishes citizens with a "high" taste for public goods from those with a "low" taste for them. It is easy to check that this implies single-peaked preferences

---

[14] Excluding multidimensional redistribution in the case of centralization means also excluding interregional redistribution; the model assumes this is possible.

over public good and tax combinations, for any local budget. The value of θ_m is known only to citizen m.

In each election, two candidates compete by promising credibly to implement particular policies after the election. In local elections, the candidates' policies consist of a local public good level and associated budget-balancing tax rate for that locality. In central elections, each candidate's policy consists of local public good levels for each district, along with the local budget-balancing local tax rates.[15] Each candidate cares only about election, which carries a payoff of R under decentralization and $2R$ under centralization (i.e., one R for each locality), which is not funded by the budget.[16] A candidate who loses the election gets 0.

The proportions of citizens with $\theta_m = \underline{\theta}$ and $\theta_m = \overline{\theta}$ in each district are not known. Denote the share with $\theta_m = \underline{\theta}$ in locality n as $s_{\underline{\theta}}{}^n$. I assume for concreteness that all players know that the median voter in each district is more likely to have a high taste for public goods: $p_n \equiv \Pr[s_{\underline{\theta}}{}^n > 1/2] < 1/2$, for $n = A, B$. Following Laffont and Zantman, I model investment in acquiring information as follows. Each candidate can choose to send an agent to investigate the distribution of citizens' preferences. The cost of investigating in one locality is K, and that of investigating in both is $2K$. With probability ξ, a given search in a locality is successful and the agent learns the local distribution of θ_m; with probability $1 - \xi$, he does not obtain any information. Candidates' investments in information are common knowledge, but the results of such information searches are known only to the candidate who conducts them (if these were common knowledge, candidates would never gain any advantage over their rivals by investigating). If a candidate has no information, she acts on the prior that the median voter is more likely to have $\theta_m = \overline{\theta}$.

Consider first the equilibrium in each locality under decentralization. Because the candidates care only about election, they will announce either the policy most preferred by those with $\theta_m = \underline{\theta}$ or that most preferred by those with $\theta_m = \overline{\theta}$. If they have no information, they will choose that most preferred by those with $\theta_m = \overline{\theta}$. If both candidates announce the same policy, each has a 50 percent chance of winning. If they adopt different policies, whichever announces the preferred policy of

---

[15] Because we have abstracted from redistribution, every local budget must balance.

[16] One could also assume that the payoff to national election is greater than $2R$ – for instance, being president might be more than twice as rewarding as being a provincial governor. This would not change the implications of the model.

Table 9.1. *Expected payoffs under decentralization in locality n*

		Candidate 2	
		Search for info	Don't search
Candidate 1	Search for info	$\frac{R}{2} - K, \frac{R}{2} - K$	$\frac{R}{2}(1 + \xi p_n) - K, \frac{R}{2}(1 - \xi p_n)$
	Don't search	$\frac{R}{2}(1 - \xi p_n),$ $\frac{R}{2}(1 + \xi p_n) - K$	$\frac{R}{2}, \frac{R}{2}$

the median voter wins. The expected payoffs to the candidates are shown in Table 9.1.[17]

Solving this, there are two Nash equilibria. If $K < R\xi p_n/2$, both candidates invest in information. If $K > R\xi p_n/2$, neither candidate invests in information. Thus, investment in information occurs only if the cost is sufficiently low, the probability of obtaining information is sufficiently high, the prior probability that the median voter has *low* taste for public goods (i.e., that the default action will get it wrong) is sufficiently high, and the benefit of winning is sufficiently high.

Under centralization, each candidate first conducts any information searches and then chooses the policy in each locality n that maximizes $U_{nm} = \hat{\theta}_n h(g^n) + (1 - \tau^n)y$ subject to $g^n = \tau^n M y$, where $\hat{\theta}_n$ is the candidate's best estimate of the median voter's taste parameter in locality n. If a candidate does not search, if the search is unsuccessful, or if he searches and finds the median voter in n has $\theta_n = \overline{\theta}$, then he maximizes $\overline{\theta}h(g^n) + (1 - \tau^n)y$. If he searches and finds that $\theta_n = \underline{\theta}$, he maximizes $\underline{\theta}h(g^n) + (1 - \tau^n)y$. Each candidate must first decide whether to send agents to investigate in one locality, in both, or in none. Consider first the case in which $p_A = p_B \equiv p_n$. The expected payoffs are shown in Table 9.2.

By comparing the payoffs, it can be shown that if $K < R\xi p_n/2$, the only Nash equilibrium is for both candidates to invest in each of the localities. If $K > R\xi p_n/2$, the only equilibrium is for neither to invest in either. The

---

[17] The expected payoffs are calculated by enumerating the possible outcomes and multiplying the payoff by its probability. For example, the payoff for Candidate 1 in the top left cell will be $R/2 - K$ unless either Candidate 1 gets information and Candidate 2 does not and the median has $\theta = \underline{\theta}$ (which occurs with probability $\xi(1 - \xi)p_n$ and implies a payoff for Candidate 1 of $R - \overline{K}$) or Candidate 1 gets no information but Candidate 2 does and the median has $\theta = \underline{\theta}$ (which, again, occurs with probability $\xi(1 - \xi)p_n$ and implies a payoff for Candidate 1 of $-K$). So the expected payoff for Candidate 1 is: $\xi(1 - \xi)p_n(R - K) + \xi(1 - \xi)p_n(-K) + [1 - 2\xi(1 - \xi)p_n](R/2 - K) = R/2 - K$.

Table 9.2. *Expected payoffs under centralization,* $p_A = p_B \equiv p_n$

	Search in	Candidate 2 0	1	2
	0	R, R	$R(1 - \xi p_n/2),$ $R(1 + \xi p_n/2) - K$	$R(1 - \xi p_n),$ $R(1 + \xi p_n) - 2K$
Candidate 1	*1*	$R(1 + \xi p_n/2) - K,$ $R(1 - \xi p_n/2)$	$R - K, R - K$	$R(1 - \xi p_n/2) - K,$ $R(1 + \xi p_n/2) - 2K$
	2	$R(1 + \xi p_n) - 2K,$ $R(1 - \xi p_n)$	$R(1 + \xi p_n/2) - 2K,$ $R(1 - \xi p_n/2) - K$	$R - 2K, R - 2K$

Table 9.3. *Expected payoffs under centralization,* $p_B < p_A < 1/2$

	Search in	Candidate 2 0	1	2
	0	R, R	$R(1 - \xi p_A/2),$ $R(1 + \xi p_A/2) - K$	$R(1 - \xi p_A/2 - \xi p_B/2),$ $R(1 + \xi p_A/2 + \xi p_B/2)$ $-2K$
Candidate 1	*1*	$R(1 + \xi p_A/2) - K,$ $R(1 - \xi p_A/2)$	$R - K, R - K$	$R(1 - \xi p_B/2) - K,$ $R(1 + \xi p_B/2) - 2K$
	2	$R(1 + \xi p_A/2 + \xi p_B/2)$ $-2K,$ $R(1 - \xi p_A/2 - \xi p_B/2)$	$R(1 + \xi p_B/2) - 2K,$ $R(1 - \xi p_B/2) - K$	$R - 2K, R - 2K$

results – and the equilibrium levels of information seeking – are the same under centralization as under decentralization.

But what if the probability that the median voter has a low taste for the public good differs across the localities? For concreteness, suppose $p_B < p_A < 1/2$. Under decentralization, if $K < R\xi p_B/2$, both the candidates in B search; if $K < R\xi p_A/2$, both the candidates in A search. Under centralization, the expected payoffs are as in Table 9.3. If a candidate invests in just one locality, obviously he will choose A because the probability of finding useful information there is higher.

The results under centralization are exactly those under decentralization. If $K < R\xi p_A/2$ and $K < R\xi p_B/2$, the only equilibrium is for both candidates to search in both localities. If $K > R\xi p_A/2$ and $K > R\xi p_B/2$, both candidates will search in neither. If $R\xi p_B/2 < K < R\xi p_A/2$, then both candidates will search in just locality A. Thus, this model also suggests that centralization and decentralization give political candidates exactly the same incentives to search for information about voters' tastes.

In sum, it does not seem that governments will be more motivated to seek out information about voter preferences under decentralization than under centralization. Rather, the extent of information search at both local and central levels will depend on the value of holding office, the effectiveness of search methods, the prior probability of making a mistake, and the intensity of electoral competition. More generally, the common intuition that political decentralization will lead to better-informed government decision making does not seem to be based on any clear and compelling theoretical argument.

9.2 Policy Experimentation

In 1932, the U.S. Supreme Court was asked to rule on a case concerning the marketing of ice in Oklahoma.[18] The state legislature had introduced a system of compulsory licensing for manufacturers and sellers of ice. Opponents complained that the legislators had been captured by the industry lobby, which – already threatened by the invention of the refrigerator – was just trying to restrict the entry of competitors. Most of the justices agreed. The majority ruled that the statute was an abridgment of market competition and a violation of the Fourteenth Amendment protection against unreasonable regulation.

Justice Louis Brandeis, however, saw a deeper issue of federalism in the case. In one of his most famous dissents, he argued that intervention by the Court would compromise the ability of state governments to seek innovative solutions to their citizens' problems. Because ice was so important to consumers, and "destructive competition" might drive all producers out of business, the state should be given leeway to experiment with new approaches. Other states might then benefit from Oklahoma's discoveries. Federalism, Brandeis suggested, was uniquely suited to such innovation: "It is one of the happy incidents of the federal system that a single courageous State may, if its citizens choose, serve as a laboratory; and try novel social and economic experiments without risk to the rest of the country."[19]

In linking political decentralization to innovation, Brandeis was not saying anything radically new. James Bryce had argued in the 1880s that federalism "enables a people to try experiments which could not safely be tried in a large centralized country" (1888, p. 353, quoted in Oates 1999,

---

[18] This section draws on Cai and Treisman (2005b).

[19] See Brandeis (1932). For a spirited critique of Brandeis's argument, see Greve (2001).

p. 1132). Woodrow Wilson, writing in 1889, also referred to the states as laboratories: "While European nations have been timidly looking askance at the various puzzling problems now pressing alike in the field of economics and in the field of politics, our states have been trying experiments with a boldness and a persistency which, if generated by ignorance in many cases and in many fraught with disaster, have at any rate been surpassingly rich in instruction" (1889, pp. 158–9). Harold Laski in the 1920s thought that federalism engendered a "spirit of experiment," and Justice Oliver Wendell Holmes had expressed similar opinions.[20]

But Brandeis's name has become inseparable from the notion that local political autonomy encourages policy innovation. More than three dozen judges have cited his *New State Ice Co.* dissent in a variety of contexts (Greve 2001). In the Supreme Court, Brandeis's ghost has been summoned to defend letting states set policy on physician-assisted suicide, jury trial procedure, the protection of rape victims, regulation of gas companies, the use of medical marijuana, sex discrimination, and gun-free school zones.[21] The argument is also common in economics and political science. Oates, in his classic work on fiscal federalism, argued that one of the three major benefits of decentralization is that it may "result in greater experimentation and innovation in the production of public goods."[22]

The idea has proved oddly attractive to scholars and politicians from opposite ends of the political spectrum. Today the case that political decentralization encourages local experimentation is often made by conservatives. But in the 1930s it was social progressives, such as Brandeis, who favored allowing the states to try new approaches in economic regulation, while libertarians, such as Friedrich Hayek, argued against such state government experimentation. In the New State Ice case, Brandeis was, of course,

---

[20] See Laski (1921, p. 52). In later life, Laski had second thoughts about federalism, worrying that the complicated division of powers weakened government to the point where it could not compete with the growing power of capitalist corporations (Laski 1939). See Chapter 8. On Holmes, see his dissent in *Truax v. Corrigan* (257 U. S. 312, 1921).

[21] On physician-assisted suicide, see Justice O'Connor's opinion in *Washington v. Glucksberg* (521 U.S. 702, 1997); on jury trial procedure, see Justice Powell in *Johnson v. Louisiana* (406 U.S. 356, 1972); on rape victims, see Chief Justice Warren Burger in *Globe Newspaper Co. v. Superior Court* (457 U.S. 596, 1982); on gas companies, see Justice Robert Jackson's dissent in *Federal Power Commission v. East Ohio Gas Co.* (338 U.S. 464, 1950); on medical marijuana, see Justice John Paul Stevens in *U. S. v. Oakland Cannabis Buyers' Cooperative* (532 U.S. 483, 2001); on sex discrimination, see *Boy Scouts of America v. Dale* (530 U.S. 640, 2001); on guns in school, see Justice Anthony Kennedy in *U. S. v. Lopez* (514 U.S. 549, 1995). These examples are discussed in Althouse (2004).

[22] Oates (1972, p. 12). See also his discussion in Oates (1999, pp. 1131–4).

defending restrictions on market freedom. Hayek (1939, pp. 266–7) complained around this time that in the United States and Switzerland separate regional economic policies were "bringing about a gradual disintegration of the common economic area" and advocated giving the federal government "general restraining powers." He did endorse "desirable experimentation" at the municipal – not state – level because vigorous competition would keep such innovation "within the appropriate limits" (ibid., p. 268).

Why might decentralization stimulate policy experimentation? Some assume that in a centralized system, the government simply cannot differentiate its policies geographically (e.g., Strumpf 2002). Given this, in a country with fifty regions, a centralized government can conduct only one-fiftieth as many experiments per period as local governments acting autonomously. Brandeis seemed to have this in mind; federalism, he wrote, permitted "courageous" states to experiment "without risk to the rest of the country," implying that in the absence of federalism experiments would have to impose risks nationwide. Bryce seemed to assume the same.

In fact, as I argued in section 3.2, central governments in centralized states can enact different policies in different localities, and do so all the time. Moreover, the governments of politically centralized states certainly can and do conduct localized policy experiments. This is true of centralized dictatorships. In the Soviet Union, Leonid Brezhnev authorized regional economic experiments, extending successful ones to other areas,[23] and so did both Mao and his successors in China. It is also true of centralized democracies. In the United Kingdom – usually considered among the most centralized – the government routinely tests policies locally before "rolling them out" nationwide. One 2003 survey identified "well over 100" such pilot schemes conducted in the previous five years and even worried that central authorities might run out of test sites: "With the growth in the number of locations that have been selected as either test or control areas for one pilot or another ... the supply of suitable 'untouched' localities may soon be exhausted" (Jowell 2003, pp. 25, 32). Localized experiments examined the

---

[23] The best-known example is probably that of Georgia under Eduard Shevardnadze in the 1970s. In 1973, in the backward Abasha region, Shevardnadze "regrouped all agricultural institutions into one management association and introduced a new system of remuneration based on a Hungarian model ... The experiment, which resulted in spectacular increases in agricultural production, was extended to other regions of the republic and became the model for so-called RAPOs (agricultural-industrial associations), created at the national level in 1982" (Ekedahl and Goodman 1997, ch. 1). Shevardnadze also experimented with commerce, permitting small, family-run private enterprises.

effectiveness of financial incentives to keep teenagers in school (in fifteen local education authorities), aid to low-income workers (in eight pilot areas), anti-smoking initiatives (in twenty-six health action zones), personal advisers to help poor single parents get jobs (in eight local areas), schemes to improve the real estate market (in Bristol), and treatment and testing sentences for minor drug offenders (in four towns).[24] The locations for these experiments were chosen carefully to ensure appropriate controls or to examine how policies interacted with different local conditions.

Given that localized policy experiments are technically possible in both centralized and decentralized regimes, the real question is whether decentralization provides stronger or weaker incentives for incumbent officials to order them. Strumpf (2002, p. 209) argues that constitutional restrictions such as the U.S. Constitution's "uniformity clause" may prevent central governments from introducing local experiments without the consent of the local communities in question.[25] However, the right of local communities to veto central policies is a feature of *decentralization*, not centralization; the U.S. Constitution is among the most decentralized in the world. Even given this, the requirement that local communities consent could not impose less policy variation under centralization than under decentralization, because any variation that local governments would themselves choose under decentralization could presumably be implemented with local communities' consent under centralization.

So how do the incentives for incumbent officials differ under the two arrangements? Cai and Treisman (2005b) examine this, focusing on democracies. We model electoral competition in centralized and decentralized orders and compare the frequency with which incumbents enact experimental policies in equilibrium in the two cases. Office-seeking incumbent officials and their electoral rivals campaign by committing themselves to a two-period program of policies to be enacted after an election.[26] In each period, they may "experiment" – that is, enact a policy the payoff of which

---

[24] See UK Office of the Deputy Prime Minister (2002), Eley et al. (2002), Jowell (2003, pp. 18–30).

[25] The "uniformity clause" of the U.S. Constitution (Article 1, Section 8,1) requires that "all Duties, Imposts and Excises [levied by Congress] shall be uniform throughout the United States." While limiting regional variation in central taxation laws, it does not require that central expenditures or non–tax-related policies be identical in each of the states.

[26] In an associated paper, we derive similar results under retrospective voting, although then there are certain parameter values under which there is more experimentation under decentralization than centralization.

to voters is not known precisely in advance – or stick to "status quo" policies, the payoff of which is known by all. Under *centralization*, a central incumbent sets policies for each of three localities and to get reelected must win a majority nationwide. Under *decentralization*, a separate local incumbent sets policy in each locality and to get reelected must win a majority within her locality.

We hold everything constant across the two cases except the manner in which the official is elected (i.e., in one district or in three). But this makes a big difference to the frequency of experimentation in equilibrium – and in exactly the opposite direction from the common intuition. Contrary to Brandeis's claim, the basic logic suggests that centralization should lead to more experimentation than decentralization. Compared with the socially optimal program – which maximizes the sum of payoffs to all voters – centralization tends to lead to too much experimentation, while decentralization leads to too little.

Several effects combine to produce this result. First, localized experiments often generate information that is valuable to other districts. Individual local governments will ignore this positive *informational externality*, and so when local governments (or populations) decide whether or not to experiment, the amount of experimentation they choose will generally be socially suboptimal.[27] Local governments will seek to free ride on the discoveries of other districts rather than experiment themselves. A central government, which must win votes in more than one district, would partially internalize the externality, resulting in greater experimentation.

Second, a *risk-taking effect* increases experimentation under centralization. Central governments do not just have more to gain from successful local experiments – they also have less to lose from failed ones. The larger is the government's jurisdiction relative to the size of the experiment, the smaller is the risk that a given failed experiment will prevent the government's reelection. A local incumbent may be sure to lose office if an experiment she conducts in her district fails. But if the country consists of one hundred such jurisdictions, then a failed policy experiment in one jurisdiction would make very little difference to a central incumbent's chance of reelection.

---

[27] Susan Rose-Ackerman, in a pioneering contribution (1980), also identified the informational externality that causes uncoordinated local governments to underinvest in innovations that might benefit other localities, and she noted the potential for wasteful duplication under decentralization. Strumpf (2002) also notes the informational externality but assumes that the central government cannot discriminate geographically.

Both the previous effects tend to increase the amount of experimentation under centralization relative to decentralization – and relative to the socially optimal level. We might expect both to become more pronounced as the number of localities increases (exacerbating free-rider problems under decentralization, and reducing the risk to a central government of some experimentation). However, two other effects pull in the opposite direction. The first can result in less experimentation under centralization than is socially optimal, although still at least as much as under decentralization. We call this the *risk-conserving effect*. In cases where experiments have a positive expected value but a high risk of failure, it might be socially optimal for all districts to experiment. However, under centralization, the incumbent needs only the votes from districts containing a majority of voters. He can do better by concentrating the risky experiments in a minority of districts and thus reducing the risk – and increasing the expected payoff – for voters in the other districts.

The positive informational externality predisposes local governments, acting separately, to experiment "too little." But there may also be *negative* interregional externalities that induce local governments to experiment "too much." Local governments might reduce pollution controls to see if this attracts investment or reduce welfare benefits to the unemployed to see if this causes them to find jobs quicker. The costs of such experiments are likely to be borne in part by neighboring localities where the pollution and unemployed workers end up. A central government, which must seek votes in more than one locality, will generally care more about such negative externalities than local governments, which benefit by exporting costs. Although this effect may lead to less experimentation under centralization than decentralization, fewer experiments of this type might be a good thing. If the external costs of such experiments are high, preventing them will increase the total welfare of voters nationwide.

One type of externality is worth considering separately. Suppose voters care about what policies are implemented not just in their own locality but in other localities too.[28] In the United States, for instance, many voters care strongly about whether abortion is legal not just in their own state but in other states as well. Voters might care about policy in other districts because

---

[28] This distinction arose already in sections 4.1.3 and 7.2.3. Calabresi and Melamed (1972, pp. 1111–12, quoted in Gillette 1997) discuss such "moralisms," or external costs that "do not lend themselves to collective measurement which is acceptably objective and nonarbitrary."

they anticipate moving to them. Or they might simply wish to impose their moral or ideological values on others.[29] If such attitudes affect voting, the central government may choose not to implement locally popular policies that alienate voters elsewhere. Banning abortion in Alabama might win the central government votes there but lose it even more in California. This might reduce the number of experiments under centralization. Would this be good or bad? Most people would resist reducing the question to a purely utilitarian calculation of the net welfare gains, as in the previous paragraph. One must also make a value judgment about whether the national majority or the local majority has the right to decide on the issue in question.

Although such *ideological spillovers* may be important, they may not imply a great innovation advantage for decentralization in practice. First, political institutions guaranteeing local autonomy must be quite robust to resist the pressure of national public opinion. In practice, even in countries with very decentralized constitutions, central authorities and national judiciaries often intervene to overrule local governments whose policies conflict with preferences of the national majority. This is true of the United States. Although the United States is among the most decentralized countries in the world, the Supreme Court regularly uses the Commerce Clause, the Eighth Amendment, and Section 5 of the Fourteenth Amendment to invalidate state laws on various grounds. The Court often explicitly rejects the "states as laboratories" argument – as, of course, the majority did in *New State Ice Co. vs. Liebmann*. To overturn state policies on grounds of "cruel and unusual punishment," the Court has invoked "evolving standards," based on its perception of nationwide public opinion. So ideological spillovers may restrain unpopular experiments even in decentralized federations. Second, if a local experiment is ideologically opposed by the nationwide majority, the potential for it to spread, if successful, is limited. Were a U.S. municipality able to experiment with legalizing heroin and found that drug overdoses

---

[29] Central governments might also be more vulnerable to pressures from national interest groups such as labor unions or business confederations, which want to secure uniform policies for their members nationwide. This might lead central governments to ignore local variation. However, national interest groups could lobby individual local governments in a decentralized system. Indeed, their threats to punish individual local governments with boycotts, etc., might be more credible than threats to stage nationwide strikes or other actions. If such groups can secure uniform policies under centralization, it seems likely they would also secure them under decentralization. Laski (1939) feared that federalism had become "obsolescent" in the United States precisely because large corporations and business groups could overwhelm local governments and could be effectively opposed only by a powerful central government.

fell, it seems doubtful that many other cities would follow. The type of experiment that decentralization protects under this argument is one that will generate the smallest benefits nationwide.

And third, in a decentralized order consisting of three or more tiers, decentralizing authority to an intermediate tier – as in a federal system – may sometimes reduce rather than increase experimentation. Voters in a given region may want to limit experiments by local governments in the region for ideological reasons. In some cases, the central authorities – or the country's national electorate – might have supported the experiments in question if given the choice. Thus, the comparison may hinge on whether regional electorates or the national electorate in a given country is more tolerant of local experiments. There does not seem to be any *a priori* answer to this question.

For instance, in the early 1990s a number of municipalities in Colorado enacted ordinances banning anti-gay discrimination in employment, education, and housing within their borders. The state electorate approved a voter intiative, "Amendment 2," rewriting the state constitution to prohibit such local ordinances. The majority of Colorado voters were thus imposing their ideological preferences onto municipalities where they did not live. The U.S. Supreme Court, showing greater tolerance toward local experiment, invalidated Amendment 2.[30] Had the U.S. constitutional system decentralized adjudication of such issues to the state level, the federal courts would not have had this option. For decentralization to guarantee protection of local experimentation, not only must local autonomy be extremely securely entrenched – such autonomy must be entrenched in the smallest subnational units.

Another possible argument concerns heterogeneity of localities. Suppose that some localities are less risk averse than others. Or suppose that voters care about not just the "success" or "failure" of particular experiments but also the policies themselves. Voters in a "left-wing" locality might have a higher payoff from experimenting with universal health insurance – whether it succeeds or fails in saving money – than voters in a "right-wing" locality. Voters in a right-wing unit might have a higher payoff from experimenting with harsh criminal penalties than those in left-wing units. It is tempting to think this might lead to greater experimentation under decentralization, because the left-wing units could choose "left-wing" experiments while the right-wing units choose "right-wing" ones. But this implicitly assumes that

[30] *Romer v. Evans* (116 S. Ct. 1620, 1996). See the discussion in Gillette (1997).

central policies must be uniform, a position I argued is hard to sustain. If central incumbents can differentiate policies geographically – and assuming there are no ideological externalities like those just discussed – they too would allocate left-wing experiments to left-wing districts and right-wing experiments to right-wing districts. To do otherwise would enable an electoral rival to offer voters a program they prefered just by reallocating experiments geographically.

Decentralization might stimulate experimentation if, controlling for the different incentives, local officials just tended to be more innovative and creative than their central counterparts. Is this likely to be the case? The great political theorists seem mostly to have argued the opposite. Tocqueville, who admired local democracy for many reasons, did not admire it for this one. On the contrary, the governments of large political units had, in his view, "more general ideas" and were "more effectively detached from the routine of precedent and from provincial selfishness." The government of a large unit typically had "more of genius in its conceptions and more boldness in its approach" (Tocqueville 1969 [1835], p. 160). Mill also worried that talent would flow to the central government: "The greatest imperfection of popular local institutions ... is the low calibre of the men by whom they are almost always carried on" (Mill 1991 [1861], p. 417). More recently, economists have often noted the lack of "state capacity" in developing countries to staff local governments with well-trained professionals.

For a given frequency of experimentation, three other effects suggest that centralization may extract and exploit information better. First, some experiments are correlated, in the sense that the "success" of one is related to the "success" of others. For instance, some types of experiment involve choosing different points on a scale. Suppose the speed limit on highways is sixty-five miles per hour. One locality might reduce its speed limit to sixty miles per hour to see how this affects traffic accidents, another to fifty-five miles per hour, and so on. The results would likely be correlated, though less than perfectly.

In such cases, the local units are not so much separate "laboratories" as separate "test-tubes," subjected to different treatments. The amount of information generated will depend on how the different treatments are selected. If local governments choose speed limits for themselves, they may bunch around certain values and duplicate one another, making it hard to estimate the underlying relationship with confidence. By contrast, a central government could coordinate its local treatments, spreading them out across the scale so that the estimates are tighter. Thus, a *calibration effect* should tend to make correlated experiments more informative when conducted under centralization.

A second *coordination effect* comes into play when governments choose between a number of experiments with different expected values. Suppose there is one experiment with a higher expected value – and higher chance of winning voter support – than the others. Under decentralization, local governments that choose to experiment in the first period will all choose this high-expected-value experiment, thus duplicating one another and perhaps neglecting other experiments that also have high expected values. Under centralization, coordination of experiments avoids this pathology and will often lead to the enactment of a wider range of experiments.

A third *communication effect* concerns how effectively experimental discoveries are analyzed, communicated, and exploited. The process of collecting and disseminating information from local experiments is likely to exhibit economies of scale. It will probably be cheaper for the central government to consolidate and analyze local reports on behalf of all the units than for each local government to gather information from all the others and conduct its own analysis. Even if experimentation decisions were made by local governments, the central government might still choose to perform this public service. But it would certainly do so if it had designed the experiments itself. As mentioned in section 9.1, John Stuart Mill advocated a vigorous central government for exactly this reason in *On Representative Government*. In *On Liberty*, he called for "the greatest dissemination of power consistent with efficiency; but the greatest possible centralization of information, and diffusion of it from the centre" (Mill 1991 [1859], p. 126).

Collecting and disseminating information about local experiments may not be just a technical matter. In some settings, outsiders may not directly observe what policy is enacted, but only the resulting government performance. Suppose, for instance, that a local government devises a new procedure for tracking waste within the local bureaucracy, and this procedure reduces costs substantially. The improved performance is evident to all, but suppose the local incumbent can keep details of the procedure secret (perhaps it requires original software). Suppose also that local voters evaluate the performance of their local government *relative* to that of neighboring localities, using "yardstick competition" (Shleifer 1985, Besley and Case 1995). Clearly, the local incumbent will wish to keep details of the experiment secret, rather than share them with other districts where the new policy could be used to reduce costs. Any improvement in neighboring districts would erode the relative performance advantage of the first. Under centralization, no such problem arises (unless the central government also uses yardstick competition to reward its agents and cannot motivate them to reveal details of policy). Thus, discoveries may be disseminated more rapidly under centralization, for strategic as well as technical reasons.[31]

Finally, the discussion so far has focused on localized policy experiments. But some experiments are inherently national in scope. A central government cannot instruct different localities to try out different foreign policies. It is also difficult to implement different monetary policies in different parts of a country. Whether experimenting on such issues is easier or harder under centralization depends on what institutional arrangements exist under decentralization. In section 8.2, I discussed various types of decentralization that increase the number of veto players in central policy decisions. For instance, "constitutional decentralization" – the assignment to subnational governments of formal roles in central policy making – can turn the subnational governments into veto players. As argued there, the greater number of veto players will tend to entrench the status quo more than under unitary government. Thus, even if political decentralization increased the frequency of local experiments, some types of decentralization might, other things being equal, decrease the frequency of central ones.

In short, the common intuition that political decentralization stimulates policy innovation seems dubious. In fact, the electoral logic suggests that decentralization should tend to lead to too little equilibrium experimentation, while centralization tends to lead to too much. In most cases, the experimentation gap between centralization and decentralization should increase with the number of districts and the cross-regional applicability of discoveries. From the perspective of social welfare, centralization appears preferable when experimentation has a high expected value, and decentralization may be preferable precisely when experiments have low expected value for voters and *restraining* local experimentation is a priority. A central

---

[31] There might be agency or communication problems for a central government trying to assemble and disseminate this information (recall the discussion in Chapter 3). But it is hard to see how such problems could be avoided in any state organization designed to gather and disseminate information about all the country's local experiments. A private survey firm might perform this function better. But if it is performed in the public sector, the choice is between a single, streamlined central survey and analysis bureau (with agency and communication problems) and multiple local survey and analysis bureaus (with agency and communication problems), duplicating each other's efforts.

government may also be better placed to design experiments optimally, and to analyze and publicize the results.

Should one conclude that decentralization actually leads to *less* policy innovation? Many of the arguments in this section would support this. However, the possibility of negative externalities makes generalizing in this direction equally vulnerable. If local experiments have strong negative externalities, decentralization may lead to more experiments than centralization – and probably an excessive number from the perspective of voters' welfare. Ideological factors that, under centralization or incomplete decentralization, cause national or state electorates to prohibit local initiatives may be quite widespread. Without knowing more about the context of a particular experiment, it is hard to say under what constitutional order it is more likely to be enacted.

Although the result that decentralization's main benefit is to limit local policy experimentation contradicts the common intuition articulated by Brandeis, it is not as surprising as it might at first seem. Indeed, one of the oldest arguments for political decentralization is that it will restrain abuses by a central government that is *too* willing to impose risky or undesirable policies on local communities. The American Revolutionary War occurred because a distant central government, in urgent need of revenues, began to experiment with new kinds of taxes without consulting local elected assemblies. The word "innovation" today has an overwhelmingly positive connotation, but not in the eighteenth century. As the American revolutionary John Dickinson wrote about the Stamp Act: "This I call an innovation; and a most dangerous innovation" (McDonald 1962). More than a decade before Brandeis compared the states to "laboratories," Justice Oliver Wendell Holmes had made an almost identical argument in *Truax vs. Corrigan*, insisting that "social experiments" – in this case, a very liberal state law on strikers picketing – should be permitted in the "insulated chambers" of the states.[32] He was rebuffed by Chief Justice William Howard Taft, writing for the majority: "The Constitution was intended, its very purpose was, to prevent experimentation with the fundamental rights of the individual."

The belief that decentralization stimulates experimentation is quite deeply rooted in American culture. As evidence, scholars often point to cases in which innovative policies at the state level have inspired later federal programs. In the 1920s and 1930s, novel state social policies and economic regulations laid the ground for much of President Franklin D. Roosevelt's

---

[32] *Truax v. Corrigan* (257 U. S. 312, 1921).

New Deal (Patterson 1969, Morehouse and Jewell 2004, Nathan 2006). However, the relevant question is not whether local innovations preceded central legislation within the United States but whether a decentralized country like the United States was quicker to innovate than its more centralized counterparts. In fact, the United States was one of the *slowest* developed countries to adopt social legislation. Among the thirty current members of the OECD, the United States was the twenty-third to pass national legislation on old age pensions, disability benefits or insurance, or benefits for surviving dependents of the insured.[33] It was outpaced by Slovakia, Ireland, Iceland, Italy, and Spain, among other countries. The United States was the last of the thirty to pass national legislation on sickness and maternity benefits. These comparisons relate to national legislation, but even if one focused on the start of state-level legislation on pensions, disability, or survivor insurance around 1920, the United States would still rank only about eighteenth out of thirty.

Indeed, it may be that policy innovations tend to come from local governments in politically decentralized countries precisely because the local governments in such orders block attempts by the central government to innovate. In Canada, the provinces have been seen by some as a "crucial incubator" of social policy initiatives, paving the way for the introduction of national hospital insurance in 1957 and national health insurance in 1966 (Gray 1991; Hacker 1998, pp. 72, 104). Saskatchewan introduced public hospital insurance in the late 1940s and was followed by other provinces. But Saskatchewan's experiment came only after the federal government had been trying to introduce health insurance for decades. Ottawa had tried to do so during the Great Depression but had been blocked by the country's top constitutional tribunal, which ruled that health insurance fell within the provinces' jurisdiction (Hacker 1998, p. 97). The postwar Liberal government of Mackenzie King tried again in 1945 but could not get the necessary agreement from the provinces (ibid., p. 98). Only after a number of provinces had introduced their own programs, following Saskatchewan's lead, was the federal government allowed to superimpose a common framework. If provincial governments in federations block all central attempts to innovate, then of course all innovations – if they occur – must start in the provinces. But this does not mean that federalism stimulates innovation.

---

[33] These data come from *Social Security Programs Throughout the World, 2004*, compiled by the International Social Security Association, in Geneva, Switzerland, downloaded from the U.S. Social Security Administration, at www.socialsecurity.gov, June 23, 2006.

Policy Experimentation

Like the United States, Canada was a laggard rather than a leader in introducing social policies. Its national hospital insurance in 1957 came extremely late compared with that of other developed countries. Among current OECD members, only Finland, South Korea, and the United States were slower to enact sickness or maternity benefits. The median date of the first sickness or maternity benefits program was 1921.

10

Ethnic Conflict and Secession

Where major ethnic or regional cleavages exist that are territorially based, the relationship is by now self-evident and axiomatic: The absence of provisions for devolution and decentralization of power, expecially in the context of ethnoregional disparities, feeds ethnic insecurity, violent conflict, and even secessionist pressures. . . . In deeply divided societies, meaningful devolution of power – typically through federalism – is an indispensable instrument for managing and reducing conflict.

Larry Diamond, Juan Linz, and Seymour Martin Lipset, (1995, pp. 44–5)

Federalism has become a very popular "solution" for problems of ethnic conflict in public discourse. In fact, ethnic federations are among the most difficult of all to sustain and are least likely to survive because constituent units based on ethnic nationalisms normally do not want to merge into the kind of tight-knit units necessary for federation.

Daniel Elazar (1993, p. 194)

As American-occupied Iraq slid into civil war in 2004–5, experts debated what political arrangements might contain the escalating sectarian violence. Many saw the best hope in the creation of a loose federation or some other kind of decentralized order. According to Dawn Brancati (2004, p. 7), writing in early 2004: "federalism offers the only viable possibility for preventing ethnic conflict and secessionism as well as establishing a stable democracy in Iraq." Around the same time, Larry Diamond (2004) predicted that: "Federalism – as negotiated and structured by Iraqis in their process of constitution making during the coming year – will provide the means to hold Iraq together permanently, democratically, and peacefully." After voters approved a new constitution in late 2005, Marina Ottaway (2005) urged the U.S. government to convince the still-skeptical Sunnis to accept a federal system. Six months later, Senator Joseph Biden and Leslie Gelb proposed a plan "to maintain a united Iraq by decentralizing it, giving each ethno-religious group – Kurd, Sunni Arab and Shiite Arab – room to run its own affairs, while leaving the central government in charge of common interests" (Biden and Gelb 2006).

In context, support for federalism was not exactly surprising. At a conference in 2002, all factions of the Iraqi opposition had united to call for a democratic, federal structure for a post-Saddam Iraq (Brancati 2004, p. 11). By 2004, the degradation of the state caused by de-Ba'athification, inept U.S. administration, and the violence of Shiite militias and Sunni insurgents had eliminated any hope of a centralized order. Given the determination of the Kurds in the North to defend their current autonomy, the only alternative to federalism was probably not unified government but rapid disintegration of the country, which would drag surrounding powers such as Turkey and Iran deep into the maelstrom. Federalism was written into the constitution that voters endorsed in late 2005.

Still, not all were confident that decentralization would help. "So far, proposed federalism for Iraq is proving to be a recipe for disaccord, not accommodation," Pietro Nivola of the Brookings Institution observed in 2005. Reaction in the Arab press was hardly enthusiastic. Qatar's *Al-Rayah* newspaper called the proposal for federalism "a political time bomb, which makes the situation in Iraq more confused than ever" (BBC Monitoring Service 2005). Former U.S. Assistant Secretary of State James Dobbins (2005) warned that: "Federalism is a concept foreign to the Arab world, representing a system of government unfamiliar to Iraqis and to the region. Federalism did not hold the Soviet Union together after the fall of communism, nor did it hold Yugoslavia together after the collapse of the Warsaw Pact. Many Iraqis believe it unlikely to do any better for their country." Most previous attempts to create federations in the Arab world – including Sudan in 1972–83 and the United Arab Republic in 1958–61 – had failed (Dunn 2005). Imad Salamey and Frederic Pearson worried that decentralizing Iraq might encourage ethnic minorities elsewhere in the Middle East to seek outside intervention to secure autonomous regions for themselves. "Depending upon how it is administered . . . Iraqi federalism could prove to be an active ingredient in regional instability and ethno-religious fragmentation" (Salamey and Pearson 2005, p. 199).

Does political decentralization tend to stabilize ethnically divided societies, making it possible for diverse groups to live together peacefully and democratically? Or does it exacerbate the internal clash of civilizations? In fact, the divergent views on Iraq mirror similar disagreements among scholars about the general determinants of ethnic violence and civil war. Some, like Diamond, Linz, and Lipset, see devolution of power as "an indispensable instrument for managing and reducing conflict."[1] Others are less sure and warn that building ethnic or religious cleavages into the structure of government can accentuate intractable divisions and empower local extremists.[2] In this chapter, I consider the arguments scholars have made relating political decentralization to the frequency of ethnic conflict and the danger of secession.[3]

10.1 Satisfying Limited Demands for Autonomy

Perhaps the most common argument is that satisfying the limited demands of ethnic minorities for some cultural, political, or economic autonomy can prevent them from escalating their objective to outright secession. One way to do this, if the minority groups are geographically compact, is to devolve power to local governments, with jurisdictions drawn so that the minority ethnic groups predominate within them. They will then be able to choose their own local leaders and exercise some self-government (Hechter 2000a, 2000b; Lake and Rothchild 2005). In Simeon and Conway's words: "conflict will be reduced by a measure of disengagement, of separation. Harmony will be increased in a system in which territorially concentrated minorities are able to exercise autonomy or self-determination on matters crucial to their identity and continued existence, without fear of being overridden or vetoed by the majority group" (Simeon and Conway 2001, p. 339).

---

[1] Diamond, Linz, and Lipset (1995, pp. 44–5); see also Diamond and Plattner (1994).

[2] Just a few generations ago, scholars – rather than considering federalism a way to manage heterogeneity – often saw cultural homogeneity as a precondition for federalism to work. According to William Maddox (1941, p. 1123), federations would not survive if the parts represented "too great a diversity in size, culture, and the level of their political and economic development." Ronald Watts (1966, p. 42, quoted in Riker 1975, p. 115) also viewed "community of outlook based on race, religion, language, or culture" as a precondition for federal stability. Such writers echoed Tocqueville, who thought even nineteenth-century France was too heterogeneous for federalism because of the large "difference in civilization" between the neighboring provinces of Normandy and Brittany (Tocqueville 1969 [1835], p. 168).

[3] A number of scholars have examined demands for secession motivated by economic differences, with no explicit ethnic component, and suggested that decentralization may alleviate such problems. In Chapter 5, I discussed a paper by Bolton and Roland (1997) on this subject, which is also discussed in Alesina and Spolaore (2003). Here I focus on arguments about how decentralization interacts with ethnic divisions.

This argument is plausible on its face, but there are three main problems. First, ethnic minorities may not be territorially concentrated. If a minority constitutes 10 percent of the national population, and 10 percent of the population of each local jurisdiction, then decentralization will not help it at all. (One might try to gerrymander districts to get around this, but sometimes ethnic cleavages run through the smallest villages, or even families.) By contrast, various other ways of protecting ethnic minorities do not require such territorial concentration. A nationwide system to defend individual rights – for instance, constitutional provisions securing the rights of each citizen to worship, obtain education in his own language, and engage freely in cultural activities – would enable members of ethnic minorities to live according to their distinct cultures and communal traditions, regardless of settlement patterns. Similarly, a consociational bargain at the center between different ethnic groups, allowing each to organize its own educational and religious systems nationwide, would also provide for ethnic autonomy. Under various historical arrangements, from the millet system of Ottoman Turkey to the national *curiae* of the late Habsburg Empire, ethnic minorities have enjoyed cultural autonomy, without any associated territorial decentralization.[4]

Second, if minorities are sufficiently concentrated geographically, decentralization will indeed empower those minorities that predominate in particular local jurisdictions. However, unless ethnic groups are perfectly segregated, this merely relocates the problem rather than solving it. Such constitutional engineering leaves new minorities within each locality powerless and creates new "protected minorities that may be local tyrannical majorities" (Duchacek 1975, p. 43).[5] If local units are more ethnically homogeneous than the country as a whole, then local minorities will tend to make up a smaller share of each local unit's population than the share of ethnic minorities in the country's population. But smaller minorities do not necessarily care less about autonomy or press their demands less violently.

---

[4] See Linz and Stepan (1996, p. 34) and Finer (1997, p. 1196). Under Ottoman rule, three non-Muslim religious communities were allowed autonomy in most matters throughout the Empire. Orthodox Christians, Armenians, and Jews constituted three self-governing communities – *millets* – under a religious leader. They could collect their own taxes and maintain internal order, and each managed its own communal institutions for religion, education, social assistance, and civil justice.

[5] One such local ethnic minority might be protected by its majority status nationwide. However, this may exacerbate tension at the local level rather than alleviate it, as suggested by the case of Serbian minorities in Bosnia and Croatia in the early 1990s. See the argument in the next paragraph.

One rejoinder to this might be that if different ethnic groups predominate in different localities, then the existence of mutual "hostages" might deter abuses: If group A abuses members of group B in region 1, group B can retaliate by abusing members of group A in region 2. However, it is not just protection from abuses that minority ethnic groups desire: Their members often want to choose policies for themselves. And, in games with mutual hostages, another equilibrium often exists in which each local majority ethnically cleanses the minority, forcing individuals to emigrate into the district where their co-ethnics already predominate. Without ethnic cleansing, one cannot usually provide autonomy for all minorities simply by reducing the scale of units.

A third problem with the argument that decentralization can satisfy limited demands for autonomy is that the demands of ethnic minorities may not be limited. The group may be secretly committed to secession. In this case, decentralization will strengthen it in its efforts to secede. Introducing local elections can give local separatist leaders the legitimacy of a popular mandate and the administrative resources of local government office. If tax revenues are decentralized, local officials may use such funds to fight the center. If law enforcement responsibilities are devolved, local separatist leaders can set up secessionist militias. As Roeder (1999, p. 870) puts it: "Every power assigned to an ethnic group is also a potential weapon to be used against another ethnic group and the state at the bargaining table of ethnoconstitutional politics."

Eaton (2005) provides a striking example. In the 1980s and 1990s, Colombia decentralized, hoping in part that this would encourage locally based left-wing guerrilla groups and right-wing paramilitaries to disarm and participate in the democratic process. Direct elections were introduced for mayors and governors, and subnational governments were given responsibilities for providing a range of local services. Both right- and left-wing armed extremists did choose to participate, but not in the way desired. The left-wing FARC came down from the mountains to extort aid from local politicians, murder mayors who refused to cooperate, and appropriate the decentralized budget flows. Right-wing militias also infiltrated mayoral and gubernatorial offices, intimidating local voters and setting up fraudulent "health service providers" to embezzle health care funds. Both have used the newly decentralized resources and powers to "reinforce and expand their domination of vast stretches of the national territory." The result has been, in Eaton's words, "a bizarre dynamic according to which part of the central state (e.g. the Finance Ministry) issues automatic revenue transfers to local governments that are controlled by armed groups at war with other parts of the central state (e.g. the military and the police)."

Even if ethnic groups' demands start out limited, decentralization itself may cause them to escalate. Local communities may evolve in different directions, becoming more and more alienated from one another as common cultural reference points fade and separate political discourses develop (Roeder 1999, pp. 869–70). Local and ethnic attachments can eat away at broader forms of patriotism. Amicable separations sometimes allow simmering resentments to cool; at other times, they pave the way to divorce. In Yugoslavia before its collapse, the divergent educational, cultural, and media policies of the republic governments had increasingly divided the population into "segregated intellectual universes" (Woodward 1995, p. 77).

Beyond such cultural drifting apart, decentralization may lead to ethnically exclusionary types of politics (Snyder 2000). Devolution to Protestant-dominated governments in Northern Ireland created, according to Furniss (1975, p. 401), "a 'hothouse' atmosphere in which traditional hatreds could flourish." Local electoral competition may create incentives for "ethnic entrepreneurs" to deliberately inflame intergroup hatred in order to out-flank their moderate rivals. The opportunistic mobilization of ethnic conflict by politicians for their own political advantage "has been a recurrent feature of electoral politics" in many developing countries (Diamond and Plattner 1994, p. xxi). In order to win in local elections, "ethnopoliticians are likely to find that they must outbid one another in their appeals to the ethnic community, making ever more extreme claims about what they will win at the central bargaining table" (Roeder 1999, p. 869).

Even if neither the ethnic community nor the opportunistic politician actually wants to secede, the process of local elections can lead to a danger-ous spiral of escalating demands and nationalist rhetoric. And the problem is not prompted just by elections. Such dramas of confrontation are also provoked by the inevitable bargaining that occurs between central and local politicians over the distribution of public property and fiscal benefits. Polit-ical decentralization empowers and motivates local incumbents to threaten and lobby their central counterparts. As Furniss (1975, p. 404) puts it: "mil-itancy pays in dealing with the modern state – provided the militancy can be assuaged by generous supplies of cash. The threat (perhaps even more than the reality) of separation or autonomy seems well suited to galvanize the center into action." In this sense, the ethnic conflicts that political decen-tralization is supposed to manage are "institutionalized and entrenched in the very design of the political system" (Simeon and Conway 2001, p. 340).

In Canada, scholars argue that federalism has exacerbated language and regional divisions "by giving the groups involved an institutional power base and creating political élites with a vested interest in bad relations with the national government" (Covell 1987, p. 75, quoted in Gagnon 1993, p. 18).

10.2 Splitting the Prizes of Politics

A second argument for political decentralization is that it can change the game of politics from a "winner takes all" contest into one in which many groups can each control some part of the governing apparatus. In Donald Horowitz's phrase, it can "proliferate the points of power" (Horowitz 1991). No group need be completely excluded. If important decisions are shared between governments at different levels, then control of the central government may not seem quite as urgent. Ethnic groups that lose national elections may be persuaded not to riot or secede by the chance of winning at subnational levels.

Dividing up authority among different levels of government may indeed reduce the stakes of any given election. There are two points to note about this. First, dividing power may prevent any group from being excluded. But if it does so, it must by the same logic increase the danger of conflict between governments at different levels that have been captured by different groups. If dividing power is a solution – because it prevents one group from monopolizing power – it is simultaneously a problem – because it engenders confrontation between levels. As in the previous section, the outcome will depend in part on whether leaders of the ethnic minority merely want some autonomy or want complete independence. If a minority, excluded at the center, is strongly separatist, then winning local power may just give it resources to attack the center and secede (Bunce 1999). The minority may indeed be better able to protect itself against central abuses. But that protection may take the form of shooting at central troops or police. Or it may involve providing safe haven for violent anti-center guerrillas in the hope of weakening the central authorities. There is no guarantee that proliferating the points of power will restrain the battle over them rather than merely extend the arenas of conflict.

Second, if dividing authority among different institutions is a good idea, it can also be accomplished – perhaps more effectively – without decentralization. Constitutions can assign each region or ethnic group formal representation in central institutions, with rights to veto certain types of legislation. Or different central offices can be reserved for members of different ethnic groups. Electoral laws can require that presidential candidates receive a threshold level of support in each region or within each community, forcing them to reach across ethnic or geographical lines.[6]

10.3 Restraining the Central Government

Related to the previous point, some argue that by dividing power among many institutions, decentralization can make it hard for the central government to act decisively in ways that threaten ethnic minorities. This is the veto players argument discussed in Chapter 8.

Preventing the central government from acting expeditiously may prevent ethnic conflict if the central government is the main aggressor. But if rival ethnic minorities win control of two local governments, the central government's intervention may be necessary to mediate or control conflict between them. In ethnically divided countries, local explosions of violence among hostile groups often require central administrative interventions to reimpose order and stop the bloodshed. If at times restraining the central government "lowers the temperature of politics at the center," as Horowitz (1991) argues, at other times it can prevent the center from putting out fires in the regions. Whether incapacitating the central government will reduce or exacerbate ethnic conflict depends on the patterns of conflict within a given country. One might argue that the weakness of the Yugsolav federal government prevented it from halting the spiral of interrepublic hostility in 1989–91 that led to civil war. Suffering a severe budget crisis, lacking resources to address the economic grievances of the Northern republics, the government of Ante Markovic was forced to rely on the Yugoslav army, which was predominantly Serb, and which confronted well-armed militias in Slovenia and Croatia. Similarly, ethnic conflict is sometimes caused not by central government repression but by the attempts of local ethnic minority politicians to secede. Incapacitating the central government may encourage such attempts, resulting in violence.

---

[6] Former UN Secretary General Kofi Annan (2000) sums this up well. Stable democracy, he argues, requires that national minorities be given a permanent share of power. "In some places that can be done by decentralization, so that national minorities can win *local* power, in regions where they form the local majority." But the same result can also be secured by "provisions giving minorities guaranteed representation at *national* level – in the legislature, or the executive, or both. What is important is not the particular device used, but the outcome."

At the same time, if preventing a centrally dominant ethnic group from oppressing others is the goal, this could also be accomplished by multiplying veto players at the center and giving ethnic minorities nationwide institutional protections. Decentralization is not necessary for this, and it will only sometimes be effective.

10.4 Socializing Politicians

Decentralization to smaller units, it is argued, may create settings in which politicians can learn the art of compromise and acquire values of moderation. Experience dealing with members of other ethnic groups at the local level can socialize politicians "in dealing with conflict in a divided society before they must do so at the national level" (Horowitz 1991). Local governments, in this view, may serve as "nodes of interracial cooperation and accommodation."[7]

Or they may not. A local government, captured by one or another ethnic group, can quite easily become an incubator for intolerance and ethnic exclusion rather than moderation and compromise. Ethnic politicians may learn from local experience that attacks on rival groups are an effective way of rallying their base. It may be racism, not reason, that spreads upward from the grass roots. This is, in fact, a version of the "civic virtue" argument discussed in section 7.1. But, as noted there, local governments can become "schools of evil" instead of "schools of good." If local governments are run by individuals committed to tolerance and multi-ethnic cooperation, they may cultivate similar commitments in new members. If they are run by bigots and violent opportunists, then the socialization they provide may be in less pacific values.

10.5 Stimulating Growth of Small Ethnic Parties

Usually, the lack of strong national parties is viewed as a political defect. But in ethnically divided societies, Horowitz (1991) argues, the opposite may be true. In Nigeria's Second Republic, the original states were broken into smaller units. This stimulated the emergence of small parties to represent the ethnic and subethnic groups that constituted the local majorities. These small parties then had to "reach across group lines" and form broad coalitions in order to contest national elections. In cases like this, Horowitz

---

[7] Slabbert and Welsh (1979, p. 129), quoted in Horowitz (1991, p. 221).

contends, decentralization may lead to negotiation and compromise among smaller ethnic groups, rather than to a politics of confrontation between homogeneous national parties.

Several comments are in order. First, Horowitz's argument is not about the degree of political decentralization – the Nigerian First Republic, which collapsed into civil war, was just as federal as the Second – but about the size of units within a federal state. For a given level of political decentralization, the Nigerian case – if it can be generalized – might suggest that increasing the number of first tier units will help to stabilize politics. This would be an interesting point about how decentralized institutions might be structured to reduce ethnic conflict, but it would not imply anything about the comparison between decentralization and centralization per se.[8]

Even then, *can* the example be generalized? Splitting the country's main ethnic groups among many smaller units could provoke less benign reactions. Small parties, formed in the regions, might, as Horowitz argues, "reach across group lines" to forge national coalitions. Or they might choose to unite with co-ethnics in other regions, reproducing exactly the same type of homogeneous national parties as before. At the same time, emphasizing the main local, rather than national, ethnic cleavages may or may not lead to greater stability. It might inflame local ethnic conflicts that are even more intense and dangerous – albeit less extended in space – than national ones. It might prompt small minority nationalities such as the Chechens in Russia or the Papuans in Indonesia to seek independent statehood. There do not appear to be any reliable general rules about what pattern of territorial units will minimize conflict.

10.6 Conclusion

Political decentralization may satisfy the moderate demands for autonomy of geographically concentrated ethnic groups. It may reduce the urgency of central political competition, providing multiple points of power that can be shared among the different communities. If ethnic minorities control subnational governments, this may help them resist discriminatory central policies and defend themselves. Local government may also serve as a training ground in cooperation and compromise, and as an incubator for small

---

[8] In a similar vein, Hale (2004) argues that dividing the nationally dominant ethnic group among multiple regional governments may render ethnofederations more stable. He does not compare ethnofederations to more centralized forms of government, however.

ethnic parties that may choose to form multi-ethnic coalitions to contest national elections. In all these ways, decentralization may at times alleviate ethnic conflict.

But decentralization may exacerbate ethnic conflict in just as many ways. It may enable local majorities to abuse local minorities and inflame ethnic cleavages that are salient at the local but not the national level. It may empower local ethnic majorities to mobilize for secession and provide havens for ethnic guerrillas. Over time, it may cause public opinion to diverge in different regions, fraying the bonds that unite all citizens and replacing national patriotism with ethnic and regional loyalties. Local elections may prompt ethnic candidates to exploit ethnic antagonisms and attack the central government in order to outflank and outbid rivals. In a decentralized state, local leaders may "play the ethnic card" to pressure the central government over fiscal redistribution. Decentralization may make it harder for the central government to intervene to stop local ethnic groups from massacring one another.

In short, any simple conclusions seem quite dubious. As Simeon and Conway write of federalism: "it is virtually impossible to make broad generalizations about the effectiveness of federalism in multinational societies" (Simeon and Conway 2001, p. 339). Nor is it easy to say, in a way that is useful in practice, under what conditions decentralization will help. Political decentralization is more likely to reduce conflict: if the demands of minorities are limited – and stay limited; if local politicians choose strategies of multi-ethnic cooperation over the politics of exclusion; and if ethnic groups do not drift apart culturally. All these "conditions," however, are not exogenous features of a particular setting but depend on how the political game plays itself out over time. In fact, they are not conditions at all but uncertainties that resist any general, *a priori* resolution. Even if political decentralization does, at times, reduce ethnic conflict, there are many ways of designing central institutions in a unitary state that would tend to achieve the same results – from constitutional protections of minority cultures and minority veto powers to electoral rules that require representation from multiple ethnic groups or regions and proportional distribution of state benefits and jobs. Once again, a general presumption in favor of decentralization seems hard to justify.

11

Data to the Rescue?

It is a capital mistake to theorize before one has data. Insensibly one begins to twist facts to suit theories, instead of theories to suit facts.

Sherlock Holmes, in Sir Arthur Conan Doyle's "Scandal in Bohemia" (1892)

Facts are stupid things until brought into connection with some general law.

Louis Agassiz, in Scudder (1874)

One response to the previous chapters might be to agree that theory is inconclusive and look to empirical research to determine whether the positive or negative effects of decentralization tend to dominate. "Where theory leaves us completely stranded," advise Dahl and Tufte (1973, p. 44), "we can be rescued only by data." It may not be possible to say in the abstract whether a decentralized constitution is better or worse than a more centralized one. But the proof of the pudding is in the eating.

There are several reasons why turning to empirical observations at this point might seem dangerous, if not perverse. First, even if we found the empirical "pudding" to be tasty, we would not know what it was we were consuming. If theory tells us not to expect a consistent relationship between decentralization and most political and economic outcomes, finding such a relationship in one data set gives us no reason to expect similar results in others. For instance, suppose one found a correlation between decentralization and individual liberty in a sample of countries. The theory in Chapter 8 showed that if local governments wish to protect one another's citizens against central abuses, there is an equilibrium in a repeated game in which they coordinate to do so. One might hypothesize that the observed correlation in the data was caused by this mechanism. But the theory tells us also that if local governments do *not* wish to protect one another's citizens, or if they fail to coordinate on a particular desirable equilibrium, then decentralization can support the worst kinds of tyranny. Unless one has a supplementary theory about how frequently – and under what conditions – local governments favor liberty (more than the central government) and succeed in coordinating, one does not know when to expect a similar result and when to expect the opposite. Contrary to Dahl and Tufte, it is not clear how data can "rescue" us in such cases.[1]

A second danger in turning to the empirical literature to fill in theoretical gaps relates to the sociology of academic publication. Null empirical results are much less likely to get published, or even reported, than positive findings (although this might be changing in the Internet age). If many scholars examine the effects of decentralization using different data and methods, a certain proportion will find positive or negative, statistically significant results purely by chance. Because no one knows how many past explorations yielded insignificant results and were aborted or rejected by journals, it is hard to judge whether the studies that do get published establish significant patterns or come from the tails of a distribution of noise. This is not a criticism of individual researchers, who may be operating strictly according to the canons of science. But knowledge can – and does – get unintentionally distorted by the system of reporting.[2]

---

[1] A strong believer in induction might argue that an observed association between decentralization and freedom is enough to create a presupposition that the two will be linked in other cases. But such radical inductionism has gone out of fashion since the attacks on it by Hume, Russell, and Popper. Anyone who has read this far is probably interested also in the mechanisms that bring about observed correlations and will find a mere assertion of empirically observed correlations unsatisfying. In any case, as this chapter will show, there are almost no robust correlations to report.

[2] Gerber, Green, and Nickerson (2001) devise a test for "publication bias" and find evidence that it has occurred in the dissemination of studies of voting behavior. Sigelman (1999) agrees that studies with significant results do get published more frequently than those with insignificant results but suggests that this might be not because reviewers and editors favor significance per se but because well-designed studies based on clear and compelling theory and using large samples are more likely both to impress the referees and to obtain significant results. This seems unlikely to apply in this case. More often, the studies that find significant results about decentralization seem to have smaller (and probably nonrandom) samples. And the analysis presented in this book suggests that the theoretical underpinnings of these studies leave something to be desired. In any case, those who test for decentralization effects and get significant results usually start from the same theories as those who get insiginificant results, so the quality of the underlying theory would not explain why the former are published more than the latter.

These concerns notwithstanding, I examine empirical studies of the consequences of political decentralization in this chapter, if for no other reason than to satisfy curiosity. I review examinations of, respectively, government quality and public service provision, economic performance, ethnic conflict, democracy, and the stability of central government policies. A survey of this kind must be selective, and I have probably omitted many worthwhile contributions, but I think even the partial review offered here is sufficient to reach certain conclusions.

I focus on cross-national comparisons that include a relatively large number of countries. Besides the works considered here, an enormous number of books and articles have examined decentralization experiences in particular countries and advanced claims about what their experience implies. Such case studies often describe a particular decentralizing reform and the economic and political outcomes that followed, and then propose these observations as a guide to what to expect from decentralization in other countries under similar circumstances. While such studies can offer fascinating insights into the political games played in particular settings, I doubt that they can produce reliable generalizations about the consequences of decentralization, and so I do not consider them here.

The main problem with such extrapolations from a sample of one or two is that there is no way to assess how likely it is that the particular associations observed in the given case arose by causation or by chance. If there is no relationship between decentralization and economic or government performance, we should expect to see performance improve after decentralization in some places and worsen in others. Since at least Hume, an element in the definition of causation has been the "constant conjunction" – or at least regular association – of a "cause" with an "effect." Most country case studies describe just one association of decentralized institutions with a particular outcome. They can, therefore, tell us nothing about whether the two phenomena are "constantly" or regularly associated.

Even if we could know that the association was causal, in any one case study many phenomena are observed in combination. It is hard to disentangle which of the possible causes of particular outcomes are the genuine causes and which are merely occurring simultaneously. And we do not usually have a way to evaluate what set of conditions are necessary for a particular relationship to hold. Thus, even if we knew that an observed association was causal, that would permit us only to predict a similar outcome in another country when the full set of conditions was reproduced there.

For example, we are taught by fascinating case studies of Argentina in the 1980s that fiscal decentralization combined with interlevel revenue sharing in a federal state causes fiscal instability. The spectacular crises of public finance in post-authoritarian Argentina are well documented (see, e.g., Saiegh and Tommasi 1999). Only if one looks at a larger set of countries does one realize that Australia, another federation with extensive interlevel revenue sharing, was as fiscally decentralized as Argentina in many years, yet did not suffer any comparable fiscal disasters. Looking more systematically, the authors of a cross-national study that I discuss below (Rodden and Wibbels 2002) found that in federal states, fiscal decentralization – even when accompanied by revenue sharing – was associated with *lower* rather than higher government deficits, the opposite conclusion from the one suggested by the Argentine case studies. This is not to question the value of case studies – which can inform about the case itself, suggest hypotheses, disprove general arguments when posed nonprobabilistically, and illustrate results derived by other means – but they are not suited to the task at hand: establishing what evidence has been found of general consequences of decentralization.

Reading available cross-national studies suggests that if the proof is in the pudding, the pudding in this case is rather insubstantial. Of course, there are enormous obstacles to constructing empirical tests for most of the arguments discussed in this book. Such practical difficulties might explain why strong results are hard to find. But a good number of scholars have set out to gather evidence of decentralization's consequences and have reported results that are mixed at best. Those papers that do find positive or negative results often rely on smaller cross-national datasets with nonrandom inclusion of countries or else fail to include appropriate controls. To date, there are almost no solidly established, general empirical findings about the consequences of decentralization. Rather, the inconclusive, weak, and contradictory results one finds in the empirical literature are very much what one would expect given the inconclusive, weak, and contradictory arguments such work aims to test.[3]

---

[3] I would apply this criticism to some of my own empirical work. In a 2002 paper titled "Decentralization and the Quality of Government" (discussed below), I examined how various measures of political decentralization correlated with measures of government performance in a relatively large, cross-national data-set. Such exercises establish patterns – or the lack thereof – in the data, but I would now resist generalizing from such analyses to countries not included in the data-set or drawing confident conclusions about the mechanisms that produce such patterns.

11.1 The Quality of Government

A number of scholars have examined whether political or fiscal decentralization affects the pervasiveness of corruption.[4] They typically use cross-national indexes of "perceived corruption," constructed from surveys of businesspeople and ratings by risk analysts. Indexes in common usage include those compiled by Transparency International (TI), a team at the World Bank (WB), and the PRS Group, which publishes the *International Country Risk Guide* (ICRG). Since the late 1990s, scholars have regressed countries' corruption ratings on a variety of possible determinants. Recently, they have tried including several measures of decentralization, which I discuss in turn.

Probably the most popular is a measure of fiscal decentralization constructed from the IMF's *Government Finance Statistics* (GFS), representing the share of subnational governments in total government expenditures (or sometimes revenues).[5] Huther and Shah (1998, p. 12) first noted that greater fiscal decentralization correlated with lower corruption, as measured by TI's 1996 perceived corruption index. Several subsequent papers reported similar findings: Fisman and Gatti (2002), which used ICRG data; De Mello and Barenstein (2001), using ICRG and WB ratings; and Arikan (2004), using TI data.

This might seem quite conclusive, except that none of these studies simultaneously controls for two factors that are both correlated with fiscal decentralization and strongly related to perceived corruption: Protestant religious tradition, and a long experience of uninterrupted democracy.[6] This raises the possibility that the apparent relationship between fiscal decentralization and corruption is spurious, produced by one or two omitted variables. For instance, the Scandinavian countries have Protestant cultures, high fiscal decentralization, and low corruption. It seems to me at least as plausible to attribute the relative honesty of Scandinavian bureaucrats to Protestant culture as to fiscal decentralization. Huther and Shah (1998) present only uncontrolled correlations between fiscal decentralization and corruption. Fisman and Gatti (2002) and Arikan (2004),

---

[4] See Bardhan and Mookherjee (2005) for a useful review.

[5] For a criticism of this as a measure of fiscal decentralization, see Ebel and Yilmaz (2002).

[6] See Treisman (2000a) for a demonstration of the significance of these variables in corruption regressions. Both extended democracy and the proportion of Protestant adherents in the population correlate with fiscal decentralization (as of the mid-1990s) at about $r = .4$; TI's 2000 corruption index (adapted so that higher scores indicate higher corruption) correlates with extended democracy at $r = -.72$ and with the percentage Protestant at $r = -.57$.

although including various other controls, do not control for Protestant religious tradition.[7] De Mello and Barenstein (2001) find fiscal decentralization significant when they control for just economic development and population. When they add a variable for Protestantism, this reduces the coefficient on fiscal decentralization to insignificance in a regression with the WB data. Fiscal decentralization is still significant (with a reduced coefficient) in a regression with ICRG data, controlling for Protestantism, economic development, and population. But I suspect it would not be if one controlled simultaneously for both Protestantism and uninterrupted democracy.[8]

In Treisman (2002), I present regressions for both the WB (2001) and TI (2000) corruption indexes. In regressions with few controls, fiscal decentralization correlates with lower corruption. But if I control for both uninterrupted democracy and Protestantism, these two controls are significant, while fiscal decentralization – although its coefficient is still positive – is not. My conjecture is that Protestant culture and a long experience of democracy support governments that are relatively clean and honest, and that the apparent relationship with fiscal decentralization is mostly illusory. One can, of course, interpret the results differently. If one has strong priors that fiscal decentralization influences the quality of government and is skeptical that Protestant culture would affect individuals' willingness to take or give bribes, then one might choose to ignore this. But however one reads the evidence, on this point it seems fragile.

The general pattern can be seen in Figure 11.1, which graphs the average WB corruption score of countries for which data were available for the years 1996–2002 against the average share of subnational governments in total government expenditure for those years during 1985–95 for which GFS data were available. I plot the purported cause of corruption (decentralization) for a period before that of the purported effect to reduce the danger of picking up reverse causation. The data, for both federal and non-federal states, sketch out a curious C-shape. At least in this data-set, at high levels of fiscal decentralization governments are either very corrupt or very clean, but rarely in between. This also highlights the danger of dropping key cases in estimating this relationship. Were a few highly decentralized

---

[7] Arikan still gets only a significant decentralization effect if he drops two of his other controls.
[8] I did not have the ICRG data to test this in De Mello and Barenstein's setup, but these other controls sharply reduce the decentralization effect using the WB or TI data, as described in the next paragraph.

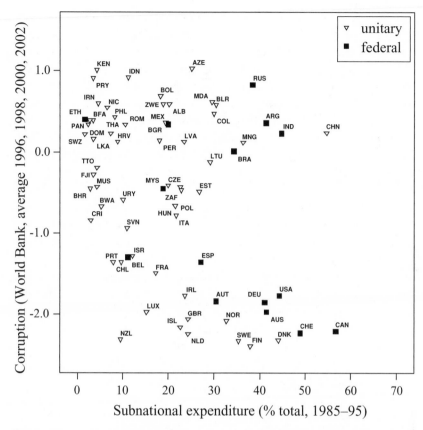

Figure 11.1. Decentralization and corruption, 1980s–1990s. *Sources*: Subnational expenditure calculated from IMF's *Government Finance Statistics* data as in *World Bank Decentralization Indicators*. Corruption data from World Bank, adapted so higher scores indicate more corruption. "Federal" as categorized by Elazar (1995), with Bosnia-Herzegovina added.

and "corrupt" countries such as China, India, Argentina, and Russia to drop out, the data would start to look much more like a downward-sloping line. Notice also that all the decentralized countries with low corruption ratings in the graph are developed countries; if one controls for national income, the C-shape turns into an upward-sloping line, indicating greater corruption in more decentralized countries.

In an interesting analysis that does include appropriate controls, Enikolopov and Zhuravskaya (2003) find some complicated conditional effects of fiscal decentralization on corruption. Among developing countries, greater decentralization is associated with lower corruption in countries that have long-established, stable party systems (as proxied by the age of the main parties), but higher corruption in countries with less well-established party systems. However, in developed countries, the relationship is reversed: Greater decentralization is associated with *higher* corruption in countries that have long-established, stable party systems, but lower corruption where party systems are less well established. The authors suggest some reasons why stable party systems might have different effects in developed and developing countries, but it is not clear why fiscal decentralization in the presence of strong party systems would have different effects at different levels of development.

Two studies explore whether smaller scale of subnational units leads to lower corruption, on the theory that horizontal competition should be more intense among smaller units. Arikan (2004) finds that the average number of local jurisdictions per 1,000 citizens is not significant; but, oddly, the average number of local *plus regional* jurisdictions per 1,000 citizens *is* significant at the 10 percent level. A larger number of local plus regional governments per capita correlates with lower corruption.[9] Treisman (2002) focuses on the average land area of local units (rather than the average population of local and regional units). I find that smaller local jurisdictions correlate very significantly with *higher* corruption. The results of these papers might differ for many reasons. Besides the different definitions of the size-of-jurisdiction variables, they use different corruption indexes and different sets of controls. My regressions include 81–114 countries, Arikan's 33–40. The relationship between size of units and corruption – if any exists – remains obscure.

In Treisman (2000), I found federal states to have significantly higher perceived corruption than unitary states (using TI indexes).[10] Fisman and Gatti (2002) do not find federalism significant (using ICRG data). This could be because three of the more corrupt federations – Nigeria, Pakistan, and Russia – drop out of their regressions because of missing data. In Treisman (2002), I investigated a number of other indicators of decentralization. I was unable to find any clear relationship between corruption, on the one hand, and subnational policy autonomy, electoral accountability of subnational executives, strong regionally representative upper houses of parliament, or the subnational share in government employment, on the

[9] The significance disappears, however, when he drops one of his controls.
[10] See, also, Goldsmith (1999) for a similar finding.

other. I did find a significant positive relationship between the number of tiers of government and the level of corruption.

Lederman, Loayza, and Soares (2005) analyzed the ICRG index of corruption in a panel for the years 1984–99. They found that once basic cultural and historical controls were included, the presence of an intermediate tier (region, province, or state) with an elected legislature and/or executive was associated with significantly higher corruption. (The difference from my results in Treisman [2002] could be due to the panel design. Or they might be picking up the effect of more tiers rather than elections per se.) They also found that larger fiscal transfers from the central to subnational governments were associated with lower corruption. These results would seem to go against the expectation that corruption can be reduced by making subnational governments more electorally accountable and fiscally self-sufficient.

Turning to public service provision, although many scholars have examined individual cases, I found very few papers that study how decentralization affects the extent or quality of government outputs in a cross-section of countries.

Burki, Perry, and Dillinger (1999) examine decentralization reforms in Latin America since the late 1970s and review a number of papers that assess these reforms. On education, they conclude that while giving individual schools greater autonomy may "contribute to higher-performing schools," the purported benefits of decentralization to local and regional governments "have not yet been demonstrated" in Latin America (ibid., p. 68). On health care, they write: "it might be argued that decentralization has damaged healthcare provision, at least in some Latin American countries" (ibid., p. 85). On infrastructure, in their assessment, the results of widespread programs to decentralize road management "have varied widely." While some countries – such as Argentina, Brazil, and Colombia – showed positive results, others – such as Bolivia and Peru – "had to seriously reconsider and reverse course" (ibid., p. 97). In short, they conclude that "Decentralization has improved services in some jurisdictions and worsened [them] in others" (Burki et al. 1999, p. 3).

Three studies look for statistical evidence of a link between fiscal decentralization and health care performance. Khalegian (2004) examined a panel of countries from 1980 to 1997. He found that greater decentralization was associated with a better record of immunizations for childhood diseases in poor countries – but a worse record of immunization in middle-income countries. Robalino, Picazo, and Voetberg (2001) studied the infant mortality rate in a panel of countries between 1970 and 1995. They found that greater fiscal decentralization was associated with lower infant mortality, especially in poorer countries. However, this study did not control for fertility, which is often thought to influence the infant mortality rate. Enikolopov and Zhuravskaya (2003) control for fertility in a similar cross-national panel for 1970–95. Fertility is very significantly related to higher infant mortality in their data. Controlling for this, decentralization is generally not significant among developing countries, although it is among developed ones. In both cases, there may be more complicated conditional relationships.

In Treisman (2002), I explored how a variety of measures of decentralization correlated in a cross-section of countries with two indicators of health care performance – the share of infants inoculated for diphtheria, tetanus, and pertussis, and the share of the population for which essential drugs were accessible and affordable. Subnational autonomy, fiscal decentralization, the size of units, number of tiers, and public employment decentralization were not significantly related to either measure of health care provision. A strong, regionally representative upper house of parliament was significantly associated with a much worse record inoculating babies. By contrast, more local electoral accountability correlated with somewhat better access to medicines.

Although there are many one-country case studies, I found almost no cross-national statistical analyses of political decentralization and public education. In Treisman (2002), I examined countries' rates of youth illiteracy (the percentage of those aged 15–24 who could not read).[11] Greater fiscal decentralization was associated with higher youth illiteracy. So was a measure of appointment decentralization (the extent to which subnational officials were chosen locally rather than appointed from above). Other types of decentralization were not significant. Enikolopov and Zhuravskaya (2003) also looked for effects of decentralization on education quality, as measured both by the illiteracy rate (for all adults) and the ratio of primary school pupils to teachers. They found some quite complicated interactive effects. For instance, in a panel (but not in cross-sections) of developing countries, greater revenue decentralization led to more pupils per teacher in countries where the main parties were less stable, but to fewer pupils per teacher in countries with more stable parties (ibid., p. 38). In a panel of

---

[11] This seemed a better measure of current education quality than the illiteracy rate for all adults, which reflects in part the quality of education many decades earlier.

developed countries, greater revenue decentralization appeared always to lead to more pupils per teacher (ibid., p. 39). One cross-sectional regression for developing and transitional countries found that (in most cases) greater revenue decentralization was associated with higher illiteracy (ibid.), but this was not significant in various other specifications. What to make of all this is unclear.

Estache and Sinha (1995) estimated the impact of fiscal decentralization on infrastructure expenditure in two panels – containing, respectively, ten developed and ten developing countries – during 1970–92. They found that the level of total per capita government spending on power, transport, and communications increased significantly with fiscal decentralization in both samples. These results prompt two additional questions. First, are the particular countries for which data were available representative of others in the relevant category? Second, is higher public spending on infrastructure – which obviously comes at the cost of something else – a good or a bad thing?[12]

Humplick and Estache (1995) address the second question more directly. They seek to assess how decentralization of responsibility for particular kinds of infrastructure affects the quality of provision. They find a positive correlation (in seventy-six developing countries) between the share of road maintenance financed by subnational governments and better maintenance of unpaved roads, but no significant relationships with other indicators of road maintenance. In the electricity sector, performance was negatively related to the degree of spatial decentralization within the electricity monopoly. They found no significant relationships with water supply.

In Treisman (2002), I examined three types of infrastructure provision – the share of the population with access to an improved water source, the percentage of the population with access to improved sanitation facilities, and the number of kilometers of paved road per thousand inhabitants. Most of the indicators of decentralization I studied were not significantly related to any of these measures of infrastructure provision. Fiscal decentralization was significantly associated with better provision of paved roads per capita, but with poorer access to sanitation facilities. A strong, regionally representative upper house of parliament was associated with poorer access to both water and sanitation and with fewer kilometers of paved roads. As in

---

[12] One concern is that the estimations appear to have been run by weighted least squares, without a correction for temporal autocorrelation, which might render the standard errors unreliable.

the case of corruption, no clear and simple patterns emerge from existing empirical analyses of decentralization and public service provision.

11.2 Economic Performance

Do politically and fiscally decentralized countries have better or worse economic performance than their more centralized counterparts? Various scholars have looked for effects of decentralization on: (a) macroeconomic stability, and (b) economic growth. I discuss these in turn.

Browsing through studies of individual countries, one quickly sees that some highly decentralized states have unusually good records of macroeconomic stability (the United States, Germany, Switzerland), while others have performed unusually badly (Argentina, Brazil, the former Yugoslavia). One might therefore expect empirical analyses to reach different conclusions depending on how many of each type of country are included in a given sample. Results certainly do vary.

Fornasari, Webb, and Zou (2000) examine a panel of seventeen developed and fifteen developing countries during the 1980–94 period. They find that in these countries, increases in subnational government spending and deficits were significantly related to increases in central government spending and central deficits the following year (ibid., p. 417). They conclude that "The process of fiscal decentralization tends to cause problems" and caution against "rapid decentralization without adequate safeguards" (ibid., p. 418). This conclusion – which Burki et al. (1999, p. 39) repeat – is a little surprising because the authors observe fiscal deficits spreading upward in a sample that includes both centralized and decentralized states and provide no evidence that the problem is worse in one than in the other.[13] In fact, the paper's regressions suggest that at least one kind of political decentralization – federal structure – can mitigate the tendency for subnational profligacy to get pushed upward (Table 3, p. 420).

De Mello (2000) studies a panel of seventeen developed and thirteen developing countries for the 1970–95 period and finds a "deficit bias in decentralized policy-making." Again, the results might support different interpretations. A number of related variables are included simultaneously in the regressions – "subnational tax autonomy," "subnational fiscal dependency," the "subnational spending share" – some in both current and

---

[13] The authors suggest that the results are driven by countries that experienced large changes in subnational spending or deficits – but such large changes could occur in countries that are either centralized or decentralized.

lagged form, along with one interaction term. Working out the net effects is complicated, but the most direct measure of fiscal decentralization – the subnational spending share – appears to be significantly related to lower rather than higher central and subnational deficits.

Martinez-Vazquez and McNab (2004) analyze a panel of fifty-two developed and developing countries between 1972 and 1997 and conclude, contrary to Fornasari et al. and De Mello, that fiscal decentralization increases macroeconomic stability. Controlling for change in the money supply, revenue decentralization (although not expenditure decentralization) was associated with lower inflation. The effect is relatively small – a 10 percent increase in the subnational revenue share is associated with just a 3 percent decrease in the inflation rate – but statistically significant.[14] Shah (2005) informally reviews some countries' experiences and similarly concludes that "decentralized fiscal systems offer a greater potential for improved macroeconomic governance than centralized fiscal systems." In Treisman (1998), I examined a panel of eighty-seven countries in the 1970s and 1980s and found no significant relationship in a worldwide sample between either federalism or fiscal decentralization (measured as either the subnational revenue or expenditure share) and inflation.

Rodden (2002) addresses the question of whether decentralization affects the size of subnational budget deficits. He uses a data-set of forty-six developed and developing countries in the period 1986–96. He identifies some quite complicated interactive effects between certain fiscal variables and subnational deficits. However, his federalism variable is not significant in any model, and his expenditure decentralization is significant (implying higher local government deficits) in only one of three models presented (ibid., p. 678).[15] He also finds no significant relationship between either federalism or expenditure decentralization and the total public-sector budget deficit. He concludes that "Fiscal decentralization and political federalism may indeed complicate macroeconomic management, but their effects are contingent on other institutional factors" (ibid., p. 683).

[14] One might wonder, though, why one would expect decentralization to affect inflation by a pathway that bypasses change in the money supply (which is included among the controls). Most arguments suppose that political pressures or institutional dysfunctions caused by decentralization result in larger increases in money emission – which, in turn, generate inflation.

[15] This regression, with subnational surplus as the dependent variable, controls, *inter alia*, for federalism, the central government surplus, the provincial surplus in federations, vertical fiscal imbalance, and an interaction term for vertical fiscal imbalance times borrowing autonomy.

Besides studying worldwide samples of countries, some scholars have analyzed developed and developing countries separately. King and Ma (2000) examined macroeconomic performance in twenty-one OECD countries. In data for 1982, they found a significant relationship between greater fiscal decentralization (measured as tax revenues) and lower inflation, although this relationship appeared to weaken in the 1990s as European countries moved toward monetary integration. Wibbels (2005, Chapter 3) studied a panel of eighty-three developing countries in 1978–2000. He found that among these countries federalism was significantly associated with both larger central government deficits and higher inflation. In Treisman (1998), I found similar contrasting results for subsamples of developing and developed countries (in the 1970s and 1980s). Whereas both federal structure and fiscal decentralization were associated with lower average inflation in the OECD countries, both of these were associated with higher inflation in the developing countries.

If it is true that decentralization correlates with greater macroeconomic instability in developing countries, but better performance in developed ones, why might that be the case? In Treisman (2000b), I suggest an answer and provide some evidence for it. I found that in more decentralized countries – whether developed or developing – relative macroeconomic performance tended to stay either good or bad over the course of years or decades. Whereas centralized countries slipped back and forth more easily between good and bad policies, their decentralized counterparts seemd to get "locked in" to historical patterns that proved highly durable. That meant that certain, mostly poorer, decentralized states with poor macroeconomic performance as of the late 1960s saw their performance deteriorate still further in subsequent decades, while other, mostly richer, decentralized states with good historical performance remained macroeconomically stable through the turbulence of the 1970s and 1980s. I interpreted this as evidence for the policy stability argument discussed in section 8.2. I return to this in section 11.5, where I discuss evidence of a link between decentralization and the durability of policies. In Figure 11.2, I plot average inflation of the consumer price index for 1995–2000 against countries' average level of fiscal decentralization in 1985–95. (Again, I plot the purported cause [decentralization] for a period before that of the effect to reduce the risk of picking up reverse causation.)

Finally, certain scholars have looked for relationships between fiscal decentralization and macroeconomic performance in samples of just federal states, arguing that such states have distinct political dynamics. Rodden

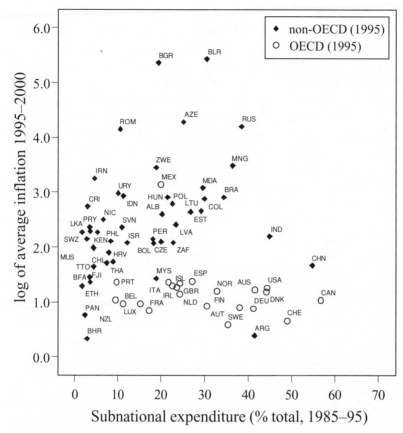

Figure 11.2. Decentralization and inflation, 1980s–1990s. *Sources:* Subnational expenditure calculated from IMF's *Government Finance Statistics* data as in *World Bank Decentralization Indicators*. Inflation of CPI from IMF *International Financial Statistics Yearbook*, 2002. One has been added to the inflation rate before taking the log.

and Wibbels (2002) studied a panel of fourteen federations between 1978 and 1996. They found that, controlling for various factors, greater fiscal decentralization was associated with smaller public-sector deficits in these federal states and was not significantly related to inflation (ibid., p. 518). The deficit-reducing effect was weaker where provincial governments were more dependent on fiscal transfers, but even at extremely high levels of transfer dependence fiscal decentralization still reduced the aggregate deficit. These results held in models both with and without country fixed effects. Wibbels (2006, 2005, p. 112), examining a panel of nine federal states in the same eighteen-year period, also found that, controlling for various factors, greater fiscal decentralization was associated with smaller public-sector deficits (but the interaction with transfer dependence was not significant). These results would seem at odds with the common claim that decentralization exacerbates fiscal imbalances; at least in federations, fiscal decentralization seemed to reduce deficits.

Several scholars have looked for an empirical relationship between fiscal decentralization and the growth rate.[16] Davoodi and Zou (1998) examined a panel of forty-six countries for the 1970–89 period, averaging growth rates over five- or ten-year periods and including country and period fixed effects. They found fiscal decentralization to be significantly associated with slower growth, both in the full sample and among developing countries, although not among developed countries taken separately. Iimi (2005) looked at average growth rates in 1997–2001 in a cross-section of fifty-one developed and developing countries. He found fiscal decentralization to be significantly associated with faster growth. The contrasting results might be due to the different design (cross-section rather than fixed effects panel), data period, or controls included in the regressions. Woller and Phillips (1998) examined a panel of twenty-three developing countries from 1974–91, including country fixed effects. They were unable to find "any strong, systematic relationship" between fiscal decentralization and growth in their sample. Martinez-Vazquez and McNab (2004) also found no significant relationship between fiscal decentralization and growth in their panel of fifty-two developed and developing countries in 1972–97. In brief, the results for growth are as difficult to read as those for macroeconomic stability.

11.3 Ethnic Conflict

As with economic performance, different examples can be used to motivate quite different conclusions about the effects of decentralization on ethnic conflict. Those who focus on the Soviet Union, Yugoslavia, Nigeria, or Sierra Leone tend to view political decentralization as problematic or even dangerous (Suberu 1994, Rosenbaum and Rojas 1997, Bunce 1999). By contrast, those who study the politics of Spain, Belgium, Switzerland, or India tend to see decentralization as a means of integrating diverse communities into a relatively harmonious single state (see, for instance, UN 2004).

Cross-national statistical analyses of this question are quite rare. Several scholars have studied the data on ethnic interactions compiled by Ted Gurr's

---

[16] For a review, see Breuss and Eller (2004).

"Minorities at Risk" (MAR) project, which monitors politically active ethnic groups around the world. The data distinguish between cases of "non-violent protest" (ranging from petitions and letter writing to mass rallies), "violent protest" (ranging from scattered sabotage to riots and local rebellions), and ethnic "rebellion" (ranging from banditry to guerrilla activity and civil war). Cohen (1997) examined these data for the 1945–89 period, focusing on just those groups located in democracies. He found that federalism was associated with less "rebellion" by minority ethnic groups, but more "non-violent protest," and he argued that federal institutions helped to moderate and redirect potentially violent conflicts. Hechter (2000b) identified a similar pattern in the MAR data, concluding that "whereas federation stimulates nationalist political mobilization, it decreases nationalist violence." Saideman et al. (2002) also examined the MAR data, this time employing a panel design and focusing on just the 1985–98 period. They also found federalism to be associated with more protests but fewer rebellions, although they cautioned that the result was not robust (see their footnote 34). Federalism was significantly associated with more rebellion only when the minority was territorially concentrated. Unlike Cohen, they found that federalism became insignificant if the sample was restricted to democracies; it was only among autocracies that federalism seemed to reduce rebellion and increase protest.

The general – although not complete – concurrence of findings would seem encouraging. However, Hug (2005) suggests that these studies are misspecified. He argues that federalism – and other kinds of political decentralization – is endogenous to ethnic conflict, a fact the studies of the MAR data fail to take into account. Replicating Cohen's (1997) analysis, he finds that the result changes dramatically when the endogeneity is incorporated into the model. In fact, federalism turns out to be associated with *higher*, not lower, frequency of rebellion, although this result was only marginally significant.

Two other studies, using different data, report mixed or inconclusive results. Brancati (2005) analyzes a panel of twenty-three democracies between 1990 and 2000.[17] She finds that, among these democracies, political decentralization had some effects that exacerbated and others that alleviated ethnic conflict. Decentralization tended to reduce conflict by giving minorities greater political, social, and economic autonomy, but it increased

---

[17] How these twenty-three were selected and whether they are more broadly representative is not entirely clear from the paper.

conflict by stimulating the development of regional parties, which reinforced minority identities and sometimes mobilized groups into ethnic violence. The net effect could vary from case to case. Hegre and Sambanis (2005) study the outbreak of civil wars and use a variation on Leamer's "extreme bounds analysis" to explore how robust various purported causal factors are to the inclusion of different sets of control variables. They include four measures of political decentralization. None of these turn out to be robust determinants of civil war.

11.4 Democracy

One of the first, informal attempts to assess the relationship between political decentralization – in this case, federalism – and democracy was that of Riker (1975, p. 156), who wrote:

It should be abundantly clear, just from looking at the list of federal governments, that not all of them are democracies or even pretend to be democracies, although their claim to be federations is indisputable. Mexico is one example, Yugoslavia is another, Nigeria was a third, before its civil war. To find an association between federalism and democracy is, on the face of it, absurd.

Some subsequent studies have seemed to bear out Riker's skepticism. Diskin, Diskin, and Hazan (2005) examined a dataset of 62 countries during parts of the twentieth century and found no empirical relationship between federalism and the likelihood of democratic collapse. Lane and Errson (2005) regressed democracy, as measured by Freedom House scores for 144 countries around 2000, separately on five alternative measures of federalism, along with various controls. The Freedom House scores may be thought of as measuring the extent of democracy on a continuum from pure dictatorship to pure democracy. In none of their regressions was any indicator of federalism statistically significant. In Figure 11.3, I plot countries' average Freedom House political rights scores for the years 1995–2000, corrected for the country's level of economic development,[18] against fiscal decentralization.

Foweraker and Landman (2002) analyzed the quality of democracy in forty countries in 1970–98, using a variety of measures of accountability,

---

[18] That is, I regress countries' average Freedom House scores in 1995–2000 on their average per capita GDP in 1985–95 and plot the residual against the subnational expenditure share in 1985–95. Because economic development is strongly related to political freedom and fiscal decentralization, this reduces the risk of observing a spurious correlation.

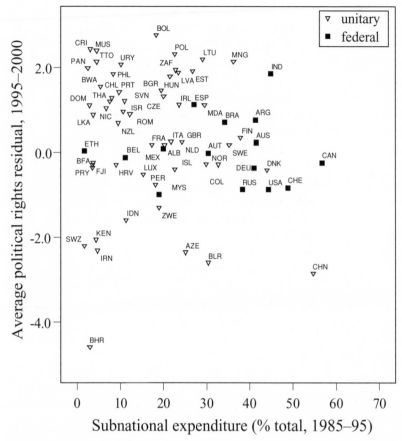

Figure 11.3. Decentralization and democracy, 1980s–1990s. Note: Average political rights residual is residual from regression of Freedom House political rights score (averaged for 1995–2000) on average per capita GDP 1985–95 (from World Bank's *World Development Indicators*). A positive residual indicates that the country had greater political freedom than predicted for its level of economic development. *Sources:* Freedom House; subnational expenditure calculated from IMF's *Government Finance Statistics* data as in *World Bank Decentralization Indicators*.

representativeness, participation, and other elements of democratic government. They found that federal countries had lower rates of participation and minority rights than unitary states in their data-set. Meguid (2003) examined how citizen participation changed in Western European countries in recent decades as some of them decentralized their political systems. She reviewed the trends in voter turnout and in the level of interest in politics and the sense of political efficacy of citizens, as judged from surveys and concluded that "decentralization has not caused overall increases in efficacy levels and interest in politics or high levels of voter turnout in the subnational level elections." Political interest did tick up in Belgium and France around the time of the first regional elections, but it soon fell again.

In contrast to all these studies, one other suggests an opposite result. Adsera and Boix (2004) report a significant positive relationship between federalism and democratic stability. They analyzed a data-set containing all democratic regimes from the mid–nineteenth century to the end of the twentieth century, where countries were classified as democratic if they had free and competitive elections; if the president was elected or the government (in a parliamentary system) was accountable to an elected legislature; and if at least 50 percent of the male population could vote. They found that among countries with per capita income under $7,000–$8,000 a year, federal structure was associated with longer survival of democracy than unitary structure. This was especially true among parliamentary regimes but also held among presidential ones. There was one exception that weakened the results slightly – Argentina, a federal country, suffered a number of coups at relatively high levels of economic development. Above per capita income of $7,000–$8,000 a year, all democracies whether federal or unitary were highly stable.

The paper offers probably the most comprehensive analysis of all democratic experiences. However, there still may be reasons for caution in interpreting the results. As the authors discuss, whether a country is federal or unitary is itself endogenous. Suppose federal structure actually makes democratic regimes *less* stable. Countries already suffering from political instability might then be less likely to adopt federal structures, and leaders of unstable federations might be inclined to convert them into unitary states. For instance, fractious politics in Uganda in the early 1960s prompted Prime Minister Milton Obote to suspend the country's federal constitution in 1966 and install a unitary presidential regime. Most federal democracies would then be stable just because all states with underlying instability would eschew federalism. Adsera and Boix address this by instrumenting for federalism with a dummy variable for former British colonies. The results are not always significant but tend to confirm their original conclusion. However, British colonial heritage does not seem a reliable instrument because various scholars have argued that British colonial experience itself predisposed countries to democracy through a variety of channels (see, e.g., Weiner 1987; Lipset, Seong, and Torres 1993).

In sum, it is hard not to agree with Kulipossa (2004, p. 778) that the strongest arguments are on the side of agnosticism or even skepticism: "a careful and detailed analysis of empirical works...forces one to question the assumed relationship between decentralization and democracy. If such a relationship really exists, it is far more complex and multi-faceted than usually thought." Or as Linz (1999, quoted in Lane and Errson 2005, p. 166) puts it: "Although there are writers who suggest so, federal states are not necessarily more democratic. To federalize might or might not be a step in the direction of democracy."

11.5 Stable Policies

The notion that political decentralization might enhance policy stability is an application of Tsebelis's theory of veto players (as discussed in Chapter 8). A number of empirical studies have found support for this theory. Most, however, focus on the number of veto players in central legislative politics or on the total number of veto players, rather than on the specific role of decentralization in creating additional veto points. Hallerberg and Basinger (1998) show that OECD countries with more veto players tended to change their corporate and personal income tax rates less in response to the U.S. tax reform of 1986. Franzese (2002, p. 187) finds that OECD countries with more veto players had greater difficulty reducing high levels of debt in the postwar period.[19] Kastner and Rechtor (2003) report that, among OECD parliamentary democracies, those with more party veto players in government enacted fewer changes to capital controls legislation during 1951–98. O'Reilly (2005) studies trade policy in twenty-three OECD countries in 1960–96 and finds that those with more institutional veto players had less change over time in the extent of tariffs and nontariff barriers.[20]

---

[19] He finds that federalism had a small restraining impact on government deficits but does not appear to have tested specifically whether federalism entrenched fiscal policy, whether good or bad.

[20] Three studies found evidence for another prediction – that greater ideological distance between veto players should result in greater policy stability. Tsebelis (1999) showed this for labor legislation in seventeen parliamentary democracies, and Tsebelis and Chang (2001) showed the same thing for the composition of central government spending in nineteen OECD countries. Basinger and Hallerberg (2004) found that countries were less likely to lower their tax rates on capital in order to compete with their neighbors if the veto players in these competitor countries were more ideologically divided (making it harder for these competitor countries to lower tax rates themselves).

The only paper I know of that examines the effect of political decentralization on the *durability* of government policies is Treisman (2000b), already discussed in section 11.2. I showed there that more decentralized countries tended to have more consistent performance in controlling inflation – whether consistently good or consistently bad. I interpreted this as evidence for the veto player–increasing effect of decentralization. I also found that federal structure tended to "lock in" the extent of central bank independence and the extent of central government net lending, both of which tended to converge to the mean more slowly in federal than in unitary states. Given the relative theoretical coherence of the argument linking decentralization to policy stability (see Chapter 8) and the encouraging empirical results on veto players and stability, more empirical work along these lines might be worth pursuing. However, decentralization is only one source of additional veto players, so the more general approach that focuses on all types of veto players – rather than just those created by decentralization – is probably preferable.

11.6 Conclusion

Many scholars have attempted to identify common consequences of decentralization by means of cross-national statistical comparisons. They have studied a range of political and economic outcomes, using different conceptualizations and measures of decentralization, different data, and different statistical methods. Some have detected complex interactive effects in particular data-sets. Others have found significant results that, however, weaken when more controls are added or the country coverage changes. Almost nothing that is robust or general has emerged.

To the seasoned empiricist with data on the hard drive, this might seem like an invitation. When the data refuse to speak in a clear voice, that might be because one has failed to ask them the right questions. Many scholars have already graduated from the search for simple linear effects to analysis of interactions between different institutional features of decentralized states. It is a matter of intellectual taste how deep into the thicket of imperfectly measured, non–randomly selected data-sets one wants to probe with multiple interaction terms. Perhaps we can find clear effects of fiscal decentralization among developing countries with parliamentary systems and small subnational jurisdictions during years of recession. But after a certain point, this sort of exercise appears to be picking up the idiosyncrasies of particular countries – or even mapping statistical noise – rather than identifying general patterns. Such efforts might yet congeal into a body of knowledge about where and when decentralized institutions perform well. Stronger empirical relationships might also emerge in new, more accurately measured and comprehensive data-sets. But it is noteworthy that many successive articles over the years have introduced their supposedly more conclusive results on this subject by pointing to the inconclusive nature of previous work.[21]

Even those inclined to favor decentralization on theoretical grounds often seem disappointed that empirical analyses turn up so little in the way of general support. Litvack et al. (1998, p. 3) complain that "Much of the discussion of decentralization reflects a curious combination of strong preconceived beliefs and limited empirical evidence." And later they seem close to cynicism: "It is not much of an exaggeration to say that one can prove, or disprove, almost any proposition about decentralization by throwing together some set of cases or data" (ibid., p. 30). The World Bank, in its *World Development Report 1999/2000*, argues strongly in favor of decentralization when it is well designed. But the report admits that empirical evidence supporting the main arguments for decentralization "is scanty" (World Bank 1999, p. 109).

To those convinced that theory in this area implies almost no general effects, the weak, partial, and inconclusive flavor of the empirical literature is not puzzling at all. It is what one would expect.

---

[21] Faguet (2004, p. 869), after reviewing some empirical studies, concludes: "The sum of these and many other findings is that 50 years of research has failed to establish clearly whether decentralization makes government more or less responsive to its citizens." He then presents a case study of decentralization in Bolivia that, although interesting in itself, cannot pretend to provide a general answer to this question.

12

Conclusion: Rethinking Decentralization

> The mania for drawing conclusions is one of humanity's most dreadful and sterile obsessions. Each religion, and each philosophy, has claimed to have God to itself, to comprehend the infinite and to know the recipe for happiness. What pride and what nothingness!
>
> Gustave Flaubert (1863)[1]

So what can one say in general about the consequences of administrative and political decentralization? It is time to sum up.

Multi-tier institutions can, as Montesquieu argued, achieve the advantages of both large and small size. Administrative decentralization makes it possible for a benevolent and wise ruler to satisfy the demands of a heterogeneous population more precisely and cost-effectively. But multi-tier government can also achieve the *dis*advantages of both large and small size. Under less benign, intelligent, or effective leadership, the outcome may be greater waste, higher costs, and more citizen frustration.

If administrative decentralization can have opposite effects, what about political decentralization? Some claim that giving local communities the right to select their own rulers and decide matters of local concern themselves will improve the quality of government. I considered a series of arguments to this effect. Many of these could hold in particular cases, but none seemed likely to hold in general. Nor could I identify a set of observable conditions under which the positive effects would outweigh the negative.

---

[1] From Flaubert's letter to Mlle. Leroyer de Chantepie, October 23, 1863. My translation from the original: "La rage de vouloir conclure est une des manies les plus funestes et les plus stériles qui appartiennent à l'humanité. Chaque religion, et chaque philosophie, a prétendu avoir Dieu à elle, toiser l'infini et connaître la recette du bonheur. Quel orgueil et quel néant!"

Under political decentralization, different policies can be chosen in different places. But the same is true under centralization: Fully sovereign central governments differentiate their policies geographically all the time. Some claim that local governments will be more sensitive to local wishes. In fact, the responsiveness of an elected government at either level will depend primarily on the intensity and pattern of competition for office. If competition in central elections is intense, the candidates will battle one another for votes throughout the country. If competition in local elections is weak, local incumbents will treat voters with indifference. If, at either level, the incumbent can get voters to compete against one another for redistributive benefits, he can use this method to escape accountability. On some divisive issues, the majority nationwide may want to impose its preferred policies on dissenting local majorities. Centralization will favor the nationwide majority in such conflicts, while decentralization will favor the local majorities. Different voters will be frustrated or satisfied in the two cases, but to say which majority *should* decide requires a value judgment.

Some think the smaller size of local districts will enable voters to coordinate better to discipline officials. But spontaneous coordination becomes unlikely when the numbers rise above a few hundred, so coordination will depend more on the efforts of the press, political parties, and other associations, which may be more or less active at either level. In any case, both central and local incumbents can preempt coordination by promising subgroups of voters selective benefits. In decentralized systems, responsibilities may be assigned neatly to particular tiers of government, making it easier to hold each to account. Or they may not. Responsibilities may also be assigned *less* clearly than under centralization; if many functions are shared across multiple tiers, it will be harder for voters to allocate praise or blame. In any case, even the smallest village governments perform multiple functions, making it difficult for voters to agree on how to judge them.

Decentralization is said to bring government "closer to the people." If this means physically close, centralized regimes can – and often do – station agents in local field offices, with just as direct a view of events as autonomous local governments would have. If "close" means sensitive to local voters' policy preferences, the counterarguments in previous paragraphs apply. If one has in mind community service – providing information to constituents, ensuring that bureaucrats treat citizens fairly, and so on – it is not clear why a member of the national parliament, elected in a local district, would be less concerned to help local voters than a mayor or councilman elected in the

271

same district. Both need local voters' support to get reelected.[2] Some point out that central governments must administer via bureaucratic agents, who may not be well monitored. In fact, almost all local governments implement policies by means of bureaucratic agents as well. A town mayor does not usually teach school, collect the garbage, and catch stray dogs herself. Whether bureaucracy is good or bad, this does not clearly distinguish the two systems. A central government might administer via a longer chain of agents, which might lead to greater loss of control as instructions pass down the hierarchy. Or it might not. There are methods – such as surveying local citizens about local services and paying all agents in the hierarchy accordingly – that can minimize incentives for agents anywhere in the chain to cheat.

Some have likened decentralized systems of government to the free market. Competition motivates firms to satisfy consumers' demands efficiently. In a politically decentralized system, local governments may have to compete against one another to attract mobile residents and capital. This might create a similar sort of discipline. Or it might not. Decentralization may fail to generate competition for a variety of reasons. If local governments *are* pressured to compete, they may compete in ways that harm citizens rather than in ways that benefit them. Or local competition, by reducing local taxation, may just increase the rents left for the central government to capture. If local competition does satisfy demands efficiently, central governments in a centralized democratic system will face incentives to replicate such competition.

Decentralization might, as Jefferson and Mill hoped, nurture civic spirit and teach political skills by involving ordinary people in the government of their communities. That is, unless local governments are more like "schools of evil" than Mill's "schools of good," teaching not civic virtue but nepotism, bribery, and partisan conflict. In any case, except in the smallest villages no more than a small fraction of the population can take direct part in government. And where all *can* in principle participate, institutions of direct self-government enable the confident, articulate, and socially privileged to dominate their more marginal fellow citizens. Indirect modes of participation – contacting representatives, voting in referenda, demonstrating, and so on – are available under centralization as well as decentralization.

---

[2] This would not necessarily be true, however, if the national electoral system were closed list proportional representation, in which case members of parliament would depend less on particular local communities.

Some assume that local governments are better informed about local conditions. But most information is either costly to acquire and analyze or can be elicited only in a strategic game. Local governments have no obvious cost advantage in acquiring the necessary information; indeed, a central government might enjoy economies of scale in data gathering and analysis. Nor is it clear that local governments would have a stronger motive to acquire relevant information or – in general – a greater ability to get citizens to reveal it. If transmitting information to the center for processing is costly, then a central government could process information in its local field offices. Under political decentralization, local units can serve as "laboratories" for policy experimentation. This might lead to greater policy innovation under decentralization – except that the same laboratories are available to a central government, which will often have stronger incentives to use them effectively and disseminate discoveries rapidly.

Some see decentralization as a bulwark protecting individual freedom. Strong local governments might coordinate to resist central abuses and defend the liberty of their citizens. On the other hand, they might coordinate to defend local abuses and prevent the central government from protecting civil rights. Or they might fail to coordinate at all. Political decentralization is sometimes thought to alleviate ethnic tensions by splitting the prizes of politics and enabling locally concentrated minorities to choose their own educational and religious policies. However, decentralization may also empower sectarian local leaders to persecute minorities and cultivate violent separatist movements. Local democracy may inflame local ethnic divisions and make it harder for central authorities to enforce peace between antagonistic groups.

Certain arguments focus on fiscal incentives. Assigning local governments a larger share of tax revenues might motivate them to support local economic growth, which would expand their tax base. But a larger share for local governments means a smaller share for the center. If fiscal decentralization of this type improves incentives for local officials, it must worsen them for their central counterparts, who will face weaker incentives to support growth. The net effect on the business environment could go either way.

All these arguments have at most highly conditional – and more often completely unclear – implications about the consequences of decentralization. But that does not mean that arguments about the dangers of decentralization are more convincing. Indeed, these do not seem to be more general at all.

Some think political decentralization encourages fiscal irresponsibility. If local governments view the central budget as a "common pool," they will wish to drain it before others do so. Their greed is beside the point, however, if the central government can just say no. Local governments may be able to pressure the central government to bail them out financially. If they pre-commit to policies the center does not like, the latter may choose to provide aid, "softening" the local governments' budget constraints. But, as I showed in Chapter 5, such attempts to manipulate the center can lead to lower – rather than higher – spending. Or they may be ineffective, if, for instance, the central government can exploit competition between the different localities, or if rich localities impose a hard budget constraint on the center. Another argument concerns vertical competition between governments at different levels whose tax bases or spending responsibilities overlap. If under decentralization both local and central governments can levy (distortionary) taxes on the same base, each may neglect the effect of the distortion on the other level, leading to a total burden of taxation that is higher than under unitary government. And the burden may increase with the number of tiers. But overlapping responsibilities may simultaneously lead to shirking in the provision of public goods, which should tend to reduce the budget.

One argument did seem somewhat more general. If political decentralization increases the number of actors whose acquiescence is needed to change policies, this will – other things being equal – tend to entrench the status quo. From a normative perspective, it is not clear whether such stability is to be valued or avoided. Entrenching the status quo may be desirable or undesirable, depending on what gets entrenched. In the long run, decentralization should tend to reduce the flexibility of government, creating continuity and predictability but impeding responses to crises.

In short, it is hard to reach any general conclusions about whether political – or administrative, or fiscal – decentralization will improve or impair the quality of government and economic performance. They will have many effects, driving in different directions on different dimensions. These effects depend on numerous conditions, many of which are difficult to disentangle in theory and to identify in practice. As one would expect, empirical studies have found almost no solid, general results about the consequences of decentralization. Decentralizing government in a particular place and time is very much a leap into the dark.

12.1 Possible Objections

These conclusions will seem counterintuitive to both advocates and critics of decentralization. As noted in the Introduction, I do not expect all readers to accept them. There may be arguments I have missed, and no doubt certain points might be defended more convincingly. These seem unlikely to change the picture that emerges of many complicated effects, pulling in different directions under different, often obscure conditions. However, a few possible objections of a more global character are worth considering.

12.1.1 No Models Are Completely General; No Institutions Always "Work"

Imagine, a critical reader might contend, that one were to subject free-market competition or democracy to the type of critique I have leveled at political decentralization. Market competition is not beneficial in all contexts. When rapid coordination is vital as in wartime, when information is asymmetrically distributed, or when natural monopolies exist, state regulation or planning may be preferable. The famous First Theorem of Welfare Economics, which establishes a presumption in favor of market competition, also makes assumptions that some would consider demanding – for instance, that a Walrasian equilibrium exists and is reached. Nor do we have a single, agreed model that shows why democracy will, in general, have better consequences than autocracy. Dictators – at least occasionally – may be benevolent, while democratic majorities are sometimes both misguided and illiberal. Should one, therefore, stop advocating market reforms and democratization?

I have some sympathy for this line of argument. It is true that no institutions work in the same way in all contexts (I return to this point in section 12.3) and that all models make assumptions, some of which may seem demanding. But I do not conclude from this that we should accept common claims made about decentralization uncritically. There are several key differences.

First, some institutions are valued not just because of their purported consequences but because they are desirable in themselves. Campaigners for democracy see in it not just an efficient mechanism to achieve some particular goal but a system that is good in itself. Security of property and freedom to trade – the foundations of free markets – are also often considered basic human rights. Advocates of political decentralization are sometimes *accused* of treating it as though it were itself a basic value.[3] But most make arguments about its consequences. If political decentralization is desirable in itself, the arguments in this book about its consequences are, of course, beside the point.

Second, the *reductio ad absurdum* argument sketched above does not necessarily lead anywhere absurd. Scholars do need to understand better the circumstances in which democratic institutions have desirable consequences (for instance, when electoral competition leads to protection – rather than persecution – of minorities). There is also plenty to learn about when market competition increases and when it decreases welfare. Much recent work in economics explores precisely how markets can fail if, for instance, information is imperfect. Examining the necessary assumptions and conditions underlying general claims for democracy and free markets has led to a deeper understanding of both. If the points raised in this book were to prompt a similar rethinking of the theory of political decentralization, yielding strong conditional arguments about its effects, it would have served its purpose. I am somewhat skeptical that such arguments will emerge for reasons discussed in section 12.1.4.

12.1.2 Models Are Tools; When They Fail, One Should Adapt Them

One response to this book's claims might be that the failure of a model to yield general conclusions is just that – a failure of the model – rather than a revelation about the world. Models are tools. When a construction worker's spirit level is broken, he repairs or replaces it; he does not give up on building houses. By the same logic, if our models of politics perform poorly at prediction or empirical validation, we should return to the drawing board and think how to modify the assumptions or techniques in a way that will yield more positive results. Just because the models I examine fail to establish general consequences of political decentralization does not mean that political decentralization does not have general consequences.

This objection would make a great deal of sense if I were using modeling to simulate the world or forecast by extrapolation. (Recall the discussion of different uses of modeling in Chapter 1.) Then, adjusting the models until they better simulated reality or fit the data might be perfectly

---

[3] For instance, Fesler (1965, p. 538) complains that "decentralization appears to have been transformed into a value in its own right, and so into an article of faith for 'right-thinking people.'"

appropriate. However, the use of modeling in this book aims at a more modest objective: to evaluate the validity and applicability of common arguments about decentralization. Most of these are based on informal intuitions, metaphors, or images. If the formalizations I use accurately capture the logic of the basic intuitions yet expose flaws in this logic or narrow bounds of applicability, then the appropriate next move is not to "fix" the models by stretching them in new directions. It is to conclude that the original intuition is unreliable as a general guide. I am not testing claims about the world in this book, although Chapter 11 turned up a notable lack of evidence of any general consequences of decentralization. I am testing the persuasiveness of a collection of often-repeated arguments. It is true that I do not prove decentralization has no general consequences in the real world; I do not purport to. I just show that there is no reason to think it would.

To an uncommitted researcher, the style of adjusting and readjusting models until they support a particular conclusion, rather than building them to see where plausible assumptions lead, can seem dogmatic and perverse. At times, scholars seem determined to show formally that decentralization is beneficial, no matter how difficult this turns out to be. They remain loyal to their initial intuition come what may, a bit like the medieval astronomers who found that planets did not move in the ways predicted by Ptolemy's theory of epicycles and so added epicycles to the epicycles. At some point, the difficulty of modeling decentralization in a way that produces general and empirically useful implications becomes a datum in its own right. If one never arrives at the desired goal, one might consider whether one is heading in the right direction.

12.1.3 Models Are Metaphors; One Should Not Take Them Literally

Other critics might contend that I have misunderstood the role of formal models in economic and political arguments. Of course models do not correspond exactly to the observable world. Of course they simplify and select, and they reach conclusions that are not general. That is their function. Formal models direct attention to some aspects of a complex reality. They isolate particular mechanisms and describe them in stark and precise language. They show similarities between superficially dissimilar phenomena. To take them literally is to miss the point. Formal models are not catalogs of the features of reality. They are metaphors – rhetorical devices scientists use to persuade others of the cogency of their arguments.

In fact, this account of modeling is quite consistent with what I have tried to do in this book. If authors are using models as rhetorical devices, one must consider whether to let oneself be persuaded by the rhetoric. It makes sense to ask two sets of questions. First, are the models valid – do they obey the rules of formal logic? Second, are they relevant – do they capture the key elements of the "real world" cases we are interested in? The question is not whether models simplify but whether they simplify in ways that bias the conclusions. For instance, has the author omitted from the game players that would change the logic, or has she assumed certain parameter values that will rarely arise in practice? If so, the model's usefulness as a guide to experience is open to question. A given model may be simple, brilliant, and aesthetically pleasing as a metaphor – and yet useless for understanding the world.

Of course, I do not just evaluate other authors' models; I build some of my own. Formalization helps to unpack the intuitions that motivate arguments and to see if they rely on a selective exclusion of important facts. It helps check that arguments observe rules of deductive logic. It can make explicit necessary assumptions that otherwise would go unnoticed and let the reader decide whether these are too demanding. In short, models can be critical tools as well as rhetorical devices, arming the consumer – rather than the purveyor – of scientific claims.

12.1.4 Of Course Decentralization Is Not Always Good; It Must Be "Well Designed" and Introduced Under "the Right Conditions"

Sophisticated advocates of decentralization have already digested the finding that political decentralization may have bad as well as good consequences. Influential articles by Vito Tanzi (1996) and Remy Prud'homme (1996) identified a number of "dangers of decentralization" that had been somewhat neglected. This prompted some scholars to make more conditional arguments. As Litvack et al. (1998, p. 26) put it: "To debate whether decentralization is good or bad is unproductive and misleading since the impact of decentralization depends on design." Or as Wildasin suggested, in a response to Tanzi's article: "the 'right' degree of decentralization depends on what it is we are considering decentralizing and on local economic, historical, and political circumstances" (Wildasin 1996, p. 325).

The analysis in this book suggests that, indeed, political decentralization can have beneficial effects under certain conditions. The problem is that the set of conditions is so complicated and hard to identify empirically as to undermine even a conditional endorsement of decentralization. Saying that decentralization is good when "well designed" or when introduced under the "right conditions" is useful only if one can specify in general and for particular countries what "good design" and the "right conditions" are.

What do those who make such arguments have in mind? I examined a number of recent papers and reports by leading specialists in search of clarification. Most authors were vague about what the necessary conditions for successful decentralization were. Some did cite particular prerequisites. But they rarely explained how these had been chosen, and the conditions mentioned seemed problematic in several ways.

First, many of the prerequisites for successful decentralization that scholars identified – transparency, popular participation, the rule of law – are actually things that would help in almost any setting.[4] Such factors may, indeed, improve governance in a decentralized state. But they would also improve it in a centralized state. They do not, in themselves, establish a presumption for one system over the other.[5] Some prerequisites for successful decentralization have the added disadvantage that they are not directly observable and can only be inferred from whether decentralization succeeds or fails. Among the "main reasons typically cited for poor decentralization performance," Paul Smoke (2000, p. 2) includes "weak political resolve." Because "weak political resolve" is usually detected only when an attempted reform fails, it does not go very far toward explaining such failures.[6]

---

[4] Litvack et al. (1998) and World Bank (1997) both emphasize the importance of transparency and community participation. See Diamond (1999) on rule of law.

[5] Diamond (1999, pp. 159–60) asserts that centralized government is "intrinsically less democratic" than decentralized government. He then qualifies this, saying it is true only if local and regional governments are themselves democratic. To ensure this, "other institutions are needed, including a well-crafted constitution, a strong and independent judiciary, and a vibrant civil society." However, in a state with a well-crafted constitution, a strong and independent judiciary, and a vibrant civil society, *centralized* government would also perform well. Decentralization is a bit like a stone that can be used to make a tasty soup – so long as one also adds carrots, onions, chicken, and spices. I would also place in this category the common prescription of public finance specialists – irreproachable in itself – that decentralization will work better if local public services are financed by user charges (e.g., Litvack et al. 1998, p. 27). User charges should have the same beneficial effects on incentives and allocative efficiency whether the government providing local public services is central or local.

[6] In another paper, Smoke does – laudably – identify countries where governments did have strong political will to decentralize in a way that is independent of the results (Smoke 2001). However, as he points out, in these cases political will did *not* result in succcessful decentralization.

Second, some of the conditions required for successful decentralization are actually benefits that decentralization is itself supposed to produce. One paper summarizing the World Bank's recent efforts cites research which "showed that decentralization can increase participation, improve the accountability and responsiveness of government, and lead to programs and projects which better match local preferences and are therefore more sustainable." The paper cautions, however, that "For decentralization programs to work well requires that . . . strong, enforceable systems of accountability and monitoring by citizens and the central government are established" (Ayres 2003, pp. 72–3). In other words, decentralization will improve accountability, so long as effective systems of accountability are established. Decentralization will also improve air quality, so long as effective systems of pollution control are established.

Some other commonly cited conditions concern not exogenous features of the setting, or particular ways decentralization might be designed, but endogenous aspects of the way the political game is played. For instance, some economists argue that for decentralization to work well, the central government must refuse to bail out local governments. "Central governments must demonstrate early on that they are committed to imposing a hard budget constraint on subnational governments" (World Bank 1999, p. 124). But whether or not the central government imposes hard budget constraints on local governments depends on whether doing so is an equilibrium strategy. As discussed in Chapter 5, it may be or it may not, depending on details of the game. If one actor "must" act against its self-interest for decentralization to work, one should probably not be optimistic.[7] In any case, this is not an exogenous condition that reformers can observe in advance or a neutral design feature they can incorporate in a reform plan.

Or, to take another example, political decentralization will work better, various scholars argue, if there are clear rules governing the division of policy responsibilities among governments (World Bank 1997, p. 127; World Bank 1999, p. 112). Clarity is surely a good thing. Clear rules were one of the many conditions I found in Chapter 7 to be necessary for voters

---

[7] In a similar vein, Bird and Vaillancourt argue that for fiscal decentralization to be successful, there should be "no funding at the margin from transfers from other levels of government" (Bird and Vaillancourt 1998, p. 12). The principle is sensible in itself. But whether there is or is not such funding at the margin seems to me to be endogenous to the game played by the two levels of government rather than a technical aspect of tax system design.

to hold decentralized governments accountable.[8] But, as I argued there, rules do not become unclear by chance or by oversight of the designers: They are deliberately obfuscated by the players. Both local and central governments have reason to blame the other for their own failures and claim credit for the other's successes. The public collaborates in blurring the rules because if a local community blames the center for a locally generated failure, this may – however unjustly – pressure the center to provide remedies. To require clear rules as a condition for decentralization to work well is, in effect, to require that the players refrain from pursuing self-interest, or that they be restrained by some rule-clarifying mechanism that no one has yet discovered.

Rules must not only be clear; they must limit government abuses. For decentralization to succeed, according to the World Bank's *World Development Report 1997*, "states" must "make sure that sound intergovernmental rules are in place to restrain arbitrary action at the central and the local levels" (World Bank 1997, pp. 129–230). Leaving aside who the "states" are that should write such rules to constrain central and local governments, it is unclear who should enforce them. Sometimes it is said that rules must be "self-enforcing."[9] This is usually taken to mean that the rules coincide with equilibrium behavior: It is in each individual's self-interest to follow the rules, given the self-interested strategies chosen by the others. But if people choose to act in a particular way because doing so is a best response to the actions of others, the rules themselves do not restrain the actors but merely describe mutually consistent patterns of behavior. Sound, self-enforcing rules under which local and central governments behave appropriately are not a condition for successful decentralization – they are a description of it.

Finally, some conditions for successful decentralization amount to requirements that the central government monitor and supervise its local counterparts and intervene periodically to stop the local governments from messing things up.[10] One essential precondition for success, according to Hommes (1996, p. 348), is that the central government have the ability "to direct reforms and to behave in a way that does not impede

---

[8] In fact, it is not just the clarity of the rules but the absence of joint or concurrent responsibilities.

[9] E.g., World Bank (1999, p. 112).

[10] Fesler (1965, p. 549) offered a devastating critique of such arguments forty years ago. See also Hutchcroft (2001, p. 44), who quotes Fesler approvingly.

decentralization." The central government must have "sophisticated polit-ical skills" and be "able – and willing – to steer the institutional change in the direction of a more democratic and efficient society." The obvious question is why – if such a sophisticated, capable, and benevolent central government exists – one needs to decentralize at all. At the same time, if the central gov-ernment retains the right to intervene at its discretion, this can only be some kind of administrative – not political – decentralization. As Prud'homme (1996, p. 357) replied in a skeptical rejoinder to Hommes: "Few developing countries have a central government that is sufficiently strong, dedicated, and efficient to perform these functions. And the few that would qualify are precisely the countries that do not need decentralization.... Where decentralization is needed (because central governments are corrupt and inefficient), it cannot be implemented. Where it can be implemented, it is not needed."

In short, this admittedly cursory review identified some factors that would help almost any political system work effectively, as well as a list of desirable things one might urge "states" to do. It did not turn up any useful guidelines to predict in what times and places decentralization will outper-form centralization. Identifying such guidelines is extremely difficult. Some advocates of "well-designed" decentralization are, in fact, admirably candid on this point. Smoke (2001) admits that some of the commonly cited prereq-uisites of decentralization – such as a clear system of laws outlining the roles and responsibilities of local governments – are actually neither necessary nor sufficient for success. Some countries have decentralized successfully without them, while others have failed despite meeting the precondition. "We may not be able to say exactly what the 'correct' form of decentral-ization is for a particular country," write Litvack et al. (1998, p. 27), "but we do know that correct institutional incentives are essential both to reveal mistakes and to provide a self-regulatory mechanism." If the correct insti-tutions are essential to make decentralization work, but one cannot say what they are, this would seem to rather weaken the case for decentrali-zation.

Or consider a remarkable admission on the last two pages of the U.S. Agency for International Development's practical handbook on decentral-ization (USAID 2000). After detailing (in sixty-four pages) how agency employees should set up decentralization programs in countries around the world, the author shifts gears suddenly to ask: "Should decentralization always be promoted?" The handbook then lists a series of problems that decentralization can generate, including inequity, local authoritarianism, and the erosion of national standards in education and health. The author concludes:

> As this section demonstrates . . . maximizing the impact of program activities on the development of democracy and improved governance demands greater understanding in a variety of areas. In the coming months and years, in its efforts to provide technical leadership for the Agency, the DG Office will be taking on many of these and other questions as they emerge. Ultimately, after all, successful programming is a continual learning process.

One cannot help wondering whether this learning process might not be more useful before rather than after hundreds of millions of dollars have been spent promoting a particular type of reform.

12.2 Explaining Decentralization's Appeal

If I am right that very little can be said in general about the consequences of political decentralization, why do so many scholars, journalists, and politicians think otherwise? What can account for the widespread, persistent belief in the superiority of decentralized government? Although this is more a question for a sociologist of knowledge than a political scientist, several elements seem to me to have combined to generate this presumption.

First, centralization suffers from a great deal of guilt by association. Historically, centralized government has been the preferred choice of dictators, empire builders, and incompetents.[11] Robespierre snarled at the "federalists" who opposed his vision of a unitary republic of virtue and sent more than a few to the guillotine. Stalin reserved special corners of Siberia for those who took the Soviet federal constitution too literally. Hitler's aim to unite the entire German people left little room for local autonomy. Not all dictators favor centralization – Mao, during the Cultural Revolution, sought to bypass the bureaucracy and decentralize terror to the villages – but most tyrants have attempted to consolidate power in their own hands. By contrast – and, in part because of this – democratic reformers often seek to dismantle centralized structures and devolve decision making to local governments. The elected leaders who replaced military *juntas* in Latin

---

[11] As Ivo Duchacek (1975, p. 46) puts it: "on the side of unitary centralism we may find such mutually antagonistic groups as, for instance, the radical right which dreams about fascism; the radical left which has been inspired by Stalin, Trotsky, or Mao; and enlightened liberals who are committed to welfare planning and an energetic struggle against parochial backwardness" – a gallery of rogues sufficient to scare most college freshmen.

America in the 1980s thought decentralization a key element in overcoming their authoritarian legacies. So did the postcommunist leaders of various Eastern European countries.

Reviewing such cases, it is hard to escape a subtle – or sometimes not so subtle – bias. Centralized institutions did not create Hitler; Hitler centralized Germany's political institutions. Stalin built his hierarchical machinery of terror himself out of the debris of post-imperial Russia. Still, one can easily slip into thinking that it is centralization which causes dictatorship, not dictators who choose centralization. The unwary observer can also misdiagnose symptoms of authoritarian politics – repressive, unresponsive bureaucracy – as maladies of centralization and mistake aspects of democracy – transparency, accountability – for benefits of decentralization.

Not only dictators and imperialists seek centralized institutions. Governments that are unable to maintain order or perform basic functions often respond by tightening hierarchical authority. This may not work, but it is a common impulse of ineffective governments. One recent example is Russian President Vladimir Putin's efforts, after the turbulent 1990s, to subordinate regional and local leaders to the Kremlin and establish a strong "vertical of power." These reforms are defended as – and probably believed to be – essential for reconstructing an effective state. That weak, embattled, and incompetent governments tend to centralize political institutions creates another misleading association in the minds of some observers. They blame the failures of government on centralization when in fact centralization may have resulted from the failures of government.

Second, the popularity of decentralization feeds off romantic images of life in small, usually rural communities. Villages and towns are often thought of as "authentic" or "natural" units, while central governments are seen as artificial and contrived. The mystique of the Athenian polis combines with images of communal barn raisings, church picnics, summer hayrides, and so on. Of course, such a view of small-town life is highly selective. Besides dancing round the Maypole, the New England townspeople found time to burn witches and pin scarlet letters onto adulterers. But the widespread nostalgia for a kind of harmonious community, where the common life is based on friendship rather than on mutual interest, predisposes people to favor small-scale political units.

In the United States, decentralization has a particular cultural resonance. There are several reasons. First, the history of isolated pioneer settlements engendered a strong attachment to the folkways of the self-governing village. "We have inherited . . . local town-meeting practices and ideas," John

Dewey wrote eighty years ago. "But we live and act and have our being in a continental nation state" (Dewey 1927, p. 113). Second, since colonial times, politics has been infused by a historically conditioned distrust of central authority. Two wars have been fought over local autonomy – one against London, one against Washington – and both left profound marks on the national psyche. Some Southerners still like to recall that "before the Civil War the phrase the United States took a plural verb" (Reed 2000). In no other country could the partisans of strong *central* government have been known not as centralists or nationalists but as "Federalists."

These historical factors pop out in unexpected places. One of the most influential modern thinkers about the benefits of decentralization is the Nobel Prize–winning economist James Buchanan, who, along with Gordon Tullock, founded the school of public choice analysis. In a fascinating account of how his upbringing affected the direction of his work in political economy, Buchanan recently recalled the cultural atmosphere of his early years:

I was born and reared in the upper South of the country, in middle Tennessee, a region that was Confederate in loyalties during the great Civil War of the 1860s, but which had never been a plantation society, as such. That war itself cannot be overlooked as a formative influence. In a genuine sense, I grew up as a member of a defeated people in a war that was still remembered by my grandparents. From this fact of history alone, any strongly held pronationalist sentiment, if translated into unquestioning loyalty or fealty to federal or central government authority, would have been near-treachery.[12]

A third great source of support for political decentralization consists of analogies to the market. Given the remarkable feats of organization and information processing markets are known to accomplish, comparing decentralized government to a free market guarantees it considerable appeal. Sometimes the comparison is explicit and literal, as in Tiebout's account of local governments competing to satisfy mobile clients. In Tiebout's world, local governments are not just *like* firms in a market – they are a special kind of firm, selling products to consumers, who can pick and choose. But often connections are drawn in a fuzzier way, confusing quite different phenomena. In the 1930s, a famous debate pitted advocates of "centralization" – meaning here state planning and economic administration – against believers in "decentralization" – meaning here individual choice and free markets. Friedrich Hayek argued, against Oskar Lange, that

---

[12] Buchanan and Musgrave (2000, p. 15).

even if the mathematical computations necessary for centralized economic control could be made, only the price system could extract and exploit the necessary "local" information from all the consumers and sellers. This debate – which these days Hayek is taken to have won – is sometimes invoked to justify political decentralization. In fact, as I noted in Chapter 9, Hayek's point had nothing to do with how authority should be distributed across levels of government: It was about the advantages of market coordination over state planning.[13]

Fourth, the affinity many people feel for decentralized politics is some-times really an attraction to diversity. The two have often been conflated, consciously or unconsciously. Diversity is associated with creativity, evolu-tionary resilience, and flexible problem solving. It is a powerful value in its own right. Unitary systems are often assumed to impose a "sterile unifor-mity" and to insist on standardized routines. Some do. But must all? Again, our intuitions are colored by the historical association of centralization with authoritarianism, and it is hard mentally to separate the two. One can cer-tainly imagine a unitary democracy whose leaders nurture local diversity by limiting the state, enlarging the sphere of local asssociations, decen-tralizing administration, encouraging a culture of tolerance, and respond-ing to local citizen feedback. Indeed, following the logic advanced several times in this book, if electoral competition at the center is strong, leaders should face powerful incentives to give local voters what they want in all its variety. At the same time, a central government should internalize the advantages diversity provides *to the entire system* – such as greater adaptabil-ity to a changing environment – that are likely to be ignored by individual local leaders. Innovative organizations, such as the Capital One corpora-tion and the U.S. Marine Corps, have found ways to encourage innovation and improvisational adaptation at the ground level without undermining the basic hierarchy of command (Meyer and Davis 2003, pp. 131–61). Although understandable, perhaps, the assumption that diversity can be found only in politically decentralized systems does not seem correct.

Finally, of course, there are the eloquent, intuitively appealing arguments of the great political theorists that this book has attempted to examine. It is not surprising that, with defenders such as Tocqueville, Mill, and Rousseau, a belief in the value of political decentralization would have found its way into the conventional wisdom. Each of these three authors was enthusiastic

---

[13] He did hold out hope in another essay that competition might restrain local governments from abusing their power (Hayek 1939).

about decentralized institutions.[14] In fairness, however, one should note that each had certain reservations and doubts.

None of the three thought a particular set of decentralized institutions would have the same, desirable effects in all countries. Despite making general-sounding pronouncements, each actually focused on the way decentralization worked in particular places and periods, and on the social underpinnings needed for decentralization to succeed. All recognized that under some conditions, decentralized forms of government could perform disastrously. They, too, would have been uncomfortable with universal or indiscriminate policy prescriptions.

Tocqueville admired the decentralized character of American government. But he thought that unique factors made such arrangements work in the American context. Far from proposing that other countries copy American institutions, he insisted that attempts to do so would likely fail. Three factors were crucial for a decentralized system to succeed: a highly educated and engaged population (in which "even the lowest ranks of society have an appreciation of political science"), cultural homogeneity, and geographical remoteness, which kept the country out of wars so it could afford the administrative inefficiencies that decentralization generated. The Mexicans had transported the U.S. Constitution to a less hospitable environment. "But when they borrowed the letter of the law, they could not at the same time transfer the spirit that gave it life. As a result, one sees them constantly entangled in the mechanism of their double government . . . shifting from anarchy to military despotism and back from military despotism to anarchy" (Tocqueville 1969 [1835], p. 165).

Even in less auspicious settings, Tocqueville did believe "administrative decentralization" was possible and desirable. (By this he meant the provision of local public goods and services by locally formed bodies.) But local liberties were a fragile growth, in continual danger of being trampled. France, too, had once had vigorous municipal institutions. In the archives researching *The Old Regime and the Revolution*, Tocqueville found records of medieval parishes that bore a strong resemblance to the New England townships. By the eighteenth century, these had been hollowed out and replaced by "petty oligarchy" (Tocqueville 1955 [1856], p. 45). If history was driving toward an ever-greater concentration of power and homogenization of society, local institutions could at most slow the process rather than reverse it.

---

[14] Although Rousseau's views on this are harder to characterize: See below.

Thus, Tocqueville's defense of American local democracy is best seen as just that – a defense of decentralization as it had evolved, with all the underlying social supports, in America. He did not think that similarly vigorous local institutions could be easily engineered elsewhere. Rather, successful decentralization occurs as a happy accident:

> [C]ommunal freedom is not, one may almost say, the fruit of human effort. It is seldom created, but rather springs up of its own accord. It grows, almost in secret, amid a semibarbarous society. The continual action of laws, mores, circumstances, and above all time may succeed in consolidating it. Among all the nations of continental Europe, one may say that there is not one that understands communal liberty. (Tocqueville 1969 [1835], p. 62)

Mill ardently advocated strong local government. But he was troubled by the dissonance between decentralization as an ideal and the corrupt and ineffective English local governments he observed in practice. In reviewing the first volume of *Democracy in America*, Mill agreed with Tocqueville that local self-government could not be introduced in Europe in the same form as in the New England towns. This, Mill cautioned, would only "throw the cloak of democratic forms over a jobbing oligarchy" (Mill 1977 [1835], p. 63). On the one hand, he believed passionately in the mission of local public service to educate and civilize the lower classes that were being mobilized into politics by the great nineteenth-century reforms. On the other, he saw that local governments could bring out the worst rather than the best in those who served in them. He found no solution to this problem.

For Rousseau, decentralization was never more than a distant second best. The virtuous city republics of ancient Greece were his ideal. When larger scale was vital for military defense, he was willing to countenance confederal alliances or even the confederal states of Switzerland or the Dutch United Provinces (Rousseau 1986 [1762], p. 100). Asked in 1769 to advise the Poles on a constitution for their country, Rousseau began by recommending that, if their neighbors did not do them this "service," they should split the country into smaller pieces.[15] Barring that, he told them to "extend and perfect the system of federal government." (Rousseau 1986 [1772], p. 183)

But it is far from clear what he meant by this. Although he writes of "federal" government, he insists that sovereignty is indivisible and held by the central diet on behalf of the entire citizenry (ibid., e.g., p. 195). Local

---

[15] Rousseau (1986 [1772], p. 182). The neighbors did oblige.

assemblies – the little diets, or "dietines" – play an important role in his scheme, but apparently as electoral colleges for selecting and instructing deputies to the central legislature. Nowhere does he assign them authority to make local laws. "[B]e sure that nothing can break the bond of common legislation which unites them, or disturb their common subordination to the body of the republic" (ibid., pp. 194–5). He is adamant that local bodies do not have the right to protest or disobey central legislation once passed, although each province has the right to veto central constitutional laws via its deputy (ibid., p. 183). Thus, it is quite possible to agree with several critics who contend that Rousseau is not an advocate of federalism at all (Riley 1973, p. 17; Nelson 1975, p. 12). Rather, the arrangement he describes sounds like one of centralized representative government, with strong protections built in for the provinces.[16]

Rousseau quite explicitly agrees with Montesquieu that particular forms of government must be adapted to the mores, history, and geography of a given country. "Just as an architect, before erecting a great edifice, observes and sounds out the ground to see if it can support the weight, the wise legislator does not begin by drawing up laws which are good in themselves, but first investigates whether the people for whom they are intended is capable of bearing them" (Rousseau, 1986 [1762], p. 46). His recommendations for the Poles were not meant to be applied loosely to other settings, regardless of conditions. Fortunately, he wrote, the constitution he recommended was "already in harmony with the spirit of [Polish] institutions" (Rousseau, 1986 [1772], p. 182). As with Tocqueville and Mill, a careful reading suggests a more conflicted and context-specific advocacy of decentralized institutions than is often appreciated.

12.3 A New Agenda?

"The question of decentralization is once more on the agenda, not just in France but in the entire world," wrote the French liberal politician Camille Hyacinthe Odilon-Barrot in 1861.[17] One could add that it has never quite

---

[16] Nelson (1975) sees this, rather, as a blueprint for a confederal state. The fact that each province may not challenge a central law that has been made with assent of its deputy – even though that deputy could have exercised his veto during the central deliberations – and the fact that Rousseau does not discuss any right of the dietines to pass local laws suggest to me that the scheme is closer to one of representative central government.

[17] My translation from Odilon-Barrot (1861, p. 18): "La question de décentralisation est de nouveau à l'ordre du jour, non-seulement en France, mais dans le monde entier; elle remplit

left the agenda since. "Since the Revolutionary War, thoughtful students of American institutions have viewed the issue of centralization versus decentralization as one of the most important – and difficult – of their problems," wrote George Benson in 1941 (p. ix). Again, the claim could have been made with equal justice yesterday. Every decade or two, advocates and critics of decentralization square off, ready to debate the issue one more time. A familiar set of arguments for and against decentralization is rediscovered, and they are dusted off and sent out to battle. Familiar tradeoffs are identified, analyzed, catalogued, and – these days – modeled and graphed from multiple angles. Apparently, the results have never seemed sufficiently conclusive for debaters to wish to stop.[18]

Although many of the same arguments turn up repeatedly – and decentralization almost always seems to "win" – the emphasis has changed over the years. Different virtues come to the fore. In the 1920s, scholars emphasized the need to reduce the congestion of business in the central organs of government in Britain, France, and the United States (Lowrie 1922). Right after World War II, the efficiency of decentralized institutions was contrasted with the waste and tyranny of totalitarian states (e.g., Benson 1947, pp. 171, 178). In the 1960s and early 1970s, decentralization was seen as a way to re-create participatory communities in the midst of rigid bureaucracies and atomized mass societies.[19] In the 1980s, support for decentralization in the United States merged with the anti-government rhetoric and deregulation crusades of the Reagan right. Libertarian arguments for individual self-help dissolved into arguments for local self-government. More recently, decentralization has found a place in the "to do" list of economic reformers, along with privatization, trade liberalization, and various other good things. Skeptics have periodically jumped in to prick the bubble – see Laski (1939), Fesler (1965), Kristol (1968), Riker (1975), and Tanzi (1996) – but with only temporary effect.

It is not only scholars who keep rediscovering and re-arguing the same questions. There are also clear cycles in the salience of decentralization in electoral politics. In a fascinating study, De Vries (2000) measured the frequency with which manifestos of the leading political parties in four

---

tous les écrits un peu sérieux sur la politique, et de plus elle se trouve au fond de tous les problèmes qui s'agitent dans le monde."

[18] It is striking how similar Benson's (1941) discussion of the pros and cons of decentralization is to typical analyses today. Few new arguments have emerged – and few have been resolved – during the past sixty years.

[19] E.g., Marcuse (1972, p. 42), quoted in Furniss (1974, p. 958).

countries – England, Germany, Sweden, and the Netherlands – discussed decentralization during the postwar period. In each country, attention to decentralization fluctuated in waves lasting about ten to fifteen years. Interest peaked in different years in the different countries – the early 1950s in Germany, around 1970 in England, the early 1970s in Sweden, the late 1980s in the Netherlands – but all showed cycles.

To replow the same ground periodically can be worthwhile, as most farmers could confirm. It depends what is harvested each time. In recent decades, new data-sets have made broad, cross-national, comparative explorations possible. Not unreasonably, researchers have looked to see whether patterns of decentralization correlated with various outcomes. At the same time, interest in formal modeling of political economy arguments has been increasing since the 1960s. Scholars have developed more refined tools to test the rigor of arguments previously expressed only informally. However, several other factors tend to keep some debates alive even after they should probably have been removed from life support.

In politics, of course, ideological beliefs and self-interest create attachments to certain arguments that go beyond logic or evidence. In the academic world, as noted in Chapter 11, the bias toward publication of strong positive or negative results means that clear results get published, even if dozens of similar analyses have turned up only noise. Policy analysts have their own reasons to resist claims that certain questions have no general answers. It is their job to tell statesmen what to do, and few rise to prominence by pleading ignorance. Political officials want answers, so answers are what they usually get. Hirschman, quoting Flaubert, called this "*la rage de vouloir conclure*" (the mania for drawing conclusions).

If one accepts the claim of this book that no robust, general consequences of political decentralization have been – or are likely to be – identified, what then? It might be tempting to take skepticism a step further and draw broader lessons. One might wonder whether any political institutions have the kind of powerful, uniform consequences that are often attributed to them. Since the 1980s, enthusiasm for the study of institutions has spread throughout political science. Scholars have related countries' patterns of economic development and the quality of their governments to institutional causes and examined how particular formal structures influence individuals' choices. However, lately some have sounded a little discouraged. Adam Przeworski writes that, reading the recent scholarship, he "was struck by how little robust, reliable knowledge we have about the impact of institutions" (Przeworski 2004, p. 528). Celebrated recent empirical studies that

291

claim to identify effects of institutions sometimes turn out not to contain measures of institutions at all. Instead, they proxy these with patterns of behavior or social psychology such as the perceived security of property rights, the frequency of bribery, or generalized trust.[20]

An argument could be made that the preoccupation with institutional explanations has gone too far. One distinguished tradition of thought has viewed political institutions as so flexible, evolving, and context-dependent in their effects as to make generalizations across periods and countries ill advised. Individual institutions work in a particular way because of the systems of which they are part. As a result, constitutions must be considered as a whole, in their historical context, rather than broken down into pieces to be held up for examination. A constitution, wrote Burke, is "made by the peculiar circumstances, occasions, tempers, dispositions, and moral, civil, and social habitudes of the people, which disclose themselves only in a long space of time." Rather than a mold that shapes society into a particular form, a constitution is "a vestment which accommodates itself to the body" (Burke 1997 [1756–95], p. 398).[21] Oakeshott also warned that one should not fix "upon an institution a falsely permanent character" (Oakeshott 1991, p. 389). Conditions like the "rule of law" are produced by complicated, mutually attuned combinations of institutions, cultural values, and skills. An arrangement that initially promotes a dispersion of power may come to be an instrument of absolutism without any change in the formal rules. Consequently, identifying the effects of particular institutional elements is impossible, and institutional engineering is both futile and dangerous. As Acton wrote: "The history of institutions is often a history of deception and illusions."[22]

I am not ready to abjure general institutional explanations on principle. In a book critical of overhasty generalization, such a blanket proscription would be out of place. A failure to find general results about one dimension of political institutions – decentralization – does not imply that such

---

[20] In a review of cross-national studies of economic development, Aron notes that the "institutional variables" that have proved useful for predicting investment and growth are "those that capture the *performance* or *quality* of formal and informal institutions rather than merely describe the characteristics or attributes of political institutions" (Aron 2000, p. 128). The point is even more true today than when she wrote.

[21] To which, Jefferson, an advocate of periodic reconsideration of the constitution, would perhaps have replied as he wrote to Samuel Kercheval in 1816: "We might as well require a man to wear still the coat which fitted him when a boy, as civilized society to remain ever under the regimen of their barbarous ancestors" (Jefferson 1999 [1774–1826], p. 215).

[22] Quoted in Oakeshott (1991, p. 389).

results cannot be found about others. More robust empirical findings and defensible arguments probably do connect democracy to aspects of government performance, and among democracies scholars have found some relationships between political outcomes and the type of electoral system (proportional, majoritarian) or the form of executive (parliamentary, presidential).[23] The presumption that institutions will *never* have general effects seems no more compelling *a priori* than the presumption that they always will. Each institution merits separate examination.

A second response to the book's claims might be to argue that meaningful and useful conditional relationships *can* be identified with a little more time and effort. If one splits the hairs a little finer, adds more boundary conditions, or throws in additional interaction terms, perhaps one would be able to make stronger claims about the effects of decentralization in narrowly defined contexts. Of course, as the list of contingent factors gets longer, the number of cases to which the generalizations apply becomes so small as to invalidate the designation "general." And convincing others that the generalization is more than a description of observed patterns becomes harder. There is nothing illegitimate about this approach, although the usefulness of claims shrinks with the narrowness of application, and the difficulties of testing may become insurmountable. One cannot test claims on the same data that prompted the hypothesis, and narrow, conditional arguments in political science rarely yield independent predictions that could be tested on different data. But even if this approach is defensible, it has not yielded useful results to date, and I am skeptical that it will in the future.

A third response might be to give up on studying decentralization completely. This would clearly be to go too far. Even if one cannot generalize usefully about the consequences of decentralization, it is both possible and important to understand the processes of politics in particular decentralized orders. Identifying the games played by political actors in given settings is interesting in itself and necessary to predict the effects of policies in those settings. One cannot assume that politics in Argentina, Russia, India, and Switzerland will follow a similar logic just because all are federations. But one cannot understand politics within each of these countries without taking into account their federal structure.

In fact, there are countless ways to study the political economy of multi-tier states without assuming common patterns at a high level of abstraction.

---

[23] See Persson and Tabellini (2003) for a recent review of the empirical evidence.

One can compare the choices of local governments in different regions within a country at different points in time. One can examine the strategies used by a central government in relations with its regions. Starting from puzzles, one can investigate how a particular framework of decentralized institutions constrained the behavior of local actors to produce an unexpected result. An empirical researcher will be intermittently struck by resemblances between political processes and outcomes in different decentralized countries. Fascinating studies of this kind have been done by too many scholars to list individually. Occasionally, speculative generalizations are tacked on to the rigorous examination of particular cases almost as an afterthought. One can be modest in generalization without making the underlying analysis any less convincing or interesting.

As for policy, the implication is conservative in one sense, but not in another. We do not – and usually cannot – know whether in a given setting political decentralization will on balance increase or decrease efficiency, accountability, and other values. But that does not imply that further decentralization should always be avoided. The probability of an improvement must depend, in part, on how "good" or "bad" the starting point is. When past performance has been particularly disastrous, experiments to decentralize – or, for that matter, to centralize – institutions make more sense. The fish that jumps out of the frying pan into the fire perhaps deserves more sympathy than criticism: However unfortunate the outcome, its other options were not appealing. Policy makers considering decentralization are in a situation similar to that of the fish. They do not know what lies beyond the pan's rim and so must choose between a leap into the unknown or staying put. When doing nothing is sufficiently dangerous or unsatisfactory, it may make sense to take a leap.

References

Acemoglu, Daron, and James A. Robinson. 2001. "A Theory of Political Transitions," *American Economic Review*, 91, 938–63.

Acemoglu, Daron, and James A. Robinson. 2006. *Economic Origins of Dictatorship and Democracy*, New York: Cambridge University Press.

Adsera, Alícia, and Carles Boix. 2004. "Constitutional Engineering and the Stability of Democracies," University of Illinois, manuscript.

Ahmad, Nuzhat, and Syed Ashraf Wasti. 2003. "Pakistan," in Yun-Hwan Kim and Paul Smoke, eds., *Intergovernmental Fiscal Transfers in Asia: Current Practice and Challenges for the Future*, Manila: Asian Development Bank, pp. 176–218.

Alesina, Alberto. 1988. "Credibility and Political Convergence in a Two-Party System with Rational Voters," *American Economic Review*, 78, pp. 796–805.

Alesina, Alberto, and Roberto Perotti. 1995. "The Political Economy of Budget Deficits," *IMF Staff Papers*, 42, 1, March 1–31.

Alesina, Alberto, and Roberto Perotti. 1998. "Economic Risk and Political Risk in Fiscal Unions," *Economic Journal*, 108, July, pp. 989–1008.

Alesina, Alberto, and Enrico Spolaore. 2003. *The Size of Nations*, Cambridge, Mass.: MIT Press.

Alpermann, Bjorn. 2001. "The Post-Election Administration of Chinese Villages," *The China Journal*, 46, July, pp. 45–67.

Althouse, Ann. 2004. "Vanguard States, Laggard States: Federalism and Constitutional Rights," *University of Pennsylvania Law Review*, 152, p. 1745.

Annan, Kofi A. 2000. "Africa's Thirst for Democracy," *International Herald Tribune*, 5 December.

Arikan, G. Gulsun. 2004. "Fiscal Decentralization: A Remedy for Corruption?" *International Tax and Public Finance*, 11, pp. 175–95.

Aristotle. 1996. *The Politics and the Constitution of Athens*, ed. Stephen Everson, New York: Cambridge University Press.

Aron, Janine. 2000. "Growth and Institutions: A Review of the Evidence," *World Bank Research Observer*, 15, 1, pp. 99–135.

Aron, Leon. 2000. *Yeltsin: A Revolutionary Life*, New York: St. Martin's Press.

Arrow, Kenneth. 1991. "Scale Returns in Communication and Elite Control in Organizations," *Journal of Law, Economics, and Organization*, 7, pp. 1–6.

Austen-Smith, David. 1997. "Interest Groups: Money, Information, and Influence," in Denis C. Mueller, ed., *Perspectives on Public Choice: A Handbook*, New York: Cambridge University Press, pp. 296–321.

Austen-Smith, David, and Jeffrey Banks. 1989. "Electoral Accountability and Incumbency," in Peter Ordeshoook, ed., *Models of Strategic Choice in Politics*, Ann Arbor: University of Michigan Press.

Ayres, Wendy S. 2003. "Supporting Decentralization: The Role and Experience of the World Bank," *Online Sourcebook on Decentralization and Local Development*, Columbia University, Center for International Earth Science Information Network, http://www.ciesin.org/decentralization/English/General/SDC_wb.html, downloaded March 24, 2005.

Banks, Jeffrey S., and Rangarajan K. Sundaram. 1998. "Optimal Retention in Agency Problems," *Journal of Economic Theory*, 82, 2, October, pp. 293–323.

Bardhan, Pranab. 2002. "Decentralization of Governance and Development," *Journal of Economic Perspectives*, 16, 4, Fall, pp. 185–205.

Bardhan, Pranab, and Dilip Mookherjee. 2005. "Decentralization, Corruption and Government Accountability: An Overview," forthcoming in Susan Rose-Ackerman, ed., *Handbook of Economic Corruption*, Cheltenham, UK: Edward Elgar.

Baron, David P. 1991. "Majoritarian Incentives, Pork Barrel Programs, and Procedural Control," *American Journal of Political Science*, 35, 1, February, pp. 57–90.

Baron, David P., and John A. Ferejohn. 1989. "Bargaining in Legislatures," *American Political Science Review*, 83, 4, December, pp. 1181–206.

Barro, Robert. 1973. "The Control of Politicians: An Economic Model," *Public Choice*, 14, pp. 19–42.

Bartlett, F. C. 1932. *Remembering*, New York: Cambridge University Press.

Basinger, Scott, and Mark Hallerberg. 2004. "Remodeling the Competition for Capital: How Domestic Politics Erases the Race to the Bottom," *American Political Science Review*, 98, 2, May, pp. 261–76.

BBC Monitoring Service. 2005. "Press Alarm over Iraq Federalism," 13 August, http://news.bbc.co.uk/2/hi/middle_east/4148214.stm, downloaded July 26, 2006.

Bebchuk, Lucian, and Allen Ferrell. 1999. "Federalism and Corporate Law: The Race to Protect Managers from Takeovers," *Columbia Law Review*, 99, 5, June, pp. 1168–99.

Bednar, Jenna. 2005. "Credit Assignment and Federal Encroachment," University of Michigan: Manuscript.

Benson, George. 1941. *The New Centralization*, New York: Farrar and Rinehart.

Benson, George. 1947. "A Plea for Administrative Decentralization," *Public Administration Review*, 7, 3, Summer, pp. 170–8.

Bergstrom, Theodore C., Lawrence Blume, and Hal Varian. 1986. "On the Private Provision of Public Goods," *Journal of Public Economics*, 29, pp. 25–49.

Berkowitz, Daniel, and Wei Li. 2000. "Tax Rights in Transition Economies: A Tragedy of the Commons?" *Journal of Public Economics*, 76, 3, June, pp. 369–98.

Besley, Timothy and Anne Case. 1995. "Incumbent Behavior: Vote Seeking, Tax Setting, and Yardstick Competition," *American Economic Review*, 85, 1, pp. 25–45.

References

Besley, Timothy and Stephen Coate. 1997. "An Economic Model of Representative Democracy," *Quarterly Journal of Economics*, 112, 1, pp. 85–114.

Besley, Timothy and Stephen Coate. 2003. "Centralized versus Decentralized Provision of Local Public Goods: A Political Economy Approach," *Journal of Public Economics*, 87, 12, December pp. 2611–37.

Bewley, Truman. 1981. "A Critique of Tiebout's Theory of Local Public Expenditures," *Econometrica*, 49, pp. 713–40.

Biden, Joseph R., Jr. and Leslie H. Gelb. 2006. "Unity Through Autonomy in Iraq," *New York Times*, May 1.

Bilinsky, Yaroslav. 1968. "Education of the Non-Russian Peoples in the USSR, 1917–1967: An Essay," *Slavic Review*, 27, 3, Sept., pp. 411–37.

Bird, Richard M., Robet D. Ebel, and Christine I. Wallich, eds. 1996. *Decentralization of the Socialist State: Intergovernmental Finance in Transition Economies*, Aldershot: Avebury.

Bird, Richard M. and François Vaillancourt. 1998. "Fiscal decentralization in developing countries: an overview," in Bird and Vaillancourt, eds., *Fiscal Decentralization in Developing Countries*, New York: Cambridge University Press, pp. 1–48.

Blackstone. 1979 [1765–9]. *Commentaries on the Laws of England*, Chicago: University of Chicago Press.

Blanchard, Olivier and Andrei Shleifer. 2001. "Federalism With and Without Political Centralization: China versus Russia," *IMF Staff Papers*, 48, 0, pp. 171–79.

Blankart, Charles B. 2000. "The Process of Government Centralization: A Constitutional View," *Constitutional Political Economy*, 11, pp. 27–39.

Bloch, Marc. 1961. *Feudal Society*, Chicago: University of Chicago Press.

Boadway, Robin and Michael Keen. 1996. "Efficiency and the Optimal Direction of Federal-State Transfers," *International Tax and Public Finance*, 3, pp. 137–55.

Boadway, Robin, Maurice Marchand, and Marianne Vigneault. 1998. "The Consequences of Overlapping Tax Bases for Redistribution and Public Spending in a Federation," *Journal of Public Economics*, 68, pp. 453–78.

Bodin, Jean. 1992 [1576]. *On Sovereignty: Four Chapters from the Six Books of the Commonwealth*, ed. Julian Franklin, New York: Cambridge University Press.

Bogart, William T. and Brian A. Cromwell. 1997. "How Much More is a Good School District Worth?" *National Tax Journal*, 50, 2, June, ppp. 215–32.

Boix, Carles. 2003. *Democracy and Redistribution*, New York: Cambridge University Press.

Bolton, Patrick and Mathias Dewatripont. 1994. "The Firm as a Communication Network," *Quarterly Journal of Economics*, 109, 4, Nov, pp. 809–39.

Bolton, Patrick and Joseph Farrell. 1990. "Decentralization, Duplication, and Delay," *Journal of Political Economy*, 98, 4, Aug, 803–26.

Bolton, Patrick and Gérard Roland. 1997. "The Breakup of Nations: A Political Economy Analysis," *Quarterly Journal of Economics*, 112, 4, pp. 1057–90.

Borck, Rainald. 2002. "Jurisdiction Size, Political Participation, and the Allocation of Resources," *Public Choice*, 113, pp. 251–63.

Bordignon, Massimo, Paolo Manasse, and Guido Tabellini. 2001. "Optimal Regional Redistribution Under Asymmetric Information," *American Economic Review*, 91, 3, June, pp. 709–23.

Bordignon, Massimo and Gilberto Turati. 2002. "Fiscal Federalism and Soft Budget Constraints in the Italian National Health Service," Universita di Pavia: manuscript.

Borsuck, Richard. 2003. "In Indonesia, a New Twist on Spreading the Wealth: Decentralization of Power Multiplies Opportunities for Bribery, Corruption," *The Wall Street Journal*, January 29, p. A16.

Brancati, Dawn. 2004. "Can Federalism Stabilize Iraq?" *The Washington Quarterly*, 27, 2, Spring, pp. 7–21.

Brancati, Dawn. 2005. "Decentralization: Fueling the Fire or Dampening the Flames of Ethnic Conflict," Harvard University: manuscript.

Brandeis, Louis D. 1932. *Dissent on New State Ice Co. v. Liebmann*, 285 U.S. 262.

Break, George F. 1967. *Intergovernmental Fiscal Relations in the United States*, Washington, DC: Brookings Institution.

Brennan, Geoffrey and James M. Buchanan. 1980. *The Power to Tax: Analytical Foundations of a Fiscal Constitution*, New York: Cambridge University Press.

Breton, Albert. 1996. *Competitive Governments: An Economic Theory of Politics and Public Finance*, New York: Cambridge University Press.

Breton, Albert. 2000. "Federalism and Decentralization: Ownership Rights and the Superiority of Federalism," *Publius*, 30, 2, Spring, pp. 1–16.

Breton, Albert, and Angele Fraschini. 2003. "Vertical Competition in Unitary States: The Case of Italy," *Public Choice*, 114, pp. 57–77.

Breton, Albert, and Anthony Scott. 1978. *The Economic Constitution of Federal States*, Toronto: University of Toronto Press.

Breuss, Fritz and Markus Eller. 2004. "Fiscal Decentralisation and Economic Growth: Is There Really a Link?" Vienna: Vienna University of Economics and Business Administration: manuscript.

Brewer, John. 1989. *The Sinews of Power: War, Money, and the English State, 1688–1783*, New York: Knopf.

Brillantes, Alex B., Jr., and Nora G. Cuachon, eds. 2002. *Decentralization and Power Shift: An Imperative for Good Governance. A Sourcebook on Decentralization Experiences in Asia*, vol. 1, Manila: University of the Philippines, Center for Local and Regional Governance.

Brosio, Giorgio. 2000. "Decentralization in Africa," Washington, DC: IMF.

Brueckner, Jan K. 1983. "Property Value Maximization and Public Sector Efficiency," *Journal of Urban Economics*, 14, 1, July, pp. 1–15.

Bryan, Frank M. 1995. "Direct Democracy and Civic Competence," *Good Society*, 5, 1, Fall, pp. 36–44.

Bryce, James. 1888. *The American Commonwealth*, New York: Macmillan and Co.

Bryce, James. 1924. *Modern Democracies*, volume II, New York: Macmillan and Co.

Buchanan, James M. 1995–6. "Federalism and Individual Sovereignty," *Cato Journal*, Vol. 15, Nos. 2–3, Fall/Winter.

Buchanan, James M. and Roger L. Faith. 1987. "Secession and the Limits of Taxation: Toward a Theory of Internal Exit," *American Economic Review*, 77, 5, December, 1023–31.

Buchanan, James M. and Richard A. Musgrave. 2000. *Public Finance and Public Choice: Two Contrasting Visions of the State*, Cambridge, MA: MIT Press.

References

Buchholz, David. 2002. *"Business Incentives Reform Case Study: Mercedes-Benz: The Deal of the Century,"* Washington, DC: Corporation for Enterprise Development, http://www.cfed.org/focus.m?parentid=34&siteid=1629&id=1653, downloaded July 8, 2006.

Bueno de Mesquita, Bruce, Alastair Smith, Randolph M. Siverson, and James D. Morrow. 2003. *The Logic of Political Survival*, Cambridge, MA: MIT Press.

Bunce, Valerie. 1999. *Subversive Institutions: The Design and Destruction of Socialism and the State*, New York: Cambridge University Press.

Burke, Edmund. 1997 [1756–95]. *Edmund Burke: Selected Writings and Speeches*, Peter J. Stanlis, ed., Washington, DC: Regnery Publishing.

Burki, Shahid Javed, Guillermo Perry, and William Dillinger. 1999. *Beyond the Center: Decentralizing the State*, Washington, DC: World Bank.

Burstein, Melvin L. and Arthur J. Rolnick. 1994. "Congress Should End the Economic War Among the States," Minneapolis: Federal Reserve Bank of Minneapolis.

Bush, George W. 1999. *A Charge to Keep*, New York: William Morrow.

Cai, Hongbin and Daniel Treisman. 2004. "State Corroding Federalism," *Journal of Public Economics*, 88, pp. 819–43.

Cai, Hongbin and Daniel Treisman. 2005a. "Does Competition for Capital Discipline Governments? Decentralization, Globalization, and Public Policy," *American Economic Review*, June 2005.

Cai, Hongbin and Daniel Treisman. 2005b. "Political Decentralization and Policy Experimentation," UCLA: manuscript.

Calabresi, Guido and A. Douglas Melamed. 1972. "Property Rules, Liability Rules, and Inalienability: One View of the Cathedral," *Harvard Law Review*, 85.

Calvo, Guillermo A. and Stanislaw Wellisz. 1978. "Supervision, Loss of Control, and the Optimum Size of the Firmm" *Journal of Political Economy*, 86, 5, pp. 943–52.

Campos, Jose Edgardo and Joel S. Hellman. 2005. "Governance Gone Local: Does Decentralization Improve Accountability?" in Roland White and Paul Smoke, eds., *East Asia Decentralizes: Making Local Government Work in Asia*, Washington DC: World Bank, pp. 237–52.

Caplan, Bryan. 2001. "Standing Tiebout on his head: Tax capitalization and the monopoly power of local governments," *Public Choice*, 108, July, pp. 101–22.

Carney, Frederick S. 1964. "Introduction," in Johannes Althusius, *The Politics of Johannes Althusius*, trans. Frederick S. Carney, Boston: Beacon Press.

Cavanaugh, Gerald J. 1969. "Turgot: The Rejection of Enlightened Despotism," *French Historical Studies*, 6, 1, Spring, pp. 31–58.

Chamberlin, John. 1974. "Provision of Collective Goods as a Function of Group Size," *American Political Science Review*, 68, 2, June, pp. 707–16.

Chamley, Christophe. 1986. "Optimal Taxation of Capital Income in General Equilibrium with Infinite Lives," *Econometrica*, 54, pp. 607–22.

Chang, Eric C. C. 2005. "Electoral Incentives for Political Corruption Under Open-List Proportional Representation," *Journal of Politics*, 67, 3, August, pp. 716–30.

Chari, V. V., Larry E. Jones, and Ramon Marimon. 1997. "The Economics of Split-Ticket Voting in Representative Democracies," *American Economic Review*, 87, 5, December, pp. 957–76.

Cheibub, José Antonio and Adam Przeworski. 1999. "Accountability for Economic Outcomes," in Bernard Manin, Adam Przeworski, and Susan C. Stokes, *Democracy, Accountability, and Representation*, New York: Cambridge University Press.

Cicero, Marcus Tullius. 1960 [70 B. C.]. "Against Verres," in Michael Grant, trans., *Selected Works*, New York: Penguin, pp. 35–57.

Clarke, E. 1971. "Multipart pricing of public goods," *Public Choice*, 8, pp. 19–33.

Coase, Ronald H. 1937. "The Nature of the Firm," *Economica*, 4, 16, November, pp. 386–405.

Cohen, Frank S. 1997. "Proportional Versus Majoritarian Ethnic Conflict Management in Democracies," *Comparative Political Studies*, 30, 5, October, pp. 607–30.

Collie, Melissa. 1988. "The Legislature and Distributive Policy Making in a Formal Perspective," *Legislative Studies Quarterly*, 13, pp. 427–58.

Covell, Maureen. 1987. "Federalization and Federalism: Belgium and Canada," in Herman Bakvis and William M. Chandler, eds., *Federalism and the Role of the State*, Toronto: University of Toronto Press.

Crawford, Harriet E. W. 1991. *Sumer and the Sumerians*, New York: Cambridge University Press.

Cumberland, John H. 1981. "Efficiency and Equity in Interregional Environmental Management," *Review of Regional Studies*, 2, pp. 1–9.

Dabla-Norris, Era and Paul Wade. 2002. "The Challenge of Fiscal Decentralization in Transition Countries," Washington DC: IMF, WP/02/103.

Dahl, Robert A. 1967. "The City in the Future of Democracy," American *Political Science Review*, 61, 4, December, pp. 953–70.

Dahl, Robert A. 1986. *Democracy, Identity, Equality*, Oslo: Norwegian University Press.

Dahl, Robert A. 1998. *On Democracy*, New Haven: Yale University Press.

Dahl, Robert A. and Edward R. Tufte. 1973. *Size and Democracy*, Stanford: Stanford University Press.

Dahlby, Bev. 1996. "Fiscal externalities and the design of intergovernmental grants," *International Tax and Public Finance*, 3, pp. 397–411.

Dahlby, Bev and Leonard S. Wilson. 2003. "Vertical fiscal externalities in a federation," *Journal of Public Economics*, 87, pp. 917–30.

Dante. 1904 [c. 1314–20]. *De Monarchia*, ed. Aurelia Henry, Boston: Houghton, Mifflin & Co.

Datta, Saikat. 1996. "On Control Losses in Hierarchies," *Rationality and Society*, 8, 4, pp. 387–412.

Davis, Otto A., Morris H. DeGroot, and Melvin J. Hinich. 1972. "Social Preference Orderings and Majority Rule," *Econometrica*, 40, pp. 147–57.

Davoodi, Hamid and Heng-fu Zou. 1998. "Fiscal Decentralization and Economic Growth: A Cross-Country Study," *Journal of Urban Economics*, 43, pp. 244–57.

De Mello, Luiz R. Jr. 2000. "Fiscal Decentralization and Intergovernmental Fiscal Relations: A Cross-Country Analysis," *World Development*, 28, 2, pp. 365–80.

De Mello, Luiz R. Jr. and Matias Barenstein. 2001. "Fiscal Decentralization and Governance: A Cross-Country Analysis," IMF Working Paper 01/71, Washington DC: IMF.

References

De Vries, Michiel S. 2000. "The rise and fall of decentralization: A comparative analysis of arguments and practices in European countries," *European Journal of Political Research*, 38, pp. 193–224.

Dewatripont, Mathias and Eric Maskin. 1995. "Credit and Efficiency in Centralized and Decentralized Economies," *Review of Economic Studies*, 62, 541–56.

Dewey, John. 1927. *The Public and Its Problems*, New York: Henry Holt and Company.

Diakonoff, I. M. 1974. *Structure of Society and State in Early Dynastic Sumer*, Los Angeles: Undena Publications.

Diamond, Larry. 1999. *Developing Democracy: Toward Consolidation*, Baltimore: Johns Hopkins University Press.

Diamond, Larry. 2004. "Why Decentralize Power in A Democracy?" Stanford University: manuscript, at http://www.stanford.edu/~ldiamond/iraq/Decentralize_Power021204.htm.

Diamond, Larry and Marc F. Plattner. 1994. "Introduction," in Diamond and Plattner, eds., *Nationalism, Ethnic Conflict, and Democracy*, Baltimore: Johns Hopkins University Press, pp. ix–xxx.

Diamond, Larry, Juan J. Linz and Seymour Martin Lipset. 1995. "Introduction: What Makes for Democracy?", in Diamond, Linz, and Lipset, eds., *Politics in Developing Countries: Comparing Experiences with Democracy*, Boulder: Lynne Rienner, pp. 1–66.

Dillinger, William, and Steven B. Webb. 1999. *Fiscal Management in Federal Democracies: Argentina and Brazil*, Washington, DC: World Bank, Policy Research Working Paper 2121.

Dininio, Phyllis. 2000. *USAID's Experience in Decentralization and Democratic Local Governance*, Washington, DC: USAID Center for Democracy and Governance, at http://www.usaid.gov/our_work/democracy_and_governance/publications/pdfs/pnach302.pdf, downloaded March 22, 2005.

Diskin, Abraham, Hanna Diskin, and Reuven Y. Hazan. 2005. "Why Democracies Collapse: The Reasons for Democratic Failure and Success," *International Political Science Review*, 26, 3, pp. 291–309.

Dixit, Avinash. 2002. "Incentives and Organizations in the Public Sector: An Interpretative Review," *Journal of Human Resources*, 37, 4, Autumn, pp. 696–727.

Dixit, Avinash and John Londregan. 1996. "The Determinants of Success of Special Interests in Redistributive Politics," *Journal of Politics*, 58, 4, November, 1132–55.

Dixit, Avinash and John Londregan. 1998. "Fiscal Federalism and Redistributive Politics," *Journal of Public Economics*, 68, pp. 153–80.

Dobbins, James. 2005. "Iraq Needs Unity," *United Press International*, December 30.

Donahue, John D. 1997. "Tiebout? Or not Tiebout? The Market Metaphor and America's Devolution Debate," *Journal of Economic Perspectives*, 11, 4, Fall, pp. 73–82.

Downs, Anthony. 1957. *An Economic Theory of Democracy*, New York: Harper & Row.

Downs, Anthony. 1965. "A Theory of Bureaucracy," *American Economic Review*, 55, 1–2, March, pp. 439–46.

Duchacek, Ivo. 1975. "External and Internal Challenges to the Federal Bargain," *Publius*, 5, 2, pp. 41–76.

Dunn, Michael C. 2005. "Why is Federalism Rare in the Middle East?" *Middle East Institute Perspective*, Washington, DC, Middle East Institute, August 12, http://www.mideasti.org/articles/doc412.html.

Eaton, Kent. 2005. "Armed Clientelism: How Decentralization Complicated Colombia's Civil War," Naval Postgraduate School: manuscript.

Ebel, Robert D. and Serdar Yilmaz. 2002. "On the Measurement and Impact of Fiscal Decentralization," World Bank Policy Research Working Paper No.2809, Washington, DC: World Bank.

Economist, The. 2001. "Does Britain Want To Be Rich?" April 14–20, pp. 18–20.

Ehrenberg, Victor. 1960. *The Greek State*, London: Methuen & Co. Ltd.

Ekedahl, Carolyn and Melvin A. Goodman. 1997. *The Wars of Eduard Shevardnadze*, University Park, PA: Penn State University Press.

Elazar, Daniel J. 1987. *Exploring Federalism*, University of Alabama: University of Alabama Press.

Elazar, Daniel J. 1993. "International and Comparative Federalism," *PS: Political Science & Politics*, June, pp. 190–95.

Eley, Susan, Kathryn Gallop, Gill McIvor, Kerry Morgan, Rowdy Yates. 2002. *Drug Treatment and Testing Orders: Evaluation of the Scottish Pilots*, Edinburgh: Scottish Executive Central Research Unit, at http://www.scotland.gov.uk/cru/kd01/green/dtts.pdf.

Emerson, Ralph Waldo. 1903 [1835]. "Historical Discourse at Concord," in *The Complete Works of Ralph Waldo Emerson, Vol XI, Miscellanies*, Boston: Houghton, Mifflin, and Co.

Enikolopov, Ruben, and Ekaterina Zhuravskaya. 2003. "Decentralization and Political Institutions," Moscow: CEFIR.

Epple, Dennis and Thomas Romer. 1991. "Mobility and Redistribution," *Journal of Political Economy*, 99, 4, August, pp. 828–58.

Epple, Dennis and Allan Zelenitz. 1981. "The Implications of Competition Among Jurisdictions: Does Tiebout Need Politics?" *Journal of Political Economy*, 89, pp. 1197–217.

Estache, Antonio and Sarbajit Sinha. 1995. "Does Decentralization Increase Public Infrastructure Expenditure?" in Antonio Estache, ed., *Decentralizing Infrastructure: Advantages and Limitations*, Washington, DC: World Bank, pp. 63–80.

European Union. 2001. *Regional and Local Government in the European Union: Responsibilities and Resources*, Brussels: European Union, Committee of the Regions.

Faguet, Jean-Paul. 2004. "Does Decentralization Increase Government Responsiveness to Local Needs? Decentralization and Public Investment in Bolivia," *Journal of Public Economics*, 88, 3–4, pp. 867–93.

Feldstein, Martin and Marian Vaillant Wrobel. 1998. "Can State Taxes Redistribute Income," *Journal of Public Economics*, 68, 3, pp. 369–96.

References

Ferejohn, John. 1986. "Incumbent Performance and Electoral Control," *Public Choice*, 50, pp. 5–26.

Ferejohn, John and Barry R. Weingast. 1992. "A Positive Theory of Statutory Interpretation," *International Review of Law and Economics*, 12, pp. 263–79.

Fesler, James. 1965. "Approaches to the Understanding of Decentralization," *Journal of Politics*, 27, 3, August, pp. 536–66.

Filgueira, Fernando, Herman Kamil, Fernando Lorenzo, Juan Andrés Moraes, and Andrés Ruis. 2002. *Decentralization and Fiscal Discipline in Subnational Governments: The Bailout Problem in Uruguay*, Washington, DC: Inter-American Development Bank.

Finer, Samuel E. 1997. *The History of Government*, New York: Oxford University Press.

Fischel, William A. 1975. "Fiscal and Environmental Considerations in the Location of Firms in Suburban Communities," in Edwin Mills and Wallace Oates, eds., *Fiscal Zoning and Land Use Controls*, Lexington, MA: D. C. Heath, pp. 119–173.

Fishel, Jeff. 1985. *Presidents and Promises: From Campaign Pledge to Presidential Performance*, Washington, DC: Congressional Quarterly Press.

Fisman, Raymond and Roberta Gatti. 2002. "Decentralization and Corruption: Evidence Across Countries," *Journal of Public Economics*, 83, pp. 325–45.

Flowers, Marilyn R. 1988. "Shared Tax sources in a Leviathan model of federalism," *Public Finance Quarterly*, 16, 1, January, pp. 67–77.

Fornasari, Francesca, Steven B. Webb, and Heng-Fu Zou. 1998. "Decentralized Spending and Central Government Deficits: International Evidence," Washington, D.C.: World Bank.

Fornasari, Francesca, Steven B. Webb, and Heng-fu Zou. 2000. "The Macroeconomic Impact of Decentralized Spending and Deficits: International Evidence," *Annals of Economics and Finance*, 1, pp. 403–33.

Foweraker, Joe, and Todd Landman. 2002. "Constitutional Design and Democratic Performance," *Democratization*, 9, 2, Summer, pp. 43–66.

Franzese, Robert J., Jr. 2002. *Macroeconomic Policies of Developed Democracies*, New York: Cambridge University Press.

Friedman, Milton. 1953. *Essays in Positive Economics*, Chicago: University of Chicago Press.

Fudenberg, Drew and Eric Maskin. 1986. "The Folk Theorem in Repeated Games With Discounting or With Incomplete Information," *Econometrica*, 54, 3, May, pp. 533–54.

Furniss, Norman. 1974. "The Practical Significance of Decentralization," *Journal of Politics*, 36, 4, November, pp. 958–82.

Furniss, Norman. 1975. "Northern Ireland as a Case Study of Decentralization in Unitary States," *World Politics*, 27, 3, April, pp. 387–404.

Gagnon, Alain-G. 1993. "The Political Uses of Federalism," in Michael Burgess and Alain-G. Gagnon, eds., *Comparative Federalism and Federation: Competing Traditions and Future Directions*, Toronto: University of Toronto Press, pp. 15–44.

Gandhi, Jennifer and Adam Przeworski. 2006. "Cooperation, Cooptation, and Rebellion under Dictatorships," New York University: manuscript.

Gautier, Axel and Dimitri Paolini. 2000. "Delegation and Information Revelation," Louvain-la-Neuve, Belgium: IRES.

Gélineau, François and Karen Remmer. 2005. "Political Decentralization and Electoral Accountability: The Argentine Experience, 1983–2001," *British Journal of Political Science*, 36, pp. 133–57.

Genet, J. P. 1981. "Political Theory and Local Communities in Later Medieval France and England," in J. R. L. Highfield and Robin Jeffs, eds., *The Crown and Local Communities in England and France in the Fifteenth Century*, Gloucester: Alan Sutton, pp. 19–32.

Gerber, Alan S., Donald P. Green, and David Nickerson. 2001. "Testing for Publication Bias in Political Science," *Political Analysis*, 9, 4, pp. 385–92.

Gierke, Otto von. 1966. *The Development of Political Theory*, trans. Bernard Freyd, New York: Howard Fertig.

Gilbert, Guy, and Pierre Picard. 1996. "Incentives and optimal size of local jurisdictions," *European Economic Review*, 40, pp. 19–41.

Gillette, Clayton P. 1997. "The Allocation of Government Authority: The Exercise of Trumps by Decentralized Governments," *Virginia Law Review*, 83, October, pp. 1347–1418.

Gimpelson, Vladimir and Daniel Treisman. 2002. "Fiscal Games and Public Employment: A Theory with Evidence from Russia," *World Politics*, 54, 2, January, pp. 145–83.

Glaeser, Edward and Andrei Shleifer. 2005. "The Curley Effect: The Economics of Shaping the Electorate," *Journal of Law, Economics, and Organization*, 21, 1, pp. 1–19.

Goldsmith, Arthur A. 1999. "Slapping the Grasping Hand: Correlates of Political Corruption in Emerging Markets," *American Journal of Economics and Sociology*, 58, 4, pp. 865–86.

Goodspeed, Timothy J. 2002. "Bailouts in a Federation," *International Tax and Public Finance*, 9, pp. 409–21.

Goolsbee, Austan. 1999. "Evidence on the High-Income Laffer Curve from Six Decades of Tax Reform," Brookings Papers on Economic Activity, 2, pp. 1–64.

Gordon, Roger. 1983. "An Optimal Tax Approach to Fiscal Federalism," *Quarterly Journal of Economics*, 97, pp. 567–86.

Gray, Gwendolyn. 1991. *Federalism and Health Policy: The Development of Health Systems in Canada and Australia*, Toronto: University of Toronto Press.

Greve, Michael S. 2001. "Laboratories of Democracy: Anatomy of a Metaphor," *Federalist Outlook*, American Enterprise Institute, 6, May.

Grodzins, Morton. 1967. "The federal system," in Aaron Wildavsky, ed., *American Federalism in Perspective*, Boston: Little, Brown and Co., pp. 256–77.

Grossman, Gene M. and Elhanan Helpman. 1999. "Competing for Endorsements," *American Economic Review*, 89, 3, June, pp. 501–24.

Grossman, Gene M. and Elhanan Helpman. 2001. *Special Interest Politics*. Cambridge, MA: MIT Press.

References

Grossman, Herschel. 1991. "A General Equilibrium Model of Insurrections," *American Economic Review*, 81, 4, Sep, pp. 912–21.

Groves, Theodore. 1973. "Incentives in Teams," *Econometrica*, 41, pp. 617–31.

Hacker, Jacob S. 1998. "The Historical Logic of National Health Insurance: Structure and Sequence in the Development of British, Canadian, and US Medical Policy," *Studies in American Political Development*, 12, Spring, pp. 57–130.

Hajnal, Zoltan L. and Paul G. Lewis. 2003. "Municipal Institutions and Voter Turnout in Local Elections," *Urban Affairs Review*, 38, 5, May, pp. 645–88.

Hale, Henry. 2004. "Divided We Stand: Institutional Sources of Ethnofederal State Survival and Collapse," *World Politics*, 56, January, pp. 165–93.

Hallerberg, Mark and Scott Basinger. 1998. "Internationalization and Changes in Tax Policy in OECD Countries: The Importance of Domestic Veto Players," *Comparative Political Studies*, 31, 3, June, pp. 321–52.

Hamilton, Alexander. 2001 [1769–1804]. *Writings*, New York: Library of America.

Hamilton, Bruce. 1976. "Capitalization of Interjurisdictional Differences in Local Tax Prices," *American Economic Review*, 66, 5, pp. 743–53.

Hansson, Ingemar and Charles Stuart. 1987. "The Suboptimality of Local Taxation Under Two-Tier Fiscal Federalism," *European Journal of Political Economy*, 3, 3, pp. 407–11.

Hausmann, Ricardo. 1998. "Fiscal Institutions for Decentralizing Democracies: Which Way to Go?" in Kiichiro Fukasaku and Ricardo Hausmann, eds., *Democracy, Decentralisation and Deficits in Latin America*, Paris: OECD Development Centre.

Hayek, Friedrich. 1939. "The Economic Conditions of Interstate Federalism," *New Commonwealth Quarterly*, 5, 2, pp. 131–49, reprinted in Friedrich Hayek, *Individualism and Economic Order*, University of Chicago Press: 1948, pp. 255–72.

Hayek, Friedrich. 1945. "The Use of Knowledge in Society," *American Economic Review*, 35, 4, pp. 519–30.

Hayek, Friedrich. 1960. *The Constitution of Liberty*, Chicago: University of Chicago Press.

Hayek, Friedrich. 1982. *Law, Legislation, and Liberty*, London: Routledge.

Hechter, Michael. 2000a. *Containing Nationalism*, New York: Oxford University Press.

Hechter, Michael. 2000b. "Nationalism and Rationality," *Journal of World-Systems Research*, 6, 2, summer/fall, pp. 308–29.

Hegre, Havard, and Nicholas Sambanis. 2005. "Sensitivity Analysis of the Empirical Literature on Civil War Onset," Yale University: Manuscript.

Henderson, Vernon. 2003. "The Urbanization Process and Economic Growth: The So-What Question," *Journal of Economic Growth*, 8, pp. 47–71.

Hinich, Melvin J. and Peter C. Ordeshook. 1974. "The Electoral College: A Spatial Analysis," *Political Methodology*, 1, 3, pp. 1–29.

Hinich, Melvin J., John O. Ledyard, and Peter C. Ordeshook. 1972. "Nonvoting and the Existence of Equilibrium under Majority Rule," *Journal of Economic Theory*, 4, pp. 144–53.

Hobbes, Thomas. 1968 [1651]. *Leviathan*, ed. C. B. MacPherson, New York: Penguin.

Hoffmann, Stanley. 1959. "The Areal Division of Powers in the Writings of French Political Thinkers," in Arthur Maass, ed., *Area and Power: A Theory of Local Government*, Glencoe, IL: The Free Press, pp. 113–49.

Holmström, Bengt. 1982. "Moral Hazard in Teams," *Bell Journal of Economics*, 13, pp. 324–40.

Hommes, Rudolf. 1996. "Conflicts and Dilemmas of Decentralization," in World Bank, *Annual World Bank Conference on Development Economics 1995*, Washington DC: World Bank, pp. 331–50.

Hooghe, Liesbet and Gary Marks. 2001. *Multi-Level Governance and European Integration*, New York: Rowman and Littlefield.

Hooghe, Liesbet and Gary Marks. 2003. "Unraveling the Central State, but How? Types of Multi-level Governance," *American Political Science Review*, 97, 2, May, pp. 233–43.

Horowitz, Donald L. 1991. *A Democratic South Africa? Constitutional Engineering in a Divided Society*, Berkeley: University of California Press, online at http://ark.cdlib.org/ark:/13030/ft0f59n6zd/.

Hotelling, Harold. 1929. "Stability in Competition," *Economic Journal*, 39, pp. 41–57.

Hug, Simon. 2005. "Institutions and Conflict Resolution: Dealing with Endogeneity," Universität Zürich: manuscript.

Hume, David. 1994 [1752]. "Idea of a perfect commonwealth," in *Political Essays*, ed. Knud Haakonssen, Cambridge: Cambridge University Press.

Humplick, Frannie and Antonio Estache. 1995. "Does Decentralization Improve Infrastructure Performance?" in Antonio Estache, ed., *Decentralizing Infrastructure: Advantages and Limitations*, Washington, DC: World Bank, pp. 81–97.

Hutchcroft, Paul D. 2001. "Centralization and Decentralization in Administration and Politics: Assessing Territorial Dimensions of Authority and Power," *Governance*, 14, 1, January, pp. 23–53.

Huther, Jeff, and Anwar Shah. 1998. "Applying a Simple Measure of Good Governance to the Debate on Fiscal Decentralization," Washington, DC: World Bank.

Iimi, Atsushi. 2005. "Decentralization and economic growth revisited: an empirical note," *Journal of Urban Economics*, 57, pp. 449–61.

Inman, Robert P. 2003. "Transfers and Bailouts: Enforcing Local Fiscal Discipline with Lessons from U.S. Federalism," in Rodden, Eskeland and Litvack, eds., *Fiscal Decentralization and the Challenge of Hard Budget Constraints*, Cambridge: MIT Press, pp. 35–83.

Inman, Robert P. and Daniel L. Rubinfeld. 2005. "Federalism and the Democratic Transition: Lessons from South Africa," *American Economic Review: Papers and Proceedings*, 95, 2, May, pp. 39–43.

Jefferson, Thomas. 1998 [1785]. *Notes on the State of Virginia*, ed. Frank Shuffelton, New York: Penguin Classics.

Jefferson, Thomas. 1999 [1774–1826]. *Political Writings*, ed. Joyce Appleby and Terence Ball, New York: Cambridge University Press.

References

Jin, Hehui, Yingyi Qian and Barry R. Weingast. 2005. "Regional Decentralization and Fiscal Incentives: Federalism, Chinese Style," *Journal of Public Economics*, 89, pp. 1719–42.

Jin, Jing and Heng-fu Zou. 2002. "How Does Fiscal Decentralization Affect Aggregate, National, and Subnational Government Size?" *Journal of Urban Economics*, 52, pp. 270–93.

Jones, Mark P., Pablo Sanguinetti, and Mariano Tommasi. 2000. "Politics, Institutions, and Fiscal Performance in a Federal System: An Analysis of the Argentine Provinces," *Journal of Development Economics*, 61, pp. 305–33.

Joumard, I. and P. M. Kongsrud. 2003. "Fiscal Relations Across Government Levels," *OECD Economics Department Working Papers*, No.375, Paris: OECD.

Joumard, I. and W. Suyker. 2002. "Enhancing the Effectiveness of Public Spending in Norway," *OECD Economics Department Working Papers*, No.343. Paris: OECD.

Jowell, Roger. 2003. *Trying it Out: The Role of 'Pilots' in Policymaking*, London: Government Chief Social Researcher's Office.

Kastner, Scott L. and Chad Rector. 2003. "International Regimes, Domestic Veto-Players, and Capital Controls Policy Stability," *International Studies Quarterly*, 47, pp. 1–22.

Keen, Michael. 1998. "Vertical Tax Externalities in the Theory of Fiscal Federalism," *IMF Staff Papers*, 45, 3, September, pp. 454–85.

Keen, Michael and Christos Kotsogiannis. 2002. "Does Federalism Lead to Excessively High Taxes," *American Economic Review*, 92, 1, March, pp. 363–70.

Keen, Michael and M. Marchand. 1997. "Fiscal Competition and the Pattern of Public Spending," *Journal of Public Economics*, 66, pp. 33–53.

Kennan, George F. 1993. *Around the Cragged Hill: A Personal and Political Philosophy*, New York: Norton.

Kessler, Anke S. and Christoph Lülfesmann. 2005. "Tiebout and Redistribution in a Model of Residential and Political Choice," *Journal of Public Economics*, 89, 2–3, February, pp. 501–28.

Key, V. O., Jr. 1961, *Public Opinion and American Democracy*, New York: Knopf.

Khaleghian, Peyvand. 2004. "Decentralization and Public Services: The Case of Immunization," *Social Science and Medicine*, 59, pp. 163–83.

King, David N. and Yue Ma. 2000. "Decentralization and Macroeconomic Performance," *Applied Economic Letters*, 7, pp. 11–14.

Kincaid, John. 1999. "Federal Democracy and Liberty," *PS: Political Science and Politics*, 32, 2, June, pp. 211–16.

Kisubi, Mohammad M. 1999. "Involving Civil Society in the Fight Against Corruption," in Rick Stapenhurst and Sahr J. Kpundeh, eds., *Curbing Corruption: Toward a Model for Building National Integrity*, Washington DC: World Bank, pp. 117–25.

Kochen, Manfred and Karl W. Deutsch. 1969. "Toward a Rational Theory of Decentralization: Some Implications of a Mathematical Approach," *American Political Science Review*, 63, 3, September, pp. 734–49.

Kornai, János. 1979. "Resource-constrained versus Demand-constrained Systems," *Econometrica*, 47, 801–19.

Kornai, János. 1980. *Economics of Shortage*, Amsterdam: North Holland.

Kreimer, Seth F. 2001. "Federalism and Freedom," *Annals of the American Academy of Political and Social Science*, March, 574.

Kreps, David M. and Robert Wilson. 1982. "Reputation and Imperfect Information," *Journal of Economic Theory*, 27, pp. 253–79.

Kristol, Irving. 1968. "Decentralization for What?" *Public Interest*, 11, Spring, pp. 17–25.

Krugman, Paul R. 1995. *Development, Geography, and Economic Theory*, Cambridge, MA: MIT Press.

Kulipossa, Fidelx P. 2004. "Decentralization and democracy in developing countries: an overview," *Development in Practice*, 14, 6, November, pp. 768–79.

Kunicová, Jana and Susan Rose-Ackerman. 2005. "Electoral Rules and Constitutional Structures as Constraints on Corruption," *British Journal of Political Science*, 35, pp. 573–606.

Lacey, W. K. and B. W. J. G. Wilson. 1970. *Res Publica: Roman Politics and Society According to Cicero*, New York: Oxford University Press.

Laffont, Jean-Jacques. 1990. "Analysis of Hidden Gaming in a Three-Level Hierarchy," *Journal of Law, Economics, and Organization*, 6, 2, Fall, pp. 301–24.

Laffont, Jean-Jacques and David Martimort. 1998. "Collusion and Delegation," *Rand Journal of Economics*, 29, 2, Summer, pp. 280–305.

Laffont, Jean-Jacques and Wilfried Zantman. 2002. "Information Acquisition, Political Game and the Delegation of Authority," *European Journal of Political Economy*, 18, pp. 407–28.

Lake, David A. and Donald Rothchild. 2005. "Territorial Decentralization and Civil War Settlements," forthcoming in Philip Roeder and Donald Rothchild, eds., *Sustainable Peace*, Ithaca, NY: Cornell University Press.

Lane, Jan-Erik and Svante Errson. 2005. "The Riddle of Federalism: Does Federalism Impact on Democracy?" *Democratization*, 12, 2, April, pp. 163–82.

Larsen, J. A. O. 1968. *Greek Federal States: Their Institutions and History*, Oxford: Clarendon Press.

Laski, Harold J. 1921. *The Foundations of Sovereignty and Other Essays*, New York: Harcourt, Brace and Co.

Laski, Harold J. 1939. "The Obsolescence of Federalism," *The New Republic*, May 3, pp. 367–9.

Lederman, Daniel, Norman V. Loayza, and Rodrigo R. Soares. 2005. "Accountability and Corruption: Political Institutions Matter," *Economics and Politics*, 17, 1, March, pp. 1–35.

Ledyard, J. O. 1984. "The Pure Theory of Large, Two-Candidate Elections," *Public Choice*, 44, pp. 7–41.

Lijphart, Arend. 1984. *Democracies: Patterns of Majoritarian and Consensus Government in Twenty-One Countries*, New Haven: Yale University Press.

Lindbeck, Assar and Jörgen Weibull. 1987. "Balanced-Budget Redistribution as the Outcome of Political Competition," *Public Choice*, 52, pp. 272–97.

Linz, Juan J. 1999. "Democracy, Multinationalism, and Federalism," in Wolfgang Merkel and Andreas Busch, eds., *Demokratie in Ost und West*, Frankfurt am Main: Suhrkamp.

References

Linz, Juan J. and Alfred Stepan. 1996. *Problems of Democratic Transition and Consolidation: Southern Europe, South America, and Post-Communist Europe,* Baltimore: Johns Hopkins University Press.

Lippmann, Walter. 1963 [1935]. "On This Rock," in *The Essential Lippmann,* New York: Random House, pp. 220–22.

Lipset, Seymour Martin, Kyoung-Ryung Seong and John Charles Torres. 1993. "A comparative analysis of the social requisites of democracy," *International Social Science Journal,* 45, 2, May, pp. 155–76.

Lipson, Leslie. 1965. *The Great Issues of Politics,* Englewood Cliffs, NJ: Prentice-Hall.

Litvack, Jennie, Junaid Ahmad, and Richard Bird. 1998. *Rethinking Decentralization in Developing Countries,* Washington, DC: World Bank.

Lizzeri, Alessandro and Nicola Persico. 2001. "The Provision of Public Goods under Alternative Electoral Incentives," *American Economic Review,* 91, 1, March, pp. 225–39.

Lohmann, Susanne. 1998. "Federalism and Central Bank Independence: The Politics of German Monetary Policy, 1957–92," *World Politics,* 50, 3, pp. 401–46.

Lowi, Theodore. 1964. "American Business and Public Policy, Case Studies and Political Theory," *World Politics,* 16, pp. 677–715.

Lowrie, S. Gale. 1922. "Centralization vs. Decentralization," *American Political Science Review,* 16, 3, August, pp. 379–86.

Loyseau, Charles. 1994 [1610]. *A Treatise of Orders and Plain Dignities [Traité des ordres et simples dignités],* ed. and trans. Howell A. Lord, New York: Cambridge University Press.

MacLennan, M. C. 1965. "Regional Planning in France," *Journal of Industrial Economics,* 13, pp. 62–75.

Maddox, William P. 1941. "The Political Basis of Federation," *American Political Science Review,* 35, 6, December, pp. 1120–27.

Madison, James. 1999 [1772–1836]. *Madison: Writings,* Jack N. Rakove, ed., New York: Library of America.

Malcomson, James. 1986. "Some analytics of the Laffer Curve," *Journal of Public Economics,* 29, ppp. 263–79.

Manin, Bernard, Adam Przeworski, and Susan C. Stokes. 1999. "Elections and Representation," in Bernard Manin, Adam Przeworski, and Susan C. Stokes, *Democracy, Accountability, and Representation,* New York: Cambridge University Press, 1999.

Mansbridge, Jane J. 1983. *Beyond Adversary Democracy,* Chicago: University of Chicago Press.

Marcuse, Herbert. 1972. *Counter-Revolution and Revolt,* Boston: Beacon Press.

Marschak, Jacob. 1968. "Economics of Inquiring, Communicating, Deciding," *American Economic Review,* 58, 2, May, pp. 1–18.

Martinez-Vazquez, Jorge and Robert McNab. 2004. "Fiscal Decentralization, Macrostability, and Growth," Atlanta: Georgia State University.

Mas-Colel, Andreu, Michael D. Whinston and Jerry R. Green. 1995. *Microeconomic Theory,* New York: Oxford University Press.

Maskin, Eric S. 1996. "Theories of the Soft Budget-Constraint," *Japan and the World Economy,* 8, 2, pp. 125–133.

Maskin, Eric. 1999. "Recent Theoretical Work on the Soft Budget Constraint," *American Economic Review Papers and Proceedings*, 89, 2, May, pp. 421–25.

Maskin, Eric and Cheggang Xu. 2001. "Soft Budget Constraint Theories: From Centralization to the Market," *Economics of Transition*, 9, 1, 1–27.

Mayhew, David. 1974. *Congress: The Electoral Connection*, New Haven: Yale University Press.

McAfee, R. Preston and John McMillan. 1995. "Organizational Diseconomies of Scale," *Journal of Economics and Management Strategy*, 4, Fall, pp. 399–426.

McDonald, Forrest, ed. 1962. *Empire and Nation: John Dickinson, Letters from a Farmer in Pennsylvania and Richard Henry Lee, Letters from the Federal Farmer*, Indianapolis: Liberty Fund, 1999, second edition.

McIlwain, Charles Howard. 1932. *The Growth of Political Thought in the West*, New York: MacMillan.

Meguid, Bonnie. 2003. "Bringing Government Back to the People? The Impact of Political Decentralization on Voter Engagement in Western Europe," University of Rochester: manuscript.

Meltzer, Allan H. and Scott F. Richard. 1981. "A Rational Theory of the Size of Government," *Journal of Political Economy*, 89, 914–927.

Meyer, Christopher and Stan Davis. 2003. *It's Alive: The Coming Convergence of Information, Biology, and Business*, New York: Crown Business.

Migue, Jean-Luc. 1995–6. "Federalism and Individual Sovereignty: Comment on Buchanan," *Cato Journal*, Vol. 15, Nos. 2–3 (Fall/Winter).

Milgrom, Paul and John Roberts. 1982. "Predation, Reputation, and Entry Deterrence," *Journal of Economic Theory*, 27, pp. 280–312.

Milgrom, Paul and John Roberts. 1990. "Bargaining Costs, Influence Activities, and the Organization of Economic Activity," in James Alt and Kenneth Shepsle, eds., *Perspectives on Positive Political Economy*, New York: Cambridge University Press, pp. 57–89.

Mill, John Stuart. 1977 [1835]. "Review of Tocqueville's Democracy in America," *London Review*, I (October 1835), reprinted in *John Stuart Mill, Essays on Politics and Society*, ed. J. M. Robson, Toronto: University of Toronto Press, pp. 49–90.

Mill, John Stuart. 1991 [1861]. "Considerations on Representative Government," in John Gray, ed., *John Stuart Mill: On Liberty and Other Essays*, New York: Oxford University Press, pp. 205–467.

Mill, John Stuart. 1991 [1859]. "On Liberty," in John Gray, ed., *John Stuart Mill: On Liberty and Other Essays*, New York: Oxford University Press, pp. 5–128.

Milner, Henry. 2001. "Political Information and Voter Turnout: A Theoretical and Empirical Analysis," paper presented at the Annual Meeting of the American Political Science Association, San Francisco, at http://www.ucd.ie/canada/papers/Henry_Milner_talk.html (downloaded Jan 30, 2005).

Montesquieu, Charles de Secondat, baron de. 1989 [1748]. *L'esprit des lois*, translated and edited by Anne Cohler, Basia Miller and Harold Stone, New York: Cambridge University Press.

Montinola, Gabriella, Yingyi Qian, and Barry R. Weingast. 1995. "Federalism, Chinese Style: The Political Basis for Economic Success," *World Politics*, 48, 1, pp. 50–81.

References

Mookherjee, Dilip. 2006. "Decentralization, Hierarchies, and Incentives: A Mechanism Design Perspective," *Journal of Economic Literature*, XLIV, 2, June, pp. 367–90.

More, Thomas. 1965 [1516]. *Utopia*, trans. Paul Turner. New York: Penguin Books.

Morehouse, Sarah M. and Malcolm E. Jewell. 2004. "States as Laboratories: A Reprise," *Annual Review of Political Science*, 7, pp. 177–203.

Morell, Merilio. 2004. "*FAO Experience in Decentralization in the Forest Sector*," Rome: UN FAO.

Morlan, Robert L. 1984. "Municipal vs. National Election Voter Turnout: Europe and the United States," *Political Science Quarterly*, 99, 3, Autumn, pp. 457–470.

Moulton, H. Geoffrey, Jr. 1997. "Federalism and the Choice of Law in the Regulation of Legal Ethics," *Minnesota Law Review*, 82, pp. 73–171.

Mueller, Denis C. 1989. *Public Choice II*, New York: Cambridge University Press.

Musgrave, Richard. 1997. "Devolution, Grants, and Fiscal Competition," *Journal of Economic Perspectives*, 11, 4, Autumn, pp. 65–72.

Myerson, Allen R. 1996. "O Governor, Won't You Buy me a Mercedes Plant?" *The New York Times*, September 1, Section 3, p. 1.

Myerson, Roger. 1993. "Incentives to Cultivate Favored Minorities Under Alternative Electoral Systems," *American Political Science Review*, 87, 4, December, pp. 856–69.

Myerson, Roger. 2006. "Federalism and Incentives for Success of Democracy," *Quarterly Journal of Political Science*, 1, 1, pp. 3–23.

Nathan, Richard P. 2006. "There Will Always Be a New Federalism," *Journal of Public Administration Research and Theory*, forthcoming.

Nelson, Ralph. 1975. "The Federal Idea in French Political Thought," *Publius*, 5, 3, Summer, pp. 7–62.

Nevins, Allan and Henry Steele Commager. 1992. *A Pocket History of the United States*, New York: Pocket Books.

Nicolini, Juan Pablo, Josefina Posadas, Juan Sanguinetti, Pablo Sanguinetti, and Mariano Tommasi. 2000. *Decentralization, Fiscal Discipline in Sub-National Governments, and the Bailout Problem: The Case of Argentina*, Washington, DC: Inter-American Development Bank.

Nisbet, Robert A. 1962. *Community and Power*, New York: Oxford University Press.

Nivola, Pietro S. 2005. "*Why Federalism Matters*," Washington, DC: Brookings Institution

Norton, Alan. 1994. *International Handbook of Local and Regional Government: A Comparative Analysis of Advanced Democracies*, Aldershot: Edward Elgar.

Nugent, John D. 2000. "State Implementation of Federal Policy as a Political Safeguard of Federalism," Connecticut College: manuscript.

Oakeshott, Michael. 1991. *Rationalism in Politics and Other Essays*, Indianapolis: Liberty Fund.

Oates, Wallace E. 1972. *Fiscal Federalism*, New York: Harcourt Brace Jovanovich.

Oates, Wallace E. 1981. "On Local Finance and the Tiebout Model," *American Economic Review: Papers and Proceedings*, 71, 2, May, pp. 93–8.

Oates, Wallace E. 1999. "An Essay on Fiscal Federalism," *Journal of Economic Literature*, 37, pp. 1120–49.

Oates, Wallace E. and Robert M. Schwab. 1988. "Economic Competition Among Jurisdictions: Efficiency Enhancing or Distortion Inducing?" *Journal of Public Economics*, 35, 3, pp. 333–54.

Odilon-Barrot, Camille Hyacinthe. 1861. *De la centralisation et de ses effets*, Paris: H. Dumineray.

OECD. 1999. *Taxing Powers of State and Local Government*, Paris: OECD.

Olson, Mancur. 1965. *The Logic of Collective Action*, Cambridge, MA: Harvard University Press.

Olson, Mancur. 1993. "Dictatorship, Democracy, and Development," *American Political Science Review*, 87, 3, September, pp. 567–76.

O'Reilly, Robert F. 2005. "Veto Points, Veto Players, and International Trade Policy," *Comparative Political Studies*, 38, 6, August, pp. 652–75.

Osborne, Martin J. 1995. "Spatial Models of Political Competition under Plurality Rule: A Survey of Some Explanations for the Number of Candidates and the Positions they Take," *Canadian Journal of Economics*, 28, 2, pp. 261–301.

Osborne, Martin J. and Al Slivinski. 1996. "A Model of Political Competition with Citizen-Candidates," *Quarterly Journal of Economics*, 111, 1, February, pp. 65–96.

Ottaway, Marina. 2005. "Back From the Brink: A Strategy for Iraq," *Carnegie Endowment Policy Briefs*, 43, November, at http://www.carnegieendowment.org/files/pb43.ottaway.FINAL.pdf.

Page, Edward C. 1991. *Localism and Centralism in Europe: The Political and Legal Bases of Local Self-Government*, New York: Oxford University Press.

Palmon, O. and B. Smith. 1998. "New Evidence on Property Tax Capitalization," *Journal of Political Economy*, 106, pp. 1099–1111.

Pandey, Kalyan and Yuri Misnikov. 2001. "Decentralization and Community Development: Strengthening Local Paritcipation in the Mountain Villages of Kyrgyzstan," *Mountain Research and Development*, 21, 3, August, pp. 226–30.

Patterson, James T. 1969. *The New Deal and the States: Federalism in Transition*, Princeton, NJ: Princeton University Press.

Pauly, Mark. 1970. "Cores and Clubs," *Public Choice*, 9, pp. 53–65.

Pauly, Mark. 1976. "A Model of Local Government Expenditure and Tax Capitalization," *Journal of Public Economics*, 6, pp. 231–42.

Persson, Torsten and Guido Tabellini. 1994. "Does Centralization Increase the Size of Government," *European Economic Review*, 38, pp. 765–773.

Persson, Torsten and Guido Tabellini. 2000. *Political Economics*, Cambridge, MA: MIT Press.

Persson, Torsten and Guido Tabellini. 2003. *The Economic Effects of Constitutions*, Cambridge, MA: MIT Press.

Pisauro, Giuseppe. 2001. *Intergovernmental Relations and Fiscal Discipline: Between Commons and Soft Budget Constraints*, Washington, DC: IMF, WP 01/65.

Plato. 1970 [350s-340s B.C.]. *The Laws*, New York: Penguin Classics.

Plutarch. 1936. "Precepts of Statecraft," in *Moralia*, vol.10, Loeb Classical Library, Cambridge, MA: Harvard University Press, pp. 798–825.

Poitevin, Michel. 2000. "Can the Theory of Incentives Explain Decentralization?" *Canadian Journal of Economics*, 33, 4, November, pp. 878–906.

References

Polanyi, Michael. 1967. *The Tacit Dimension*, Garden City, NY: Anchor Books.

Polybius. 1979. *Historiae*. English and Greek, trans. W. R. Paton, Cambridge: Harvard Universtiy Press.

Potters, Jan and Frans van Winden. 1992. "Lobbying and Asymmetric Information," *Public Choice*, 74, pp. 269–92.

Powell, G. Bingham Jr. and Guy D. Whitten. 1993. "A Cross-National Analysis of Economic Voting: Taking Account of the Political Context," *American Journal of Political Science*, 37, 2, May, pp. 391–414.

Proudhon, Pierre Joseph. 1979 [1863]. *Du principe fédératif et de la nécessité de reconstituer le parti de la révolution*, trans. Richard Vernon, Toronto: University of Toronto Press.

Prud'homme, Remy. 1995. "On the Dangers of Decentralization," *World Bank Research Observer*, 10, 2, pp. 201–20.

Prud'homme, Remy. 1996. "Comment on 'Conflicts and Dilemmas of Decentralization,' by Rudolf Hommes," in World Bank, *Annual World Bank Conference on Development Economics 1995*, Washington DC: World Bank, pp. 354–9.

Przeworski, Adam. 2004. "Institutions Matter?" *Government and Opposition*, 39, 2, pp. 527–40.

Qian, Yingyi and Gérard Roland. 1998. "Federalism and the Soft Budget Constraint," *American Economic Review*, December, 88, 5, pp. 1143–62.

Qian, Yingyi and Barry R. Weingast. 1997. "Federalism as a Commitment to Preserving Market Incentives," *Journal of Economic Perspectives*, 11, 4, Autumn, pp. 83–92.

Radner, Roy. 1992. "Hierarchy: The Economics of Managing," *Journal of Economic Literature*, 30, 3, Sept., pp. 1382–1415.

Radner, Roy. 1993. "The Organization of Decentralized Information Processing," *Econometrica*, 61, 5, Sept., pp. 1109–46.

Rau, Johannes. 2003. "Plenary Speech to International Conference on Federalism 2002, St Gallen, Switzerland," published in Raoul Blindenbacher and Arnold Koller, eds., *Federalism in a Changing World – Learning from Each Other*, Montreal: McGill-Queen's University Press, pp. 524–33.

Reed, John Shelton. 2000. "The Decline of Localism – and Return?" *American Enterprise*, January.

Revesz, Richard L. 1997. "Federalism and Environmental Regulation: A Normative Critique," in John Ferejohn and Barry R. Weingast, eds., *The New Federalism: Can the States Be Trusted?* Stanford: Hoover Institution Press, pp. 97–128.

Reynolds, Susan. 1984. *Kingdoms and Communities in Western Europe, 900–1300*, Oxford: Clarendon Press.

Richter, Wolfram F. and Dietmar Wellisch. 1996. "The Provision of Local Public Goods and Factors in the Presence of Firms and Household Mobility." *Journal of Public Economics*, 60, pp. 73–93.

Riker, William H. 1964. *Federalism: Origin, Operation, Significance*, Boston: Little Brown.

Riker, William H. 1975. "Federalism," in Fred Greenstein and Nelso Polsby, eds., *Handbook of Political Science*, volume 5, pp. 93–172.

Riker, William H. 1993. "Federalism," in Robert E. Goodin and Philip Pettit, eds., *A Companion to Contemporary Political Philosophy*, Cambridge, MA: Blackwells Publishers, pp. 508–14.

Riley, Patrick. 1973. "Rousseau as a Theorist of National and International Federalism," *Publius*, 3, 1, Spring.

Riley, Patrick. 1976. "Three 17th Century German Theorists of Federalism: Althusius, Hugo and Leibniz," *Publius*, 6, 3, pp. 7–41.

Ringquist, Evan J. and Carl Dasse. 2004. "Lies, Damned Lies, and Campaign Promises? Environmental Legislation in the 105th Congress," *Social Science Quarterly*, 85, 2, June, pp. 400–19.

Robalino, David A., Oscar F. Picazo, and Albertus Voetberg. 2001. "Does Fiscal Decentralization Improve Health Outcomes? Evidence From a Cross-Country Analysis", Washington, DC: World Bank.

Rodden, Jonathan. 2002. "The Dilemma of Fiscal Federalism: Grants and Fiscal Performance around the World," *American Journal of Political Science*, 46, 3, July, pp. 670–87.

Rodden, Jonathan. 2004. "Comparative Federalism and Decentralization: On Meaning and Measurement," *Comparative Politics*, July, pp. 481–500.

Rodden, Jonathan and Gunnar S. Eskeland. 2003. "Lessons and Conclusions," in Jonathan Rodden, Gunnar S. Eskeland, and Jennie Litvack, eds., *Fiscal Decentralization and the Challenge of Hard Budget Constraints*, Cambridge MA: MIT Press, 2003, pp. 431–65

Rodden, Jonathan, Gunnar S. Eskeland, and Jennie Litvack. 2003. "Introduction and Overview" in Jonathan Rodden, Gunnar S. Eskeland, and Jennie Litvack, eds., *Fiscal Decentralization and the Challenge of Hard Budget Constraints*, Cambridge, MA: MIT Press, pp. 3–32.

Rodden, Jonathan and Erik Wibbels. 2002. "Beyond the Fiction of Federalism: Macroeconomic Management in Multitiered Systems," *World Politics*, 54, July, pp. 494–531.

Roeder, Philip G. 1999. "Peoples and States after 1989: The Political Costs of Incomplete National Revolutions," *Slavic Review*, 58, 4, Winter, pp. 854–882.

Roland, Gérard. 2000. *Transition and Economics: Politics, Markets, and Firms*, Cambridge, MA: MIT Press.

Rom, Mark Carl, Paul E. Peterson, Kenneth F. Scheve, Jr. 1998. "Interstate competition and welfare policy," *Publius*, 28, 3, Summer, pp. 17–38.

Romer, Thomas and Howard Rosenthal. 1978. "Political Resource Allocation, Controlled Agendas and the Status Quo," *Public Choice*, 33, 4, pp. 27–43.

Rose-Ackerman, Susan. 1980. "Risk Taking and Reelection: Does Federalism Promote Innovation?" *Journal of Legal Studies*, 9, pp. 593–616.

Rosenbaum, Allan and Maria Victoria Rojas. 1997. "Decentralization, local government, and centre-periphery conflict in Sierra Leone," *Public Administration and Development*, 17, pp. 529–40.

Rothschild, Michael and Joseph Stiglitz. 1976. "Equilibrium in Competitive Insurance Markets: An Essay on the Economics of Imperfect Information," *Quarterly Journal of Economics*, 40, pp. 629–49.

References

Rousseau, Jean Jacques. 1986 [1762]. *Du Contrat Social*, translated in *Rousseau: Political Writings*, translated and edited by Frederick Watkins, Madison, WI: University of Wisconsin Press.

Rousseau, Jean Jacques. 1986 [1772]. *Considérations sur le Gouvernement de Pologne*, translated in *Rousseau: Political Writings*, translated and edited by Frederick Watkins, Madison, WI: University of Wisconsin Press.

Rubinfeld, Daniel. 1987. "The Economics of the Local Public Sector," in Alan Auerbach and Martin Feldstein, eds., *Handbook of Public Economics*, vol.2, Amsterdam: North Holland, pp. 571–645.

Russell, Bertrand. 1961 [1922]. "Introduction," in Ludwig Wittgenstein, *Tractatus Logico-Philosophicus*, New York: Routledge, pp. ix–xxv.

Sabatini, Christopher. 2003. "Latin America's Lost Illusions: Decentralization and Political Parties," *Journal of Democracy*, 14, 2, April, pp. 138–50.

Saideman, Stephen M., David J. Lanoue, Michael Campenni, and Samuel Stanton. 2002. "Democratization, Political Institutions, and Ethnic Conflict: A Pooled Time-Series Analysis, 1985–1998," *Comparative Political Studies*, 35, 1, February, pp. 103–29.

Saiegh, Sebastian and Mariano Tomassi. 1999. "Why is Argentina's Fiscal Federalism so Inefficient? Entering the Labyrinth," *Journal of Applied Economics*, 1, May, 165–209.

Saiegh, Sebastian and Mariano Tommasi. 2001. "*The Dark Side of Federalism*," CEDI: Buenos Aires.

Salamey, Imad and Frederic Pearson. 2005. "The Crisis of Federalism and Electoral Strategies in Iraq," *International Studies Perspective*, 6, pp. 190–207.

Salmon, Pierre. 1987. "Decentralization as an Incentive Scheme," *Oxford Review of Economic Policy*, 3, 2, summer, pp. 24–43.

Samuelson, Paul. 1954. "The Pure Theory of Public Expenditure," *Review of Economics and Statistics*, 36, 4, Nov, pp. 387–89.

Sanders, Lynn M. 1997. "Against Deliberation," *Political Theory*, 25, 3, June, pp. 347–76.

Saxonhouse, Arlene W. 1993. "Athenian Democracy: Modern Mythmakers and Ancient Theorists," *PS: Political Science and Politics*, 26, 4, September, pp. 486–90.

Schneider, Aaron. 2003. "Decentralization: Conceptualization and Measurement," *Studies in Comparative International Development*, 38, 3, Fall, pp. 32–56.

Scudder, Samuel H. 1874. "In the Laboratory with Agassiz," *Every Saturday*, 16, April 4, pp. 369–70.

Seabright, Paul. 1996. "Accountability and decentralisation in government: An incomplete contracts model," *European Economic Review*, 40, pp. 61–89.

Shah, Anwar. 1998a. "Indonesia and Pakistan: Fiscal Decentralization – an Elusive Goal?" in Richard M. Bird and Francois Vaillancourt, eds., *Fiscal Decentralization in Developing Countries*, New York: Cambridge University Press, pp. 115–51.

Shah, Anwar. 2005. "Fiscal Decentralization and Fiscal Performance," Washington, DC: World Bank, Policy Research Working Paper 3786.

Shapiro, David L. 1995. *Federalism: A Dialogue*, Evanston, IL: Northwestern University Press.

Shepsle, Kenneth. 1979. "Institutional Arrangements and Equilibrium in Multi-Dimensional Voting Models," *American Journal of Political Science*, 23, pp. 27–59.

Shepsle, Kenneth and Barry R. Weingast. 1981. "Structure-induced Equilibrium and Legislative Choice," *Public Choice*, 37, pp. 503–19.

Shleifer, Andrei. 1985. "A Theory of Yardstick Competition," *Rand Journal of Economics*, 16, 3, Autumn, pp. 319–27.

Shleifer, Andrei and Robert Vishny. 1993. "Corruption," *Quarterly Journal of Economics*, 108, August, pp. 599–617.

Sigelman, Lee. 1999. "Publication Bias Reconsidered," *Political Analysis*, 8, 2, pp. 201–210.

Simeon, Richard and Daniel Patrick Conway. 2001. "Federalism and the Management of Conflict in Multinational Societies," in Alain-G. Gagnon and James Tully, eds., *Multinational Democracies*, New York: Cambridge University Press, pp. 338–65.

Singh, Hoshiar. 1994. "Constitutional Base for Panchayati Raj in India: The 73rd Amendment Act," *Asian Survey*, 34, 9, September, pp. 818–27.

Sinn, Hans-Werner. 1997. "The Selection Principle and Market Failure in Systems Competition," *Journal of Public Economics*, 66, pp. 247–74.

Slabbert, F. Van Zyl and David Welsh. 1979. *South Africa's Options: Strategies for Sharing Power*, New York: St Martin's Press.

Smoke, Paul. 2000. "Beyond Normative Models and Development Trends: Strategic Design and Implementation of Decentralization in Developing Countries," New York: UNDP.

Smoke, Paul. 2001. "Overview of Decentralization and Workshop Theme Linkages," New York: UNCDF, at http://www.uncdf.org/english/local_development/documents_and_reports/thematic_papers/capetown/DLGA_sec2.php#3, downloaded June 4, 2006.

Snyder, Jack. 2000. *From Voting to Violence*, New York: Norton.

Sonin, Konstantin. 2003. "Provincial Protectionism," New Economic School, Moscow: manuscript.

Spengler, Joseph J. 1950. "Vertical Integration and Antitrust Policy," *Journal of Political Economy*, 58, 4, August, pp. 347–52.

Stepan, Alfred C. 2001. *Arguing Comparative Politics*, New York: Oxford University Press.

Stiglitz, Joseph. 1991. "Symposium on Organization and Economics," *Journal of Economic Perspectives*, 5, 2, Spring, pp. 15–24.

Storing, Herbert J., ed. 1981. *The Anti-Federalist*, Chicago: University of Chicago Press.

Strumpf, Koleman. 2002. "Does Government Decentralization Increase Policy Innovation," *Journal of Public Economic Theory*, 4, 2, pp. 207–41.

Suberu, Rotimi T. 1994. "The Travails of Federalism in Nigeria," in Larry Diamond and Marc F. Plattner, eds., *Nationalism, Ethnic Conflict, and Democracy*, Baltimore: Johns Hopkins University Press.

Tanzi, Vito. 1996. "Fiscal Federalism and Decentralization: A Review of Some Efficiency and Macroeconomic Aspects," in World Bank, *Annual World Bank*

References

Conference on Development Economics 1995, Washington, DC: World Bank, pp. 295–316.

Tanzi, Vito. 2001. "Pitfalls on the Road to Fiscal Decentralization," Washington, DC: Carnegie Endowment for International Peace, Working Paper No. 19.

Ter-Minassian, Teresa, ed. 1997a. *Fiscal Federalism in Theory and Practice*, Washington, DC: IMF.

Ter-Minassian, Teresa. 1997b. "Decentralization and Macroeconomic Management," Washington, DC: IMF, WP/97/155.

Thomas, Kenneth P. 2000. *Competing for Capital: Europe and North America in a Global Era*, Washington, DC: Georgetown University Press.

Tiebout, Charles. 1956. "A Pure Theory of Local Expenditures," *Journal of Political Economy*, 64, October, 416–24.

Tocqueville, Alexis de. 1969 [1835]. *Democracy in America*, J. P. Mayer, ed., New York: Harper Perennial.

Tocqueville, Alexis de. 1955 [1856]. *The Old Regime and the French Revolution*, trans. Stuart Gilbert, Garden City, NY: Doubleday.

Treisman, Daniel. 1998. "Decentralization and Inflation in Developed and Developing Countries," UCLA: manuscript.

Treisman, Daniel. 1999a. *After the Deluge: Regional Crises and Political Consolidation in Russia*, Ann Arbor: University of Michigan Press.

Treisman, Daniel. 1999b. "Political Decentralization and Economic Reform: A Game Theoretic Analysis," *American Journal of Political Science*, April,.

Treisman, Daniel. 2000a. "The Causes of Corruption: A Cross-National Study," *Journal of Public Economics*, 76, June, pp. 399–457.

Treisman, Daniel. 2000b. "Decentralization and Inflation: Commitment, Collective Action, or Continuity?" *American Political Science Review*, 94, 4, December, pp. 837–57.

Treisman, Daniel. 2002. "Decentralization and the Quality of Government," UCLA: manuscript, available at http://www.polisci.ucla.edu/faculty/treisman/.

Treisman, Daniel. 2005. "Fiscal decentralization, governance, and economic performance: a reconsideration," UCLA: manuscript.

Treisman, Daniel. 2006. "Fiscal decentralization, governance, and economic performance: a reconsideration," *Economics and Politics*, 18, 2, July, pp. 219–35, Blackwells Publishing.

Trudeau, Pierre. 1968. *Federalism and the French Canadians*, New York: St Martin's Press.

Tsebelis, George. 1999. "Veto Players and Law Production in Parliamentary Democracies: An Empirical Analysis," *American Political Science Review*, 93, 3, pp. 591–608.

Tsebelis, George. 2002. *Veto Players: How Political Institutions Work*, New York: Russell Sage Foundation and Princeton: Princeton University Press.

Tsebelis, George, and Eric Chang. 2001. "Veto Players and the Structure of Budgets in Advanced Industrialized Countries," *European Journal of Political Research*, 43, 3, May, pp. 449–76.

Tullock, Gordon. 1970. "A Simple Algebraic Logrolling Model," *American Economic Review*, 60, 3, June, pp. 419–26.

Turgot, Anne-Robert-Jacques. 1775. *Mémoire sur les municipalités*, in Keith M. Baker, ed., *The Old Regime and the French Revolution*, Chicago: University of Chicago Press, 1987, pp. 97–123.

Turkish State Institute of Statistics. 1999. *Statistical Yearbook of Turkey*, Istanbul: State Institute of Statistics.

UK Office of the Deputy Prime Minister. 2002. *Evaluation of a Pilot Seller's Information Pack: The Bristol Scheme, Final Report*, London: Office of the Deputy PM, at http://www.odpm.gov.uk/stellent/groups/odpm_housing/documents/downloadable/odpm_house_601730.pdf.

United Nations. 2004. *Human Development Report 2004: Cultural Liberty in Today's Diverse World*, New York: United Nations.

UNDP. 2002. "A Global Analysis of UNDP Support to Decentralisation and Local Governance Programmes 2001," New York: UNDP.

USAID. 2000. *Decentralization and Democratic Local Governance Programming Handbook*, Washington, DC: USAID, pp. 65–6, downloaded March 22, 2005, from: www.usaid.gov/our_work/democracy_and_governance/publications/pdfs/pnacp339.pdf

Velasco, Andrés. 1997. "Debts and Deficits with Fragmented Policymaking," Cambridge, MA: National Bureau of Economic Research, WP 6286.

Vernon, Richard. 1979. "Introduction," in Pierre Joseph Proudhon, *Du principe fédératif et de la nécessité de reconstituer le parti de la révolution*, trans. Richard Vernon, Toronto: University of Toronto Press.

Volden, Craig. 2005. "Intergovernmental Political Competition in American Federalism," *American Journal of Political Science*, 49, 2, April, pp. 327–42.

Vollers, Maryanne. 1999. "Razing Appalachia," *Mother Jones*, July/August.

Von Hagen, Jurgen and Barry Eichengreen. 1996. "Federalism, Fiscal Restraints, and European Monetary Union," *American Economic Review: Papers and Proceedings*, 86, 2, May, pp. 134–8.

Watts, Ronald L. 1966. *New Federations: Experiments in the Commonwealth*, Oxford: Clarendon Press.

Webb, Steven B. 2003. "Argentina: Hardening the Provincial Budget Constraint," in Rodden, Eskeland and Litvack, eds., *Fiscal Decentralization and the Challenge of Hard Budget Constraints*, Cambridge, MA: MIT Press.

Weiner, Myron. 1987. "Empirical Democratic Theory and the Transition from Authoritarianism to Democracy," *PS*, 20, 4, Autumn, pp. 861–866.

Weingast, Barry R. 1979. "A Rational Choice Perspective on Congressional Norms," *American Journal of Political Science*, 23, 2, May, 245–62.

Weingast, Barry R. 1995. "The Economic Role of Political Institutions: Market-Preserving Federalism and Economic Development," *Journal of Law, Economics, and Organization*, 11, 1, April, pp. 1–31.

Weingast, Barry R. 1997. "The Political Foundations of Democracy and the Rule of Law," *American Political Science Review*, 91, 2, June, pp. 245–63.

Weingast, Barry R., Kenneth A. Shepsle, and Christopher Johnsen. 1981. "The Political Economy of Benefits and Costs: A Neoclassical Approach to Distributive Politics," *Journal of Political Economy*, 89, pp. 642–64.

References

Wheaton, William C. 1975. "Consumer Mobility and Community Tax Bases: The Financing of Local Public Goods," *Journal of Public Economics*, 4, 4, pp. 377–84.

White, Michelle J. 1975. "Firm Location in a Zoned Metropolitan Area," in Edwin Mills and Wallace Oates, eds., *Fiscal Zoning and Land Use Controls*, Lexington, MA: D. C. Heath, pp. 175–201.

Whitehead, David P. 1986. *The Demes of Attica, 508/7-ca.250 B.C.: A Political and Social Study*, Princeton: Princeton University Press.

Wibbels, Erik. 2005. *Federalism and the Market: Intergovernmental Conflict and Economic Reform in the Developing World*, New York: Cambridge University Press.

Wibbels, Erik. 2006. "Corrected Table 4.2," University of Washington: manuscript, online at http://faculty.washington.edu/ewibbels/data/book.mht.

Wildasin, David E. 1996. "Comment on 'Fiscal Federalism and Decentralization: A Review of Some Efficiency and Macroeconomic Aspects'," in Michael Bruno and Boris Pleskovic, eds., *Annual World Bank Conference on Development Economics 1995*, Washington, DC: World Bank, 323–8.

Wildasin, David E. 1997. "Externalities and Bailouts: Hard and Soft Budget Constraints in Intergovernmental Relations," Vanderbilt University: manuscript.

Wildasin, David E. and John D. Wilson. 2004. "Capital Tax Competition: Boon or Bane?" *Journal of Public Economics*, 88, 6, June, pp. 1065–91.

Williams, Philip. 1957. "Political Compromise in France and America," *The American Scholar*, 26, 3.

Williamson, Oliver E. 1967. "Hierarchical Control and Optimal Firm Size," *Journal of Political Economy*, 75, 2, April, pp. 123–38.

Wilson, James Q. 1970. "Corruption: The Shame of the States," in Arnold J. Heidenheimer, ed., *Political Corruption: Readings in Comparative Analysis*, New York: Holt, Rinehart and Winston.

Wilson, John D. 1996. "Capital Mobility and Environmental Standards: Is There a Theoretical Basis For a Race to the Bottom," in Jagdish Bhagwati, and R. Hudec, eds., *Harmonization and Fair Trade*, vol 1, Cambridge, MA: MIT Press, pp. 395–427.

Wilson, John D. 1999. "Theories of Tax Competition," *National Tax Journal*, 52, pp. 269–304.

Wilson, Woodrow. 1889. "Bryce's American Commonwealth," *Political Science Quarterly*, 4, 1, March, pp. 153–69.

Wintrobe, Ronald. 1990. "The Tinpot and the Totalitarian: An Economic Theory of Dictatorship," *American Political Science Review*, 84, 3, September, pp. 849–72.

Woller, G. and K. Phillips. 1998. "Fiscal Decentralization and LDC economic growth: Am Empirical Investigation," *Journal of Development Studies*, 34, 4, pp. 139–48.

Wood, Gordon S. 1969. *The Creation of the American Republic, 1776–1787*, Chapel Hill: UNC Press.

Woodward, Susan L. 1995. *Balkan Tragedy: Chaos and Dissolution after the Cold War*, Washington, DC: Brookings Institution.

World Bank. 1997. *World Development Report 1997*, Washington, DC: World Bank.

World Bank. 1999. *World Development Report 1999–2000*, Washington, DC: World Bank.

World Bank. 2005. *Indonesia Policy Brief: Supporting Small and Medium Enterprises*, Washington, DC: World Bank, downloaded August 15, 2006 from: http://www.worldbank.or.id.

Wrede. 1999. "Tragedy of the Fiscal Commons?: Fiscal Stock Externalities in a Leviathan Model of Federalism," *Public Choice*, 101, pp. 177–93.

Wrede. 2000. "Shared Tax Sources and Public Expenditures," *International Tax and Public Finance*, 7, pp. 163–75.

Yates, Douglas. 1973. *Neighborhood Democracy*, Lexington, MA: Lexington Books.

Yates, Douglas. 1978. *The Ungovernable City*, Cambridge, MA: MIT Press.

Zhuravskaya, Ekaterina V. 2000. "Incentives to Provide Local Public Goods: Fiscal Federalism, Russian Style," *Journal of Public Economics*, 76, 3, June, pp. 337–68.

Index

Index

Index

Other Books in the Series (*continued from page iii*)